Discover Your Destiny:

The Soul, The Self, and The Search

Dr. Timothy L. McNeil

Copyright © 2010 by Timothy L. McNeil

All rights reserved. No part of this book shall be reproduced or transmitted in any form or by any means, electronic, mechanical, magnetic, photographic including photocopying, recording or by any information storage and retrieval system, without prior written permission of the publisher. No patent liability is assumed with respect to the use of the information contained herein. Although every precaution has been taken in the preparation of this book, the publisher and author assume no responsibility for errors or omissions. Neither is any liability assumed for damages resulting from the use of the information contained herein.

ISBN 0-7414-5541-2

Published by:

INFINITY
PUBLISHING.COM

1094 New DeHaven Street, Suite 100
West Conshohocken, PA 19428-2713
Info@buybooksontheweb.com
www.buybooksontheweb.com
Toll-free (877) BUY BOOK
Local Phone (610) 941-9999
Fax (610) 941-9959

Printed in the United States of America
Published January 2010

Discover Your Destiny

The Soul, The Self, and The Search

is dedicated to the memories of my grandmother,
Lily Bozeman Holloway;
my mother,
Dorothy Holloway McNeil;
and former pastor, mentor, and friend,
Dr. Paul L. Hartsfield.

"For God has not given us a spirit of fear,
but of power, and of love, and of a sound mind."

Contents

Foreword	7
Chapter 1: The Search for Safety	17
Chapter 2: The Search for Meaning	66
Chapter 3: The Search for Justice	108
Chapter 4: The Search for Competence	152
Chapter 5: The Search For Connection	205
Chapter 6: The Search for Healing	264
Chapter 7: Transcendence	335
Epilogue: The Dumbo Dilemma: Taking the Leap toward Transformation	392
Appendix: Narcissistic Personality Disorder	396
Notes	398

Foreword to: *Discover Your Destiny*
The Soul, The Self, and The Search

This expedition begins in St. Augustine, the nation's oldest city and the birthplace of Christianity in the New World. St. Augustine was founded over 400 years ago on September 8, 1565. It was named after this early church father because it was on the feast day of St. Augustine that the debarkation took place. Pedro Menendez de Aviles was commissioned by King Phillip II to plant the dual flags of Spain and the Roman Catholic Church, and to expand both Kingdoms, the empires of the temporal and the eternal.[1]

The voyage to the New World began in the Canary Islands off the coast of Morocco. During the expedition, the sailors faced perilous odds as they fought to fulfill their destiny. The flotilla of ships nearly sank as they encountered a hurricane on the high seas.

> Up to Friday, the 20th (of July), we had very fine weather, but at ten o'clock that day a violent wind rose, which by two in the afternoon had become the most frightful hurricane one could imagine. The sea, which rose to the very clouds, seemed about to swallow us up alive, and such was the fear and apprehension of the pilot and other sailors that I exerted myself to exhort my brethren and companions to repentance. I represented to them the passion of our Lord Jesus Christ, His justice and His mercy, and with so much success that I passed the night in confessing them.
>
> Very often the sea washed completely over the deck where we were gathered, one hundred and twenty men having no other place to go, as there was only one between-decks, and that was full of biscuit, wine, and other provisions. We were in such great danger that it was found necessary to lighten the vessel, and we threw a great many barrels of water into the sea, as well as our cooking apparatus and seven millstones which we were taking with us. Most of the reserve rigging and the great ship's cable were cast overboard, and still the waves continued to break over us. The admiral then resolved to throw all the chests of the men into the sea, but the distress of the soldiers was so great that I felt constrained to throw myself at his feet and beg him not to do it. I reminded him that we ought

to trust to the great mercy of our Lord, and, like a true Christian, he showed confidence in God, and spared the luggage. When Jesus Christ permitted the return of day, we looked at each other as if men raised from the dead, and, though our suspense during Saturday was no less than that of the preceding night, light itself was a consolation to us; but when night, however, found us again still in the same dangerous situation, we thought we must surely perish, and during this whole night I preached to the crew, and exhorted them to put their trust in God. Sunday morning came, and your Lordship can fancy how we rejoiced to see daylight once more, although the storm continued unabated all day, and until noon of the following Monday, when our Lord deigned to have compassion and mercy on us, and calmed the fury of the winds and waves. [2]

Docked in the safety of the harbor and preparing to embark on their expedition from the Canary Islands, did they lay awake wondering what was waiting beyond their known horizon? Did these sailors feel a pull to remain in the safety of their sameness or were they compelled to journey into the mysterious and the unknown? Their apprehension captures our imagination: the tension that exists between risk and safety. The sojourner is driven to discover his or her destiny when the expedition means risking the instinctual need for safety and willfully navigating uncharted waters.

With crude maps, sun and moon, sextant and stars, the early explorers faced perilous odds and encountered the unexpected as they charted and followed the course to a new land. To pause, to reflect, and to imagine, allows us to experience the tension and the terror the journeymen must have felt. What was it like to be one of those sailors on board as they prayed in fear for their lives? What was it like to be knocked down by waves and to cleave for their own survival? What was it like to throw everything essential for future survival overboard in hopes of keeping the ship afloat and staying alive for the next five minutes?

We are the descendents of those who stood watch at the helm and navigated unchartered waters. Just like them, each one of us is on a search; we are all on a journey. Every person on the planet is a pilgrim. Just as those sailors who left the Canary Islands and founded St. Augustine, we live our lives in the tension between risk and safety.

This book is about your journey, *your* quest. Your quest begins when your search for meaning takes precedent over your need for safety. The quest begins with questions. Why am I here? What am I supposed to be doing with my life? Is there something I am missing? When do I set sail? How can I board this ship?

Our contemporary dilemma for a new adventure is that sailing ships and space ships have already circumnavigated the earth. Our planet no longer provides us with new lands to pioneer, divide, and conquer. In our place and time in history, *we can no longer expand as explorers of old*. We can only divide, conquer and re-conquer what already exists. The expansion we so desperately seek today can only be found in an *expansion of consciousness*.

The very survival of the planet may depend upon whether we *make an inward journey*. Ralph Waldo Emerson once wrote, "What lies behind us and what lies ahead of us are tiny matters *compared to what lies within us*." What did Emerson mean? What lies within us? Does he allude to the soft whispering of the soul?

Is what lies within us more important than past or future? How can we move beyond a false identity based on distorted images of the self? How do we discover a deeper sense of identity that transcends family, tribe, or nation? We must make way for the inward journey *to discover our destiny*: "Out there" holds false promise. It is not "out there" but it is "in here." It is not without but within. To *live in the mystery* is to Discover our Destiny *within* the Soul, the Self, and the Search. Wherever you are at this very moment, you are standing on the gangplank that will launch you and your life into a brave new world! Are you ready?

My pilgrimage drew me to St. Augustine in August of 1993. As a local church pastor for fifteen years, my profession took an unexpected turn in a new direction. Just as the initial pilgrims found their way to St. Augustine by tacking and zigzagging to catch the wind, our journeys follow similar patterns. Moses *tacked* for 40 years across the wilderness. Spiritual journeys rarely follow a straight path. In spiritual discovery, we tend to zigzag, sometimes pushed and other times pulled, until we finally reach the destination, the target, X marks the spot.

In 1993, I accepted a position as the Director of Operations in a not-for-profit organization. During the previous year, I earned a doctorate in pastoral counseling. I never dreamed I would ever leave my work as a local church pastor, but here was my new reality, staring me in the face. The organization ran two small nursing homes, an emergency assistance program for people in need of food, clothing, and medical attention, and a counseling center. My job was to provide supervision and oversight for all three operations.

During my first year, I would take my lunch and drive my truck to the *Shrine of Our Lady of la Leche*.[a] From there I would walk to the towering 20 story cross, a cross that commemorates the landing of Menendez in 1565, and sit in the shadows. I would eat my sandwich and thirst for that same milk; I would weep and pray. I asked God the agonizing question: "Why am I here?" I felt enormously conflicted when I accepted the new position. I remained that way for some time. I rarely, if ever, felt more than 70% *certain* this vocational shift was the direction I needed to follow.[b] I recall packing my study in preparation for the move; I grieved as I stored away 15 years of sermons in a box. At my core, I knew if I did not take the new position I would always wonder if I turned my back on an opportunity I would later regret. Over the course of this first year I began to reflect on my work as a local church pastor as a time when I was a servant of the *institutional* church. As a new purpose

---

[a] This shrine is the first in our nation dedicated to Mary and to the breasts that fed Jesus.

[b] Faith journeys do require faith. Beware of those who are 100% certain of their certainty, for they may lead you to Jonestown, Guyana. . .

10

came into focus, I began to understand my vocation as a laborer in the *servant* church, caring for the needs of the elderly, the poor, and the broken hearted. My service in this position was a different manifestation of the same church, the Church Universal, the body of Christ. In the evolution of my own understanding, I learned to trust that I was where I needed to be.

I spent the next six years acquiring valuable experience in organization, management, and administration. During this time, Flagler College invited me to teach *Death and Dying* as an adjunct faculty member. More important, as my workload increased as a trained and licensed psychotherapist and pastoral counselor, I noticed some consistent themes with persons who came from both sacred and secular backgrounds. In 1998, I moved out of the not-for-profit position and transitioned to full time work as a pastoral counselor. In my heart, I see my work as a pastoral counselor as doing the work of an evangelist. Matters of the heart always lead us to the soul.

M. Scott Peck came to a realization about spiritual values while writing his best seller *The Road Less Traveled* in 1980. This is where I begin. I have attempted to integrate the work of spirituality and psychotherapy in a way that will be clear and concise to the reader, although the movement from psychotherapy to spirituality is intentionally gradual. This work promotes a lifestyle of non-violence and moves us away from conquest into cooperation and connection.

This book emerged from my work as a psychotherapist and pastoral counselor for over a decade. As Eckhart Tolle states, *"both the teacher and the taught become the teaching."*[3] I have been both teacher and student in this process. My experiences through this began to set a new direction in my work, which I see like points on a compass. Sojourners who I traveled with in my practice began to recognize their own personal latitude and longitude markers and compass points. They began to use these compass points to map their own quest to move out of their mazes of meaninglessness and emerge from chaos into coherence and thus into a completely new world. I have briefly outlined each theme below and these will function as compass points to establish direction for our expedition as well as serving as the nautical chart for this book. These compass points are *safety, meaning, justice, competence, connection, healing, and transcendence.*

Safety is the first compass point. It is our number one need. Simply put, if we do not feel safe, *nothing else matters.* We react *instinctually* to threat in this way. Anger and anxiety are reactive emotions we experience to a real or imagined threat to our safety.

The economic tsunami caused from the bursting housing and credit bubbles has sent us on a cycle from boom to bust not seen since the great depression. The automotive industry has been the bell weather economic indicator for the stability of capitalism for decades. Do you remember, "How General Motors goes, so goes the nation?" Revelations of corporate greed have sent shock waves from Wall Street to Main Street. The current digital photo of western capitalism captures an astonishing and staggering image of one huge Ponzi scheme.

As for our individual health, we await the coming of each new pandemic from bird flu to swine flu with dread. As for the health of our planet, our carbon footprint has created the fungus of global warming that promises to make our planet as inhabitable as a soiled and smelly tennis shoe.

Our foundations for safety have been forever destabilized. Prior to 9-11-2001, the United States could depend on its geographical boundaries to insure a modicum of safety. Terrorism always happened "over there." We now know that our safety is no longer an inalienable guaranteed constitutional right. We now know what the rest of the world knows: safety can no longer be taken for granted. We now know that 9-11 is a dividing line in history, marking time "before" and "after." The "new normal" continues to raise anxiety to new levels. Our collective consensus is not *if* there will be another terrorist strike but *when and where.* Fighting a war on terror without boundaries and borders may well mean that our nation and the world will now be in a state of war *in perpetuity*. We have notched up both anxiety and anger through isolated and prolonged acts of "holy violence."[4]

We cannot live purposefully, creatively, and with passion if we are stuck in a protective mode. Our *psychological* safety needs trigger anger and anxiety when there are real or imagined threats to issues of justice or competence.

Meaning is our next compass point. Meaning involves our attempts to find "purpose" through career, companionship, and vocation as we wrestle with life choices. Meaning involves the facts of our lives and how we *interpret* these facts. "Our baby died," might be a fact: but what does this mean? We strive to make our meaning making *conscious* and to develop our own theory, philosophy, theology, or ideology about how to make sense out of our experience. It may be as simple as the Golden Rule or as complex as Aristotle or Augustine.

Justice involves our attempts to achieve balance in relationships. We each carry our own internalized compass that points toward what we believe to be just or fair. We want to get *out* of our relationships what we put *into* them: to get what we give! The basis of many relationships frequently involves unconscious bartering, "If I do *this* for you, you are supposed to do *this* for me." When these expectations are not met, resentment eventually builds to implosions or explosions. Reactivity frequently follows real or imagined threats to interpersonal or social injustice.

Competence is our need, drive, and desire to be competent with who we are and in what we do. From the time we are born until we die, we strive to achieve and maintain competence. Reactivity frequently follows real or imagined attacks on our competence. In this controversial chapter, the reader will witness the dismantling of a popular cultural and psychological myth: *there is no such thing as self-esteem.* Self-esteem describes *symptoms*: what is the cause?

Connection is our need to be in relationships where

we experience unconditional love, acceptance, and approval. The old television show "Cheers" began with, "I want to go to a place where everybody knows my name." We are all creatures of community. We are born into families and we journey our way through many places of belonging, where we receive nurture, challenge, and identity. Are our sources of connection life giving or life denying?"

Healing is our bodies' homeostasis of health. This is why we have an immune system. Research will continue to establish a direct link between emotional, spiritual, physical health, and well-being. In this chapter, I present my work with sojourners who experience healing in relationships. I also present some of my own findings, which add to the research of other professionals establishing a link between emotional illness and disease, how emotional healing may facilitate physical healing, and documented incidences of spontaneous healings. Forgiveness and healing are intricately connected.

Transcendence is our search for God. Transcendence is not about finding orthodoxy but orthopraxy. It is not about "talking the talk" but "walking the walk." God is not so much interested in right belief as in right relationship. When we get into an aligned relationship, the right belief seems to take care of itself. (Jeremiah 31:31-34) Discovering our destiny is about *recovering* the divine image hidden below the self and *discovering* our adoption that connects the soul to the divine. (Romans 8:12-17) An encounter with transcendence is an invitation to experience transformation.

Although I have seen these compass points repeatedly in my work, let me clearly state there are no formulas or set maps to faith and thus to transcendence. This is not about discovering seven "how to's" or seven steps to salvation or seven blueprints for the soul. More than anything else, I believe **abundant life is hard work.** (Philippians 2:12-13) Your point of encounter with God is precisely where you may struggle with any or all of these compass points. It is a fundamental affirmation of a fundamental truth that *God meets us where we are in our sojourn.* This book will challenge the reader to say "yes" to the miracle of transformation, pull anchor, and chart a new course as you begin mapping your own quest. The more intense the struggle, the more you will be pushed into discovering who you are in God. What holds your ship together is learning how to hold the tension of your two natures, human beings made in the divine image, and to become whole persons. The ongoing work of transformation is to transform the individual and connect us into the global consciousness of God.

Albert Einstein once stated, *"No problem can be solved by the same level of consciousness that created it. We have to think with a new mind."[5]* Unless we enter into a new consciousness, the anger and anxiety that have now been unleashed create the possibilities of our own self-extinction. Unless there is a radical breakthrough of this consciousness, civilization, as we now know it, may be hanging by a thread.

This book is written for persons who are spiritual seekers. It is written for persons who are interested in taking the inward journey and are seeking to discover their identity as human and spiritual beings. It is written for persons who are interested in an authentic, integrated spirituality.

I envision this book being used in classrooms, churches, and synagogues as a tool for personal and spiritual growth. The potential applications are numerous and unlimited: When I presented portions of this material at the Candler School of Theology at Emory University in the fall of 2007, a delegation from the Bahamas expressed interest in this work as a method for helping to deal with the growing problems associated with gang violence in their country. In June of 2008, I presented portions of this material to the First Annual Conference of the Society for Spirituality, Theology & Health at Duke University. Emotional, physical, and spiritual health is intricately connected. My hope is that this work will make a contribution in the field of wholeness, health, and well-being.

No words can adequately express my gratitude and appreciation for the persons who have shaped my life and influenced this process. Dr. C. Fred Hall was my first Clinical Supervisor in Clinical Pastoral Education at the Candler School of Theology at Emory University and his timely presence many years later was the signal that sent me in a new direction in ministry. I want to thank Dr. Larry Lake, my working partner for six years in St. Augustine. His encouragement of me to enter the pastoral counseling training program at the Samaritan Center in Jacksonville, Florida in 1989 opened windows of opportunity that I never dreamed or imagined. I would also like to thank Dr. John Rutland-Wallis, my first clinical supervisor at the Samaritan Center who introduced me to the Psychology of the Self and the genius of Heinz Kohut. Dr. Jon Connelly revolutionized my practical skills with his insightful and dedicated work. Rev. Phil Roughton, Rev. Chris Akers, Rev. Bill Owens, and the staff of the First United Methodist Church of Ormond Beach have provided affirmation and confidence in my work and have kept me busy. Demcie Re, Dr. Harry Black, Rev. Melynne Rust, Dr. Jay Rust, Rev. Leslie Avchin, Nancy Edwards, Karen Iseman, Yvonne Newcomb-Doty, Ruth Westwood, Rebekah Krahe, Brenda McNeil, and Lisa Carboni have spent countless hours reading, proofing, and bouncing around ideas in helping me to improve the manuscript. Kathleen Andrews has been a benevolent supporter of this work. Sarah Gerace and Sean McNeil worked together in designing the cover. Brenda, my spouse, and my children, Sean and Rebekah, have been my greatest teachers of all. I am deeply appreciative of their love and support in this project.

    Most important of all, I wish to thank the hundreds of fellow spiritual pilgrims who have allowed me the sacred privilege of joining them on their expedition. Those with whom I have been privileged to work have been my teachers. Mutually we have worked to establish the creation of new meanings as we have sought to *Discover our Destiny* in the great exploration of *The Soul, The Self, and The Search.*

Chapter 1
The Search for Safety

> "The desire for safety stands against every great and noble enterprise."
> Roman Historian, Orator, and Senator Publius Cornelius Tacitus (55-117)

It is hard to imagine what those early explorers thought when they left the Canary Islands and day after day they sailed toward the sunset. Did they feel the excitement of a new adventure? Did they believe they were fulfilling their destiny? Were they running away from failed relationships, problems with the law, or even themselves? Did they grieve loved ones left behind?

What happened, when without notice or warning, the seas began to swell and the skies turned black? What happened when they began to feel the stinging pellets of driving rain and the winds howled with gale force terror? Were they filled with regret and fear – regret for having boarded this God forsaken ship and fear of being swallowed by an angry sea?

Safety First

Safety is the first order of business, and what those sailors knew, we also know: if we do not feel safe, then nothing else matters. Those sailors did two things when they encountered the hurricane: they threw cargo off the boat to lighten the load and they prayed. It may have felt futile, like using a peashooter to kill a charging elephant, but they had to *do something* to make them feel safe in such perilous conditions. Similarly, today we might see hundreds of volunteers filling sandbags to hold back raging river floodwaters. We want to show our teeth and face down the forces of nature. By comparison, those forces loom so large and we are so small. Doing *something* in the face of such odds fights off feelings of helplessness and hopelessness.

In Abraham Maslow's *Hierarchy of Needs*, safety is located at the base of the pyramid. All other needs are stacked on top of this need. If we do not feel safe, nothing else much matters. I doubt any of the crew was sport fishing or the captain was writing poetry when gale force winds started to howl and the seas began to churn twenty feet swells. Similarly, never would anyone call to a friend and say, "Do you hear something that sounds like a train coming? Since we live twenty miles from the nearest railroad track, I wonder if a tornado might be heading our way. And by the way, would you mind fixing me a tuna fish sandwich?" Eating, having sex, or going to the movies will not matter if a tornado is bearing down on your house. Safety is our first order of business.

As geographical descendants of those first sailors, Floridians are well aware of the six-month period during June 1st until November 30th of each year when like sitting ducks we try to dodge those West African, Caribbean, and Gulf of Mexico bullets known as hurricanes. We have the advantages with all the latest advanced web technologies, satellite infrared images, computer models, and air reconnaissance flights, which are now a part of the modern meteorological arsenal those sailors could not possibly have ever imagined. In spite of it all, 20 different computer models will predict 15 different potential pathways for the storm track. For us, the guessing game has become far more sophisticated but still a crapshoot. With this in mind, we watch the Weather Channel with fear and awe when a tropical depression becomes a named storm and suddenly matures into full adult storm fury.

I was born and raised in Jacksonville, Florida, just 40 miles north of where the Spanish expedition landed and where the dual flags were stuck in the ground claiming the land for the King of Spain and the Catholic Church. I have lived in the Sunshine State most of my life, with the exception of three brief years of graduate school in Atlanta. Depending upon the direction and the intensity of a storm, Floridians operate with a full checklist of survival drills in preparation for the arrival of the counter-clockwise buzz saws of chaos.

During the "red alert" phase flashlights, batteries, candles, canned goods, and bottled water are cautiously purchased 96 to 72 hours in advance of an approaching named storm. 48 hours prior to a near or direct hit, important documents such as insurance papers, family photo albums, and passports are placed in one location for easy access and safe removal if an evacuation is ordered. Pre-cut plywood to cover windows is installed. If the storm is within thirty-six to twenty-four hours from landfall, the family vehicles will be gassed up and ready to go. Escape routes and lodging are planned in the event we have to move temporarily inland. A last minute decision is made whether to leave or to weather out the storm.

During this phase, all other activities diminish in priority and importance. If the yard is not mowed, if the house is not spic and span and the rooms are not all straightened up, or if "normal" day-to-day household maintenance items are delayed, it truly does not matter. And although we thoroughly enjoy our home, and we hope to continue to make mortgage payments and live in it, when it comes right down to it, the house doesn't matter that much. What matters, more than anything else, is the survival of the family and feeling as safe as we possibly can under these conditions.

Whoever coined the phrase, *Safety First*, was not kidding. If we do not feel safe, nothing else matters. Heeding hurricane warnings and the preparations that necessarily follow are a part of disasters we can anticipate. This allows us time to create and implement preemptive plans for securing our homes, to evacuate if necessary, and thus to insure our safety. What about incidents and accidents we cannot see coming? What happens when we have to make life or death decisions with no time to anticipate or plan? Do you swerve to avoid the mother pushing the baby in the stroller and hit the semi truck coming head on? Life sometimes comes at us fast!

I experienced this lesson in reality 28 miles off the coast of St. Augustine. I was scuba diving with a close friend and coworker whom I have known and trusted for many years. We were experienced divers and teamed together on several previous occasions. We did not anticipate any problems on what was to be our next dive. The seas were choppy when we entered the water, and it took a great deal of effort for both of us to snorkel and swim in full gear to the front of the boat. We found the anchor line and slowly began our dive down to 100 feet. We carried spear guns and anticipated spear fishing for grouper, amberjack, and snapper. We made it safely to the ocean floor. Visibility was poor and less than 10 feet. We had been down only a few minutes when Larry began frantically pointing to his regulator. I was puzzled by his behavior and I did not understand what he was trying to tell me. He again repeated the gesture, this time, with an increased sense of urgency in his eyes. I still did not get it. Finally, in desperation, he reached out, grabbed my mouthpiece out of my mouth, and began breathing. This time I understood. He was out of air!

We slowly began our ascent back to the surface, stopping every 30 feet to avoid the bends, taking turns and buddy breathing. About 15 feet from the surface, my tank pressure gauge read empty; we were both out of air. We floated to the surface, swam to the boat and climbed to safety. Once aboard we helped each other out of the equipment, lay down exhausted and stared at the sky. Oxygen was no longer a problem. We had all we needed. Almost on cue, we both erupted spontaneously into uproarious laughter. Without stating the obvious, we knew we had come close to being kissed by the angel of death. With this came a renewed sense of awe for the beauty of the day, the wonder of the clouds, and an intense feeling of gratitude and appreciation for being alive!

Larry explained he had panicked on the way down, with the choppy seas and murky visibility, and he had sucked all 3000 lbs. of air out of his tank. About this time, a sobering thought hit me. We were both 100 feet below the surface on the bottom of the ocean floor. Someone I cared for very deeply was pulling my life-giving oxygen out of my mouth and I held a loaded spear gun in one hand.

Whom are we kidding? Are we trying to fool ourselves? If we peel back the veiled veneer of civilization, and expose the raw reality and red meat of human nature one law is revealed. In the Darwinian jungle or the Darwinian ocean, the law is the same: survival of the fittest. The strong survive and the weak perish. I was the strong. I held the gun. Now I shuddered and wondered if I would have been capable of murder if it had come down to either him or me. How would I have been able to live with myself if I had pulled that trigger in a moment of panic? Would I have been charged with manslaughter or would the courts have ruled it a justifiable homicide? Would I have spent 20 years in prison tormented by the last look on Larry's face? These were the "afterthoughts" that were deeply troubling for me. Fortunately, none of that mattered. Darwinian reactions to survival can be tamed and transformed. My training acted preemptively. What we both learned in our diver's certification training equipped us for this emergency. We worked cooperatively and not competitively. Safety came first!

Severe threats to our health and well-being signal threats to our safety needs. As a rule, there are no atheists waiting to receive biopsy reports. With the time bomb of a tumor attached to bone or organs and buried beneath the skin, you will live in a constant state of "readiness." This became evident to me as I witnessed how the early onslaught of the H.I.V. epidemic was wreaking havoc, hysteria, and mayhem in the late 1980s and early 1990s. The plague is currently annihilating the continent of Africa. An individual cannot feel safe when a viral time bomb is ticking in the bloodstream, decimating the t-cells, and leaving the person feeling vulnerable as a host for infections. Full-blown AIDS means your immune system has no fight left. Twenty years ago, an H.I.V. diagnosis was the equivalent of receiving a death sentence.

A handful of us who shared a vision overcame many obstacles for launching a support group for P.W.A.'s, or persons with A.I.D.S. We started the group in a church and quickly found we were fighting a two-front war. For persons in the church, they were fearful of the newcomers. Church members would not sit in the seats the group members sat in for fear of catching the disease. For many with the disease, the church was not a symbol of acceptance but a source of institutional prejudice and fear. Television preachers created skewed, reactive, and distorted meanings by calling it "The Gay Plague" and concluded this was God's judgment on their wicked lifestyle. The only thing our support group could do was model acceptance ourselves. We educated the church members, the doors were opened, and those who needed the group faced their fears and came.

It had been eight years since I first met Tony. Tony was one of the founding members of the core support group I had been involved in helping to launch at the height of the outbreak of the epidemic. I was startled when he identified himself over the phone and asked me if I remembered him. Tony was an unforgettable person: if you met him, you would never forget him. He wanted to make an appointment to see me so we set something up for the following day.

We spent time catching up and reviewing the whereabouts of the members of the original group. Tony informed me as a matter of fact: "No one in the group is left but me and John, and John is in Ft. Lauderdale." I was stunned. The group had grown exponentially at first, starting with four persons who were infected with the virus. In four months, we had reached 70 persons and had broken into two groups. Two out of 70 survived eight years! One by one, as I would mention names, Tony would recount tales of tears and would report the stories of each death.

Together we remembered Lonnie, one of the first four members who came to the initial meeting. Lonnie had the distinction of being the first member to die. I remembered walking into the cardiac intensive care unit the day of his death. In fact, he had already died four times that day, but his mother would not sign a "do not resuscitate" order. Every time his heart would stop beating, the medical team would revive him. Lonnie's physician pulled me into a small charting room and literally begged me to plead with his mother to sign a D.N.R. order. It did not matter. The fifth time Lonnie coded his heart would not jump-start. The D.N.R. was no longer an issue.

I conducted the graveside service for Lonnie, consisting primarily of the fellow members of the PWA support group. Lonnie felt community with this group, and the collective pain was prevalent and pervasive. The mood was somber and serious, and carried over into our next group meeting. Lonnie's chair was empty. Each member of the group sat in silence for what seemed like an eternity. Denise, a young African-American woman, finally broke the silence and verbalized the thoughts of the entire group. She said, "I wonder where the empty chair will be next?" Her comments were prophetic. Denise's chair was the next to become empty.

Now Tony reports all but two of the chairs were empty. Each story of death dealt a staggering blow. With each name mentioned, Tony told a corresponding story of death. Carrol, an eccentric man of high drama, had died four years ago. Cheryl, who was HIV positive, had given birth to a baby girl who had been born HIV negative. I baptized this child on Christmas Eve in the context of a bigger story about another baby who had been born and pushed aside. The following year Cheryl left for New York City. H.I.V. had not claimed her. She had died a violent death, having been stabbed to death in a back alley.

Tony was near tears the entire time. He shifted and began to discuss his own story and the events of the last five years. Tony had survived the H.I.V. death sentence but narrowly escaped murder from domestic abuse. Tony smiled, and through the lips of a man approaching 60 years of age, he was showing off his new set of dentures. His lover had beaten his previous set of teeth, anchored by implants, out of his mouth. Tony was almost beaten to death. Prior to this attack, there had been two previous incidents of domestic violence. In each incident, the violence became more brutal. Tony knew he had to leave or he would be killed. He fled to a domestic abuse shelter in Key West. One of the counselors told him to read a particular book, which he now clutched in his hand. "The book has stirred up a lot of issues for me, issues I thought I had taken care of, but apparently I have not."

Tony was lucky. He had fled and found safety. He had moved to St. Augustine in order to get out of harm's way. He told me he did not have to look over his shoulder any more to worry if his former partner would be stalking behind him to exact another pound of flesh. Tony was indeed safe, but he was still a victim of the trauma. His post-traumatic stress flashbacks made him re-live the terror in much the same way he lived through it the first time it happened. He questioned why he had not fought back, why he had "taken it" and wondered aloud if this was his source of shame. The beatings were over, but now Tony relived the brutality, as it played non-stop in his mind. He did not have memories: his memories had him! His wounds were as raw and as real as the day it first happened. Although Tony did not have to look over his shoulder or worry if his former partner would be stalking him, the trauma he endured activated an internal switch that he was unable to flip to the "off" position. In the following chapter, we examine why this occurs as we explore *meaning* in more detail.

Unfortunately, Tony's situation is not at all unique. Prior to the O.J. Simpson murder trial, police called to the scene of domestic violence would try to deescalate or defuse the situation. Someone might be asked to leave. Today, when police are called to the scene of domestic violence someone goes to jail. Pete, a 37-year-old computer information technician with a government agency, came to see me. His lip was split, one eye was swollen, and he had several cuts and lacerations on his face. When I asked him the obvious question he said, "My wife beat me up." When I asked why he did not defend himself he said, "I felt like I deserved it." He had purchased a pre-paid cell phone and called a late night chat service advertised on television. He "met" several women via the chat line although they never met in person. They began "sexting," exchanging lewd sexually explicit photos via cell phone. Pete's phone vibrated indicating he had a new photo and he went out to the garage to view the latest picture. His wife followed him, grabbed the phone, and saw all the pictures, including the ones he had sent of himself. She went berserk and beat him with phone and fists. The police were called. She went to jail.

Unfortunately, home no longer represents the peaceful haven most of us desperately need. We collect and carry home the stress from every corner of our culture. Home is where boundaries are blurred and where we are frequently most vulnerable. Stressors on family life have grown exponentially. The stress of raising children, with all the challenges in our Post Modern Age, creates constant chronic frustration. I worked with a 42-year-old professional who called after his second wife informed him she did not love him anymore and wanted a divorce. He had adopted the daughter of this woman and continued to exert a positive influence on the child's life after the divorce with his now limited contact. After spending a year working through the pain of this divorce, he sent the following e-mail concerning the 13-year-old girl:

> Hi Tim,
> Well, Susan got into it again this weekend. The highway patrol pulled over a car at midnight on Saturday with two boys, Mandy and her girlfriend (Whom she was supposed to be spending the night with). The boys had pot, condoms, and other assorted party favors. Apparently Susan was extremely belligerent with the police and her mother. I've convinced her mother to agree to have her get some counseling. I don't remember if you said you work with adolescents or if you think it would be a good idea for you to see her since you are seeing me, but if not, could you recommend someone? Someone who can see through her act? Any help would be appreciated.

The rate that girl is turning my hair white I am going to look like Santa by Christmas!

Tony's struggles with H.I.V. and domestic violence, Pete's issues with graphic pornographic "sexting," and Susan's acting out and the aging effects it is having on her step-father may be more of a function of larger family dysfunctional living. Does it also have something to say about our contemporary American culture?

When the Check Engine Light Stays ON

In contemporary American culture, work, volatile economies, unemployment, gas prices, recession, downsizing and out-sourcing, war, and global terrorism have created an emotional climate approaching those who live in war torn societies. Anger and anxiety have reached pandemic proportions and our collective "readiness" button remains stuck in the "on" position.

On a quiet Sunday afternoon, I was trying to teach my daughter how to drive my truck. The truck was equipped with a standard manual transmission. Rebekah was having an extremely difficult time getting all the varied motor skills working in synchronicity in her attempts to orchestrate the movements between the gearshift, the clutch, the gas pedal, the brake, and the steering wheel. I sat next to her in silence and occasionally tried to offer advice, encouragement, and suggestions about what could possibly create improvement in our present situation. Secretly, I realized what a crash test dummy felt like as I was jerked around inside the cab of the truck. I checked the tension on the seat belt, noticed the air bag light was on, and the driving lesson continued. The truck lunged forward, chortled, wheezed, jerked, and stalled in different combinations of this sequence for a total of 23 times. After the 23rd, not only did I automatically begin reciting the 23rd Psalm, I also noticed the **"Check Engine"** light began to illuminate in bright yellow on the dashboard. I suggested to Rebekah what this meant was that the truck was tired and that it needed a rest. She seemed to accept this line of reasoning, although it was clear in my mind that I was projecting on to the truck what I was feeling, and we agreed to give both Dad and the truck a rest and to resume the lesson another time.

The next morning, when I began my commute, I noticed the **Check Engine** light was still burning brightly on the dashboard, impossible *not* to notice. I wondered how far along I-95 I would get before the engine blew up!

Our autonomic nervous system was not designed to withstand the ongoing bombardment of chronic stress that keeps our **Check Engine** light constantly burning. For those, like Tony, who suffer from PTSD, the images continue to play on the internal screen and the **Check Engine** light never fully goes out. Whether as victims or victimizers, predators or prey, the hunter or the hunted, our bodies were not designed to endure high levels of stress for long periods. Readiness requires us to be constantly dumping adrenalin and cortisol into our endocrine system. In chronic conditions where the threat is ongoing, the heightened sense of "readiness" remains "on." During the hurricane season of 2004, Floridians endured direct hits from four named storms, and the net effect for many of the residents of our state was that the hurricanes felt like predators, and we felt like the prey. Interestingly enough, residents of New Orleans who survived the devastation of Katrina were frequently referred to as "the *victims* of Hurricane Katrina." Although insurance companies paid out over 11 billion in claims, many survivors experienced additional victimization from insurance carriers because of claims settled at pennies on the dollar. In certain situations, human beings may eventually be able to adjust to these chronic states, for example, during times of war. Both soldiers and civilians move into this heightened state of awareness, and only the most acute conditions of one's immediate ability to survive will alert anxiety. War can seem like a distant, unpleasant reality, until the day a best friend has his head blown off in the line of fire. Since most of us do not have to live in war zones, we may find it difficult to cope with stress related to survival on an ongoing basis

For many people, life in our contemporary culture involves chronic stress, strain, and anxiety. Once the switch flips for these emotions, clarity through the "windshield" becomes difficult. Again, behavior is either purposeful or protective, and once stuck in the protective mode, the only emotions available are anger and anxiety.

After working hard in counseling for six months, Pamela, married for 18 years, business owner and 44-year-old mother of two began to gain some new insight into the constant state of "readiness" that had been driving her life until this point. She writes:

> I am figuring out that I have operated much of my life from fear - for as long as I can remember. So many fears: fear that I cause bad things to happen in good people's lives, fear of God, fear of honesty, fear that God finds me un-loveable, fear of my feelings, fear of expression, fear of anger, fear of blowing up, fear of crying, fear of mental anguish, fear of dying, actually fear of losing, a fear of re-living my life, a fear of facing my past. So many fears, so many that I decided to invert my selection. Instead I asked myself what is NOT motivated by fear in my life. I am not afraid of myself. I am not afraid of my mind. I am not afraid: of being alone, of failure, to love myself. I will not be afraid to live - but I am afraid that my desire to live will make me seem selfish to those (my kids and family) that have no understanding of my desire to be 'set free' inside.

Pamela's pain comes in recognizing the force that has been driving most of her behavior throughout her life – fear! As you might expect, Pamela occasionally struggles with panic attacks. She further explains her fear and having to live in a constant state of "readiness":

> When I ask myself late at night 'what is the matter with me?'........ I think that this is the source of my polarized thoughts. I am internally fighting the readiness... I am tired from it. I dream and write about floating, flying, riding.... soaring and I long to just be what God created

me to be! Though it probably sounds hokey or something, but when you are constantly in "ready stance" as we used to call it in Taekwondo - even if the fight never comes, the ready stance itself burns the energy like some kind of fuse. And on the other side, I am experiencing such excitement and fever with learning about myself, God, school,.... it is the reverse of the other feelings. It is very complex.

The Taekwondo Grand Master used to make us close our eyes and stand in ready stance for thirty minutes or some times longer - and you never knew when he would sweep you off your feet or throw you on your back. With every breath you anticipated it - in fact, you altered even your breathing for it. By the end of the exercise I would feel totally faint! How can we even think normally or allow peacefulness if you think at any moment the enemy is going to take your ass out? I think you are right... We were never meant to live in a constant state of readiness!" Tell me how this happened to our human race...

Once the triggers are tripped, a full-scale emotional hijacking takes place in the form of phobic reactivity. All phobias, in one way or another, identify an object, a circumstance, a situation, or a person with a fear of death. Anxiety levels reach chronic proportions. Racing hearts and chest pain often replicate symptoms associated with heart attacks. Emergency room personnel see these persons daily. When EKG's and cardiac enzyme levels are normal, they usually will administer a shot of Demerol and send these tortured souls back out until the next episode triggers another event, or until they are able to get help and break the cycle.

Unlike a war, our current epidemic that combines personal and cultural stressors has created a chronic state of readiness most of us experience on an ongoing basis. Our government has created ways to either measure or mandate the anxiety by such means as color-coding potential terrorist attacks. We are collectively driving down life's highway with the **Check Engine** light illuminated on the cultural dashboard. As a result, we live in a chronic state of anger and anxiety. The *collective cultural self* stays in this continual state of "readiness," standing on guard to defend against what is seen or perceived as threat. The result is a state of constancy in which stressors, real or imagined, are seen or perceived as a threat to our safety. If we do not feel safe, nothing else matters.

The Role of Anger and Anxiety

All behavior is either *purposeful* or protective. If purpose drives our behavior, then we have an intentional goal or a target we are trying to hit. In this state of being, there is energy, synergy, and potential for creativity. Our work with other persons will be teamwork, and the environment we will create is one of cooperation. Our behavior develops meaning because the behavior is in service to our purpose.

If our behavior is *protective*, the driving force is anger and anxiety. Simply put, when we are living in a protective mode, we cannot live purposefully! This is why we do not make tuna fish sandwiches when a tornado is coming. This is why the captain does not write poetry when his ship may sink in a hurricane. Making tuna fish is purposeful. Writing poetry requires creative expression. Creativity and chaos cannot occupy the same space at the same time. Either a squirrel will be gathering nuts, which is purposeful, or running away from predators, which is protective. We cannot do both simultaneously. We cannot be gathering nuts and running away from predators.

We human beings share the same reality with squirrels! We cannot be purposeful and protective at the same time. Think back to a time when you were summoned by your boss to attend a meeting, without any information regarding the purpose of the meeting. This use of power creates an intentional imbalance with intimidation and fear as a way of creating control. Did you suddenly find yourself panicky and paranoid? Did you wonder, "What have I done wrong?" Did you begin to obsess and track over a list of things you may have screwed up over the last 30 days?

Think back to a time when you had an appointment with a supervisor to receive a performance evaluation. Did you wake up that morning with excitement or dread? Were you eager, receptive, and at ease or did you feel protective and vulnerable to being attacked?

We cannot be purposeful and protective in the same moment. Let me further explain. Hal Marchman has been a legend in the Daytona Beach area and has been one of the most recognizable leaders in this community for more than a generation. A retired Baptist preacher, Hal was the only chaplain the Daytona International Speedway had ever known from 1959 until his retirement in 2005. The baton was passed to me during Speed Weeks in January and February 2005.

The prayer given before the start of each race is not to exceed 25 seconds. The short prayer helps choreograph all of the pre-race ceremonies, including the National anthem, and the usual fly over of jet fighters, helicopters, or other symbols of military strength. If the prayer is too long, the timing is off, the singer is still singing the anthem, and the jets fly by. It makes for bad television.

I had watched Hal pray his pre-race prayers for years. I am usually a non-anxious individual; I did not think this would be a big deal. On most days, my anxiety level runs at minus two on a scale of one to 10. Things were no different until it was around 10 or 15 minutes before I walked up to the microphone prior to my first prayer at the Budweiser Shoot-Out. My anxiety shot up about 15 points. The Shoot-Out is a Saturday night race for drivers who have won pole-qualifying races. The pole winners from the previous season race against each other for cash prizes. There were around 90,000 people in the stands and a much larger television audience tuned in.

I was later unable to recall and had no idea what I said at the microphone that evening. It was an out of body experience. I could hear the two-second reverberation with the sound bouncing off the grandstands and back at me while I was praying. The first face I saw after I opened my eyes was the producer. Brian's eyes were as big as saucers as he stared at his stopwatch in disbelief. All he could say was, "38 seconds." My first shot out of the cannon, my invocation was 13 seconds over the limit. Fortunately, the Armed Service does not perform flyovers at night. We were eight days away from the premier event, the Daytona 500, also known as "The Super Bowl of Racing," and the rookie chaplain just wet his pants.

It does not take a licensed psychotherapist to diagnose his own case of performance anxiety. The anxiety of the speedway staff, and now, I was told, the Fox Television executives, came not only because I had missed the 25 second mark, but because of what I had also proposed to the vice president of the track. I asked, "What if I invited those 200,000 in attendance for the Daytona 500 and the thirty-seven million watching worldwide if they would like to join me in a prayer for peace in Afghanistan and Iraq?" One executive said to me, *"What do you think this is, Church?"* From their response, I understood that what I was proposing to NASCAR fans might be confusing - praying for peace while also flying weapons of war overhead to whip the crowd into a patriotic fury!

One of the executives decided the way to manage *their* anxiety was to script *my* prayers. I protested. I received the following e-mail correspondence from one of the top executives of the International Speedway Corporation. It came late on the Wednesday before the "Great American Race" on Sunday. ISC owns the Daytona International Speedway and a dozen other tracks on the NASCAR circuit.

> Tim,
>
> Sorry for the delay in responding.
>
> As you mentioned, being on the "other side" offers a whole new perspective. It's an environment that is complex, challenging, controversial, and above all entertaining.

That's right--it's all about the show. From the time the fan leaves his home until the time he/she returns or from the TV tune in until the TV tune out...it's all about the show. For us...it's about planning, promoting executing, timing, and servicing. Whether it's me, you, the vice president of operations, ushers, parkers, security.....well we are all "scripted". The only thing that's not is the race itself. If we disregard "scripting", we will fail in our mission--to entertain. I know this might feel uncomfortable for you (prayer as part of a larger entertainment concept) but those 25 seconds-- which still can be from the heart--must be scripted. It's the same for any other large sports gathering, especially when internationally televised live.

Tim, I've been in the sport now for 22 years. Anxiety is part of the job description in television--you can't manage it--it's what they thrive on. There is an understanding, however, that once the pre-race plan is agreed to by the track and TV, we cannot deviate.

Let's focus on "nailing" it the next four days and we can debrief after the event."

It is all about the show! I guess it was silly of me for thinking this was supposed to be about prayer! I had struggled with "race prayers" for years. Race prayers seemed like a mysterious mixture of wrapping God, the American Flag, and civil religion all rolled into one. Praying to "bless our troops" always felt strange to me. My son was in the Air Force at the time. I had personal interest in "blessing our troops." I wanted God to do what I could not do: protect my son. This I could understand: so what happened when this divine protection policy did not work? What happens when the military vehicle pulls up in your driveway, the uniformed soldiers knock at your door, and the first words spoken are, "I regret to inform you but your son or daughter..."Did this mean God was a slacker and had left the post? Did this mean our prayers for safekeeping were not earnest enough; is it our fault our son or daughter was killed? I was convinced God grieved whenever there was the needless death of a son or daughter regardless of the theory, ideology, philosophy, or theology that was playing behind the scene while these soldiers were pulling the triggers. The prayers often seemed to imply, "keep ours safe and help us kill more of theirs." Praying for the safety of the drivers was also strange to me. How do you pray for the safety of someone who is driving an 800 horsepower billboard traveling two hundred miles per hour aerodynamically hooked together bumper to bumper in a 43-car train? God does not suspend the laws of gravity or physics, and is not responsible for the flaws in human error in order to grant us "safety." Once, I was asked to pray at the start of a rodeo and to pray for the safety of the cowboys. How do you pray for the safety of people who intentionally place themselves in harm's way? All of this seemed to say, "We're going to place ourselves in situations of needless risk *for your entertainment* and we want God to cover the bets in the event it goes bad." It all seemed flawed, childish, and it continued to embed in the minds of the masses a magical understanding of God.

In my naiveté, I was hoping to take "race prayers" in a new direction. Perhaps this was magical thinking on my part, but 37 million people praying for peace might just set the global frequency vibrating at a higher level. However, I understood their anxiety. Hal Marchman had been doing this for 46 years. They never had to worry. I was an unknown entity, and now I was seen as a loose cannon. They needed to control me until I became as predictable as Hal. What I could not get them to understand was *my* anxiety. My protest was not because I wanted to sneak something by them. It was a logistical problem. I could not pray from the heart if my heart was filled with fear. If I am anxious, my brain does not work. No amount of memorization could manage my anxiety. In fact, I might even stand up and call something else out from memory, like the Gettysburg address, Rudyard Kipling's poem, "If," or my name, rank, and serial number like a prisoner of war. What I needed was time, experience, and a learning curve that allowed me to be able to manage my anxiety and re-engage my brain so I could learn to be "comfortable being uncomfortable" in front of the crowds. The bottom line was this: I could not be purposeful and protective at the same time.

When we experience threat to our individual self, family, clan, tribe, team, or nation and the threat bypasses the brain, we will react with anger, anxiety or both. In my experience at the Daytona International Speedway, I felt vulnerable in a new situation where I might potentially fail. I have been professionally involved in public speaking for more than 25 years. I have done public speaking hundreds of times in front of hundreds of people. However, the level of scale did not match the level of experience. 25 years did not translate to 25 seconds in front of massive numbers of people. From an evolutionary perspective, I had been a seasoned and experienced rabbit hunter and I now had to take on a charging saber-toothed tiger. My anxiety was instinctively preparing me to *run* in the opposite direction!

Anger and anxiety are protective emotions. **Protective** behavior is driven by anger or anxiety. On the anger end of the continuum, "Road Rage" provides us with a prime example. It also sells tickets to NASCAR races. If a driver wrecks and his/her car is unable to make a complete lap around the track he/she must go to the infield care center. If the driver has suffered no apparent injuries, his/her head and neck support (HANS) device and helmet show no signs of damage, then the driver is released. In less than five minutes, the driver will be out the door and perched in front of live microphones and cameras.

I have been in the infield care center when drivers are treated under these circumstances. I have seen their "road rage" when they were wrecked by the actions of another driver. Just like anyone else, a driver can become irate when another driver is unfair on the track or driving incompetently. Other sports hold press conferences after the game. Athletes have time to shower first and then meet the press. Not so in NASCAR, drivers have no down time to reflect on this game. The lights on the television cameras are illuminated, and the microphones are shoved in their faces.

The drivers express anger in front of the cameras, but they are prohibited from the use of threatening or profane language.

After witnessing this, I suggested to the executive staff that it might be helpful to assist in deescalating the anger before the drivers got in front of the cameras. From a risk management standpoint, does NASCAR have a responsibility to discourage road rage? What will happen if a road rage death occurs after a NASCAR race? A skilled attorney will use road rage as their point of attack. Attorneys would show film clips of race wrecks and drivers having words, shaking fists, occasionally throwing punches, or intentionally ramming their cars into an offending party. NASCAR might win the case, but it would potentially cost millions of dollars in attorney fees and bad publicity. What if drivers were encouraged to have a cooling down period? What if they were de-briefed before they got in front of the cameras? What if the American Automobile Association (one of the sponsors) did a few safety advertisements, making the distinction between what happens on and off the track? NASCAR could preemptively say, "This is what we have done to discourage road rage." I was basically told that driver drama sells tickets. It allows the fans to fume along with the drivers and pick good guys and bad guys. In short, road rage entertains.

Off the track and on the highways and interstates, road rage is serious business. Road rage is an expression of chronic cultural stress acted out in dangerous ways. When the safety switch is flipped, even mild-mannered individuals behind the wheel of an automobile are capable of becoming stark-raving lunatics. Unless we are driving a Smart Car or a Prius, an automobile can make us feel powerful. The power of the engine somehow travels up the steering column into the hands grasping the wheel. In addition, conscious or unconscious meaning exists between an owner and his/her automobile. An automobile for many persons may be a status symbol. It may be an expression of how I see myself. In my son's late adolescence, he spent a small fortune on his truck, lowering the chassis, chrome rims, big tires, neon lighting, and stereo systems with speakers powerful enough to bring down small airplanes. In and out of his subculture, his truck screamed like a strutting peacock, "NOTICE ME." An automobile can be seen as an extension and expression of my own identity, depending on the make, model, and the price tag. An automobile also provides us with an entitled place where we believe we are supposed to feel safe. We tend to believe we are supposed to feel safe in "our own space," which includes our automobiles. The activation of the rage sensor occurs when a fellow motorist rides too closely to our bumper, cuts us off, or gives the one-finger salute. When this happens at interstate speeds of 70 miles per hour or higher, the immediate reaction of anger, or "rage", is because our need for safety has been disrupted and destabilized by the blatant injustice or incompetence of another driver. Although the incident may serve as a reality test for safety, there is already enough free-floating anger and anxiety on the planet without a test such as this. Free-floating anger is chronic anger looking for a target to attack. Persons carrying free-floating anger are like thunderclouds ready to discharge lightning bolts. Road rage is often an incident from a random encounter. Someone you do not know becomes the target for all the free-floating anger and anxiety going on in your life. With a constant state of chronic stress, anxiety, and anger floating around, a sudden threat to safety is escalated by the heightened reaction of a driver or passenger with his/her finger on the trigger of an automatic weapon or the vehicle itself becoming a 3000-pound battering ram. Violence, if not diffused, will always escalate. This free-floating anger is dangerous and needs to be cured at the core.

Our Darwinian Default Dilemma: The DNA of Human Nature

Human beings share two basic drives with other animals and reptiles: sex and aggression. Freud would call this the "Id" in human beings. Our reptilian brain sits on the top of our spinal cord. When a reptile looks at another subject, the reptile is asking one of four questions based upon these two drives:

1) Is it going to eat me?
2) Am I going to eat it?
3) Is it going to want to have sex with me?
4) Am I going to want to have sex with it?

We human beings forget we have a million years of evolution prior to moving out of the jungle and barely 12,000 years developing civilization, as we know it today. From excavations, archeologists tell us the first cities were established around 10,000 years Before the Common Era. The evolution has involved developing language, farming, trade, art, and mathematics. Hunters and gatherers in time settled and built cities, city-states, and eventually nations or they were driven to extinction by those who did.[c] Hunting and gathering no longer works when land is stolen, surveyed, titled, and a deed is issued to indicate, "This is mine." At times, it has been evolution and in other times, it has been de-evolution, three steps forward, two steps back.

As we look backward in time 12,000 years is only the blink of an eye in the history and development of our species. Humankind, in the modern era, has not come to terms with the fact we have yet to transcend our animal nature. If we don't wake up soon, there may only be a precious few of us left who will then be driven back to the jungle to complete our de-evolution and the few will be forced to start over again. We are wired for life in the jungle. Will it be a remnant that will return to the jungle? Would our world begin to look like the one depicted in Cormac McCarthy's novel, *The Road*?[6] Civilization is merely a veneer that barely covers our collective human dysfunction, like a tank top inadequately hiding the overhang of a well-

---

[c] Native Americans were nearly decimated by the expansion of the United States in all directions.

maintained beer belly. In the last 100 years, we have made technological advances that have surpassed all previous technologies including the domestication of fire and the invention of the wheel. However, we have done pitifully poor at solving our Darwinian dilemma and dealing with the DNA of human nature.

The only game played in the jungle is "survival of the fittest." The weak are eliminated; the strong survive. You can watch it on the Discovery Channel any time you turn on a television set. Salmon struggle to get upstream to spawn, and bears wait in the water to load up on fresh fish. Sea lions hunt down, kill, and eat seals. Our species has learned how to civilize, sanitize, and domesticate the death of other animals we eat for food.

Blood lust and the thrill of the kill is an entirely different matter. Our species is the only one that kills for entertainment. Boxing is sanctioned and socially acceptable. Pugilists receive multi-million dollar purses. Main event promoters sign pay-per-view contracts so the public can watch in the privacy of their own homes while secretly satisfying their lust for blood. Ringside celebrities and spectators add glamour and glitz. They wear evening gowns and black ties, which provide an aura of sophistication. Las Vegas odds makers set the odds and gamblers place their bets. With the ringing of the bell, the battle begins. After each three-minute segment a scantily clad woman with bulging breasts wearing six inch heels will provocatively parade around the canvas holding aloft numbered signs to signify the next round. Directors of marketing know that connecting the dots between sex and aggression, our Darwinian default, sells, promotes, and packages their products. Other than these brief interludes between rounds, the battle will not end until someone is bloodied beyond recognition and unable to continue or knocked unconscious. Death occurs intermittently, but it does happen. If the fight goes the distance, ringside judges decide the fate of the fighters and a draw or a winner is declared. Our species is the only one that kills for entertainment. Boxing is sanctioned and acceptable, while other expressions of the same forms of violence are not.

When breaking news events periodically remind us of the savagery human beings are capable of committing, I am frequently amazed at the amazement of others, as was the case with NFL quarterback Michael Vick and the entire dog fighting to the death scandal. When someone does something to remind us we are animals, we act appalled, incensed and are quick to assign shame and humiliation. Is dog fighting just one vicarious step away from watching gladiators or boxers fighting to the death, substituting dogs instead of humans, wagering on the winners, and exterminating the losers if they are not killed in the process? Does this happen in nature when two bears, lions, or elk are fighting for supremacy? Is it because this venue is forced and controlled? Does cruelty to animals touch us in a deeper place than cruelty between humans? As students of human nature we must ask, "Why the uproar?" Do we connect things done in secret with being shameful or even illegal? Does either of these venues satisfy the same lust for blood?

Our Darwinian dilemma and the DNA of human nature is that the default setting resets to our basic drives: sex and aggression. Aggression in its extreme is "kill or be killed." Stress management, in this model, involves the sadistic satisfaction of retaliation and revenge. An eye for an eye and a tooth for a tooth is a basic tenet of retaliatory justice: it limits retaliatory justice so that the boundaries are not exceeded. Retaliation tends to exceed and go beyond the original injury. "If you take my eye, I will take both of yours. If you attack my village, I will burn yours to the ground and make slaves of your women and children."

The following email, one of those forwarded types, is designed to give the reader a grin, because it hits a crude truth. The scenario is designed to offer peaceful, serene, guided imagery meditation. The punch line comes at the end. Here is the intro:

"Just in case you are having a rough day, here is a

stress management technique recommended in all the latest psychological journals. The funny thing is that it really does work. Think about each step below. The entire process can be successfully accomplished in less than one minute."

1. Picture yourself lying on your belly on a warm rock that hangs out over a crystal-clear stream.
2. Picture yourself with both your hands dangling in the cool running water.
3. Birds are sweetly singing in the cool mountain air. No one knows your secret place.
4. You are in total seclusion from that hectic place called the world. The soothing sound of a gentle waterfall fills the air with a cascade of serenity.
5. The water is so crystal-clear that you can easily *make out the face of the person you are holding underwater.*

In this imaginary meditative moment, holding an adversary underwater and watching him or her drown is supposed to make me feel better by creating a fantasy of retaliatory revenge: a terror-filled face with eyeballs bulging, lungs sucking in water, and bubbles bursting the silent screams as they break the surface of the water. Is this sadistic scene supposed to make me feel better? Revenge is always about communicating to other persons how their actions make us feel. The *intent* is purposeful. It makes sense. The *method* is what causes problems! Why does the author of this meditation say it is "a funny thing that works?" Perhaps it is because in the default mode of human nature there is a sick sadistic sense of enjoyment that comes from watching someone who *caused* the pain to suffer the same hurt with even greater intensity.

Retaliation and revenge is also, unfortunately, one of the basic tenets of foreign policy. Retaliation and revenge can even be anticipatory! You can retaliate *before* you are hit! What if you were never hit? How would you know? Ooops? While coaching a client running for political office, the client inverted the Golden Rule and revealed the rationale for pre-emptive strikes: "Oh, so I am supposed to do unto others *before* they do it unto me." I do not believe I can remember the great icon of American cinema, John Wayne, ever using pre-emptive strikes.

One of the most influential spiritual teachers of history stood in the middle of the tradition of retaliatory justice and reinterpreted it:

> "You have heard that it was said, 'An eye for an eye and a tooth for a tooth.' But I say to you, do not resist one who is evil. But if any one strikes you on the right cheek, turn to him the other also; and if any one would sue you and take your coat, let him have your cloak as well; and if any one forces you to go one mile, go with him two miles. Give to him who begs from you, and do not refuse him who would borrow from you."[d]

This spiritual teacher radically reinterprets this foundational Darwinian principle. I do not think he is saying to Tony and others involved in domestic violence to stay in the environment and take their beating. What I do believe he is saying is that at some point we have to choose not to react to violence. Whatever we oppose, we strengthen. Reacting to violence only increases the reaction in the other. Violence regroups, re-strengthens, and returns bigger, meaner, and stronger than before. It happened in Germany after World War I. It moved to the Soviet Union after World War II. I shudder to think what will happen in the days ahead as the United States continues to fight the war on Global Terrorism, a war without borders or boundaries. Author Karen Armstrong has written, "What happens in Afghanistan or Iraq today will somehow have repercussions in London or Washington tomorrow."[7]

Human beings have been created to transcend our basic drives and our identity as animals. Over the last million years, we evolved four more brains on top of the reptilian brain. Transformed consciousness is about getting all five

---

[d] Jesus, quoted in the Sermon on the Mount, from the Revised Standard Version of the Bible, Matthew 5: 38-42

brains hooked up on the same page working together in synchronistic fashion. Transformed consciousness is more like synchronized swimming than watching toothless ice hockey players bloody up the ice while carrying lethal weapons and fighting over a three inch round black disc. On the other hand, perhaps it is more like the integrated sounds of syncopated jazz than the blatant rage of gangster rap.

Beyond Anger Management

I frequently receive telephone calls from members of the community who will inquire if the Genesis Counseling Center offers courses on "anger management." A local county mental health department refers these persons or they have been mandated to receive anger management through the judicial system. Persons mandated to receive anger management through the court system are usually facing charges of domestic violence or assault and battery.

The term "anger management" has always struck me as being somewhat ludicrous. Is anger something to be "managed"? "Manage" is derived from the Latin word *manus*, which translates as "hand." The original meaning associated with the word manage was "to train a horse in his paces." By definition, are they asking me to place a bit in their mouths and walk them around in their paces until their anger is "managed"? The anger may still be there, but the bit in the mouth and the harness over their heads keeps it controlled. This may be an improvement, but is there more to it? Could it involve a question of one's core feeling of safety?

In a business model, anger management conjures up a corporate or business application to the emotion of anger for the purposes of productivity and efficiency. In the behavioral model, which dominates many managed-care psychotherapies, Mr. Smith or Mrs. Jones is given a treatment plan with attainable goals. These goals are measured and documented in order to demonstrate improvement. What is the plan and how do we get there? Although treatment plans and goals are an integral part of reimbursement scenarios with many insurance companies, measuring the effects in psychotherapy may be more difficult to plot on a graph and at times appear ridiculous. "When provoked, Mr. Smith or Mrs. Jones will be able to successfully remain calm and at ease in six out of eight times in the next six to eight weeks." This may be the goal, but why are we provoked in the first place? What are the underlying triggers that bypass the brain and create instinctual survival reactivity? These underlying triggers will be exposed later, but for now let it suffice to say that the overall plan is a process. The period of accomplishment may be a lifetime!

Anger is not meant to be a *managed* emotion. In a higher state of consciousness, anger is meant to be *transformed*. Anger and anxiety provide the necessary heat to fuel, inflame and incinerate the false self. When we discover how to *hold* these emotions, we begin a lifelong journey churning in a cauldron of change and transformation. We then set out to discover our destiny *beyond* our Darwinian heritage and to *recover* our identity as spiritual beings.

Karen Armstrong, in her book *The Great Transformation: The Beginning of Our Religious Traditions,* has written:

> "Human beings are probably conditioned to self-defense. Every since we have lived in caves we have been threatened by animal and human predators. Even within our own communities and families, other people oppose our interests and damage our self-esteem. So we are perpetually poised verbally, mentally, and physically for counter-attack and pre-emptive strike. But if we methodically cultivated an entirely different mindset, the sages discovered, we experienced an alternative state of consciousness." [8]

In review, anger and anxiety are autonomic and automatic responses to the experience of threat. The Darwinian solution to *every situation* is:

1) Kill or be killed
2) Run or be killed

Let us look again at our Darwinian default, explore our instinctual wiring, and see what we are attempting to transform as we seek to arrive at an "alternative state of consciousness." When Joe and Josephine Caveperson walked out of their cave on a sunny day and they saw a saber-toothed tiger at the entrance, they would either do one of the following:

1) Move the club off his or her shoulder and whack the tiger on the head *or*
2) Run back into the cave and hide

Our first instinctual response is to eliminate the threat, either by destroying it or by eluding it. In this situation, Joe and Josephine Caveperson do not want to end up as *lunch* for the saber-toothed tiger. The firing of the neurological networks that dilate our arteries and veins and inject our bodies with adrenaline and cortisol do so to prepare us to alternatively swing the club or head for the hills.

Granted, real circumstances arise that do require us to protect, defend, or to get out of harm's way. Even our cave dwelling ancestors experienced these circumstances. However, the mind does not always receive a clear interpretation of the threat. Consider phobic reactions to such benign objects as bridges or ladders. A key component is trauma associated with these objects. Bridges infrequently collapse. Why would a news spectator a thousand miles away develop a phobia about bridges while someone whose car plunged into icy waters does not? We frequently struggle with understanding whether or not a threat is real or imagined. This same Darwinian mechanism also fires into action from our *learned* responses to threat whether the threat is real or imagined.

Purposeful and Protective: Our Learned Responses: Introducing a Working Model

During the book writing process, I began to develop a working theory, a "theory about theory." I also began testing the theory in my counseling with individuals, couples, volunteer organizations, businesses, hospitals, and churches. In the following paragraphs, I will introduce the theory and offer a more in-depth explanation of this model in the next chapter.

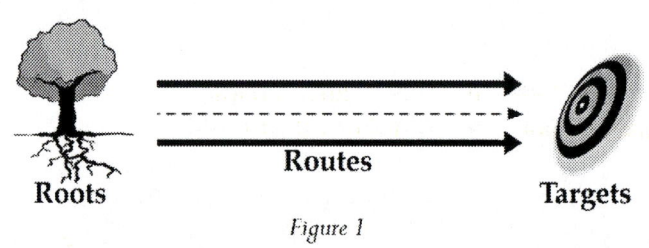

Figure 1

Roots, Routes, and Targets

First, our stories are rooted in our *history* and *experience*. If you visit a cemetery, you will see the names of persons buried in graves or entombed in mausoleums. Underneath the name, you will see the date of birth and the date of death. Between the two dates is a dash. Our history and experience is the "dash between the dates." This dash carries with it our own unique collection of stories. These stories involve a specific location of time and place. The stories involve parents who were absent or present. They involve siblings and schools. The experiences involve childhood, adolescence and adulthood. They chronicle where we have been and what we have done. Our stories involve comedy and tragedy, success and failure. This is our unique history and experience; it is our own story. One day, our story will be singularly summarized as a dash between two dates.

Our stories reveal our roots. Our roots ground us in ways that are either purposeful or protective. The root systems of the yellow pine and the palmetto have adapted through evolution in order to insure survival of the species when bolts of lightning ignite forests and set them ablaze. The southern yellow pine, indigenous to the Southeastern United States, grows three to five years underground before it erupts out of the soil with its first bushy explosion of green growth. Saw Palmettos are one of the quickest scrub plants to respond after a fire. After a palmetto burns, the charred stem can produce a new leaf within a week of a fire. Because the stem is so well protected, it never burns below the ground. Roots are foundational. Roots keep us grounded. They reach down into the earth to draw nutrients from the soil.

Wisdom, integrity, and character provide strong purposeful roots that feed the soil of the soul. A wise teacher once compared and contrasted the difference between building a house on sand or rock. Without a solid foundation, a tree or a structure is unstable especially in times of threat or danger. In Florida, houses built on sand do not survive storm surges unless they are constructed on 18-foot stilts. If roots are not deep and foundations are not solid, a crisis will create an implosion of the self and erosion of the soul.

Secondly, *our roots inform our routes.* Our roots will pave the pathways we take to reach our destination. If our roots are rooted in what is principled and purposeful, there will be energy and synergy for the journey. Our roots shape, mold, inform, adapt, and adopt the ongoing development of our own particular theory, philosophy, theology, or ideology of life. New experience provides the opportunity for the modification and continuous improvement of our own theory, philosophy, theology, or ideology. Our roots allow us to draw forth a consciously developed theory that explains, orders, prioritizes, clarifies, and improves the "why" of why we do what we do and the targets we are attempting to hit.

Thirdly, our pathways or our *routes* provide the linkage between our roots and our destination, or rather, our *targets.* Our routes will be either purposeful or protective and will involve the development of our own particular philosophy, theology, or ideology and the methods we consciously choose to hit targets. Our roots help to determine our routes and pathways for decision making, setting our course and direction, and hitting targets.

If not driven by reactivity, anger, and anxiety, our routes will become purposeful pathways to hitting targets. Targets must have a built-in intrinsic value. *Energy flows where our attention goes.* These targets will function like magnets. If our targets are effective, they can draw us toward them. There must be a compelling component about the target for this to happen. When we see them we will have an "aha, that's it" moment of internal recognition. This compelling component creates an internal ignition to create motivation, motion, and movement. At some point, these two areas intersect between an internalized energy that pushes us and a compelling target that pulls us.

In the following illustration, I add the two additional components of purposeful and protective. Purposeful behavior pushes us forward and pulls us toward reaching our destinations. Protective emotions cannot meaningfully sustain behavior. A coach may use these emotions to fire up a team to beat a rival, but they cannot replace skill, timing, and execution necessary to work synergistically as a team. Anger and anxiety are regressed states, and they generally move us backward.

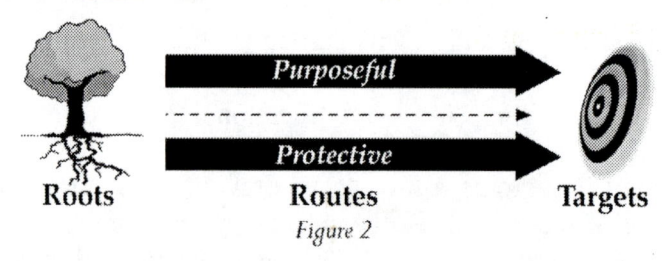

Roots   *Purposeful* / *Protective*   Routes   Targets

Figure 2

The model begins with our roots, which are our own unique history and experience. Our history and experience in turn creates ideas and beliefs that shape the *lens* of how we see the world. Our lens will be different if we are raised in Baghdad, Bangladesh, or Boulder City, Colorado. Our families, our faith, our schools, our education, our socioeconomic backgrounds all work together to establish the color of our cultural corneas.

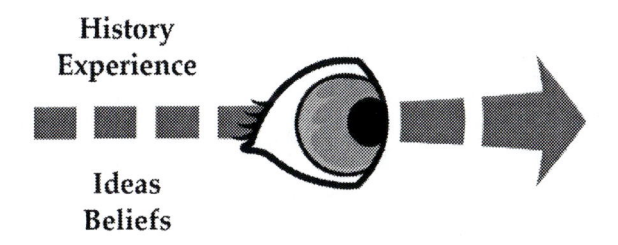

History
Experience

■ ■ ■ 👁 ➡

Ideas
Beliefs

Figure 3

Frequently our history and experience creates a lens that makes us see the world in ways that are skewed, reactive, and distorted. *Learned* responses to threat from childhood, adolescence, and adulthood become embedded in our brains. This involves our experiences with parents, siblings, peers, and all previous relationships. This involves encounters we have had with persons in authority, people we have admired and persons we have loathed. This involves specific circumstances and general encounters we have lumped together in huge emotional hairballs. These cumulative learned responses to threat have shaped our history and experience. Because of the skewing that takes place, we may perceive threat when no threat exists or the threat is minimal. In other words, the saber tooth tiger may just be a Siamese cat!

Given a choice most of us would not choose to live reactively with our **"check engine"** lights constantly aglow and with anger and anxiety waiting to erupt, like molten lava, just below the surface. We end up living this way when we become stuck and immobilized in unconscious patterns. These unconscious patterns are rooted in our history and experience. Our vision will be distorted when our personal history and experience has created ideas and beliefs through an unclear lens. We will look at the world in ways that are skewed and reactive. Before proceeding with this model in the next chapter, we will take a brief detour to look at what happens when we become stuck and why.

From Enmeshment to Disengagement, Reflection, and Re-engagement: When We Become FRICKed

```
        Enmeshment
      ↗           ↘
Re-engagement   Dis-engagement
      ↖           ↙
        Reflection
```

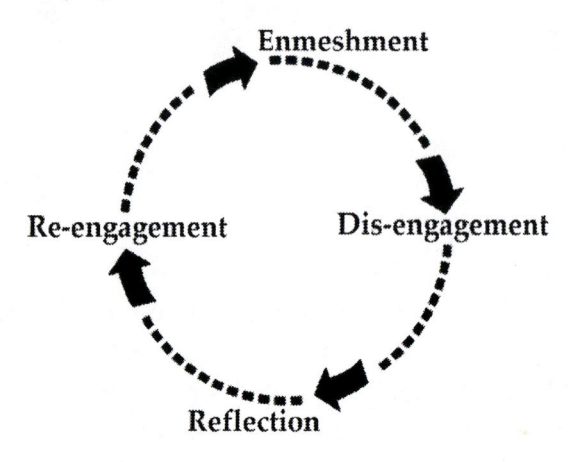

Figure 4

Enmeshment creates immobilization. When we are immobilized, we are stuck. So how do we get unstuck?

One of the popular "sports" among teenagers and young adults in my area is "mudding." This involves four-wheel drive vehicles, mud bogs, and a "Dukes of Hazard" lifestyle. Think about this model as if you were driving a 4x4 truck and you were stuck in the mud. You could dig out around the tires, strategically place 2"x 4" studs under the tires, and slowly drive your way out of the mud, rocking back and forth until you gained the necessary traction. Alternatively, you might need to call a tow truck or a friend with a power winch to pull you out. Once safely dislodged from the mud, you look over the terrain and determine what you *would* and *would not* do over again. Would you need waders to determine how deep the mud is before you attempt to drive through again? Would you adjust your speed slower or faster? In other words, what did you learn so you can avoid being stuck again? With this newfound wisdom, you turn the ignition key, fire up the truck, and re-engage the mud with newly gained knowledge.

We may go through this process ten times a day in rapid succession dealing with one problem-solving challenge after another. It may be as simple as finding your car keys or because of an accident, finding an alternative route to work. We momentarily disengage, think it through, and start over again. It may be altogether different if you get a pink slip, your spouse tells you she does not love you, or your daughter announces she is pregnant. Depending on the circumstance, the situation, the issue, the intensity, and the individual, some people are able to work things out on their own. A turtle stuck on its back may eventually be able to rock back and forth and roll over onto its feet. Far more think they can do this on their own when actually they need the willingness to ask for help. Men especially struggle with asking for help. We somehow believe we are weak if we cannot work it out on our own. The most competent thing we can do is to know when we need to ask for help. Vulnerability is a pre-requisite for emotional and spiritual growth.

We are social beings. We are not wired for isolation. We need community and connection, which will be the focus in Chapter 5. Connection is crucial to the process of disengagement and entering into purposeful reflection. A spouse, a wise friend, support groups, twelve step recovery groups, or any other small community of individuals who spin networks of healthy and effective relationships are critical to the creation and maintenance of connection. One of the most common questions I am asked is, "How long will this take?" I never know what to say. I conducted an intervention with the employees of a bank after a robbery. It took one day. For intensive reconstructive work, it may take a year or two. A large majority of the work takes three to six months. Unfortunately, third parties, such as insurance coverage, often dictate the limits of the process – or at least how much they will cover.

Counseling and consulting consistently begins with the presentation of one or more issues where an individual, couple, family, or system is stuck. So how do we know when we are stuck? This is what I call the **"FRICK"** principle. How do you know when you are **FRICK**ed? The acronym stands for:

1) **Frustration,** which is externally focused at an object, person, situation, or a circumstance when you cannot get "it" to do what you want it to do. I blame someone or something else.
2) **Reactivity,** when current situations evoke strong emotions from unresolved issues in the past. Hysterical is always historical.
3) **Internalization**, when frustration is interjected within the self. I blame myself.
4) **Conflicted thoughts, feelings, or emotions**, when I am thinking one way and feeling another way and I am struggling to resolve the internalized conflict.
5) **Knowledge**, or self-awareness that one or more of these four things is going on.

When we are **"FRICKed,"** we have lost our inner homeostasis or balance. The **"F"** in **FRICK** is **frustration**. Frustration is anger projected onto an object, a circumstance, a situation, or an individual when you cannot get it to do what you want it to do. For me, this would include golf clubs and computers. The strength of golf clubs becomes compromised once they are wrapped around a tree. Over the last 20 years, I could not tell you how many times I have turned on a computer only to encounter *"The Blue Screen of Death."* If it would provide an ecological benefit, I would advocate throwing all golf clubs and computers into the ocean in order to build a fishing reef. Eventually coral would begin forming and an ecological habitat would begin to grow. However, even fishing can become suspect. If you have ever been fishing, you have experienced those moments when you have encountered a "bird's nest." This type of "bird's nest" is not the variety you would see if you were navigating a skiff through backwater creeks, admiring a natural item of beauty, a miracle of engineering carefully constructed on the branch of a tree or in the hollow of its trunk. I am attempting to describe what you would be holding in your hands. A bird's nest occurs in that moment when casting the rod and releasing the thumb from the reel does not synchronize. The result is a tangled mess of fishing line that clearly resembles a bird's nest. Before fishing can resume, skill and patience are required to untangle the mess. When this happens to me, I immediately hand the rod over to the most experienced angler on the boat and plead for help.

Frustration is often an expression of anger when we are feeling overwhelmed. The frustration is often directed at the object that is "uncooperative", whether it is a bird's nest or a relationship. When we were living in Hollywood, Florida, a retired gentleman attended the church where I worked as an associate pastor. He was a gentle and hospitable man, and occasionally I would spend an afternoon at his home, drinking iced tea, discussing life, and shooting pool. As a hobby, he enjoyed repairing bicycles for neighborhood children. He would also build bicycles from scraps found in trash heaps and on curbsides and give them away to needy children. I owned a bicycle in need of repair, and he offered to fix it. I brought him the bicycle and a paper grocery sack full of spare parts. In a week or two, he performed his miracle and called me to tell me my bicycle was repaired and ready to go. When I was loading the bicycle into the trunk of my car and expressing my gratitude, he waited for the right moment to ask me a probing question. He grabbed what I thought was the empty sack and said to me there were a few extra parts he did not know where to attach. Curiously, I approached him and asked what did not fit. "Where does this go?" Creating more drama and curiosity on my part, he reached into the sack and slowly pulled out a ball peen hammerhead. I had broken the hammerhead in my furious attempts to loosen the pedals and had mistakenly added this "extra part" to the others in the sack. I was busted! My face flushed with embarrassment, but

I soon recovered, and we both got a good-natured laugh out of my frustration. When the frustration focuses on the *object*, we are usually blaming the object, circumstance, situation, or person for our frustration.

The **R** in **FRICK** stands for **reactivity**. Reactivity occurs when something in the present touches old pain that is lying just underneath the surface. The dormant, unresolved pain from the past is awakened like a screaming giant. If someone says to you, "Have a nice day," and your response is, **"WHO IN THE HELL DO YOU THINK YOU ARE TO BE TELLING ME WHAT TO DO?"** Sure as shootin' something else is going on just underneath the surface! When we are stuck, or immobilized, we find ourselves consistently living in a reactive mode. As previously indicated, anger and anxiety are protective behaviors, and they are *always in response to threat.* When we are stuck in reactivity, we have no choice, and we will only react. When a physician strikes the little rubber hammer just below the knee, and the knee jerks up, the reflex is a reaction to the stimulus. No cognition is involved. When certain circumstances or situations create emotional reactions (similar to the knee-jerk reaction), no cognition is involved. Disengagement requires *slowing down reactivity* in order to bring this into the realm of conscious awareness, cognition, and choice. Awareness creates options. Options establish choice. In any given moment, we may have 30 to 50 different options from which to choose. If we are not aware of being stuck, chances are slim to none anything will change. We move from enmeshment toward disengagement the moment that consciousness creates awareness about being stuck.

This moves us toward the "**I**" in **FRICK,** the third indicator of being stuck. Whereas frustration is the *projection* of anger and blame onto an object, a circumstance, a situation, or a person, when we *interject* the frustration, we *internalize* it. In other words, we *internalize* blame rather than *externalize* it. This internalizing or interjecting of blame creates an instant formula for feelings of hopelessness, helplessness, and despair. Internalization is a direct route to depression. The clinical indicator occurs when these experiences last for longer than two weeks. Untreated, prolonged experiences of enmeshment elongate, distort, and exaggerate the past. The past is then projected into the future and the loop is completed. The present becomes bracketed between the horrible past and an anticipated more-of-the-same dismal future. "It has always been (past) bad, it is always going to be (future) bad, and it is bad now (present)!" After one sojourner experienced a step forward, she began the backward slide into the descent of despair. When I asked if she had noticed what had happened when she began the decent, she replied in an e-mail correspondence:

> i have no idea. There has just been a steady slide since mid-afternoon. i can't believe i have been stupid enough to think that things were actually getting better. i feel awful right now. There is no way that things can get better. This is what i deserve and nothing else. i don't know what has been happening over the last couple of days. i have come back to the reality. How did i ever think that i could get away from what i have been… it will never change. The urge to use a knife has just hit me so strongly. There is so much pain still inside and i don't know what to do with it. i don't know how to face it, to feel, to let it go.[e]

Unless we are chronically and chemically depressed, periodic experiences of enmeshment and the feelings that accompany these experiences are normal. Although enmeshment is not the preferable state of existence, enmeshment can be a purposeful component of human experience. These wilderness experiences are often necessary times of healthy incubation. No living organism can sustain growth indefinitely. All organisms require

---

[e] Notice the self-reference with her refusal to capitalize "I," which seems directly connected to her own sense of insignificance. She constantly battles feeling diminished and "feeling small".

periods of dormancy, restoration and renewal.

The "C" in **FRICK** stands for the fourth indicator of being stuck. The C stands for *conflicted thoughts, feelings, or emotions.* If you can understand this sentence, you will understand precisely what this is about: I may be thinking one way and feeling another way and wishing I were feeling different from the way I am feeling and I do not like the way I am feeling. It is like having two 375-pound Sumo wrestlers in your head. One is wearing a red mawashi, the other is wearing a blue mawashi, and one is trying to throw the other one out of the ring.

Conflicted thoughts or emotions may indicate where we are out of alignment with the *principles* that guide our journey. Psychopaths or persons who are emotionally autistic do not experience conflicted thoughts or emotions. The rest of us do! The nature of human existence is that we are always drawn into dilemmas! Take a hypothetical situation involving two events competing for your time. Suppose your son's soccer league calls an organization meeting. A friend has pressured you into presiding at the meeting and organizing the event. You are getting dressed, sputtering around with angst and dread, angry with your friend for pressuring you and mad at yourself for taking on something you did not want to do. Another friend calls and says he just lucked into two courtside tickets for a Boston Celtic home game. The tip-off is at 8:00 p.m. and he wants you to go with him. How would you handle this dilemma? Have you ever found yourself caught in a similar situation? Have you ever had to decide between honoring a commitment driven by duty and obligation, and being enticed by something that would be selfish and fun? Would you call in "sick" at the last minute and head for the game? Would you call and tell the truth and head for the game? Would you go to the meeting feeling you had lost a moment you deserved, feeling angry and resentful? Would you have declined the invitation to the game and headed to your commitment with joy and excitement?

Deadlines require decision. Depending on the immediacy of the issue, the decision may take increments of our lives from moments to months, to triage the event, thought, or emotion and evaluate, discern, and determine which way we need to go. Decisions may heighten feelings of anxiety, especially if we sense our character is at stake. How do you process two conflicted thoughts or emotions? What principles would guide your decision and how would you resolve this dilemma? What is your set of criteria for decision-making? Detaching from enmeshment, creating new learning and insight, and re-engagement may take milliseconds or millennia.[f]

The **K** in **FRICK** stands for knowledge, or self-awareness in knowing one or more of these things are going on at the same time. Frustration, reactivity, internalization, and conflicted thoughts, feelings, or emotions may lead to breakthroughs in awareness of our enmeshment and entanglement. Denial is penetrated at this point, and we are ready to get on our Apollo radio and proclaim, "Houston, we have a problem." When we become entangled, the line usually involves two or more of the seven areas explored in this book. When we find we are in a full-blown bird's nest, this may involve all seven! Something becomes ensnared in the areas of our life that involve safety, meaning, justice, competence, connection, healing, or transcendence.

We may be able to get it untangled on our own, or we may begin to look for the most experienced angler on our

---

[f] As for millennia enmeshment, since the beginning of time we have wrestled with the dilemma of human evil. During the 20th century we humans killed 100 million of our own species. Although there are hundreds of thousands of individual triumphant victories, as a species, our enmeshment in the human condition has not demonstrated improvement. As Eckhart Tolle states, "It used to be humans were able to kill ten or twenty people with a club, so is it progress now when we can kill ten to twenty million people with the push of a button?" If we do not learn to raise the level of consciousness and effectively confront our individual and collective denial, enmeshment, and expressions of evil, our technology now makes possible the annihilation of planet earth and the extinction of our own species. Natives in the global village must become restless and demand change!

boat who may help us get our life untangled. Establishing therapeutic rapport and a covenant of care facilitates the beginning work of unraveling the entanglement. A wise friend, counselor, consultant, or coach creates a safe environment for holding and nudging the individual or system in its entanglement. *Holding* is established through empathy, care, competence, and the development of trust. *Nudging* involves raising awareness, consciousness, and confronting with truth. I have seen this happen very quickly with individuals, and I have seen it take a year or more when the persons involved have deeply repressed traumatic experiences involving ongoing sexual abuse. When these dynamics are in place, disengagement begins, and we begin to move toward reflection and re-engagement.

When counseling is effective and purposeful, the therapeutic relationship provides the embodiment of this process of getting "unFRICKed" and moving from enmeshment to disengagement, reflection, and re-engagement. Here is a situation to demonstrate how this worked for Scott and his family. Scott discovered in the early years of mid-life he was mismatched in his career. He felt frustrated and confused and he wanted to discover and move in the direction of his passion, which now was elusive and undiscovered. His spouse wanted him to come to therapy to help him learn how to deal with his fits of rage. Her family lived in South Florida, and she reported times of intense fear when riding in the car with Scott. When Scott got behind the wheel, he used the automobile as a means to express his free-floating rage at excessive rates of speed and at anyone who appeared to be a threat. She not only feared for her life but for their two sons.

Scott was the third of four children. His parents were retired and living close by. His remaining siblings were scattered throughout the country. Scott, his wife and children lived in a comfortable home in an affluent subdivision. Scott was a very likeable person with a great sense of humor and a history of deep personal pain. Scott wanted to adopt a third child into their family, and his wife, from a family of nine children, was opposed. Gina had an ideal working relationship with her company, and she commuted via Internet to her office a thousand miles each working day. Scott owned his own business and worked out of his home. Scott was unhappy with his work, was generally depressed from time to time, and vocationally he felt he needed to be doing something else. A turning point came in his work with me when Gina came to a session and reported she did not *feel safe* with Scott, although he had never done anything to physically harm or threaten her. Scott was stunned when he heard Gina tell him this. He was increasingly becoming more reactive, barking and snapping at Gina and their two sons. On a recent trip to Miami, she told him she did not feel safe and wanted to get out of the car when he was driving overly aggressive. Gina told Scott that she felt constantly intimidated by him. Scott was stunned. He realized feeling intimidated was the way he felt growing up with his father. Scott was repeatedly the target of many of his father's frequent and violent expressions of anger. He recalled an incident when he was a teenager and working at an ice cream shop. One evening the owner wanted to take his employees out for pizza. Scott tried to call home and ask permission but could not reach anyone, so he went out with his friends and his employer. Scott came home an hour and a half after his curfew. His father met him in the driveway in a blind rage and hit him over the head with a two-by-four!

    Scott began to face the rage he had with his father. He realized it was getting in the way of him being successful in his role as a husband and father, and perhaps it might have something to do with the lack of meaning he felt vocationally. When he looked at his family of origin, he realized he had never communicated with his father. The pattern was for his mother to be the one who would "mediate" between both him and his father, and she became the key interpreter for both of them to each other. On one occasion while working with Scott, I commented on this pattern and suggested to him the idea that his mother functioned as the "family kidney." She functioned as a dialysis machine by purifying the poison between the two of them. Scott received this comment as if I had hit him with a taser. He felt stung by the shocking truth of this family dynamic.

Scott realized he never "looked up to" or idealized his father. He realized he did not like being in sales since this was not his natural way of relating to people. His father had been in sales, and he had always seen his father as being inauthentic and fake, a way he was now beginning to feel about himself. He also knew "being his own boss" had a great deal to do with problems he had with authority. Working for someone else always created constant conflict with persons who were in authority over him. Scott could now avoid this problem by being self-employed and by owning his own business. Being self-employed and owning his own business also involved Scott's desperate need to be successful, something he wanted to *prove* to his father.

After toying with the idea of changing careers, he looked in depth at the possibility of becoming a physician's assistant. He ultimately decided he wanted to teach. He loved kids, and one source of emotional oxygen he received throughout this entire process was the volunteer work he did as the coach of his son's soccer team. He enjoyed the idealization he received that came with being "coach". I warned Scott this would not repair the damage or frustration that came with his inability to idealize his own father.

Scott began to see his father differently, and he became far more tolerant with him than he had ever been. When Scott first began counseling, he had written his father a letter to express that he had forgiven him for the harsh mistreatment he received during childhood and adolescence. Although he truly wanted to feel the forgiveness toward his father he had written in the letter, his emotions had not yet caught up with his intent. He was experiencing the "C" in FRICK. He was thinking one way and feeling another. After reading the letter, his father's response was, "What harsh treatment?" Scott's father was never able to acknowledge the damage he had done. Scott held out for the longest time, in hope that his father's ability to see how his behavior affected others would be miraculously healed. He desperately wanted his father to acknowledge the hurt he had inflicted. It never happened. He never did see it, and Scott got to the point where it was o.k. if he did not. He no longer needed his father's blessing. He had discovered it within himself.

Scott's mother eventually divorced her husband when she finally had enough. The precipitating incident occurred when Scott's father verbally attacked, berated, and humiliated a teen-age granddaughter at the dinner table. It was an incident Scott, his 2 brothers, and his sister had endured while growing up a thousand times. In six months, Scott's father remarried having now truly found "the love of his life", divorced a short time later, and remarried for the third time.

Scott had already gotten a handle on his anger and was relating differently to both Gina and his sons. Their marriage was working again. Scott learned in counseling that his history and experience had created ideas and beliefs that shaped how he saw his world. He learned his lens often made his perceptions of reality skewed, reactive, and distorted. It was his birthright and something he had environmentally inherited from his father. His career path in sales was an unconscious attempt to follow his father's example and to earn his father's acceptance and approval. He had unconsciously adopted and adapted many of his father's skewed, reactive, and distorted ways of seeing the world. Through our work together, healing took place, and a new vision for his future emerged out of this work.

Freed from trying to please his father, he set his sights on a new vocational target. Having already received his bachelor's degree many years earlier, Scott checked with the local school board and discovered he only needed six classes to teach at the elementary school level. With this target drawing him forward, his passion ignited as he set his sights. He sold his business, headed back to school, and finished his pilgrimage with me.

Through the work of disengaging from his enmeshment, Scott learned how to slow down his automatic trigger points of rage. Through the process of reflection, he took a pilgrimage through his family of origin and saw how many of these experiences over time had layered and clouded his perceptions of reality. Scott grieved, released the pain, and he began to heal. With new insight, awareness, and behavior, he began the process of re-engagement with his wife, his sons, and his career.

Whereas enmeshment feels like *descent*, as if we have been thrown into a miry bog, disengagement and reflection feel like *ascent*, as if we are climbing the stairway to heaven. Often an individual feels *relief* when he or she successfully disengages from enmeshment. Imagine carrying around a 50-pound backpack for days, weeks, months, or even years and being able to loosen the straps and let it fall to the ground! With relief comes release. You are no longer carrying around the extra weight! Does that feel better? No longer weighed down, we experience relief and release. We replace these feelings with emotions that enable us to feel light, airy, and spontaneous joy.

Disengagement and reflection create the potential for experiencing new emotion and perspective. When we are disengaged, we are able to *see* the forest. Prior to disengagement, we would not be able to see the forest for the fires. One reason couples, families, and systems have difficulty breaking out of their dysfunction internally, is because they are too close to the situation. The closer we are to the situation the higher the probability we are at risk for being stuck. Someone must act out for the situation to be clearer. Seeing the forest, we gain perspective and grasp the bigger picture. Forest rangers ascend towers to keep visual vigils over the threat of fire. Ancient civilizations built watchtowers so guards could stand watch from a higher vantage point. We seek higher ground in order to see the lay of the land. One thing is certain. No matter how effective we may be in this model, in some way, shape, or form, enmeshment will *always* return! Needing help and asking for help is a good thing and asking for help does not indicate weakness. It may be the first step we take toward being real and discovering an authentic integrated spirituality.

This first component of our Search is the *Search for Safety*. The reality of threat in the civilized world still exists even though the threat of the saber-toothed tigers no longer exists. Most of us will go out of our way to avoid certain areas or parts of cities we do not deem to be safe. There was a time we thought schools were safe, but since the massacres at Columbine and Virginia Tech, we have learned angry and hurt children or young adults are capable of carrying automatic weapons in these environments and performing premeditated and random acts of murder on teachers and fellow classmates.

I worked with a middle-aged woman for several years as she grieved the death of her youngest son. Wayne was the youngest of her three children. He was within four months of graduating from Southern Methodist University in Dallas, Texas. One evening, while out with friends, he was returning to his car about 1:30 a.m. As they were about to drive off, a young man leaned into the car, put a gun to Wayne's head and demanded money. His date screamed, the gun went off, and Wayne ended up for three days on life support. Wayne was pronounced dead and his organs were harvested. Transplant recipients of a heart, kidneys, liver, and corneas were called to receive a gift that cost Wayne his life. His mother and father went home to try to make sense out of what was senseless. The transplant recipients and their families must have seen it otherwise. Wayne's murderer has never been apprehended.

In South Florida, two senior members of a faith community were mugged walking up the steps to their church. Both women had their purses snatched. One was pushed to the ground, causing her agonizing pain. Her perpetrator had broken her arm. A woman of great strength and dignity, she was absolutely bewildered and broken by the experience. She could not fathom how such an incident could happen in the shadow of a steeple. Church may not be a safe place. Gun toting parishioners frequently fire on pastors, church members, or doctors who perform abortions. In other parts of the world, suicide bombers target mosques in Kabul and Baghdad. Global terrorism, home invasions, drive by shootings, road rage, gang activity, and hate groups all remind us *there is no place we can go to ultimately be safe.*

In summary, our world is not safe. Today we are witnessing the veneer of civilization being torn and ripped, readily revealing our Darwinian heritage. We are human beings, but we are also animals. The law of the jungle is the law of survival of the fittest. This law divides the world between predator and prey. We live in a time when the cultural "check engine" light remains on. The increase of cultural stressors will only ratchet up activity among the crazy, the criminal, and the insane. Once we identify the insanity, we must each decide if we will participate in the chaos or choose an alternative pathway. Our *roots* may help to determine the *routes* we take for the journey we make. These roots, or rather our history and experience, create ideas and beliefs that establish a lens and shapes how we see the world. When we are in a protective mode, our behavior will be driven by anger and anxiety. We cannot see it if we are embedded in unconsciousness. Being "unstuck" involves a predictable pattern of crawling out of the quicksand, (or being pulled out with the help of another!) disengagement, reflection, and re-engagement. When we become "FRICKed," we lose our homeostasis and inner balance. However, awareness creates choice. We can intentionally choose to move out of protective behavior and into purposeful living. When we are purposeful, we discover an internal synergy that is *pushing* us from within while *pulling* us toward the target.

Our physical safety is just one component of our safety needs. Safety issues relate to either internal or external threats to our safety. We may or may not have any control of our external situation, but we are capable of regulating the internal. The triggering of our psychological safety needs occurs when there are real or *perceived* threats to our sense of justice or competence. Both of these areas will be explored in detail in Chapters 3 and 4. We will next explore our Search for Meaning. What does it mean that we are *homo sapien sapiens* and what separates people from pigeons?

Chapter 2
The Search for Meaning

> Zorba: "Why do the young die? Why does anybody die? What's the use of all of your damn books if they can't answer that?"
> The Boss: "They tell me about the agony of men who can't answer questions like yours."
> Zorba: "I spit on this agony"[9]

> "I don't wanna die: I sometimes wish I'd never been born at all."[10]

> What if the Hokey Pokey *really is* what it's all about?[11]

What Separates Pigeons and People?

Pigeons fly and we do not. Pigeons have feathers; we have skin. Pigeons lay eggs; we birth our young. We are *homo sapien sapiens*. The verb *sapere* is from the Latin. It means "to taste or to know." We are the species that knows and knows that it knows. We have awareness and the awareness of awareness. We can target, reflect and interpret experience that clearly separates us from pigeons and other creatures of creation.

Robert Kegan relates a story concerning the work of behavioral psychologist B.F. Skinner in his book, *The Evolving Self*. Skinner boasts that pigeons could be taught to bowl:

> "Behavioralists put pigeons in miniature bowling alleys and allow them to behave as they wish. Eventually they happen to stand where the bowler rolls the ball, and at this moment they are rewarded with food. They then go about their business but eventually return to the bowler's position, where they are again rewarded. Before too long they begin to hang around at the bowler's spot, and eventually in their random body movements they lower their heads toward a miniature bowling ball; at this moment they get an even bigger reward. Before too long they not only spend most of

their time where a bowler stands, they also have their heads down ready to push the ball. Eventually, of course, they actually push the ball, and - well, you get the idea. As Skinner said, *"Getting them to bowl strikes takes even longer, but is no more complicated."* [12]

Although, according to Skinner, teaching pigeons to bowl may be possible, but the important question is, "would it mean anything to the pigeon?" If we were to consider going out for an evening of bowling, we would make the decision based upon our value of this form of sport and entertainment. Value involves meaning. What would I hope to get from an evening of bowling? A quick checklist might include:

1) Enjoyment of the sport
2) Improving skill development
3) Competition of trying to bowl better than other individuals or teams
4) Connecting with friends, family, coworkers, or acquaintances.

If the pigeon is preparing to bowl, her target is to find ways to be rewarded with pellets. The pigeon does not share our experience of value and meaning. Pigeons generally hang around park statues. Pigeons have never been sighted at bowling alleys, giving high fives and slapping each other on the back after throwing strikes.

We, of course, are not pigeons, stool pigeons, or otherwise. Men and women do not live by pellets alone. We hunger for meaning, and choose to become engaged in experiences we target and anticipate will be meaningful and intrinsically rewarding.

We Are Makers of Our Own Meaning

Making sense out of human existence is an essential component of human experience. Our very existence as human beings means we are makers of our own meaning. We are constantly scanning our surroundings and interpreting what we see, think, or feel in order to make sense out of our own experiences. The more we become aware of this ability, the more we will notice we are doing it every day in ways that are at times innocent, subtle, and profound.

We were leaving the parking lot of a grocery/retail mega store when a traffic light stopped my wife and me. Brenda noticed three empty grocery carts on the sidewalk directly adjacent to a canopied bus stop. She stared at the carts for a few moments, carefully observing and studying the scene, like the forensic student of reality she happens to be. I, on the other hand, must have been daydreaming, lost in space, and waiting for the light to change. Finally, the awareness all came together in a rush of insight. She offered the following interpretation: "I bet those people bought their groceries at the grocery store, pushed the carts down to the bus stop, took their groceries out of the carts, and got on the bus." I sat behind the wheel in stunned silence. She was thoroughly present in the moment and making sense out of why there were three grocery carts at the bus stop. I was off somewhere orbiting another planet. In all probability, she was right on target in her assessment of the situation. The question is "why?" Why do we do this? Is this just an instinctual need we have to scan continually our surroundings in order to determine if the coast is clear and our safety is intact? Is it more than this? Why are we constantly trying to make sense and figure out life around us? Why do we have a need to organize and structure reality in some way that "makes sense?"

After solving the random shopping cart mystery, are there any bigger mysteries left? What is there to life after the bills are paid, the lawn is mowed, and the groceries are toted, shelved and refrigerated? Do we live by bread alone? Is there more to life than the ongoing maintenance of the mundane? What choices do we have other than deciding between paper or plastic, pleasure or principles? Why am I here? What is my ultimate purpose? Are we randomly rambling in our race toward death, or is there a design to all the drama? Do we possess an internal spiritual compass that points our inner being to look for ways within and beyond the self so our life has order, explanations for our experiences, and meaning that provides coherence? Why do we desperately yearn to exist in a reality that holds life together?

These questions have teased and tortured men and women since we have been able to capture thoughts, articulate speech, and express emotions. These are the questions theologians, philosophers, and other meaning makers have been asking since the advent of civilization and the dawn of time. This is the quandary in the quest and our search for meaning.

How the Mind Processes Experience

Although first impressions may be inaccurate, Malcolm Gladwell in the best-selling book *Blink* documented research, which indicated that our intuitive, innate methods of decision-making are more accurate than those involving extensive research and systematic logical processes.[13] Conventional logic can leave us feeling overwhelmed with "TMI" (too much information).

How we react in a crisis may have a great deal to do with our comfort level with chaos. Many people thrive on chaos; they feel energized by the challenges chaos brings. We all have varying degrees of comfort with turmoil. What happens if we exceed the mythical limits, begin feeling radically overwhelmed, and do not know how to deal with the crisis? What happens when new information arrives and we cannot sort the details?

As a freshman and sophomore in college, I worked in the mailroom of an insurance company. Monday through Friday, my coworkers and I would arrive for work before 7:00 a.m. and sort the company mail. Each insurance division had a set of boxes: fire, life, and auto. Within each division, there were boxes for the top executives, division leaders, and so on. In addition, color-coded envelopes representing three different states arrived containing premiums. After a few months, I could stand in front of a row of post-office box sized cubes, take a stack of mail, and sort the letters at breakneck speed. I could perform the task like a machine until I came across an unfamiliar name or a letter addressed to a category, employee, or division that did not exist. This dilemma immediately shut the process down. I had to stop, track down a supervisor, and attempt to figure out how to route mail that had no clear target or destination. Occasionally I would go for days or weeks without a single rogue piece of mail, happily sorting envelopes and vying to break the Guinness World Record for mail sorting.

The mailroom process of organizing and filing information is very similar to the daily human process involved in organizing experiences. The unconscious mind is automatic until we encounter something that does not fit any of the pre-existing categories. The result is a *crisis of meaning,* which cannot place the experience, like a square peg into a round hole. A trauma can create a crisis of meaning.

When a Crisis Occurs: File System Error and Sensory Overload

External life experiences have the ability to affect our *internal* capabilities to process the situations and may create "file system errors." Sensory overload occurs when our internal capabilities are flooded with more information than we can route in any given moment. This event sends our meaning-making systems into shock or shutdown.

An insurance company called me and asked me to perform a "de-briefing" for a bank. An armed robbery had traumatized several of the employees. After the robbery, several of the employees were having a difficult time putting their lives back together. The robbery occurred on a Friday at closing time. I was called on the following Tuesday, and met with the employees on Wednesday, the next day.

Each of the employees began by telling the story of what happened. From their collective experience, I learned the robber entered the bank 15 minutes before closing at 5:45 p.m. He presented himself as a legitimate customer. He sounded like a definite "professional" and knew what he was doing. He told one of the assistants he wanted to open a business account for his cleaning business. He was dressed as a security officer and did not raise any suspicions. The bank employee was not knowledgeable about the type of account he requested. The robber was told he would have to wait for the assistant manager. The manager was tending to an enraged customer, possibly an accomplice, who was making a scene in the bank. The assistant manager came over to offer help after all the customers left and he locked the door. The robber went into an office with the investment counselor and assistant manager, showed them a gun in his briefcase, and indicated a robbery was taking place. The robber then told the assistant manager, "If anything goes wrong, if any buttons are pushed or any dye capsules are thrown in the bags, someone will be hurt, and **you** will be responsible." Money was gathered and given to the robber, and he made his getaway without a hitch. No one was physically harmed.

Five days after the robbery, three of the employees reported they had barely slept since the event. Each of them reported an increase in relational, marital and familial difficulties over incidents that seemed trivial or exaggerated. Each victim reported feeling tense when he or she arrived to work on Monday morning. All of the employees reported a sense of relational awkwardness with their coworkers. No one knew what to say to each other or how to begin the process of recovery from what had happened. Little was said about the proverbial elephant in the room. No social rituals exist to manage these types of scenarios. Hallmark does not produce "sorry you were robbed" cards. The bank opened on Monday with a "business as usual" attitude.

The three employees having the most difficulty each reported the robbery "kept playing over and over again in my mind" and it would not stop. Each of these three reported a great deal of "Monday morning quarterbacking" as they questioned what plays they should or should not have made and what they did or did not do. "Why didn't I turn the lights off inside the bank so I could identify the car and get the tag number?" Anger was triggered from the severe and criminal violation of justice issues. "He did not *deserve* to get that money; he did not *earn* it, and it was just too easy. It's going to happen again." The initial anxiety they felt concerning the violation of their safety needs turned to rage as each of the employees created fantasies about what he or she *could* have done differently so the robber *would* have been caught. The scenes kept playing over in their minds.

Let us look at the internal dynamics of what caused the distress for the bank employees who faced this robbery. First, a bank robbery is a clear threat to safety, and when we do not feel safe, nothing else matters. States of anger and anxiety become agitated and can remain this way indefinitely, or until the unconscious mind understands the event is over and we are safe. Secondly, the employees were struggling to find meaning and make sense out of what had happened. There were no prior experiences to help the employees with meaning making. There were no "mail slots" to file the experience of "bank robbery." At this point, we no longer think our own thoughts. We become hijacked by obsessive thinking. Obsessional thinking is a key component and an identifier of the depth of a crisis.[g]

Obsessive thought occurs when we do not like the

---

[g] Obsessional thought processes might literally hijack our brains in times of crisis. We don't have a way of organizing the experience and it doesn't fit into prior existing knowledge banks. After September 11th, television news coverage kept playing the video of the planes flying into the World Trade Center buildings *over and over and over* again. Why? We don't know how to make sense out of planes flying into buildings! Planes are supposed to land on runways and not fly into buildings. The news networks simply played back over and over again the same scene, which is what we do when we can't make sense out of our experiences. We keep playing the trauma over and over again, often editing the story with what we "ought" or "should" have done. We do this because we find it difficult to accept the outcome. We attempt to edit the story to change the ending so the outcome is favorable and easier to accept.

outcome of an event, and we have a difficult time accepting the reality of what happened. To replay an event is usually an intention of the psyche to find a way to "edit" the story. Mentally replaying the event is an attempt to look for ways to insert new clips of what *could* or *should* have been done differently. By "editing" the clip, we attempt to come up with an alternative outcome, one easier to accept. Afterward, we will ask questions of ourselves we never thought of at the time of the crisis. An employee asked both himself, and me, "Why didn't I turn the lights off inside the bank so I could identify the car and get the tag number?" If they could now alter, edit, and insert this small detail into the story, the entire course of events may have changed. In the edited story, the robber could now be apprehended. This moves us to the next point.

Thirdly, anger issues returned. In this instance the anger aroused, irritated, and inflamed their innate sense of what was unjust. Notice when the employee said, "He did not *deserve* to get that money; he did not earn it, and it was just too easy. It's going to happen again." For this employee, the robber not only violated safety needs and created internal and external chaos and confusion; he also violated a basic principle of justice. Adhering to principles of justice is part of the foundational glue that helps hold culture and society together. Stealing is unlawful and dishonest. Money should be earned, not stolen at gunpoint. Criminals should be apprehended and brought to justice or "It's going to happen again." What happened simply was not fair. We will delve deeper into this dilemma in the next chapter, the Search for Justice.

There are times of crisis when families may or may not have the ability to "sort it all out" and make meaning out of what is happening in their lives. During these times our personal "filing systems," our ways of organizing our life's experiences, may not fit into our present reality. A deacon in the church and a staunch pro-life supporter discovers his sixteen-year-old daughter is pregnant, and the family opts for an abortion. The company you have worked for has offered you a promotion, but it means relocating to another city. A devoted husband for many years comes home one day and tells his wife he is no longer in love and wants out of the marriage. Your teen-age son starts staying out beyond his curfew. His grades drop, his friends change, his pupils are constantly dilated and his eyes are bloodshot. The company you work for tells you your position has been eliminated and your services are no longer needed. An unexpected death occurs to a close friend or relative. Your child is diagnosed with leukemia. Your last child leaves home and the parents become empty-nested.

Our history and experience creates our own unique methods for meaning making. Our methods of meaning making often remain hidden, vague or unconscious until they are exposed by a crisis. A crisis experience will expose these methods to reality. When life is running smoothly, we do not ask questions of meaning, but when the natural process of reflecting, filing, and organizing information becomes flooded and overwhelmed, questions of meaning-making arise. In these moments of crisis, we feel intense pressure, force, and stress to reconcile conflicted thoughts or emotions.

As indicated earlier, if the target is to maintain our equilibrium, we will fail. Expected and unexpected life situational changes create destabilization. Becoming "FRICKed" is built into human experience.

Purposeful and Protective:
A Working Model for Meaning Making and Synergistic Solutions

During the process of writing this book, I began to develop a working theory and tested this theory in my work with individuals, couples, volunteer organizations, businesses, and churches. Like me, the theory is not a finished product, more of a work in progress. I frequently present this theory to individuals, groups, and organizations and I continue to utilize new input to improve the model. In essence, I offer a theory about theory. This theory has a wide range of applications that are limited only by the energy, synergy, and creativity of those individuals who seek to apply it to their own circumstances. While leading strategic meetings, planning retreats, and brainstorming sessions I have felt a deep sense of satisfaction when I see an illumination of the internal light bulbs on the faces of those in attendance.

Roots* >>>>>>> *Routes* >>>>>>> *Targets

Chapter 1 introduced the theory as roots, routes, and targets. Our life stories are rooted in our *history* and *experience.* Our roots direct our life routes. Our roots ground us in ways that are purposeful or protective. Our roots pave the path to our destination. Our pathways, our ***routes,*** provide a link between our roots and our destination, also known as our ***targets.***

In this next section, the model is broken down into five smaller sectors. Roots involve our history and experience. As the model is expanded, our history and experience creates ideas and beliefs that will establish the trajectories we will travel.

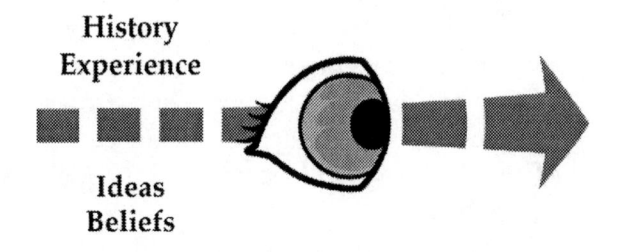

History
Experience

Ideas
Beliefs

Figure 5

A Caucasian male stockbroker raised in Boston and working on Wall Street sees the world differently from the single mother, a migrant farm worker, picking tomatoes in Homestead, Florida. One individual is not superior to the other. They are different due to their history and experiences.

An Al-Qaeda terrorist raised and trained in the mountains of Afghanistan sees the world differently than a former governor from the state of Texas. Two radically different histories and experiences create divergent ideas and beliefs about the world in which they both live.

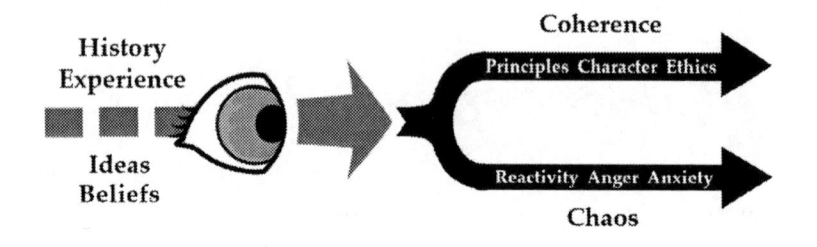

Figure 6

Now, add a second component to the model. The second component will determine whether an individual's behavior is predominantly coherent or chaotic. If we are shooting straight, our trajectory will travel the pathway of coherence. The bowstring that propels these arrows will be powered by our character, ethics, principles, and ideals. The energy that drives this behavior is motivated with synergy and cooperation. The whole is greater than the total sum of the parts. Conversely, if our history and experience create ideas and beliefs that cause us to draw the bow back with reactivity, the energy propelling this projectile will be anger or anxiety. These are damaged arrows: bent arrows, missing feathers and fletching, will create an imbalanced flight. The trajectory of these arrows will be erratic, chaotic, and will cause us to miss the mark.

As history and experience create ideas and beliefs, the *method of organizing* these factors becomes an individual's personal theory, philosophy, theology and ideology. Now, let us take a broader look at what happens in the development of theory, or what I refer to as the *theory of theory*. All experience is involved in the development of theory, and theory is the engine for sorting experience.

Clear — Focused — Purposeful — Synergistic — ▶

Coherence

History
Experience

Principles Character Ethics → Theory
Philosophy
Theology
Ideas
Beliefs

Reactivity Anger Anxiety → Ideology

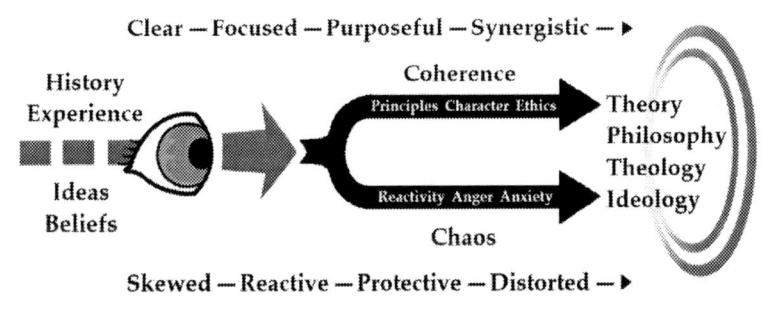

Chaos

Skewed — Reactive — Protective — Distorted — ▶

Figure 7

    Now, let us add the third segment to the model. Let us say we came home at the end of every day and dumped our loose change into an empty five-gallon water jug. Over an extended period, the jug fills, and we eventually decide to cash in our spare change at the local grocery store. We carry the jug to the store and pour the coins into a large funnel at the top of the sorting machine. The mechanism begins to ingest the coins and a digital readout flashes the amount of money we poured into the machine. The coins are automatically sorted and rolled. This machine provides a *method* for sorting and organizing coins.

    Once an experience is sorted and organized, we begin to see reality through that method of organization. This method of organizing experience potentially evolves into a personal theory, philosophy, theology, or ideology. An individual's theory, philosophy, theology, or ideology in turn becomes a way of synthesizing existing experiences and shaping the way we see new experiences. The machine is set to read pennies, nickels, dimes, quarters, and half-dollars. This is all the machine knows to look for and organize. The machine is not programmed to read Euro dollars, drachmas, or currency from other countries.

    Our theory, philosophy, theology, or ideology becomes the lens that shapes and limits what we see. If our lenses are tinted blue, then everything will appear with a hint of blue. Lenses tend to shape reality and distort reality, depending on the circumstance. A photographer selects specific lenses to "narrow" the subject matter to exactly what should be the focus of the picture. By choosing what to photograph, and where to focus, we also choose what *not* to photograph. By enhancing the focus on a humming bird dipping its beak into a red hibiscus, we fail to see the shot of the grasshopper hiding behind the stem further down from the flower.

In the development and formation of my own theory, philosophy, theology, or ideology I may choose to synthesize certain beliefs with established schools of thought. In order to increase my voice, circle of influence, and my own personal sense of power, I can align my own theory, philosophy, theology, or ideology with those of Republicans, Democrats, Conservatives, Liberals, Terrorists, Racists, Communists, or Capitalists. Jews, Catholics, Protestants, Muslims, and Buddhists perceive through complex cultural, historical, and theological lenses. Each group can be broken down into smaller subsets. I gain the rights, duties, privileges, and liabilities of group identity.

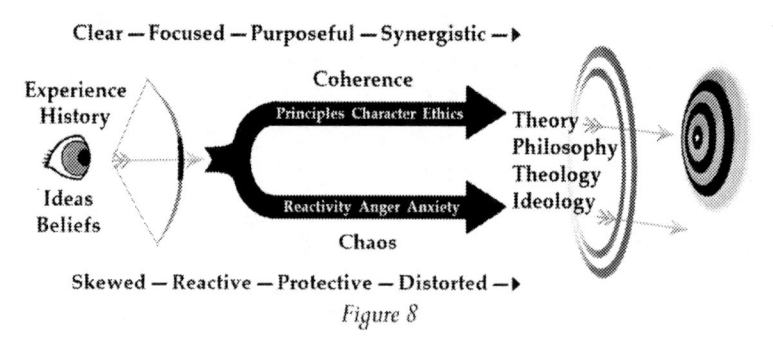

Figure 8

Targets

The fourth segment of the model adds a target. Purposeful pathways require targets guided by personal theory, philosophy, theology, or ideology. Whether we are raising a family, guiding a volunteer organization, or leading a corporation, the principle is the same. If our routes and pathways are *purposeful*, we will constantly ask others and ourselves what effect we desire in any given circumstance. What is our intended outcome? Is our behavior driven by our purpose? Is our present activity guided by our theory, philosophy, theology, or ideology, and does it effectively assist us to achieve the desired results?

In February and July, the city of Daytona Beach swells beyond capacity as thousands of race fans come to the World Center of Racing for the annual speed weeks. The Daytona 500, The Super Bowl of Racing is proudly titled, "The Great American Race." More than 40 million viewers worldwide convene around televisions to watch this event. The Daytona 500 is the inaugural event that kicks off the NASCAR season the second Sunday in February. As I mentioned previously, Hal Marchman was the track chaplain at Daytona International Speedway for 45 years. I felt privileged to step in and assume his role as the speedway chaplain when he entered retirement. The Director of Fan Appreciation gave me the grand tour during my orientation session. He stopped the car at the north entrance to the speedway just under the grandstands. My guide pointed north to the crosswalk spanning Daytona International Speedway Blvd. and over to the other side of the street. Making parking available for 200,000 fans has been an ongoing challenge. Most of the parking is offsite and miles away. Buses and trams transport the fans to designated drop-off areas. Although the fans were being shuttled by buses within a mile and a half of the speedway, the walk is still long especially lugging the necessary fan equipment: seat cushions, cameras, coolers, and scanners.

For several years, the buses dropped off fans at the entrance of a local elementary school. From this vantage point, the two and one-half mile oval speedway was not visible. The speedway takes the feedback of the race fans seriously. The Fan Appreciation Office had received numerous complaints about the length of the walk. Pointing to a building about one block closer, my guide beamed and proudly announced, "This year, we're going to be dropping off the fans at the orange building. What we have discovered in our research is that the fans do not mind walking the distance to the speedway as long as they can see the target. *If they cannot see the target, they'll complain, but if they see the target, they do not mind walking until they get there."*

As one wise person said, "Without a vision the people perish." Effective targets are targets that get our attention. The word attention comes from the Latin *attendere,* which means, "to turn or stretch towards."[14] Effective targets can pull us forward, and make the journey worthwhile. In other words, effective targets are targets that both grab our attention and inspire motivation. *Energy flows where our attention goes.* Effective targets both push and pull. As the speedway officials learned, effective targets can muffle discontent. We will not mind taking the extra steps if the steps are purposeful and help us hit the target. Behavior is either *purposeful or protective.* If behavior is protective, the prevailing energies that drive the experience are anger and anxiety. This principle is universally applicable, whether we are analyzing the downturn of Fortune 500 companies or American Foreign policy following September 11th. Reactive behavior is *always* protective and driven by anger or anxiety.

Targets are what we seek to hit with intention and purpose. It may be true that even a blind squirrel will occasionally find a nut. Targets, however, are not about random activity that intermittently works by accident. Targets are about envisioning a desired outcome and must be compelling enough to motivate, inspire, and to dedicate hard work. The poetry in motion of a skilled fly fisherman is to place the lure in the proximity of the prey. It does not happen with the first or the five-hundredth cast. The seemingly effortless movements of a violin virtuoso do not reveal the ten thousand hours of practice it takes to assimilate the mastery of the instrument. When Phil Mickelson is winding up his back swing with his head down the target he is aiming for is the pin on the green. He started aiming toward this target about the time most of us were riding bicycles or playing in Little League.

What is the target? What are we trying to achieve? What is the goal we are trying to reach individually or collectively? As indicated, our theory, philosophy, theology, or ideology will either follow pathways that provide coherence or chaos. The chaotic, reactive track supplies the individual with a real or an ideological enemy. Opposition provides a method for organizing identity and creating individual or group coherence. Political parties often utilize this method. "We know who we are because we know whom we are against." The 13 independent colonies only became the United States in opposition to a common enemy – the British. The creation of enemies, real or imagined, is essential for meaning making in the chaos track. This is why chaos causes the arrow to miss the target and why the arrow hits the bull's-eye on the coherence track. The track of coherence does not need to create enemies. The organization, group, or self does not need reactivity or opposition to create coherence. The energies driving these two sets of behaviors are entirely different.

To summarize, as we sort history and experience through the development of ideas and beliefs and enter the evolution of personal theory, philosophy, theology, or ideology, we move toward the conscious development of routes and pathways. If the routes and pathways are *purposeful*, they will be driven by cooperation, creativity, energy and synergy. Purposeful pathways require targets. Our theory will be shaped by our character, ethics, principles, and ideals that inform and develop our theory, philosophy, or theology. If the routes and pathways are *reactive*, our theory, philosophy, ideology, or theology will be driven by fear, anxiety, and anger. Reactive pathways require enemies. The shadow side of the self is projected onto others and this common enemy creates group coherence. If the behavior is reactive, our lenses will be covered with cataracts, and the perception of reality will always be distorted and skewed.

The Evaluation of Meaning: Targets, Reflection, and Interpreting Experience

This is the fifth and final segment of the model. If

targets are what we seek to hit intentionally we must evaluate whether or not we effectively hit the target. Let us say Bob and Mary invites me to go bowling. It is my turn to bowl, and with my first ball, I am going to approach the line, follow through, release the ball, and intentionally attempt to hit between the number one and three pin in order to increase my probability of throwing a strike. My target is to throw strikes, and when I make strikes, the activity is purposeful because I am hitting the target. If I missed the strike zone, was it because of my follow-through? Did I release the ball with adequate spin or was there too much spin? What do I need to do to improve for my next ball?

  Targets without *reflection* are meaningless. How will we know if we are hitting or missing the target? Whenever I agree to a speaking or teaching engagement, I usually try to recruit the assistance of two or three "truth tellers" to give me honest feedback. I do not need flattery. I need to know if I hit the target in order to know what I must improve for the next presentation. I cannot improve my work if the feedback is not helpful. I frequently have to check myself for trying to say too much in a short period. "I asked for a drink of water and instead you turned on the fire hose." Getting feedback and engaging in reflection should be a regular practice, preferably with structured intentionality.

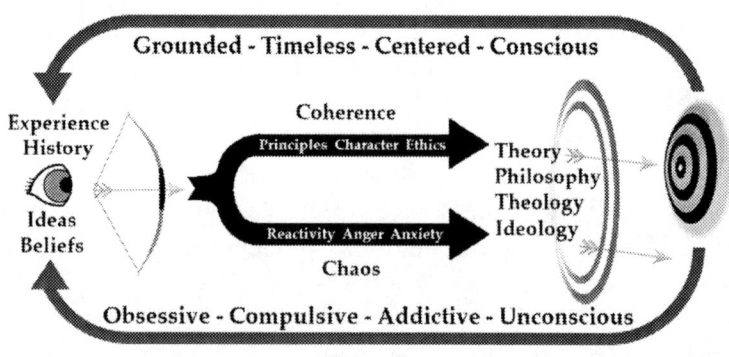

Figure 9

  The arrows in the graphic indicate a feedback loop. New experience creates the opportunity to determine whether I hit the target. What needs to change in order to improve? All feedback provides the opportunity to improve either my methods or my theory.

Reflection can be unstructured or structured, but either way it must be intentional. Intentional reflection is an attempt to improve the probability of a purposeful strike on target. It creates a feedback process for continuous improvement and effectiveness. Are we hitting our target? Why or why not? When we intentionally reflect on our experience, the purpose for doing so is to improve effectiveness. *Intentional reflection increases the probability of future improvement.* The value for creating *improvement* causes us to be more *effective* at successfully hitting our targets. When I am reflective about experience and invite other constructive input, I choose to learn and improve my methods.

Here is an example of unstructured reflection: Let us say Bob and Mary invite me to go bowling. We bowl four games. After bowling, we go to the Waffle House for coffee. We may hash over the games we bowled, speak about current events, gossip, discuss Nietzsche, Marx, or Adam Smith, or just simply shoot the breeze. Unstructured reflection is sort of hit or miss.

Structured reflection increases intentionality and therefore increases the probability for future improvement. For example, Mary has an average bowling score of 220, and my average is 150. Why do I keep throwing gutter balls? What do I need to improve? Over coffee, I ask Mary if she could see ways I could improve my form, follow through, or release. Mary tells me she would be happy to offer suggestions on how I can improve my release and follow through. Bob has a creative moment and says, "I know, why don't we get off early next Tuesday afternoon, come back and bowl a few games, and I'll bring my digital video camera. I will video your delivery; we will play it back on my laptop, and Mary can make suggestions on how you can improve. Then you can get back up the next frame and see how it works!" Formal reflection increases the likelihood of creating new methods for making assessments, determining accuracy, and making corrections.

This process of creating feedback for continuous improvement may be applied to all relationships including families, churches, synagogues, mosques, businesses, government, and any place where systems are operative. The secret for the success of maintaining methods of intentional continuous improvement is directly correlated to sustaining an environment that remains purposeful and not protective. This is why most grievance procedures do not work; they institutionalize an environment of attack and therefore place us into a protective mode. These procedures encourage an environment that stipulates, "Let me tell you what is *wrong* with you." Grievance procedures tacitly convey, "You are entitled to bitch and we are obligated to listen." They create defensiveness by inviting negative, even destructive feedback. By negative, I specifically mean the dumping of toxic emotions by complaining or blaming. This procedure is devoid of intent to create improvement. "Getting things off my chest" provides temporary catharsis but not continuous improvement.

If I perceive feedback as an attack on my competency, my reaction will be reactivity rather than receptivity. If I become reactive, my behavior is driven by anger and anxiety. As a result, an organization, system, institution, or individual will immediately fall into protective mode. Improvement, creativity, insight, and synergy never occur in an environment inflamed with anger or driven long-term by anxiety.

Built-in methods for creating intentional reflection give us the ability to determine whether we hit the target and what needs to happen to create effectiveness and improvement. Intentional reflection provides us with opportunities to determine if we are in alignment with our theory. Reflection also provides us with an added component of being able to determine if our *theory* needs to be improved. We interpret reality based on our theory, philosophy, theology, or ideology. Mary looks at Bob's video and assesses my form, follow through, and release based on her knowledge, theory, and experience of bowling. Mary offers suggestions to improve my effectiveness; I assimilate her feedback, make corrections, and my bowling score improves. Mary's knowledge, theory, and experience of bowling becomes the lens by which Mary assesses my bowling skills (interpretation); she offers suggestions for improvement (reflection), and I am able to assimilate this new learning, which enables me to be more effective at hitting the one-three pocket and making strikes (targets). However, what happens if Mary looks at the digital film, offers suggestions, I ignore the suggestions, but I improve anyway? Mary might then conduct her own in-depth study of the film and conclude I have discovered a new way of bowling that improves her theory. Mary then uses new experience as a way of modifying her theory. Reflection not only provides us with an ability to assess and correct effectiveness at hitting targets, it may provide new information for us to improve our theory.

Synergy: The Energy to Purposefully Hit Targets

Synergy is the energy driving purposeful behavior when we are living in an environment of cooperation. The origin of the word synergy is from the Greek, *sunergos*, and it means cooperation, working together.

1) The interaction of two or more agents or forces so that the combined effect is greater than the sum of their individual effects.
2) Cooperative interaction among groups, especially among the acquired subsidiaries or merged parts of a corporation, that creates an enhanced combined effect.

Creativity, insight, and new ideas abound in this type

of atmosphere. Persons often feel valued, appreciated, and experience deep personal satisfaction and joy. Questions about meaning frequently become obsessions when life does not feel meaningful. Rarely do individuals express concern about life's meaning when he or she lives inside the realm of empowerment.

Unless we consciously choose to do otherwise, the moment an individual or a system determines another individual, group, or situation to be a threat to safety, synergistic energy shuts down. If we have not learned how to move beyond this reactionary dynamic, the individual, group, or system will automatically move into a protective mode. Leaders are the individuals who have evolved in self-development and consistently live within their own synergy regardless of extenuating circumstances or situations. These persons are not subject to the usual dynamics of the inflation and deflation of the self and are capable of intentionally responding to adversity rather than reacting. When we *react* to a situation, we bypass cognitive development and processes. Our behavior bypasses the brain and becomes instinctual. When we *respond* to a situation, we increase our effectiveness by working with purposeful intentions to hit a predetermined target.

Synergistic empowerment is an organically shared power that works effectively in relationships and organizations. Organizations are organisms. An organism is vital, alive, connected, and linked together with a collective purpose and a common target. We live, move and function inside an existing dynamic between organism and organization. In this instance, an organization is an attempt to structure and harness the energy of an organism. The age-old tension between structure and spirit lives in every organization, corporation, and institution. To celebrate and embrace the tension means the organism is able to remain purposeful, effective, and relevant in changing markets and changing times.[15]

Let us look at some of the contrasting ways power is used and how the distinctions help to clarify the differences between the two dominate forms of power, coercive or persuasive. Persuasive power is purpose driven and seeks to motivate through principles, precepts, or other intrinsic values. When power flows from the top down, signals interpreted as threat or coercion may be sent throughout the organization, system, or institution. These signals in turn will trigger protective behavior among those who do not share in the power.

If a vice-president, manager, or supervisor calls an employee into the office without disclosing the nature of the meeting, coercive power is already in use to create intimidation and fear. Coercive power manages by control and the ability to reward or punish. This type of power generally operates from the top down or from a clear position of authority. Notice when we drive on a city street or an interstate highway, and traffic suddenly slows down for no apparent reason. Curiously, we pass the area of congestion and spot a police officer hanging out of her cruiser or leaning over her motorcycle with a radar gun, clocking the approaching speed of the oncoming traffic. A remarkable event happens. Regardless of age, stage, or station in life, all drivers automatically begin to comply with the speed limit. How long does this last? Usually it lasts until the driver is safely out of range of the radar gun!

Coercive power moves from the top down in systems or institutions when organizational patterns are in a pyramid or hierarchical order, such as in the military. Less obvious are organizations that seek to motivate by manipulating value laden terms such as duty, responsibility, obligation, and accountability. These methods provide veiled forms of coercive power through the manipulation of guilt. The method and the message remain the same: "If I make you *feel bad,* you will *do the right thing."* For example, certain religious institutions will deploy these methods of conscious or unconscious manipulative motivation. The damage suffered to unsuspecting, trusting, and innocent persons is especially severe for those who are vulnerable and who carry a wounded self. Religious institutions that deploy these methods of manipulative motivation would cease and desist if they were charged, tried, and convicted for spiritual malpractice!

These systems are not effective in this model of meaning because power does not flow from the top down. Synergy is impossible to achieve in an atmosphere of threat or an environment where behavior is protective instead of purposeful. In this model, the organization seeks to *harness the synergy of the organism.* Leaders work to enable, facilitate, and use the purposeful *release* of synergy as the energy and passion to hit desired and agreed upon targets. The atmosphere in these environments is contagious and exciting![16] New ideas and new methods are encouraged. New product development is welcome from any direction. Workers feel valued and appreciated and *want* to come to work. Systems seeking to motivate, organize, and improve by using methods motivated by responsibility, obligation, and accountability will experience certain levels of success. More often than not, the by-products of these methods create an atmosphere of control, drudgery, and dread. Dread cascades negative emotions and releases the reactive fight/flight toxins inside our bodies. Dread and joy cannot occupy the same place at the same time. If we increase joy, we diminish dread. If we increase dread, joy is eliminated.

Tennessee Ernie Ford made famous a song written by Merle Travis eight years earlier. In October of 1955, eleven days after the song was released, more than 400,000 singles had been sold. The title of the song was "Sixteen Tons," a ballad about shoveling coal for a living and a life lived through hopelessness, drudgery, and dread. The refrain went as follows:

> You load sixteen tons, and what do you get?
> Another day older and deeper in debt
> St. Peter don't you call me, 'cause I can't go
> I owe my soul to the company store

It is hard to imagine that 400,000 coal miners went out and bought the single. What the song expresses is the universal experience of drudgery and dread connected with pointless work with no potential benefit other than survival. How many millions of people were able to substitute shoveling coal with their daily occupation and end up feeling the same way?

As Malcolm Gladwell states in his best seller *Outliers*, vocational meaning has a direct connection between autonomy, complexity, and a correlation between effort and reward.[17] Shoveling coal does not provide autonomy if you have to work under the watchful eye of a supervisory taskmaster. There is no complexity to shoveling coal. Anyone with a strong back can do it. If you are loading sixteen tons and still deeper in debt, there is obviously no correlation between effort and reward. I worked one summer on a General Motors Assembly plant in Doraville, Georgia, a plant that is now closed. I installed carpet in each of the new vehicles: one carpet per car every sixty seconds, five hundred and forty on a nine-hour shift. There was no autonomy or complexity with this job. There was a correlation between effort and reward.

Preparing to teach *Death and Dying* my first semester at Flagler College, I read the course text. I discovered one of the greatest projectors of longevity, more so than even genetics, is job satisfaction. In other words, if I find *meaning* in my vocation, my work has the net effect of adding *years* to my lifespan. If we are shoveling coal, emptying bedpans, or driving a bus, our work has the potential to evoke meaning *if* we see what we are doing as being purposeful, beneficial, and meaningful. In some parts of this country and throughout the world, there would be no energy or heat without coal. Certified nursing assistants are doing the work of angels when they are caring for persons who cannot take care of themselves. I know. I have seen them provide extraordinary care, complete menial tasks, and work for low pay. Bus drivers provide safe, affordable, and dependable transportation and make it possible for the consumer to conserve energy. My father was a bus driver. In my own work experience, I have shined shoes, thrown newspapers, worked in the fast food industry, and worked in a car wash. I have bussed tables, been a short-order cook, a laboratory-charting clerk, and a histology technician. I have sorted mail, been a file clerk for an insurance company, sold paint, and I have done bill collections. I have worked on an automobile assembly line, and I have been an intern and investigator for the State Campaign Financial Disclosure Commission. I have been a local church pastor, managed and operated two nursing homes, a college professor, and I have been a licensed psychotherapist. I have learned extensively from each of these vocational experiences, and I sincerely love what I am doing now. People often tell me they cannot imagine how I could listen to people's pain day in and day out and still maintain my sanity. I love what I do. Nothing is more meaningful to me than to be present with individuals where life matters most. In my office, there is very little discussion about news, sports, and weather. When I am privileged to sit with individuals or couples, I enter into sacred moments when they allow me the privilege of being with them in their pain. There is a phenomenal energy of *being in the now* when I am concentrating and intently listening to every word being spoken, feeling the emotions in the room, and holding the pain of another human being. When I am participating in these sacred moments, I find I am holding and being held by a force of energy that is difficult to articulate. Through all of these experiences, I have learned that in any given moment we only have three options:

1) We can be where we are and accept it (*not a valid option if abuse is a factor*)
2) We can be where we are and be miserable
3) We can change

These are the only options. Monks in the monasteries teach if we are baking bread, then bake bread. If we are sweeping the floor, then sweep the floor. If we are washing the dishes, then wash the dishes. If we truly accept ourselves, where we are, and what we are doing, we learn to be present in each moment. Our happiness, well-being, and even longevity may depend on it.

Changing Targets through the Passages of Time

Some predictable and more pronounced times in life cause the quest and the questions to become more intense. At young adulthood, middle age, and just prior to or after retirement, we focus on these three areas: What will be my vocation? Who will be my mate? What will be my philosophy or theology of life?

At young adulthood, we usually receive training to enter the job market, career development, or vocational markets, such as college or trade school. Young adulthood is the testing ground for the age-old question, "What am I going to be when I grow up?" Having taught four years of undergraduate school, I have seen college sophomores, juniors, and seniors agonize with discovering and hitting career targets. We live in an era of rapid change when job markets quickly fluctuate. Many of these students have seen one or both parents "downsized" out of career positions not only once but sometimes two or three times. As a result, they have been uprooted and forced to move in order for a parent to follow a new job or career path.

With relationships, young adults are often involved in the Neanderthal dance of compatibility. This is the painful process of trial and error and deciding whom to choose as a partner. Young adults are often timid in relationships, and many are terrified of commitments. Most come from blended families, and carry scars and wounds. These young adults cautiously emerge from the failed marriages of their parents, and they carry many fears. They often fear making the mistakes their parents made; they fear failure in relationships, and do not want to perpetuate the same mistakes by raising children in fragmented families. In other words, they do not want their children to be raised in situations they endured, and they do not want them to face the pain they had to face.

This is also a time of sorting out personal beliefs about the self and the world, the articulation of one's own core beliefs, values, philosophy, theology, and the ongoing development of character. Many young adults will experiment with different values and lifestyles during this developmental phase. At times unsure of what they believe, they will often be searching for a theory, philosophy, theology, or ideology to interpret their experience of self and world. During this phase, they may experiment with models that were similar or different from what was modeled or absent in their families of origin. The intensity of this process can carry significant pain, but also bears great promise, as young adults move toward internalizing these components of the self and seek ownership of their own ambitions and ideals. In coffee shops, classrooms, and hanging out with friends the development process for the self begins to foment, ferment, and churn. These are delivery systems developing and under construction that will be used to propel the self to hit targets.

As many parents do, my wife and I watched our son agonize through this process. After high school, Sean floundered through several jobs and one failed attempt at college. Through a considerable struggle, he opted to enlist in the United States Air Force and entered basic training in October of 2000. From basic training, he was sent to tech school where he was trained as a plumber. He was stationed at Shaw Air Force Base in Sumter, S.C., when the tragedy of September 11th happened, and like many Americans who felt helpless, he wanted to respond. He volunteered for clean-up duty at the site of the World Trade Center, but other units were sent. Sean's unit served one tour of duty in Turkey after the invasion of Afghanistan, and three months after he returned home, the invasion of Iraq began. As this second war progressed, and no weapons of mass destruction were discovered, Sean increasingly became deeply disillusioned with American Foreign Policy and the War in Iraq. He was not sure he could kill another human being; he wrestled with the concept of potentially dying for a cause he did not support. After months of personal agony, he considered the option to apply for a change of status as a conscientious objector. In his research, Sean discovered the Air Force was over-staffed for persons in his rank and classification. Through this process, he applied for and received an honorable discharge.

With his values and beliefs in turmoil, Sean had already started back to school while still in the Air Force, and he began to reset his targets. Upon receiving his discharge, he made plans to enter Santa Fe Community College in Gainesville, Florida, and embark on an educational journey that would enable him to work in the field of water systems management. It was an area congruent with his ethical and moral commitments for the preservation of the planet. He made arrangements for housing with friends he had known from high school who were attending graduate school at the University of Florida. He moved to his new setting May 1st. After a month of living in this new environment, Sean discovered he was no longer compatible with old friends. He had traveled the world, and they had lived in academic settings and fraternity environments. They had climbed the academic ladders, and he was just beginning. He experienced verbal humiliation when he expressed ideas and thoughts and was overcome by their snobbish sense of academic superiority. He began to doubt his ability to perform academically, and he began to experience anxiety at the thought of re-entering the arena of formal education. Two more months lay ahead before classes started. He questioned whether or not he was motivated or if he wanted to follow this academic track. A part-time job created additional misery for Sean, and he sank into a spiral of despair. An early morning e-mail message followed by phone calls to both his mother and me clearly indicated he was in trouble.

Initially Sean wanted to come home, to return to a protective environment, and his mother and I were not sure if this was the right call. We were more than happy to have him home but not if he came home feeling humiliated and defeated. Having been intentional with both of my children to being their father and not their therapist, I called a trusted friend and asked if he would see Sean. They both agreed. They met together, and immediately Sean began to reverse the downward spiral and move back up. They met several times, talked by telephone, and eventually Sean did temporarily move back home for several months.

Sean's sense of competence and confidence had been severely shaken, a component that will be discussed in Chapter 4. More important, the experience proved to be beneficial as Sean discovered he was *trying to hit the wrong target*. His passion in high school had been photography, along with graphic arts and design, and he had taken all the electives in these areas during those years. He began to redirect his efforts to hit this target and enrolled in photography school at Daytona State College. As he reset his sights to hit this new target, the anxiety ended and he began to relax and look forward to this new adventure. His previous target of following a career in water systems management was not compelling enough to create the appropriate amount of synergy to motivate and inspire. Effective targets are targets that both grab our attention and inspire motivation. Effective targets both push and pull. *Energy flows where our attention goes.* Before finishing his schooling, he was hired as a contract photographer by the Daytona Beach News-Journal to do random assignments the staff photographers were too busy to cover. His superiors were impressed with his work, and three months later, he was offered a full time position to shoot magazine advertising. Less than a year later, he was promoted out of advertising to become a staff photojournalist. He was now improving his aim and consistently hitting the bulls-eye.

Who will be my mate? What will be my philosophy or theology of life? What will be my vocation? At middle age, certain "adjustments" are made. At times these adjustments are minor and amount to nothing more than resetting the thermostat a few degrees. At other times, these adjustments are radical revisions, such as divorce, changing mates, changing careers, to name a few.

Much of what happens in a person's life can be easily masked in day-to-day rituals and routines. The alarm rings, and we stumble down the driveway to get the paper, pour the coffee in our cup, and the breakfast we eat. The bus we ride to school, the route we drive to work. The teams we cheer to win. Our rituals often indicate that we seek safety in sameness and order in continuity. We want yesterday to be like today and tomorrow to be like the day after. Is our desire for sameness our own quiet way of maintaining control? Is our desire for continuity our own way to be in charge? Do we stumble into the subtle ways of safety and emerge with a belief that we may be masters of our own fate and dealers of our own destiny?

Targets at Mid-Life

Mid-life sounds the alarm to step out of rituals and into relationships. We yearn for a safe place to reveal our hopes, dreams, and fears. Couples who target their marriage as an utmost priority, learn to establish an effective blueprint for maintaining their relationship, create cooperation and agreement on how to manage stress, deal with conflict, solve problems, balance power, and raise children, will increase the probability of a successful transition through the class four rapids middle age presents. If couples have spent little time maintaining the relationship and more time maintaining the rituals, a seismological shift in the relational plates may occur.

The life situational changes associated with age and stage changes begin to occur with higher levels of intensity and frequency. Teenagers get into trouble, career or job changes may require relocation to another city, the medical and housing needs of aging parents, changes in physical, emotional, or spiritual health, children leaving the nest, increasing financial pressures, all these issues begin to create different levels of stress, and they demand our time and attention. Mid-life tends to expose these issues if we have not looked at them. The longer we wait, the greater the probability our "mid-life" experiences may become more intense.

Trevor, a handsome, intelligent, and energetic 39-year-old man, came to see me for professional counseling and coaching. His initial concern was a need to obtain more balance in his life. Trevor was very successful in his business ventures and was prepared to take his company public on the New York Stock Exchange. Although he had been very successful in business, he had one failed marriage, and he was now facing failure in a relationship he hoped would lead to a second marriage He was dating a 21 year old recent college grad, but he had become restless and bored with her and her lack of maturity. Trevor realized he wanted a family and wanted to have children. His intensity to want to settle down was frightening to the younger woman, nearly half his age. Because of his age and stage in life, Trevor was hearing and feeling the approaching hoof beats of middle age. In fact, he was already choking in the cloud of dust from the first set of the charging bulls running past.

He spoke fondly of his younger brother, the father of his two nephews. At this stage in life, he was willing to trade everything for what his brother had. Trevor's driven nature in business made it very difficult for him to succeed in relationships. His first wife tired of trying to compete for his attention. By his own admission, Trevor was married to his work and his wife was more like a mistress. She eventually told him she wanted out of the marriage. Trevor later discovered that a third party gave her all the time and attention she desperately desired. Early in our work together, he mentioned he was looking for the one woman who would be so irresistible to him that he would give up his preoccupation with his work and fall into her arms.

As the trust in our working relationship developed, I challenged some of Trevor's assumptions. We began to probe some of Trevor's drive and determination. We often admire these values in Western civilization. However, these values may be pathological when driven by overzealous safety issues, the need to win approval, or fear of creating disappointment in others. I pointed out to Trevor that he can not hit these targets. How much money is enough to create safety? Trevor's father had worked hard and had gained and gambled away two fortunes in his lifetime. Trevor readily recalled the effects of bankruptcy on himself, his mother, and his younger brother. Was Trevor trying to fix the instability of his home life, retroactively, by sheer determination to be a financial success? Trevor partially created an aversion identity, and a goal "not to be like my father." Again, I asked Trevor, "How do you hit the target of "not being like my father?" It is a negative way of establishing identity. If someone were to ask Trevor, "Who are you?" would he say, "I don't know, but I am not my father." As you might expect, there was pain, serious pain, around these issues.

How do we hit a target and know at the close of the day, we have won approval and not been a disappointment? I explained to Trevor that he established targets impossible to hit because his targets are moving daily. The self inflates or deflates daily based on whether one is successful with winning approval. Targets are fixed and stationary. They may become moving targets at different ages and stages in life, but these movements are more gradual than drastic and dramatic. Targets are set, adjusted, and re-adjusted, as we make course corrections throughout our journey.

When Trevor stated he knew he would find the right woman when she could take him away from his work obsessions, I told him I thought he was looking for a stronger drug that would take him temporarily from his drug of choice, work. The romantic notion of falling in love, glamorized by Hollywood, has a narcotic effect sustained only as long as we are "getting the buzz." When the buzz wears off, relationships become disposable, and people are turned into objects. "Falling in love" is a state of emotional regression that cannot be sustained longer than six to 18 months. I explained to Trevor that love requires hard work and involves choice. I also explained how his goal would not work because he was looking for the target to pull the trigger. He wanted the allure of this mystical, magical, and mythical creature to have the power over him, rendering him irresponsible for making the decisions and changing the priorities in his life, something he could not do on his own volition and free will. Is there something to this in our quest for meaning? Is there a spiritual passion underneath this desire? Do we long for someone or something more powerful than we are to come into our life and to re-establish our priorities, the targets we are trying to hit, and to change our identity, and our destiny?

A wise mentor once told me, *"When you hit forty, you realize you have played the front nine and you are teeing up on number ten."* During this age and stage of life, we become more conscious of the sands of time slipping through the hourglass. We become increasingly aware that life does not stand still. The distant drums of existential anxiety draw closer and beat louder. As we made headway into the year 1900, the average age life expectancy in the United States was 47.[h] What we now call middle age was once old age! Hormonal changes create menopause for both sexes. Men and women who feel stuck in their marriage, family, career, job, or vocation often begin experiencing feelings of restlessness and agitation. If men or women are feeling lonely, afraid, sad, and alienated, they may have a difficult time learning how to identify and express these emotions if they have not learned how to do so prior to now. Instead, they begin to focus and become more critical of their spouse's physical appearance. When men or women see each other, and all they see is the cellulite, the wrinkles around the eyes, increasing amounts of hair coloring, the gut hanging over the belt, varicose veins, baggy triceps, and other telltale signs of aging, they may focus on their spouse's aging and

---

[h] Due to advances in medical technology, antibiotics, surgical care, and preventive medicine, we have added more than 30 years to our lifespan!

mortality while literally running away and avoiding facing their own.

This scenario plays both ways. When Mrs. Robinson (Anne Bancroft) seduces Benjamin Braddock (Dustin Hoffman) in the 1967 classic, *The Graduate*, she may have been the forerunner of the current phenomena of "Cougar" women hunting down younger men, primarily to satisfy voracious sexual appetites.[18] Cougars may ask, "How many times will twenty-one go into forty-nine?" The question is not about mathematics but rather sexual stamina. The answer for the Cougar woman is *"Numerous times!"*

In the reverse, when the stereotypical older man looks into the face of a younger woman he sees the Fountain of Youth and not his own signs of aging. When he looks at the younger woman, he will see youth and beauty, not his own thinning hair, the bags under the eyes, and abdominal muscles that look more like a keg and less like a six-pack. At the gym where I exercise, groups of women in their early to mid-thirties work out every morning. They are slender, sleek, and siliconed to perfection. They drive nice cars. Toward the end of their workout with their professional trainers, I see men in their fifties and sixties, coming in to speak briefly and to check up on their progress. The relational trade-off is clear. "I'll give you anything you want as long as you stay young and beautiful and make me feel young and beautiful. If you gain weight, make demands, or in any other way become undesirable to me, the sugar daddy deal is off, and you're disposable." Author Greg Baer calls this "Imitation Love," in which we barter for pleasure, praise, power, and safety. In this scenario, the women exchange pleasure and praise for power and safety.[19]

All this is driven by the existential anxiety Paul Tillich spoke of as the awareness of non-being. This is a feeble attempt to avoid hearing the approaching footsteps of the grim reaper and the increased awareness of our own finality.

Targets in Retirement

Who will be my mate? What will be my philosophy or theology of life? What will be my vocation? These three issues are again visited with some level of intensity just prior to or after retirement. Although it certainly is not exclusive in any age group, this stage may be death instead of divorce ending a marriage. Hannah is a 62-year-old woman who moved to Florida with her husband five years ago. Her husband had been an executive with a major corporation gobbled up through a hostile takeover. After 30 years, he was downsized. He lost his vice-presidential position in the company. Now out of work, he took his available financial resources, retired early, and they moved to a gated country club community, complete with an 18-hole golf course. It was here they planned to spend the remainder of their days meeting new friends, traveling, and playing golf. Less than a year after his layoff, he dropped dead of a massive heart attack. The year following his death, this lively and attractive woman rarely left home. Four years later, she came to see me because she "could not get past the grief" for her late husband. To complicate the matter further, a man eight years older was pressing her to get married. Hannah did not feel confident entering into a new marriage when she still contained such overwhelming sadness for her former husband.

In terms of philosophy and theology, the adjustment involved in pre and post retirement involves extensive self-evaluation. These are evaluative years. Nothing quite captures the dark side of this better than Arthur Miller's *Death of a Salesman*. In a review written by Brooks Atkinson of the New York Times when the play originally premiered on Broadway, Atkinson summarizes:

> It is the story of an aging salesman who has reached the end of his usefulness on the road. There has always been something unsubstantial about his work. But suddenly the unsubstantial aspects of it overwhelm him completely. When he was young, he looked dashing;

> he enjoyed the comradeship of other people--the humor, the kidding, and the business.
>
> In his early sixties, he knows his business as well as he ever did. But the unsubstantial things have become decisive; the spring has gone from his step, the smile from his face and the heartiness from his personality. He is through. The phantom of his life has caught up with him. As literally as Mr. Miller can say it, dust returns to dust. Suddenly there is nothing.
>
> This is only a little of what Mr. Miller is saying. For he conveys this elusive tragedy in terms of simple things-- the loyalty and understanding of his wife, the careless selfishness of his two sons, the sympathetic devotion of a neighbor, the coldness of his former boss' son--the bills, the car, the tinkering around the house. And most of all: the illusions by which he has lived-- opportunities missed, wrong formulas for success, fatal misconceptions about his place in the scheme of things.[20]

The timeless quality of Mr. Miller's work is a testimony and a tribute to the relevance, meaning, and message embedded in *Death of A Salesman*.[21] The haunting nightmare at the end of this road is the nagging question; *"What happens if we get to the end, and it did not mean anything?"* Individuals who are able to shift effectively into retirement have often built into their life and lifestyle targets for ongoing continuous improvement in advance. By making course corrections along the way, we can prevent the end of the journey leaving us alienated and disheartened. This proactive approach is one way to avoid the pain *Death of A Salesman* depicts or predicts. The shift into retirement is often difficult if auxiliary targets have not been developed, especially if one's vocation has been the primary and sole focus. The absence of a paycheck, the camaraderie of coworkers, and the loss of productiveness can be a painful source of loss and grief.

Dan, a square-shouldered no-nonsense kind of guy whose physical appearance reminded me of Popeye the

Sailor, came to my office one day with his wife. His retirement was to begin in one month. Dan worked in the newspaper business for 40 years with a number of major newspapers across the United States. This tough guy began to weep quietly as he spoke about retiring. Eventually his weeping broke into deep sobs. "The newspaper business is the only thing that I have ever known how to do! What am I going to do with my life?" Dan's work and his life had been synonymous, and he had no other interests and never developed additional goals, dreams, and aspirations. In all my days consoling individuals through their last days on this earth, I have never heard one person say, *"I wish I would have worked more."*

Retirement is a relatively recent phenomenon in the course of history. The term "retirement" represented the ones who were the slowest in the herd. In tribe standards, you only had to be faster than the slowest tribe member to keep from "retiring." Thanks to the advent of social security, pension plans, and 401k's retirement is a household word. Prior to this grandparents and great-grandparents were parts of extended families. They simply spent more of their time on front porches participating in Zen-like activities such as rocking in chairs, shelling peas and pecans. The elderly were never considered retired. They participated in the life of families and were an integral part of the family fabric. They still contributed to the family and society, but did a little less and worked a little more slowly. Rest Homes, still visible in the landscape of rural communities, are now assisted living facilities. Congregate care retirement homes, assisted living facilities, and nursing homes are recent additions in the pages of current history.

We are now witnessing the beginning of a mass exodus from the workforce by retiring Baby Boomers. Many have the means to retire younger than ever before. Those able to make this shift to retirement begin to develop targets that have been secondary or dormant. Ongoing purposeful targets expand our circle of influence and create the potential to make a difference in someone else's life. Retirement can provide a plethora of possibilities. I frequently see adults entering into this stage of life with a "been there, done that" attitude, tired and bored from travel and golf. Without ongoing spiritual and emotional homework, individuals can become resentful, disillusioned, and even mean if they carry around unresolved anger and resentment. Retirement is not entitlement. Retirement is a gift, as all of life is a gift. We do not get retirement because we have earned it, or deserve it. In my observation, the happiest retired people are those who continue to feel useful and purposeful and do useful and purposeful things. Retirement is not a time to withdraw; it is a time to engage. So many opportunities are available to the fortunate souls given the gift of extra time to contribute. If we are skilled with tools, Habitat for Humanity creates new housing possibilities one house at a time. If we are gifted in relationships, certain organizations and institutions are begging for capable volunteers to mentor students or to be a Big Brother or Big Sister. If we can drive a car, we can deliver meals on wheels. It is all about relationships! People matter!

There is a tendency to evaluate careers and relationships to "see how everybody turned out" and to evaluate success or failure in the parenting process. If persons enter this stage of life in good spiritual, physical, and emotional health, they have targeted and have been intentional about maintaining the components of well being in each of the previous ages and stages. As a result, they may be able to enjoy an active lifestyle for several decades to come.

One of my dearest friends is Gladys, an 89-year-old woman who lives independently. Almost every Tuesday I have lunch with Gladys, unless she is out of town visiting with family and friends. Gladys drives her own car, plays bridge every week and is a voracious reader. She is lively, sharp, and fun. She grew up the youngest of five children and the daughter of a minister in Iowa. She was a nurse, married a doctor, and raised three children. After a long and successful medical practice and a few years of enjoying retirement and a second home in the North Carolina

Mountains, her husband was debilitated by colon cancer and a stroke. He died several years ago after a long tenure in a nursing home. Just over a year ago, her middle child died suddenly at the age of 62 of a massive heart attack. She has known great joy and faced heartache and suffering and has done so with dignity and style. Her grandchildren and great-grandchildren fight over who gets to come and stay with her. She is actively involved with them and stays connected in nearly all their lives. She lives one day at a time, as we all should, and Gladys consistently hits her targets.

Before basketball legend Michael Jordan retired, a national Nike add campaign featured children of all shapes and sizes saying, "I want to be like Mike." Although I thoroughly enjoyed his acrobatic basketball career, I do not want to be like Mike. Not me. I want to be like Gladys. Gladys is my hero. I have set my target. Like Gladys, I want to keep my mind sharp; I want to maintain my health to the best of my ability, and I want my children and grandchildren to spend time with me, not out of obligation or duty, but because they feel loved, cared for, valued, and appreciated, and want to be with me.

The Agility Test: Focus and Balance

When we look at meaning making from the perspective of targets, a key principle involves understanding the difference between focus and balance. Focus creates balance. If the goal is to maintain balance and equilibrium, we will always fail. The previous discussion in the model of *meaning* guarantees this. Our goal is to maintain focus on the target. Think about this in terms of logrolling. We may be very good at logrolling, and won log rolling championships in lumberjack competitions, but eventually, we will fall off the log! As best as I can tell, the log always wins! Something will always knock us off our log, even if we are logrolling solo. Choosing a life partner, raising children and teenagers, tackling careers and job changes, assuming debt, moving to a new city or a different location, going though the break-up of a relationship or divorce, struggling with illness or disease, moving through the different stages of life, the death of loved ones or struggling with our own mortality are all life situations designed to knock us off our log. These situations are destined to undermine our sense of self-sufficiency. When we are willing to seek help, we begin to discover an evolving sense of our own collective connection to life and make conscious choices about living in agreement with life. When we consciously choose to live within this matrix of reality, we discover what Joseph Chilton Pearce calls *The Cosmic Egg of Meaning*.[22]

When we experience enmeshment, we may lose both our vision and focus. One key factor in the movement from the descent of enmeshment toward the ascent of disengagement, reflection, and re-engagement is the return or re-establishment of focus. Focus involves maintaining our sight on the target. My wife takes a Pilate's class several times a week. Pilates is an exercise routine that utilizes a variety of skills, including breathing and balance, in order to strengthen the abdominal muscles. The degree of difficulty to master the different postures determines either student placement in the beginner, intermediate, or advanced level. Brenda has advanced her own skill development through hard work in these classes. Through her, I have learned one of the key components to holding a particular pose for a determined length of time involves the ability to concentrate on a single spot on the wall. The spot on the wall becomes the target, and we achieve balance through focus.

When we maintain our sight on the target, we stay focused on the purpose. Earlier, I stated that behavior is either purposeful or protective. When behavior is purposeful, we consciously choose to move out of a protective mode (dominated by anger and anxiety) and to respond in a more highly evolved level of consciousness. Living purposefully, we work to hit targets with intention. We have adopted the consciousness of cooperation. Synergy is the energy of cooperation and creativity. To establish targets means we seek to align our behavior with our ethics, principles, and ideals. The target provides the pull and the ethics, principles and ideals provide the push. This tension evokes the making of *meaning*. This method provides an automatic ongoing evaluative proponent of meaning making. What targets are we trying to hit? Why are we trying to hit it? Are we on course for hitting the target? If not, what do we need to do in order to improve?

In summary, our search is a *search for meaning.* The founder of Self-Psychology, Heinz Kohut, offered two contrasting images to clarify and simplify the options in our modern world. He called these two models ***tragic man*** and ***guilty man***.[23] Guilty man is concerned predominately with the issues of pleasure, and its antithesis, the emotion of guilt. Tragic man embraces human mortality, understands the relative nature of our existence, and pursues a life involving the evolution of meaning.

This chapter has been about the evolution of meaning. Our history and experience creates ideas and beliefs that will establish the trajectories we will travel. If we are shooting straight, our trajectory will travel the pathway of coherence. The bowstring that propels these arrows will be powered by our character, ethics, principles, and ideals. Conversely, if our history and experience create ideas and beliefs that cause us to draw the bow back with reactivity, the energy propelling this projectile will be anger or anxiety. These are damaged arrows: bent arrows, or missing feathers and fletching create an imbalanced flight. The trajectory of these arrows will be erratic, chaotic, and will cause us to miss the mark. Meaningful targets have the ability to pull synergistic energy from us so we can hit these targets. These targets act as magnets to draw us toward them!

Ongoing issues faced in each age and stage of life becomes accentuated at young adulthood, middle age, and just before or after retirement. We discover meaning in our vocation when that vocation is an ongoing expression of our passion. We are constantly involved in asking questions of meaning in the evaluation of our day-to-day experiences. When we ask, "What does this mean?" we are engaged and involved in the ongoing work and the interpretation of experience. How do my experiences fit into what I already know and believe about my self, the world, or God? What targets am I seeking to hit? Am I living purposefully or protectively? How does new experience modify, change, and improve my theory, philosophy, and theology?

Two additional components for creating meaning-making involve our search for justice and our search for competence. These two areas are capable of triggering emotional hijackings that will leave our relationships in ruin if we have not begun to evolve in our own self-awareness toward a new reality.

Chapter 3
The Search for Justice

"Defensiveness is always rationally cloaked as common sense, while revenge is always cloaked as justice."[24]

"The imitation involved in revenge tends toward more violence, for it tends to repay the violence it avenges "with interest." It tends to escalate the violence. The ancient injunction, "an eye for an eye, a tooth for a tooth," was an attempt to keep revenge from spinning out of control."[25]

As stated in Chapter 1, when a real, perceived or imagined threat to one's safety exists, the individual feels anxious or angry. If no immediate threat to physical safety exists, the perceived attack will manifest as a threat to our psychological, emotional, and spiritual safety. In Chapter 1, I described the "FRICK" principle. What happens when we become stuck, embedded, or enmeshed? To review, "FRICK" is an acronym representing:

1) **Frustration,** which is externally focused at an object, person, situation, or a circumstance when you cannot get "it" to do what you want it to do. I blame someone or something else.
2) **Reactivity,** when current situations evoke strong emotions from unresolved issues in the past. Hysterical is always historical.
3) **Internalization**, when frustration is interjected within the self. I blame myself.
4) **Conflicted thoughts, feelings, or emotions**, when I am thinking one way and feeling another way and I am struggling to resolve the internalized conflict.
5) **Knowledge**, or self-awareness that one or more of these four things is happening

In this chapter, you will explore what happens when you become hijacked by anger and anxiety. Frustration and reactivity are the key components of the FRICK principle that will help you to understand the *externalization* of anger or anxiety. In other words, you will learn what places you in an "attack" mode. The dynamics created by *internalization* and conflicted thoughts, feelings, and emotions will deepen your understanding of depression. You will learn the dynamics of what places you in a "withdraw" mode.

You will begin to learn how to circumvent these chaotic emotional states by receiving your own heart "bypass." You will begin to learn how to create the awareness necessary to remain conscious, purposeful, and to become empowered as a peacemaker. We will begin this process by asking two questions that are intended to help you create and establish awareness:

1) "Is there something happening that feels unbalanced or unfair to you?"
2) "Is there something that has been said that questions your competence and makes you feel like you have been minimized, put down, or made to feel stupid?"

The next chapter explores the issues involving question two, our search for competence. We all have basic needs to be successful with who we are and what we do. When we encounter circumstances in which we do not feel capable, we may become frustrated. This frustration will be directed internally or externally. Without a path to succeed, the wounded self creates an internal bind. We will feel safe, protecting our wounded competence, but we will also fail because we will not try.

The human brain has evolved over time. At the top of our spinal cord rests the reptilian brain. This is the same brain of alligators and snakes, and operates through four questions to interpret experience in accordance with our two major drives: sex and aggression.

1) Is it going to eat me?
2) Am I going to eat it?
3) Is it going to want to have sex with me?
4) Do I want to have sex with it?

As mammals, we developed a limbic brain that sits on top of the reptilian brain. This brain enables us to *nurture* our young rather than to *eat* them. The development of the neocortex and the cortex evolved into our "thinking" brain. Threats to our physical safety have evolved with our brains to higher functioning states of our emotional, spiritual, and psychological safety. If we are angry, and there is no clear immediate danger to our physical safety, 99% of the time the anger involves a perceived attack to our *competence* or issues of *justice*. This is the search for justice.

The Cultural Oxygen We Breathe: The Blame Game

Earl Hunt, former president of Emory and Henry College at Emory, Virginia, tells a story about a colleague and his transition as the replacement for a resigning president of a college. The new president was eager to receive suggestions by the former president, who offered this advice: "I've placed two envelopes in your drawer. After the honeymoon phase is over and when circumstances become difficult and you begin to doubt if this was the right position for you to accept, open the first envelope. If you discover later your situation continues to deteriorate, open the second envelope." The advice seemed rather somber; nevertheless, the new president accepted these words and expressed his gratitude for the cryptic message. He threw the envelopes in the top drawer of his desk and promptly forgot about them.

About a year later, controversy erupted over the colleague cleaning house and firing faculty who were incompetent and ineffective but nevertheless, well connected politically with members of the community and the board of trustees. He received a flood of phone calls, and a flurry of e-mails, followed by restless and sleepless nights. The repercussions of restructuring the faculty were more serious than he anticipated. Then, he remembered the two envelopes. Out of despair and curiosity, the new president opened the desk drawer and fiddled with the envelope labeled #1. He grabbed a letter opener, sliced the envelope open, and pulled out the letter to read the contents. In bold 36-point type, the letter offered two words, "Blame Me!" Taking the advice of his predecessor, the new president did damage control. The new president placed phone calls and answered e-mails, stating that he was simply following the advice of his predecessor, which may have been weak and ineffective. The furor temporarily died down, and calm returned.

Six months later, and another losing season on the gridiron, the alumni called for the head of the coach and the new president. During the tenure of his predecessor, the team produced 10 winning seasons, three conference championships, and six major bowl appearances. The alumni were furious, the coach blamed the president, and matters turned worse. Alumni threatened to withhold giving. A student constructed a "Fire the President" website that registered over 25,000 hits in less than a week. In desperation, the college president opened the desk drawer and nervously fiddled with the envelope labeled #2. With an element of frenzy, he jerked out the contents, unfolded the letter, and in 36 point bold type he read three words: "Write two letters."

By establishing blame, we attempt to establish culpability, responsibility, negligence, or fault. In the minds of the alumni, the new president was culpable, responsible, negligent, and at fault for another losing season on the football field. In Roman times, Caesar's "thumbs down" would mean decapitation. In our current culture, the options might include termination of employment (an occupational death sentence) or ex-communication (having to leave the community in shame). In criminal courts, when any of these factors are established, and a person is convicted of a crime, the guilty party is punished through some form of retributive justice, which may include fines, prison, or in capital cases, even the loss of life. In civil courts of law, when any of these factors are established, punitive damages in the form of financial compensation are assessed as a means of retributive or restorative justice. Pharmaceutical companies producing drugs causing harmful side effects, tire manufacturers producing defective tires causing accidents, injury, or death, or fast food restaurants without warning labels on coffee cups are all liable. The aggrieved parties are entitled to some form of financial compensation based upon the severity of the injury and the loss of future earning potential. This principle boils down to "You hurt me; you pay!" Our judicial systems, particularly the civil courts, are driven to discern fault. Who is responsible, and who will pay. If you do something wrong to me, and I can prove it, I can sue you in court. If the jury or judge agrees with my accusation, then I must be compensated. Since the only way I can be compensated is through financial remuneration, somebody is going to have to pay.

In the Western World, we live in a litigious culture. I have worked with a variety of professionals, including physicians, dentists, architects, and chiropractors subjected to years of investigations from alleged malpractice, code violations, or disciplinary action from regulatory boards. The more seasoned and cynical veterans of this process annually set aside liability premiums as well as legal fees as a presumed cost of doing business. Several years ago, I worked for a not-for-profit organization in St. Augustine, FL. My professional portfolio was risk management for several programs, including two small nursing homes. Our staff proudly maintained "superior" ratings in both homes from the State of Florida during annual inspections. We had an outstanding reputation in the community for the excellent care we provided for our residents. A seasoned core of our employees had worked for the organization for 20 years or longer. We provided the highest staff to resident ratios and far exceeded the minimum State of Florida required standards. Nursing homes, however, are the second most regulated industries in the United States, ranking just behind nuclear power plants. The administrators and directors of nursing shouldered with me the responsibility of daily critical evaluation of the facility operation with one question in mind: "How can we *not* be sued today?"

I met a police investigator in one of our homes one morning at three o'clock. Earlier in the evening, a female resident had got out of bed to go to the bathroom. She tripped and fell on her walker and bruised her pelvic area. As a precautionary measure, she was taken to the local emergency room and examined by an emergency room physician. The physician concluded that the wound looked suspicious; and, in his judgment, the injury could have been the result of sexual abuse. The doctor alerted the police, and I met the investigator at the nursing home, where he conducted an investigation into these allegations. The investigator interviewed the staff, took notes, and later concluded the resident's injury was the result of a fall, as had been reported. Certainly, situations arise when an emergency room physician will be the crucial link in reporting the possibility of some types of abuse, including the sexual abuse of the elderly. If such incidents were not reported and there in fact, had been abuse, the E.R. doctor would have shared in the liability. The point I am making is this: In all fields of medicine as well as the nursing home industry the problem is not a matter of *if* you will be sued, but *when*.

Risk management is a sophisticated way of speaking of living in a constant state of "readiness." The culture is sensitized through bizarre and isolated incidents or experiences that receive national exposure and the flood of television advertising that comes from ambulance chasing attorneys who ask, "Have you or a loved one been injured in a nursing home? Call Dewey, Cheatum, and Howe for a free consultation. We only get paid if you win!" In the nursing home industry, we *knew* we were going to be hit; we just did not know from *which direction* the hit was coming. When they are truly out to get you, the reality is not paranoia. The wide range of possibilities include patients, patient families, employees, volunteers, agency nurses, physical therapists, occupational therapists, and speech therapists.

Risk management requires employees to receive in-service training covering a range of topics from correct hand washing procedures to prevent the spread of infectious diseases, to proper handling of bio-hazardous materials to prevent H.I.V. infection, or even appropriate methods for feeding patients or lifting techniques to avoid back injury. You name it we did it. If an employee reported a back injury, the course of action went something like this: Was the employee wearing a back brace? We would produce the records indicating the employee attended the training for proper lifting and safety techniques on the job and signed the form stating, *"I have attended this training and by my signature I agree that I will wear a back brace for my safety when lifting patients or any item over twenty pounds."* Did the supervisor mandate the employee to surrender a urine sample at the time of the incident? If a urinalysis detects drugs or alcohol, the employee would immediately be disqualified from receiving workers' compensation benefits. The diligence of in-service training and documentation can shift the responsibility for the injury. The choice not to wear the back brace, resulting in injury, is employee negligence. The nursing home may not avoid a worker's compensation claim, but we could certainly avoid paying unemployment. Workman's compensation attorneys retained by the nursing home would regularly order the carrier to pay out "nuisance claims," generally $10,000 or less. The attorneys weighed legal fees and court fees against the lump payment and would often just settle. What eventually passed to the consumer is the bottom line cost of doing business in a litigious world. Right or wrong, no matter how frivolous or fictitious, every incident is taken seriously. Investigating accidents and injuries helps determine who is culpable, responsible, negligent, and at fault. Risk management attempts to anticipate and avoid these scenarios and correct liability *before* accidents or injuries happen. What we try to circumvent is this: "You hurt me; you pay!" This is the current cultural reality; you can like it or loathe it, but *it is what it is*!

What pervades western consciousness is the application of this mindset, not only in matters of law and culture, but also in relationships. Each of us have individual and collective embedded images, symbols, and icons to determine what is fair and balanced in relationships. The blind lady of justice is embedded in the collective psyche of western human beings.

In matters of law, when there is a determination of who is culpable, responsible, negligent, and at fault, restorative or punitive damages are required to offset the injustice. In matters of relationships, this same principle applies: "You hurt me; you pay!" This may especially be applicable in matters of divorce when one spouse or the other believes his or her suffering or perceived injustices should be financially compensated. Florida, which is a no-fault state, avoids this drama and simply divides the assets down the middle. What I am attempting to outline is not so much a matter of capital, assets, or possessions. What I see is an emotional law of restitution. I may not be able to sue my spouse or my children for damages, but I can take a pound of flesh out of their butts! Retributive justice appeals to a basic sense of human fairness. Ancient Judaism, from the time of Moses, stated the concept this way, "An eye for an eye and a tooth for a tooth." It follows very closely the logic I previously described. "You hurt me; you pay." However, how does this principle translate into ordinary day-to-day interaction in our tangled web of relationships?

Whose Fault Is It, Anyway? The Role of Blame, Resentment, and Revenge

The basic human need to determine what is just, fair, and balanced permeates our relational transactions. When an individual perceives a violation of these principles, there is a reactive firing sequence: blame, resentment, and revenge. The cultural oxygen we breathe is the assumption if something is wrong, someone must be at fault. Someone must be blamed but whom?

The world of blame has two kinds of people: those who *assign* blame and those who *accept* it.

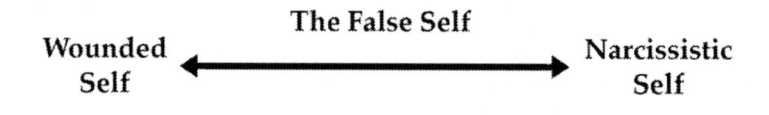

```
                     The False Self
    Wounded        <————————————>      Narcissistic
     Self                                  Self
```

Figure 10

Earlier, I described at length the Darwinian Dilemma and aspects of the human condition. Later we will explore what it means for human beings to be created in the *Imago Dei,* and how these two natures live in tension to bring about the transformation of human consciousness. In this construct of spiritual, psychological and cultural anthropology, what I would like to suggest to the reader is that the Imago Dei is soon covered with the development of the false self. The false self tends to develop in one of two directions on opposite ends of a continuum. This involves the splitting of human consciousness toward the development of either a wounded self on one end or a narcissistic self on the other end. [m]

With persons who have developed a narcissistic false self, these individuals assign blame to others. "If something is wrong, it must be *your* fault." They have an idealized image of their own perfection because of their accomplishments, achievements, possessions, status, power, wealth, or physical beauty. The narcissistic individual lives with a feeling of entitlement. They are special. They know it and others must acknowledge this fact. They demand to be treated this way and others walk on eggshells to avoid becoming the target of their narcissistic disdain, disgust, or

---

[m] A discussion of narcissistic personality disorder is found in Appendix #1

rage. Although I have a personal aversion to putting bumper stickers on my vehicle, I do have one in my office, which reads, *The Universe Rearranges Itself On A Daily Basis to Accommodate Your Picture of Reality.* This is the credo for the narcissistic individual.

On the other end of the continuum is the wounded self. If something is wrong, it must be *my* fault. At very early developmental stages for both of these individuals, a "split" occurs within the self, best described as an establishment and formation of one's internalized image. These images are *reactive* because they are formed in reaction to the environment. For the narcissist, the internalized image is expressed as, "You are bad for not recognizing how important I am." The wounded self involves a different image. Rather than *externalizing* the blame, blame is *internalized.* This image is expressed as, "I am bad because I am not able to get what I need."

Let me illustrate how splitting works. My daughter was home from college and had three weeks off until she was to begin an internship at a summer camp. When she arrived home, we were informed of her initial plans. She was going to return to school to visit Sorority sisters, spend the night, and head down to south Florida to attend a concert. The only glitch was she did not have enough money to attend the concert. I sympathized with her and told her I thought that was too bad, but I did not take the hook and swallow the bait. The next morning she was more direct and asked if she could use my credit card to buy her ticket online. I agreed to her request; she ordered her ticket, and off she went to Lakeland and then to the concert in West Palm Beach. When she returned home, she informed her mother and me that she was next planning a trip to Tallahassee, and after that, her plans were incomplete. She was criss-crossing the state at our expense, and our response to her was that we thought it would be helpful if she could establish her plans in dialogue with us so we could decide what we could or could not afford and put together a budget for the remainder of her stay until she went to camp. Our daughter fumed, spun on her heels, and headed back to her bedroom. I waited five minutes, and went to her room, and we shared in a discussion about what had just happened. She quickly apologized, and I told her I was the same Daddy who had given her my credit card for the concert as the one who was now asking her to work with us in establishing a budget for the remainder of her time home. The "split" in terms of how she saw me *was in her mind.* I was the "good" Daddy when I gave her what she wanted; I was the "bad" Daddy when I withheld.

This dynamic of external/internal blame was illustrated to me when I was becoming a certified LEAD consultant under the direction of Tim Savage.[26] He described outward blaming people as skunks. Skunks, as we know, will raise their tail, and we will be blasted when they feel threatened. My daughter was being slightly skunky with me. Savage described inward blaming people as turtles. Turtles are just as powerful as skunks, but their weapon is their ability to hook your guilt. When threatened, they will withdraw into their shell. "You do not have to worry about me. I will be here all by myself with no one to talk to. I may be a bit lonely, but that's okay. You go ahead and have a good time. Please now, run along, and do not worry about my angina pain and my heart condition. If anything happens, I'll just call 911."

Let us look more closely at this phenomenon of inward blaming/outward blaming skunks and turtles. Let me introduce you to a skunk. We were leaving a July race at Daytona International Speedway close to eleven-thirty at night, and the first wave of fans scurried out of the speedway like ants rushing out of an anthill. The rush was a frenzied attempt to beat the three-hour traffic quagmire that was soon to follow. We were hurrying, walking almost at a jog to cross International Speedway Boulevard in order to catch a shuttle bus. Another couple was scurrying in the same manner close to us but just ahead. The woman, walking next to her male companion, was looking back and not watching where she was going. She walked directly into one of those walk/don't walk concrete posts. Her shoulder and right side hit the concrete hard, and she stepped back, her eyes momentarily glazed, like a prizefighter hit with a hard body shot and about to go down on the canvas. She recovered, and her dazed look was quickly replaced with anger as rage raced through her veins. I literally noticed the veins in her neck began to bulge. She glared at the post as if it had jumped out in front of her to purposely block her path and cause her pain, followed by a verbal assault and a string of profanities. The absurdity of her verbal abuse of an inanimate object stunned me. What an unpredictable universe we live in when immovable objects suspiciously become mobile with an intention to impede our progress in life! The scene was ludicrous. What is the result? Someone or something else must be to blame! It could not possibly be my error, my mistake, or my stupidity. In relationships, one of the unconscious assumptions with casting blame is: "If I make you feel bad, you will do the right thing." Blame is an ineffective tool for problem solving. Even with guilt adjudicated and punishment established, you still have to figure out what the problem is and how to fix it. Guilt will not fix the problem.

Recently I saw a picture of an automobile accident on the front page of our newspaper. A man drove his van off an overpass, and landed in a small canal. Rescue workers were hoisting the man up over the embankment while he was strapped on a stretcher. I tried to imagine how this would play out if two skunky rescue workers attended to the scene and began by yelling and belittling the man, "Hey buddy! How did you manage to do that? Boy, you must have been on the cell phone, the fax machine, shaving, and cooking a hot dog on that George Forman 12 volt plug-in grilling machine you've got down there on the floorboard! You are supposed to be paying attention. You are such an idiot!" Meanwhile the driver is half-conscious and injured. At this point, does it matter how the accident happened and who is to blame? What matters is fixing the problem and getting this man the medical attention he needs.

In the world of blame, skunks blame others and turtles blame themselves. This is the bottom line: when something is wrong he or she will *accept* or *project* the blame. Blame will either be interjected or projected. When our son Sean was five, we were living in a two-story home. He was taking a shower in the downstairs bathroom, and suddenly to his horror, the sewer line backed up. Raw sewage backed up into the shower. It was not a pretty sight. Sean jumped out of the shower, grabbed a towel and ran into the family room repenting, "I'm sorry, I'm sorry, I'm sorry!" He assumed that *he* caused the problem, and sewage backup was *his* fault.

Millions of people operate from the psychological mindset stemming from the wounded self. Although the *wounded self* is not named in any creeds or statements of faith, mainline religious traditions often service this need. The wounded self believes that he or she deserves to be punished. Pastor William was a likeable man, easy going, with a good sense of humor and a warm heart for the two small rural Florida churches he served as pastor. He did a good job behind the pulpit. He spoke with warmth and insight. Every January the laity of the churches performed an annual review to recommend to a denominational official whether or not a pastor should stay another year or move on. Pastor William called me feeling extremely distraught and conflicted after the committee vote. One of his churches wanted him to stay and the other wanted him to leave because "he just was not tough enough when it came to preaching the gospel." In other words, Pastor William did not preach shame or fear through his message. His congregation preferred him to use humiliation as the dominant sense of coherence. Pastor William spoke about the grace of God rather than the wrath of God. When he preached, his congregants did not "feel the fear" of being sinners in the hands of an angry God. Pastor William was a turtle, and they wanted a skunk! Masochistic spirituality mistakes the experience of *shame* as feeling close to God. This is an erroneous assumption. Guilt may induce temporary compliance; however, guilt is usually accompanied by shame and humiliation. This set of emotions will never move toward energy, synergy, and cooperation as a means and method for making successful relationships.

Turtles tend to be highly adaptive people pleasers and passive-aggressive when dealing with anger. In general, turtles are tender, caring and empathic but experience difficulty making decisions. Turtles assume responsibility for the unhappiness of others and avert being the focus of blame by polling others before making a decision. Savage's research indicates that 66% of turtles marry skunks. The tradeoff seems to be that skunks need the tenderness of turtles and turtles need the assertiveness of skunks. Thirty-three percent of the time skunks marry other skunks, and this rarely renders peace in the home. Turtles never marry other turtles because nothing would ever get done! A fictitious dialogue between two turtles might go this way: "What do *you* want to do tonight, honey?" "Gee, sweetheart, I don't know, what do *you* want to do?" "I don't know; I guess we could go to a movie?" "Yes, I know, we could, but movies are so violent, and the language is always so bad." "Yes, you are right; the language is so bad. Maybe we could go out to dinner. Where would *you* like to go?" "I don't know; what would taste good to *you*?" "I'd really like to go where *you'd* like to go?" You get the picture!

When taken to an extreme, skunk (outward blaming) and turtle (inward blaming) relationships typify one of the core dynamics involved in abusive relationships. Skunks feel justified in heaping abuse, whether verbal or physical, and turtles feel they deserve the abuse. "It's really my fault he got angry and hit me. If I had his shirts ironed, or the dinner on the table when he came home, or bought the beer and had it in the refrigerator like he told me to, everything would have been okay. I know he did not really mean to hit me. I know he's really sorry and it won't happen again." Nevertheless, it will happen again, and again, and again! Statistically, the abused leaves the abuser an average of six to eight times before leaving for good. Some leave sooner while others never leave. Others are tragically murdered and they become the latest statistics of domestic violence.

In relationships, projected blame creates a position of power and establishes emotional or financial entitlement. To put it succinctly, blame is expressed, *"You owe me."* When marriages are ending, retainers are charged, and attorney fees are paid, this emotional energy may fuel the fight for as long as it takes or until the money runs out. This is a full-bore expression of the win-lose dynamic, when polarities are charged and ensuing bitterness can last a lifetime. I worked with a couple divorcing after four years of marriage. Her primary list of complaints: her husband was not the Christian man she thought he was, he was a narcissist, she was the major breadwinner, and he did not bring enough finances to the table. He was a liability rather than an asset. His primary complaints were she was cold, critical, judgmental, and he always felt he was walking on eggshells. He could not "get it right" or please her. He refused to rent movies because when anything she deemed to be morally objectionable, she would look at him with disgust and say, "What would Jesus say if he was sitting here on the couch?" (Jesus would obviously agree with her viewpoint and would not approve - a true turtle statement.) Once a family member expressed an admiration for her faith and in return, he received a condescending lecture for 45 minutes about his shortcomings, completely shutting him down. (Switching into skunk mode, which we are capable of doing when we are playing the win or lose game)

In the early 1990s, she purchased a former crack house for $67,000 and began restoration. He owned a townhouse on a golf course. After marriage, they both agreed to quitclaim deed each property to the other and create joint marital assets. They paid off his debt with the sale of the town home. Six months after they were married, due to meticulous renovations and a neighborhood fighting back, the $67,000 home she lived in was appraised at $340,000. By the time they divorced, the house was worth 1.1 million dollars! When he asked for half of the equity in the house *since the marriage*, she became belligerent and went ballistic. With both names on the deed, he legally could have asked for half the value of the entire house, but he did not. "You mean you are going to make me pay you? What kind of a Christian man would do that?" I interpreted her comments to mean, "If you do not see the situation the way I do, then I will assault your character and integrity because you do not agree with me." The home held a base meaning we worked to uncover. In my mind, a house is a house. The emotional meaning connected to the house was something else. In her mind, the house was an icon of stability and safety. She was raised in a home with an alcoholic father, and a great deal of moving around. The house represented an image of success. She bought it for next to nothing and transformed it to the present value. The house was hers, represented her life and soul. She felt entitled to this home. It was how Scarlett O'Hara felt about Tara in *Gone With The Wind* when Rhett Butler left and told her, "Frankly my dear, I don't give a damn." He was not leaving like Clark Gable, but he was leaving, sort of, or eventually. Although they remained cordial, he lived in the basement and she upstairs during this time of estrangement. She began to gather boxes and to force him to move out. Every day she would come down into the basement and launch into verbal harangues. He would try to get her to calm down, to remain cordial, but the pretense finally broke when she squared off and said, "I feel like I have to treat you like the enemy." (Back into skunk mode)

    As we see with skunks and turtles, blame either externalizes or internalizes the problem by projecting or interjecting. The person, circumstance, or situation does not meet the expectations of the individual. Frequently these expectations are an "understood" agreement between two parties. These unconscious expectations are based upon relational assumptions of *quid pro quo*. If I do something for you, you are supposed to do something in return.

    One afternoon when our daughter was home from college, I decided to wash the McNeil fleet of family vehicles. I washed my daughter's car, my wife's car, and my truck. When I noticed the water failing to bead on my wife's car, I decided to go ahead and apply a coat of wax. I had been outside for nearly three hours, listening to books on MP3's, while enjoying this activity. Brenda came out to check on me and noticed I was waxing her car. She said in a troubled tone, "Why are you waxing my car?" I was mildly stunned, but managed a reply and said, "Because it needed it and because I thought you would appreciate it." She closed the door at the entrance of the garage and went back inside. I shrugged it off, went on and finished the job, and went into the house and headed to the kitchen to get something to drink. When I got to the kitchen, Brenda was scurrying around with beaters and mixing bowls, and I asked her, "What are you doing?" She said, "I am making you those breakfast muffins you said you wanted." My response was, "That was three weeks ago, why are you doing it now?" Unconsciously, Brenda felt she had to do something to balance what I had done for her, even though I never expected anything in return.

  This is the way our mind works to create balance and to establish scenarios of justice. We have no right to "expect" something from someone else, unless an agreement or a promise was made. Moreover, we should not have to feel obligated to do something in return when someone gives us a gift. Over the years, I have heard from hundreds of women who have complained and lamented that when they receive flowers from their husbands, sex is the expectation that arrives with the bouquet. "If I do this for you, you are supposed to do this for me. Now we are even. Now it's fair." Duty, obligation, and responsibility are hardly ignition switches for passion!

  This principle of *quid pro quo* not only has a magical way of balancing the present, but may also be used (by turtles) as an insurance policy to keep from *feeling guilty in the future!* A woman I was working with told me a story about her husband. He was calling from a south Florida community where he had gone to visit his mother who was critically ill and dying. He told his wife she needed to go visit *her* mother in a neighboring town. The woman had many unresolved issues with her mother and did not particularly want to go. He suggested she visit so that "when she dies, you won't feel guilty." What an amazing piece of logic! Let us see if we have it! If I perform out of obligation *now*, I will not feel guilty in the *future*. This is the mind's precarious balancing act in the search for justice, as if there is some type of mental abacus. If we slide these beads over, this action will counterbalance the beads on the other side. Meanwhile, this delicate universe may fall and shatter in any given moment – the precarious balance. The ego is at work to protect us from the steady drip of taking intravenous guilt trips.

When the principle of *quid pro quo* is operative in a relationship, this dynamic imposes an impossible burden to keep the relationship in a position of delicate and fragile balance. Relationships rarely operate at a constant 50/50 balance. A relational thermometer does not exist and 50/50 is not the 98.6-degree measurement for normal. Although this makes sense intellectually, our emotional intelligence may see this differently. *Quid pro quo* encourages score keeping, and in all probability, someone is always in arrears. You are always going to "owe" me something or I will be in debt to you. This does not mean that couples should not equally divide household duties and day-to-day responsibilities. What it does mean is that if keeping score is about debits or credits, which one is behind or ahead, a finger will always be on the trigger of resentment. If the whole is greater than the sum total of the parts, couples will find ways to work together as a team, with energy, synergy, and cooperation.

Let us take the non-verbal concept of *quid pro quo* and create a verbal statement to use as an example. Follow the next statement slowly and carefully. *I may not know what it is I am supposed to do for you, but you assume I know and when I do not follow through with what you think I am supposed to do and I am not doing, you will be resentful, you will withdraw, or there will be some other form of punishment. I will instead go ahead and reject you first.* If you did not get it the first time, try it again! This contorted statement highlights the unconscious assumptions that are regressed states of awareness. "If you really loved me, you would *know* what I want," is the way this is expressed. This takes us back to a time when everything we needed was automatically delivered without asking, in the womb.

Resentment

Resentment is the slow boil that takes place when conflict is not resolved and remains under the surface, capable of rearing its ugly head at the drop of a hat. How do we define resentment? If we feel resentment, chances are something is eating away below the surface. Resentment means to feel bitter, indignant, or offended. It means we are holding an unresolved grievance against another person, circumstance, or situation. Address the problem, release it, and let it go. Turtles tend to bury resentment or to stuff it back down. Skunks tend to spew resentment in all directions. Resentment usually follows with shutting down and withdrawal until something trips the trigger, and the torrent of toxic emotions: hate, rage, disgust, and shame or humiliation uncork from the bottle and spew all over the walls. I remember my mother cooking black-eyed peas in a pressure cooker when the top blew off the pot and the contents exploded all over the kitchen. Fortunately, no one was injured, but black-eyed peas covered every square inch of the kitchen! Unspoken anger and resentment is toxic and pollutes the emotional atmosphere in our relationships, just like the pressure cooker. I have seen flowers begin to droop in my office when there is intense toxicity in the room. If the flowers are sagging, can you imagine what the relationship is experiencing? Resentment is toxic. Loosen the grip and release it. You would not walk around with plutonium in your pocket or purse, would you? This is why forgiveness, discussed in Chapter 6 on Healing, is essential for emotional and spiritual growth. Forgiveness is not just for the big issues; forgiveness is a daily practice.

We know as adults that life is not fair. We tortured our children with the same verbal ammunition our parents tortured us with: "Life isn't fair. Get over it!" Just because we were told this as children and because we repeat it as parents does not mean we necessarily believe it is true. What we know in our head does not always translate to the heart. This is where we may find ourselves in the "C" in FRICK with conflicted thoughts, feelings, and emotions. We want to be free from hurt, anger and resentment. We want to heal from past grievances we may still be holding and needlessly carrying around. How did we ever manage to lug our luggage through airports? Did a luggage company need to hire a caveman to figure out *the wheel* had already been invented?

We do not want our life to be unfair. How do you judge what is fair or unfair? What is your own subjective list or personal criteria for fairness? The following is a checklist to determine if you may be carrying around excessive luggage. Are you or someone you love carrying around excessive baggage from the past? How many of your present moments become hijacked and preoccupied with these thoughts? What is the "it" in your life that is not fair?

- My life isn't fair; I should be somewhere else and I am stuck here with you . . .
- My husband isn't fair; he doesn't treat me the way I want to be treated . . .
- My wife isn't fair; see response above. . .
- The children aren't fair, they are selfish, they don't do anything around the house, and all they do is demand more
- My boss isn't fair. No matter what I do, it's never enough. The only recognition I get around here is negative. They don't pay me what I am worth...
- My relatives aren't fair. If it weren't for us, the family would never get together. We end up having to do all the work, the clean-up, and they just eat and leave...
- The guy giving me the finger across five lanes isn't fair...

- My retirement plan isn't fair. Because of the stock crash, my 401k is now a 201k and I'll probably have to work at Wal-Mart and be a greeter after I retire because there won't be enough money and the price of gas and mortgages is too high...
- What "they" did to me was not fair; I am the victim and they are the perpetrators...
- It isn't fair, it's your turn to put up the dishes, initiate sex, take the trash out. I did it last time...
- It isn't fair because I did not get to go where I wanted to go on vacation; instead we went where *you* wanted to go...
- My illness isn't fair...

Alleged or actual violations of these internal principles (often thought to be universally understood) trip the switches which can cause normally sane human beings to become highly reactive, volatile and momentarily crazy. I have witnessed this firsthand. Purposeful behavior shuts down, and protective behavior takes over. Protective behavior is always chaotic and driven by anger and anxiety.

I worked with a couple in marriage counseling and during the first session, the wife, a highly respected accountant, turned to her husband and screamed at the top of her lungs, "Why do *I* have to go get the milk? Why don't *you* ever go get the god*#@m milk?" As you might expect, this attack had nothing to do with milk. It had everything to do with her perceived sense of imbalance in the relationship. A justice principle had been violated. In her mind, they were peddling a marital bicycle built for two over a bridge. She was in the front, doing all the pedaling, and he was on the back, with his feet on the handlebars, enjoying the sights. She felt neglected, taken for granted, and she felt she worked twice as hard to make the logistical components of the household work. She over-functioned with duties, tasks, and responsibilities, pleaded and nagged for help, but never got what she wanted or needed. She was hurt, angry, and frustrated. She regularly accrued resentment and made deposits in her resentment bank while she quietly boiled, simmered, and stewed. In the safety of the counselor's office, she now felt safe enough to go ahead and let 'er rip.

Revenge

When these neurons fire and ignite the sequence involves blame, resentment, and revenge. Positive and negative polarities are now fully charged resulting in the discharge of emotional lightening. This firing sequence ignites oppositional energy. Revenge is about communicating to another human being about being hurt. The intent of revenge makes sense, "I want to communicate to you how I feel." The *method* is what comes under fire. "Therefore I am going to run over you with an Amtrak train so you'll know how much you hurt me."

Retaliation and retribution does not *fix the problem*. Not only do we have one person who is blind and toothless, now we have two persons that are blind and toothless. In some magical way, the second person becoming blind and toothless is supposed to offset what happened to the first one. Phrased this way, we can see how absurd revenge sounds. However, the logic is related to the principle of justice. An eye for an eye and a tooth for a tooth means that retribution and retaliation is fair. If you cause suffering to me, I am entitled to hurt you back to the same degree. This transaction is one of vindication. Hurting you the way you hurt me balances the scales, and the blind lady of justice smiles with approval. Justice is served.

Chad, in his late thirties, a computer wizard and I.T. specialist was a very bright man. His spouse entered counseling first. Several months later, he approached me about coming to counseling. Chad's concerns involved the dual firing of both anger and anxiety. He could flip into either emotional state from one moment to another. His rage would approach intensity to the point of contemplating murder, while his severe anxiety would send him into accelerated panic attacks. As Chad spoke about injustices in his life, recalling the slightest incident could trigger a flood of emotions. I experienced a slight sense of unease when I was with Chad. He reminded me of Jack Nicholson in the movie, *The Shining*. He matched the profile of someone who would go "postal" in a crowded mall with an automatic weapon and randomly fire at anyone or anything that moved. Chad was always serious and intense.

During one of our sessions, he recalled a story about his father going out into the street and chasing down teenagers drag racing up and down the road. His father nearly got himself killed when he stood in the road, raging and pointing his finger at the teenagers when they drove by, narrowly missing him. We all have a visual image of the Chinese student in front of the tank at Tieneman Square in Beijing standing before injustice. This was hardly the same picture.

I received several e-mails from Chad when he was in the midst of one of these conflicted episodes, torn between rage and anxiety. The scenario involved an elderly neighbor, who according to Chad had attacked the hedge separating their two properties. Infuriated by this obvious act of injustice, Chad fumed about what to do to rectify and retaliate. I asked Chad, "Have you thought about going over and having a conversation with your neighbor, maybe get to know him, see what his likes and interests happen to be, and then perhaps bring up to him about the hedge and express your concerns?" Chad had not considered dialogue. In his mind, the neighbor was a threat. Although he was in his 80s, he was the enemy. Chad spent an entire weekend consumed and fuming about the hedge.

> Tuesday, September 21 11:34 PM
> Tim,
>
> Until about five minutes ago, I was doing OK since the last time I wrote. For the most part, I've had bigger things to think about than the hedge. A few minutes ago, I started reflecting on how the hedge looks and the fact that one vine is growing into the old man's hedge next door. Nothing big, but small things get his atten-

tion. I started panicking over him noticing it and him cutting down more of mine. I got angry to a point where if that miserable old shit tries anything, I'll retaliate by chopping down his stuff wholesale. I'm tired of taking his bullshit without a response.

I've asked my wife to help me clean out the corner so he hopefully doesn't have anything to get bothered about. She's agreed to help me, which is a good thing because I need it. Emotionally, it's hard for me to approach that corner of the yard and I've let it affect me.

Since I've been sitting here typing, most of this is dissipating. I feel somewhat better about it now after only a few minutes. I'm remembering what you told me and I am feeling better. I need to inquire about my application for the fence. No, nothing else has happened in that corner for some time. This is the panic coming back and I think I see it.

Is retaliation in kind a proper response i.e. by cutting his stuff if he cuts down mine?

Chad

Sunday, October 24 2:33 PM

Tim,
I am in the middle of another panic attack right now. Over landscape. No reason for it. I started leading up to it yesterday hearing a neighbor's chainsaw as he was cutting up a stump on his property. I've been sweating, heart palpitations and trouble breathing.

I'm not even sure where this is coming from. I'm trying to work through it and get my act together, but it's hard. Like it's coming out of the clear blue sky. I'm trying to come down from it, but it's not going away easily.

Chad

Chad's question to determine if retaliation was a "proper response" indicates he was beginning to question his thought processes. He was beginning to recognize his reactivity was way over the edge, or perhaps, way over the *hedge*. Anger made Chad feel powerful, in control, and in charge. It also made him look at the world through a distorted lens. When he became angry, his posture reflected retaliation, "I am going to get them." When he flipped into anxiety, his position changed to paranoia, "They are going to get me."

Hedges are boundaries. In Chad's mind, the neighbor violated the boundaries, what he perceived as "his," and he planned to defend his right to protect his space. It was an over-exaggerated violation of Chad's sense of safety. The man was eighty years old and not a threat. Although Chad continued to struggle with his rage, he did calm down over the hedge.

> Saturday, April 09 3:36 PM
> Tim,
>
> Hope all is well with you. I've been doing much better overall since starting the new job. I don't have the constant dread of life in general I used to. For the most part, the panic attacks have stopped.
>
> Noticed something today. I went out to trim the end of the hedge *(the one my neighbor cut back two years ago)* because it was getting kind of scraggly. When I got there, I saw the long stragglers were gone and there were a bunch of cut branches on the ground. I believe my neighbor has been out there again. It's hard to believe. I don't really anticipate doing anything about it because we won't be here long-term, but I have great difficulty believing he would keep doing it.
>
> It initially triggered a brief attack and then I figured, "It still looks good and hasn't substantially changed. Of the whole property, it's very minor and with the repairs and steady progress, it looks fine." An observation, I guess, if nothing else. Never quite ran into something like this before.
>
> Chad

Chad would alternately flip from anger into anxious paranoia. He struggled with the fear of a conspiracy against him. These issues expanded to his work environment. These feelings were further intensified as he recalled visiting a pornographic web site on his computer. Although Chad had struggled with an Internet pornography addiction in the past, two and a half years had passed since he had engaged in this behavior. He panicked at the thought Florida Department of Law Enforcement agents may be monitoring his activity, ready to pick him up and haul him to jail. For the casual observer, this thought pattern may seem like the toast is burning, but for Chad, this felt like the entire house was on fire. Someone needs to call 911!

As Chad rolled up his sleeves to work through these issues, we started by looking at Chad's "back yard." We explored his history and experience and the ideas and beliefs that evolved into his story. Chad was the oldest of four children and had become the emotional caretaker for his mother and his younger siblings. His father had been largely absent, due to travel for work. Chad remembered his father as a man who could step into rage at the drop of a hat. The story of the neighborhood teen racing his car up and down the road exemplified the extreme measures his father took when rage struck. He placed his own life in jeopardy as part of his rage. His father taught him repeatedly, *"people are always out to get you"* and *"you've got to look out for yourself because everyone is going to try and take advantage of you."* When Chad's father turned his anger on him, he would have to stand and take the verbal abuse and the scorching of his soul. To make matters worse, Chad's small stature made him prey to neighborhood bullies and frequent beatings.

Counseling is often a pilgrimage through skewed meanings. It involves the reworking, reorganizing, restructuring, and the repairing of skewed meanings. Psychotherapy is also a process of discovering new meanings. Nothing about the past can be changed, but we can change the *impressions* and meaning these events hold.

Revenge, reactive as with the accountant, or calculated and planned, is "hurting back" because you have been hurt. You may have heard the well-traveled urban legend about a male executive who ran off with his secretary. He headed for the Caribbean and left a message for his wife to sell his expensive sports car and send him a check for half of the proceeds, which the judge had mandated in the settlement. Two weeks later, he received a check for 50 dollars from his ex-wife and a letter explaining to him how happy he had made a college student when she sold him his Porsche for 100 dollars. "Enclosed you will find a check for half of the proceeds of the sale." Another story involves a woman who stuffed frozen shrimp heads in the curtain rods on the day she left their marital home. Several days later, her ex-husband began to notice a pungent smell. The attic was searched, exterminators were called, the house was fumigated, and nothing fixed the problem. Chemicals, deodorizers, scented candles and assorted fragrances all failed to mask the stench. Frustrated and angry, he put the house on the market, but no one would make an offer on the smelly house. He repeatedly slashed the price and finally agreed to sell the house to his ex-wife for one-half of its appraised value, since no one would make an offer on the house because of the putrid stench. After closing on the house, she promptly removed the curtain rods, and presented the rods to him as a gift so he could take the smell with him to his new home.

A biker friend and fellow gym junkie reported to me on a monthly basis the number of child support payments he was counting down until he was going to buy his Harley. One day in the gym, he proudly showed me the "book" he was going to have published, and sell during Bike Week. The title of the book was "The Rights of Husbands After A Divorce." After opening the binding and cover page, the rest of the "pages" were blank. The blank pages bound in the book were Kleenex tissue! Every time he wrote the child support payment, he was reminded of how much he hated his ex-wife. He was hoping to be able to live long enough to see her buried so he would be able to defecate on her grave.

Dealing With The Difficult Emotions: Hate, Rage, Disgust and Shame/Humiliation

These issues and emotions, as difficult as they are in families and close relationships, are no different when we apply the same dynamics as students of history, political science, and foreign policy. When toxic emotions such as hate, rage, disgust and shame and humiliation combine with the lust for power and greed, the result can be viewed as a condensed formula for a brief history of the world. Roman Catholic teacher and theologian Father Richard Rohr stated, *"The history of the world is the history of who killed who."* The chaos track will inform, develop, and articulate a theory, philosophy, theology, or ideology to justify and ratify the genocide and "ethnic cleansing" in the killing fields of human history.

We may smile at the planned, calculated, and premeditated revenge antics of the women who "got even" by outsmarting ex-husbands, one by selling the car and the other stuffing the curtain rods with frozen shrimp. Our pentagon regularly updates these planned, calculated, and premeditated revenge tactics against "rogue states" and member nations of the "axis of evil." In foreign policy we call these contingency plans for tactical military intervention through the creation of "shock and awe" and boots on the ground. These relational dynamics are the dynamics of history when the most difficult of human emotions are stirred and brought to the surface. These are volatile emotions, known as hate, rage, disgust, and shame/humiliation. Whether these emotions become embedded in the psyche of an individual or the collective psyche of a group, clan, tribe, or nation, this collective dysfunction is passed on from generation to generation like a genetic disorder implanted in our DNA. We are all capable of inheriting hate. We are also capable of transcending it!

Krista Tippett, with American Public Media's *Speaking of Faith*, interviewed Dr. Villa-Vincio, a former member of South Africa's Truth and Reconciliation Commission. Dr. Villa-Vincio had been in charge of research on the 17-member commission. "The Commission (TRC), held public sessions from 1996 to 1998 and concluded its work in early 2004. In an attempt to rebuild its society without retribution, the Commission created a new model in our time for grappling with a history of extreme violence. The basic premise of the Commission was that any individual, whatever crime he or she had committed, was eligible for amnesty if he would fully disclose and confess his crimes."

> "Victims were invited to tell their stories and witness confessions. Through the TRC, many families finally came to know when and how their loved ones died. By the end of the hearings, the Commission took statements from more than 20,000 victims of Apartheid and received applications for amnesty from 7,100 perpetrators. For decades apartheid in South Africa justified itself with Christian theology, and a religious leader. Archbishop Desmond Tutu, led the Truth and Reconciliation Commission to redress apartheid's wrongs."[27]

During the interview, Krista Tippett asked Dr. Villa-Vincio what effect hearing the truth about the atrocities had on him. He responded:

> "Whoa! Let me preface that by saying that I think anger, I think hatred, I think a desire for revenge is a most understandable human emotion and response. I can fully understand it. *I think at a communal, at a political, at a nation-building level, it is a very dangerous thing.* And so you ask what impact did it have upon me. You know, I sat and listened to hearings and some of the most horrendous stories told by victims and, goodness knows, told by perpetrators, you know, and I'd find myself sitting there and saying, 'My goodness,' you know, 'Where do we go from here? What do we do with this person?' And I think I come away from the commission perhaps learning two things, and that is, one, that human beings in certain circumstances are

capable of the most outrageously treacherous deeds. And I would like to emphasize that we're talking about human beings. We're not talking about Nazis in the Second World War. We're not talking about white Afrikaners in South Africa. We're talking about human beings. *Every human being—American, South African, Christian, Muslim, Jew—we have within us the capacity to commit some dreadful deeds.* We have a little perpetrator within each one of us. And placed in the right context, that little perpetrator becomes an outrageously powerful perpetrator."[28]

What Dr. Villa-Vincio alludes to is the shadow side of human existence and the human condition. I was in undergraduate school at the University of North Florida, majoring in political science, when I enrolled in a history elective. The course focused on Germany since World War I, Hitler's rise to power and German Socialism. The first day of class, the instructor commanded us to stand up and march across the campus, goose-stepping in the style of German soldiers and singing "Three Blind Mice." She marched us into another instructor's class beaming with pride. She stated to the other professor, "See, I told you I could make them do it." I felt shame for being easily duped into participating in her ploy.

We will do things in groups that we would not do individually. We can lose our identity in a group and follow the commands of a leader without being critical or questioning. History has repeatedly taught us this lesson, from the antics of the Imperial Knights of the Ku Klux Klan to the wholesale slaughter of an entire village in the My Lai massacre. What happens when the group grows in size and becomes a clan, a platoon, a tribe, or a nation? History has also taught us the answer to this question as well.

The Polarization of Consciousness

On September 11, 2001, the pre-meditated, articulately planned, and successfully executed heinous acts of terrorism suffered on American soil, continued the succession of murder established in the twentieth century. On our planet, over 100 million persons were killed through acts of war and violence in the twentieth century. Turning the page to a new millennium did not mean we had turned the page of human nature.

September 11th clearly re-energized the polarities we now live in.

The Polarization of Consciousness

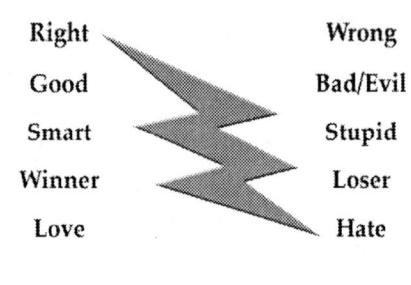

Right	Wrong
Good	Bad/Evil
Smart	Stupid
Winner	Loser
Love	Hate

Figure 11

Globally, these polarities had collapsed with the implosion of the Soviet Union and the end of the cold war. The maintenance of these polarities in our country was important enough to mandate high school seniors take a course called, "Americanism vs. Communism". As a foreign policy initiative since the end of World War II, the United States no longer had an undeclared enemy to fight in order to contain communism. The Soviet defeat in Afghanistan and the fall of communism coincided with the growth of the Internet and the economic boom of the dot.com industry. We were living in a time of unparalleled optimism. We had no enemies. The wheels were already coming off this era of optimism, and 9-11 finished the job. Gil Bailie, in somewhat of a prophetic position, stated, "At the end of the 1980's, the Cold War ended abruptly – a miracle no one thought possible – and, just as abruptly, the world that had been stabilized by cold war doctrines began to fall into confusion, animosity, and violence. Our world is now convulsing with disorder and violence, vivid scenes of which are beamed into our living rooms and burned into our sensibilities every day."[29]

Three planes hit the intended target. The fourth plane failed due to the heroics of the passengers sacrificing their lives and saving the lives of others on the ground. President Bush responded to this act of war and declared a Global War on Terrorism. With a different enemy, the polarities become re-ignited, and life is lived and understood within the either/or contrasts visually represented in Figure 11.

New York City Mayor Rudy Giuliani calmed and soothed his city and our nation with his caring, empathic, and pastoral presence. Our nation went into a period of deep grief and mourning in response to this horrific event. Grief can be a bridge to healing, but creates feelings of helplessness and hopelessness. We did not stay in this mode very long. Retaliation would be sure and swift. There was nearly a global consensus and coalition of support as the United States prepared to invade Afghanistan, overthrow the Taliban government, and search out Osama Bin Laden. The Bush administration hurried to draw a new global map of the evil empire and spoke of entering into a crusade, clearly the language of the split between good and evil.

September 11th will be remembered forever as a decisive act of evil. The sympathy of the world and coalition support radically shifted when the focus turned from Afghanistan to Iraq. The promised weapons of mass destruction never materialized and were apparently a mirage in the desert. Nevertheless, President Bush continued in his public statements across the nation to energize the polarization of consciousness in the splitting of good and evil, right and wrong, to gain support in order to accomplish his goals and objectives. The maintenance of this split began to crumble when the Army launched an investigation and determined between October and December of 2003 there were numerous instances of "sadistic, blatant, and wanton criminal abuses" at the Abu Ghraib prison. In March of 2004, the U.S. Army announced 17 soldiers in Iraq, including a brigadier general, had been removed from duty after charges of mistreating Iraqi prisoners. By the end of April, some of the pictures of the abuse were made public.[30]

I was fascinated at the outcry we witnessed with the release of those photographs of the Iraqi prisoners. The humiliation and abuse they received by their American captors was atrocious. These actions are indeed deeply disturbing. This does not explain my fascination. What captures both my imagination and my fascination is that at the core of the shock is the radical confrontation that our soldiers are capable of such actions.

To live in a split consciousness, or to direct foreign policy out of this split, the possibility that *we* could be capable of such actions is inconceivable. This is true as individuals, a group, a platoon, a clan, a class, a race or a nation. Only *they* are capable of such atrocities. This is how the split manages in order for the good versus evil polarity to work. With the release of the photos, we had to confront our own evil, and this is painful. It is easier to project it *"over there"* rather than to *see it within our selves or our own nation*. This is why Jesus said, **"Why do you see the speck that is in your brother's eye, but do not notice the log that is in your own eye?"**[i] Something I do not like in someone else is usually easier to see *in them* and therefore, *easier to hide in me*. When I minimize someone else, I temporarily feel bigger. When I am being critical of someone else or attacking him or her, this is a seductive way to enhance my own sense of self and temporarily inflate my own ego. This process makes the ego feel bigger than, more than, or superior to the other person.

Human nature is, after all, human nature. We carry with us the legacy of the last century and all the way back to the very dawn of human history. Every human being has the capacity and capability of being both good and evil. We all have a shadow, and if we are going to undergo an evolution of transformation, we must identify this in ourselves first. Since the dawn of civilization, we have faced this issue:

---

[i] Revised Standard Version, Matthew 7:3

"How do we *confront* evil without *becoming* evil?" If we are not able to confront our own shadow, we will find ways to project it onto others to inflate our own sense of superiority. This activity of projection is always the work of the ego and never the work of authentic spirituality.

The polarization of consciousness, left unchecked, ultimately leads to the demonizing of the other. This is a necessary step in order to invoke the gods to re-institutionalize the rites and rituals of holy violence.[31] For Muslim extremists, "We must kill you in the name of Allah to rid the earth of infidels who are the descendents of the Crusaders. You set up puppet governments to exploit our lands, to export our oil, and to import into our sacred land the Western way of life, which is full of vile, filth, and greed." What is our response to this? "They are terrorists," which means, they are not human, they do not think like we think, they do not value life like we do, so we have to hunt them down and kill them like the animals they are." September 11th re-ignited, re-defined, and re-established our current global polarities. As we certainly know, our dilemma is that terrorism, unlike Communism, has no defining borders or boundaries. It cannot be geographically contained. After WW II, the allied nations re-drew the map of Europe and soon thereafter, the cold war began. The Soviet Union exploded their first nuclear device in 1948, upping the stakes. When the CIA botched the Bay of Pigs invasion in our attempts to overthrow the Castro regime, a geographical embarrassment in our own hemisphere just 90 miles away from Key West, Castro asked for help from Mother Russia, and she obliged. Our spy planes captured on film the deployment of nuclear missiles on this tiny island nation, and the world held its collective breath. On October 16, 1962, the showdown began. With Mayport Naval Station, Craig Field, and the Naval Air Station located in and around the city of Jacksonville, Florida, where I grew up, even as a child I knew our city would be on the list for a first strike. Air raid sirens would sound at the Hogan Spring Glen Elementary School, and we would go through the drill of putting our heads between our legs. Teachers reminded us not to look at the flash of bright light, which would cause blindness. I suppose this would have saved us the agony of seeing the blaze of firestorm that would soon cremate us while we were alive. We were right at the edge of what Gil Bailie called, "Deadly reciprocity: *two death machines, each on a hair trigger, ready to replicate and reciprocate the morally reprehensible acts of the other and, if necessary, destroy the whole world.*"[32] I pleaded with my father to follow the advice of President Kennedy and to build a bomb shelter so we could survive such an attack. I remember vividly his response. He folded his paper, smiled, and said, "Son, I don't think you would want to live in a world after something like that happened." It was not the answer I wanted to hear: I wanted more than anything to feel safe, and I did not.

Although there were brief moments in the formation of unions during the 1930s, and the sensationalism of the McCarthy era in the 1950s, Communism has never been a domestic threat. With the exception of the initial invasion of Afghanistan, we will increasingly find it difficult to point missiles at terrorism. In this way, terrorism is able to exploit the fear factor. We live in a world now where nowhere feels safe. Acts of terror are unpredictable and may occur anywhere or anytime. It eventually took 50 years of missile pointing for the previous global polarity of consciousness to break down. We had a brief reprieve of 13 years before the new global polarity emerged to become our present reality. We may not have the luxury of time this go round. Terrorists are patient, and his or her resolve does not fluctuate with the polls. Our present path is a path of mutual destruction. In the full energy of these polarities, with either side seeing the other through projected demonizing, the horns of this dilemma are forever locked into a win-lose battle that cannot be won. The more of them we kill, the more they will recruit to their cause. In the logic of justice, "You hurt me; you pay," the stakes are much higher. We ante into this game with human lives and spend billions of dollars to kill thousands more. Each time the bets are called, the stakes are raised; the body count will go up. "If you kill me, I will kill you back, only meaner and stronger and with more shock and awe." In the polarization of consciousness, both sides see the other as the perpetrator, and each see themselves as the victim.

The time has come for the insanity and madness to be exposed so we can forge new pathways of understanding, reconciliation, and to become instruments of a new reality. Political leaders who mobilize the masses through rhetoric and by inflaming the polarities must be called to accountability. Leaders who will lead us into a new reality will do so by modeling an alternative consciousness that transcends holy violence and Darwinian logic. Throughout the course of history, some form of crisis has always driven evolutionary leaps. Some species have died off, and others adapted, evolved, and survived. The transformation of human consciousness and the survival of our species may very well be running on a parallel course. This discussion will continue in Chapter 7.

Risk Management in Relationships: Creating Consciousness and Stopping Reactivity

As I stated in the beginning of this chapter, in your ongoing attempts to evolve into a new reality toward a higher state of consciousness, you will find it helpful to *slow down* reactivity by driving a wedge between the stimulus and response. Reactivity will *always* lead you into chaos. Drama always feeds on more drama, and so it goes, on and on, ad nauseum. Our target is to eventually stop reactivity altogether. What would happen if there were no horns honking in New York City? What would happen if there were no obscene gestures or waving of pistols in rush hour traffic? What would happen if we would first stop and try to understand the skunks of this world rather than to react to them? What would happen if we were secure enough in the knowledge of whom we are? If others are being unfair or treated us in condescending ways, would it be necessary for us to *react* to them?

You are responsible for maintaining your own zone of sanity. If you become easily insulted or offended, you will set yourself up to continuously play the role of the wounded victim. Neither do you have to accept being treated rudely or like a doormat. Confrontation does not have to be confrontational and therefore escalate reactivity or ignite oppositional energy. Confrontation is about understanding and being understood. If confrontation becomes about winning and loosing, oppositional energy will be ignited, both persons will become unconscious, and everyone loses.

Reactivity is always unconscious: reactivity is contagious and will stimulate reactivity in other persons. If verbal reactivity remains unchecked, it will escalate into physical violence. By diffusing reactivity, we will remain conscious and purposeful and avoid the chaotic states when others are emotionally hijacked by anger and anxiety. In the Darwinian jungle, reactivity reigns. To live in a state of being which is non-reactive requires strength of character and spiritual discipline. At the beginning of this chapter, I posed these two questions as a way to begin creating mindfulness and consciousness in relationships. These two questions will function as a wedge and heighten our sense of consciousness and awareness:

1) "Is there something happening that feels unbalanced or unfair to you?"
2) "Is there something that has been said that questions your competence and makes you feel like you have been minimized, put down, or made to feel stupid?"

Again, we do not start with "them" or "those people." You must first start with yourself. If you are stuck in reactivity, the counsel of wise friends, 12 step groups, or counseling may provide the necessary context to dig deeper into your history and experience. Here you may discover, buried from awareness, unconscious ideas and beliefs that have become embedded in your psyche, holding you hostage, and controlling your life. The world becomes a safer place each time one person stops living in reactivity. If we increase the one person exponentially, living in a new reality will continue to grow and increase, and will soon blossom and flourish. We will cease to pollute our collective consciousness with the emotional bile expressed by toxic emotions: hate, rage, disgust and shame/humiliation.

When you learn how to stop reactivity in yourself, you will be able to apply this wisdom to stop reactivity in your circle of influence. Your circle of influence first includes your family, where your influence matters most. Beyond your family, the circle includes an ever-widening band of concentric circles to include co-workers, friends, neighbors, relatives, and acquaintances. Opportunities will arise to defuse the shadow side of human existence and peacemakers become ambassadors of reconciliation in this evolved state of awareness and consciousness.

When we are working to interrupt reactivity, we initiate a *process* by first seeking to create awareness. What follows in this process will be learning how to assess the threat, stopping reactivity, holding the reaction, and healing the pain, which will be presented in Chapter 6. For now, let us take a brief preview at how this process works. By diffusing reactivity, we remain conscious and purposeful and avoid the chaotic states when others are emotionally hijacked by anger and anxiety.

Donald Goleman tells the story about a friend of his, Terry Dobson, who was one of the first Americans to study the martial art aikido in Japan. One afternoon he was riding home on a suburban Tokyo train when a huge, bellicose, and very drunk and begrimed laborer got on. The man, staggering, began terrorizing the passengers: screaming curses, even took a swing at a woman holding a baby, sending her sprawling in the laps of an elderly couple, who then jumped up and joined a stampede to the other end of the car. The drunk, taking a few more swings and missing, grabbed the metal pole in the middle of the car with a roar and tried to tear it out of its socket.

At that point, Terry, who was in peak physical condition from daily eight-hour aikido workouts, felt he should intervene, lest someone get seriously hurt. However, he recalled the words of his teacher: "Aikido is the *art of reconciliation. Whoever has the mind to fight has broken his connection with the universe.* If you try to *dominate* people, *you are already defeated.* We study how to resolve conflict, not how to start it."

Indeed, Terry had agreed upon beginning lessons with his teacher never to pick a fight and to use his martial-arts skills only in defense. Now, at last, he saw his chance to test his aikido abilities in real life, in what was clearly a legitimate opportunity. So, as all the other passengers sat frozen in their seats, Terry stood up, slowly and with deliberation.

Seeing him, the drunk roared, "Aha! A foreigner! You need a lesson in Japanese manners!" and began gathering himself to take on Terry.

Just as the drunk was on the verge of making his move, someone gave an earsplitting, oddly joyous shout: "Hey!"

The shout had the cheery tone of someone who had suddenly come upon a fond friend. The drunk, surprised, spun around to see a tiny Japanese man, probably in his seventies, sitting there in a kimono. The old man beamed with delight at the drunk, and beckoned him over with a light wave of his hand lifting, "C'mere."

The drunk strode over with a belligerent, "Why the hell should I talk to you?" Meanwhile, Terry was ready to fell the drunk in a moment if he made the least violent move.

"What'cha been drinking?" the old man asked, his eyes beaming at the drunken laborer.

"I been drinking sake, and it's none of your business," the drunk bellowed.

"Oh that's wonderful, absolutely wonderful," the old man replied in a warm tone. "You see, I love sake, too.

Every night, me and my wife (she's 76, you know), we warm up a little bottle of sake and take it out into the garden, and we sit on an old wooden bench ..." He continued on about the persimmon tree in his backyard, the fortunes of his garden, and enjoying sake in the evening.

The drunk's face began to soften as he listened to the old man; his fists unclenched. "Yeah, I love persimmons, too... ," he said, his voice trailing off.

"Yes," the old man replied in a sprightly voice, "and I am sure you have a wonderful wife."

"No," said the laborer. "My wife died ..." Sobbing, he launched into a sad tale of losing his wife, his home, his job, of being ashamed of himself.

Just then the train came to Terry's stop, and as he was getting off he turned to hear the old man invite the drunk to join him and tell him all about it, and to see the drunk sprawl along the seat, his head in the old man's lap.[33]

Notice how the older man refused to get caught up in *reacting* to the belligerence of the laborer on the bus. He did not *oppose* the man, which would have created oppositional resistance. He did not let the belligerence of the laborer set the agenda for how he was going to feel about himself or the laborer. Instead, he remained in his own zone of sanity. He maintained his cheerfulness, which had the effect of confusing the laborer and absorbing the man's rage. Each time he responded with cheerfulness, the belligerence softened. The older man did not allow the external hostile situation determine his inner state of consciousness. He chose instead to connect with the man. He did not condemn the man as a drunk, heaping shame on his shoulders, but instead identified with him in his appreciation of sake, and reframed the usage of the drink in a moderate amount to enhance his enjoyment of his wife and his garden. When he asked a creative question about the laborer's wife, the façade broke. His rage was a mask for his pain. Underneath all the bullying behavior, was a man crying out and drowning in his own pool of pain.

The Counter-Intuitive Pathway: Discovery of the Ethics of Non-Violence

George F. R. Ellis, Professor of Applied Mathematics at the University of Cape Town, recipient of the Templeton Prize, and the author of many books, including *On the Moral Nature of the Universe: Cosmology, Theology, and Ethics*, was interviewed by American Public Media for a radio program. The theme for the program was "Science and Hope."[34]

Ellis believes mathematics and physics are fields of science we discover and not something we invent. These laws are embedded in the very structure of the universe. We discover how these principles work, but we do not invent them. Newton did not *invent* gravity; he *discovered* gravity! Gravity already existed. In much the same way, Ellis argues that laws of ethics are discovered and not invented. If we were to have visitors from another galaxy, our two common areas of discussion would be mathematics and ethics since these two areas are universally true. Visitors from another galaxy would have presumably already discovered what we have discovered.

What we would hold in common with our extra-terrestrial neighbors would be our common ethical discoveries of this new reality, the counter-intuitive way that responds with intentional purposefulness rather than reactivity. This is the ethical principle of *kenosis*, a Greek word that means, "To empty." It is selfless sacrifice. It works in subways, homes, schools, and even on the battlefield. During a presentation before a live audience in Philadelphia, Ellis read an e-mail he received from a man named David Christie. The e-mail came after he had received the Templeton Award.

> In 1967 I was a young officer in a Scottish battalion engaged in peacekeeping duties in Aden town in what is now Yemen. The situation was similar to Iraq, with people being killed every day. As always, those who suffered the most were the innocent local

people. Not only were we tough, but we had the power to pretty well destroy the whole town had we wished.

However, we had a commanding officer that understood how to make peace, and he led us to do something very unusual, not to react when we were attacked. Only if we were 100 percent certain that a particular person had thrown a grenade or fired a shot at us were we allowed to fire. During our tour of duty, we had 102 grenades thrown at us, and in response the battalion fired the grand total of two shots, killing one grenade-thrower. The cost to us was over 100 of our own men wounded, and surely by the grace of God only one killed. When they threw rocks at us, we stood fast. When they threw grenades, we hit the deck and after the explosions we got to our feet and stood fast. We did not react in anger or indiscriminately. This was not the anticipated reaction. Slowly, very slowly, the local people began to trust us and made it clear to the local terrorists that they were not welcome in their area.

At one stage neighboring battalions were having a torrid time with attacks. We were playing soccer with the locals. We had, in fact, brought peace to the area at the cost of our own blood. How had this been achieved? Principally because we were led by a man whom every soldier in the battalion knew would die for him if required. Each soldier in turn came to be prepared to sacrifice himself for such a man. Many people may sneer that we were merely obeying orders, but this was not the case. Our commanding officer was more highly regarded by his soldiers than the General: one must almost say loved. So gradually the heart of the peacemaker began to grow in the man and determination to succeed whatever the cost. Probably most of the soldiers, like myself, only realized years afterwards what had been achieved.[35]

We can only speculate what might have been different if the United States would have chosen to follow the principle of avoiding reactivity and make use of this ethic of kenosis after 9-11. Ellis reported a conversation with Revy Romin, a friend of his, who stated,

"This situation would have been totally different if the following had happened. If the President of the United States, once it had been established that Al Qaeda was responsible had said, 'I do not understand why you did this. I want to understand and meet with you in some neutral country so that you can tell me why you acted in the way you did.' If this had happened, it would not have been the reaction Al Qaeda would have expected. It would have been totally the opposite.

"It may not have changed things, but at least it would have had a chance of producing a totally different outcome. This is the power that releases the potential for transformation, not the power that leads to destruction."[36]

The last paragraph is worth repeating. "It may not have changed things, but at least it would have had a *chance* of producing a totally different outcome. This is the power that releases the *potential* for transformation, not the *power that leads to destruction*." The power is released when we choose counter-intuitively to *respond* to threat and overcome our instinctual default of *reacting* to threat through the usual methods of retaliation, retribution, and revenge.

In review, we have learned if we are angry or anxious, and there is no apparent danger to our physical safety, we will have registered a threat to our psychological safety needs. When we fall into the chaos track, it will be because there is a real or imagined threat to either our sense of justice or competence.

This chapter has been about our search for justice. Each of us has a unique, internalized sense of what is fair and balanced, or unfair and out of balance in our relationships, our families, our culture, our community, and our world. Blame is the default component for the human condition. As we see with skunks and turtles, when we live in a reactive state of consciousness by projecting or interjecting blame, we externalize or internalize our emotions. Enemy formation demonstrates the polarization of consciousness and the demonization of other persons, groups, tribes, or nations in order to activate retaliation, revenge, or to create a false sense of unity.

The stories told about the anonymous Japanese gentleman who diffused escalating violence on a train and David Christie's experience in Yemen capture Einstein's statement, "No problem can be solved by the same level of consciousness that created it. We have to think with a new mind." The theme for this new consciousness may be, *"The transformation of humanity: one mind, one hand, and one heart at a time."* This new consciousness can spontaneously erupt on trains, subways, and airports. Peacemakers are ambassadors of this new consciousness.

The healing serum of this new consciousness has the potential to inoculate us from our collective inherited and infected human dysfunction. In order to provide a cure for the human condition we desperately need the light of this consciousness to encourage new healing spores of possibility to multiply and create a healthy new mind, body and soul. This probiotic form of consciousness can flourish and spread with an infectious *healing* for our culture and society. The applications are endless when we seek to inoculate our homes, our schools, our workplaces, and our halls of justice. Once we learn to create awareness, assess the threat, stop reactivity, hold the reaction, and heal our pain, we can do amazing things, like defusing violence on a train or stopping the tossing of grenades on a battlefield.

Now, let us turn to our search for competence.

Chapter 4
The Search for Competence

> "My job, as I see it, is to enable a patient to solve his or her own problems in the always idiosyncratic context of that person's life. In this way, I set the stage for psychotherapy as a search for competence in the patient and not a search for answers from me. The search for competence is the basic motivation for behavior (a view shared by such eminent researchers as the psychologist Robert W. White [1959] and the psychoanalyst George S. Klein [1976]), and is of fundamental importance for the theory of psychotherapy I advance in these pages."[37]

> Splitting the atom requires great intelligence. Using that intelligence for building and stockpiling atom bombs is insane, or at best, extremely unintelligent. Stupidity is relatively harmless but *intelligent stupidity* is highly dangerous. This intelligent stupidity for which one could find countless obvious examples, is threatening our survival as a species.[38]

We are all born with a need, drive, and desire to feel competent about who we are and what we do. No one embarks on a journey with intent to fail. We all want to succeed in life's endeavors. It only takes a few successes to jump-start our expedition. At times, failure is a necessary component for us to be able to discover our competence.

This chapter is about our search and our quest for competence. Our quest for competence will create purposeful behavior. Each stage of development carries unique challenges for the expression and development of competence, but no phase is more perilous than childhood. The quest for competence tends to collect emotional scar tissue and skewed meanings. Skewed meanings create reactive behavior by distorting our vision.

Self-Esteem: True or False? – The Myth and the Reality

What happens when we fail? Why do some people just give up? One theory on the effects of failure comes from the current cultural myth of low self-esteem. Self-esteem only describes *symptoms*. It does not define the *cause*. As disturbing as this may be for some people, in reality *there is no such thing as self-esteem.*

Practitioners in mental health and counseling have used the diagnosis of "low" self-esteem like leeches to suck the blood out of clients and money from their wallets. If you have "low" self-esteem, when does it fill back up? A sojourner with unmet dependency needs would answer NEVER! Self-esteem has been a trendy fad in pop psychology that has outlived its usefulness and needs a fitting eulogy and burial.

Back in the early 1980's, I received a complimentary copy of a new book by television evangelist Robert Schuller, titled *Self-Esteem: The Next Reformation.*[39] The fact of the matter is Dr. Schuler's prediction was *wrong*. A reformation based on self-esteem never occurred. Countless self-help books have been written on this subject. The pop culture diagnosis of poor self-esteem is the potpourri explanation that sounds profound, but means very little. I feel for new persons who come to an initial appointment and they bring a sincere, serious, and humble admission of having "low" self-esteem. There is a great deal of shame associated with this self-diagnosis. It would seem for them to be easier to admit having gonorrhea or syphilis. Using little eye contact, sojourners attempt to explain something they do not understand in the hope that I will.

The dictionary defines self-esteem as "Pride in oneself; self-respect." Seems simple enough, but self-esteem attempts to define an *intangible, unsubstantial and vague* reality. How much self-esteem is too much? How much is not enough? Is too much self-esteem narcissism? Is too little depression? If self-esteem is low, can you add a quart? Have you ever tried to encourage someone feeling defeated, deflated or depressed? Did it work? Was it like trying to pour water into a colander?

Naming symptoms provides the means to *have power* over the unknown. Early in human history, ancient Neanderthal warriors painted images of the animals they intended to hunt on the walls of caves. Cultural anthropologists theorize this ritual "captured the spirit of the animal" prior to the hunt. In this mindset, the hunters slay what had already been captured! Organizing reality in this way met primitive needs to take control over a situation. This same dynamic is also operative in naming an illness or a disease. It will fend off feelings of powerlessness. There is power in knowing! Knowing provides a sense of coherence, a mastery and dominion over the circumstance or situation.

Low or poor self-esteem provides the *illusion* of giving mastery over the unknown but as a diagnosis, it is vague, unclear, and non-specific. It is ambiguous, ethereal and mysterious, like the shadowy mist rising from the swamp. "You have a tumor in your lung." "You have cirrhosis of the liver." Tumors and cirrhosis are clear, specific and identifiable on a CT scan. Self-esteem is not. My years as a counselor have given me the opportunity to work with many different physicians including specialists, family practice doctors, and surgeons. My favorite question to ask physicians is, "Have you ever *seen* the self-esteem? Where is it located? Is it near the cerebellum, kidneys, spleen, or the appendix?" I usually get a quizzical stare, a shrug of the shoulder, or even a philosophical statement with a finger pointing to either the head or the heart.

Naming the symptoms provides the ability to *organize the experience.* However, this is true only when the symptoms are used to diagnose a clear and identifiable *cause.* As an example, a patient presents the physician with a list of symptoms such as nausea, headache and fever. The physician assesses the symptoms, conducts a battery of diagnostic tests and determines the patient has a "mass." A respected, credentialed, and competent physician gives the symptoms a *name* and identifies the *cause.* The diagnosis now organizes what was previously vague and unclear. A team of physicians would then establish a treatment plan. A surgeon might remove the tumor, a radiologist might bombard it with radiation, or an oncologist might poison it with chemotherapy. If we *name* the demon, the demon can now be cut out, burned, or poisoned.

Unmasking the Mystery

One of the components of our search is our basic need to be competent. Competence and confidence represent an essential need that begins at birth and continues until death. When a sojourner tells me he is suffering with a self-esteem problem, it is a cue that he feels incompetent to handle or manage a *particular* situation in the immediate *present*. In response, I usually ask, "Is there something going on in your life <u>right now</u> that you do not feel competent or confident to manage?" The question seems to elicit shock and a certain level of nakedness, as though I were a mystical clairvoyant. "How did you know?" I am not clairvoyant, so let's unmask the mystery. The unconscious mind does not separate the past from the present very well.

Simba and Rafiki are characters from Walt Disney's classic film *The Lion King*. A scene unfolds around Simba, heir to the kingdom, as his Uncle Scar plots and kills Simba's father, Mufasa. Simba, who idealized his father, feels empty and depressed after his death. He flees his land to live in exile with Pumbaa, the warthog, and his manic friends. Simba adopts the laid back "no problem" lifestyle of the warthogs and turns his back on the responsibilities of his father's throne, now his. Rafiki, the wise monkey, pays Simba a visit with instructions to return to become King. Simba refuses and tells Rafiki he is happy and plans to stay with his warthog friends. At this moment, Rafiki reaches back and slaps Simba as hard as he can. Simba says to Rafiki, **"*Why did you do that?*"** Rafiki shouts back at Simba and says, **"*Shut up! It's in the past!*"**[40]

Because the unconscious mind does not do well separating the past from the present, the slap was in the past, but the sting continued into the present! The unconscious mind confuses past and present experiences because it resists the structure of linear time. These experiences may be entirely different in content but the emotional response feels the same!

Being called to your employer's office for a consultation begins to feel similar to the way you felt in fourth grade and when called to the principal's office. You *know* it is not the fourth grade, and you *know* it is not the principal, but the feeling is the same! A husband expresses his displeasure with his wife's over-involvement in activities outside the home, and she begins to feel the same way as when her mother withheld her love and approval because she was involved in cheerleading and sports as a teenager and was gone all the time. A husband's drinking patterns begin to awaken fear in his spouse due to an eerie familiarity of feelings from her father's heavy drinking when she was seven.

In this way, the unconscious mind links together a collection of experiences that are like or similar and the emotions that are connected to these experiences. With self-esteem, the focus is on the *symptoms* but not the *cause*. Symptoms cannot be cut out, burned, or poisoned. The diagnosis is in of itself a poison. It creates an internalization of meaning that is skewed, reactive, and distorted. "I have low self-esteem" is comparable to saying, "I am an incurable, defective, and pathetic human being." This demon cannot be cast out.

If self-esteem is the symptom, what is the cause? The symptoms associated with low self-esteem are actually indices of something else: a wounded self. On the other hand, if the person is externally blaming, constantly seeking to live in the inflated mode and demanding to be the center or the universe, the diagnosis would be a narcissistic self.

Most persons carry aspects of both a wounded self and a narcissistic self but one tends to be dominant. Like self-esteem, a wounded self or a narcissistic self cannot be seen on a CT scan, any more than you can see Freud's id, ego, or a superego. However, we can uncover evidence to indicate the existence of either a wounded self or a narcissistic self. Sir Isaac Newton did not *invent* gravity but he *discovered* its existence. Let us briefly put on Newton's lens to look for evidence of the wounded self and its development.

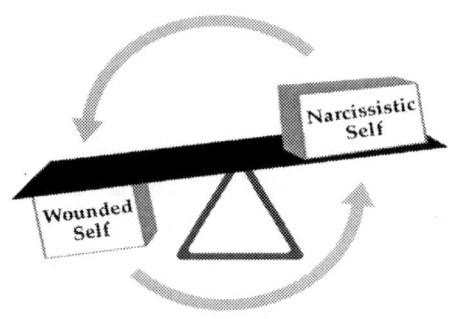

Figure 13

One indicator is the default position of the false self. The default posture for the wounded self is *deflation;* conversely, the narcissistic self constantly maneuvers to remain in the position of *inflation.* The narcissistic self expects "special" treatment, often resorting to some form of rage when this expectation is not met. Narcissists constantly seek to be the center of attention, yet in counseling they complain about feeling empty, a fraud, and a fake.

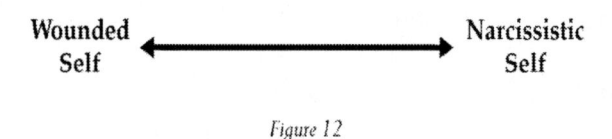

Wounded Self ←————————→ Narcissistic Self

Figure 12

In the preceding chapter, I introduced the development of the false self. On a continuum with the development of the false self, the individual who assigns blame to others tends to be narcissistic. If something is wrong, *you* must be at fault. They carry an idealized image of their own perfection because of their accomplishments, achievements, possessions, status, power, wealth, or physical beauty. Blame is externalized and will be attached to someone or something else. Individual responsibility is rarely a factor in the equation. On the "right" end of the continuum, a narcissistic self forms and *externalizes* blame.

On the other end of the continuum, the wounded self *internalizes* blame. The wounded self knows when something is wrong: *it is my fault*. Because of the inability of the conscious mind to segment time, we collect these experiences and organize the self around what is familiar.

Barry, a college instructor, began to spin downward when the sudden breakup of his current marriage collected the pain of a previous marriage and divorce. Barry's first wife also left him abruptly which felt like "déjà vu"! Thought patterns from past and present became fused. Barry expressed his feelings like this: "I failed at this relationship, and I failed at my previous relationship so . . . I must be a failure." The psyche begins to organize around this trauma thus creating the wounded self. At very early developmental stages for both these individuals, a "split" occurs within the self, which I describe as the establishment, formation, and foundation of the false self. These two individuals correlate to the skunks and turtles from Chapter 3.

In Chapter 7, these concepts are brought together in detail. For now, let us look at the developmental components of competence through the different ages and stages of our expedition. How does a wounded or narcissistic self become established and embedded?

Competence Under Construction

Faces are extremely important. When holding and feeding a child there is an 18-inch facial gap between the mother and baby. This small distance creates a magical bond based on love, care and nurturing. This bond is hard-wired in the baby's brain.

In Michael Basch's book, *Understanding Psychotherapy,* a series of photographs showed in a split frame format focuses on two faces.[41] One is the face of a tiny infant, and the other a hired professional model. Tiffany Field, a renowned expert in infant research, conducted the experiment. In the first picture, the model is simply smiling. The baby looks at the model and mirrors the same smile. The second photo shows the model expressing a look of worry and concern. The opposing frame exhibits the baby with a similar pout and an extended lower lip. The final photo demonstrates the model's expression as happy and a bright countenance. The baby's face also brightens with an expression of joy and amazement. The most amazing aspect of Field's experiment is the infant is only *36 hours old!* The infant's ability to mirror the emotion of the adult model emphasizes the very essential foundations established as the infant seeks to connect, create attunement, and to learn the gratification of acceptance and approval of an adult.

Faces are extremely important. Research shows almost every child taking those first steps, turns to look at his or her mother's face. We begin to experience our self as significant, coherent, and competent, and literally step out to the unfamiliar and unknown. Children discover this naturally when they take those first steps and learn to walk. What is the meaning behind this visual "checking?" The eye contact does not ask, "Did I do it right?" The eye contact exclaims "I did it right!" The child senses he or she *did* do it right. In order to *integrate* our sense of self, significance, competence, coherence, and new emerging abilities, we need to *see* these components reflected or acknowledged in the faces of another human being. The human mirror *enables us to see ourselves* and in turn empowers us to see our own significance. Deprived of this positive empowerment, the self can create destructive ways to satisfy the need to feel significant. In the logic of the developing self, *negative attention is better than neglect.*

Toddling away literally and figuratively is the initial step in our quest for competence. The toddler risks moving farther away from an attentive parent or caregiver, and suddenly realizes he or she is alone. The child will often let out a cry, feeling temporarily abandoned, followed by instant relief as the familiar face enters the room. Faces are extremely important. The face offers re-coherence and a sense of security. A child may meander out of a room and occasionally sneak back for a "peek" at the caregiver. The returning for reassurance offsets the fear associated with being out of sight.

We all want to be seen and affirmed in our quest for competence. Those first steps that bridge an infant to a toddler are steps toward autonomy, independence, and competence. First, the infant gains mobility and becomes a toddler; the toddler achieves speech and develops into a young child. Each step in the process, coupled with tenderness and affirmation, builds confidence and competence to take on new challenges. Other challenges include toilet training, picking out clothes, bathing and grooming, holding silverware, riding tricycles and bicycles, and tying shoes. We learn how to hold a ball, throw a ball, dribble a ball, and later throw it through a hoop, kick it into a net, kick it through goal posts, or knock it out of the park! Young children discover how to make sounds, mimic the sounds of others, speak words, put them together in sentences, talk non-stop, and write those sentences with big fat pencils. We conquer cursive writing, typing skills, word processing, and surfing the Internet! We attend school, acquire degrees, and accessorize our name with initials in front of and behind our names to project our competency. Everything we do builds layer upon layer of confidence and competence. Our entire maturation process involves a need to be seen and appreciated for mastering skills, managing situations or handling problems in a competent manner.

During the initial days of intense supervision and training, a member of my training program relayed a story about dropping off his two young daughters that morning at pre-school. Lauren was six years old, and Emily was two years old. Larry parked the car to help young Emily carry her lunch box to class. However, Emily quickly jerked the lunch box out of his hand. She was following her older sister who was effortlessly carrying her lunch box off to class. Emily lagged behind, dragging her "Gunch Ba" on the ground across the sidewalk. Larry offered help to his younger daughter, but she refused and pushed him away. *Emily wanted to be strong and competent just like her older sister.* She wanted to carry her own lunch box!

We are born with a drive and desire to be competent. The initial years of our life possess a progressive movement toward autonomy and independence. Home, school, and peers serve as the main laboratories for testing and growth in our competence as children, teenagers, and young adults. Young adulthood often involves the selection of a mate or companion, the establishment of personal skills in jobs, an occupation, calling, or career, and may include the early phases of starting a family. Middle age provides opportunities to adjust our course, or re-establish our direction, at a time when our competency in jobs or careers can begin to peak. Middle-aged adults can be sandwiched between helping to launch children's lives, and caring for aging parents. Aging parents now turn to their children to meet certain needs, as our own children move to establish their own pilgrimage.

Retirement age presents changes in lifestyles, and meaning often shifts from *doing to being.* Productivity and purpose undergo major shifts. If we enjoy relatively good health and well being, the retirement years can provide a time of meaningful activity, volunteer work, discovery of hobbies, and the enjoyment of family, friends, and travel. Eventually older adults face issues of declining health, and the slow progression of loss in terms of personal independence and freedom. After I was transferred to a small North Florida community in the early 80s, my new 86-year-old secretary greeted me on the first day at the office! Oneta was bright and cheerful and insisted *"I am not old; I've just been around a long time."* One day her manual typewriter broke, and she cried when we insisted she switch to a word processor. She wanted that familiar old typewriter fixed. She retired the following year "because it was time to let the young people take over." Whenever I would see her faded green 1967 Chevrolet on the road, I pulled over to give her plenty of room! The day the Florida Highway Patrol came by to pick up her driver's license was a sad one for Oneta. In this country, losing a driver's license represents a real and symbolic loss of independence and freedom. Our quest for competence remains as a lifelong adventure. Each age and stage provides unique challenges in managing issues of our personal, professional, emotional, and relational competence.

The Wounding of Competence

The toxic emotions of hate, rage, disgust, shame and humiliation have reached epidemic proportions in the wounding of our children. Parents who attack their children with these toxic emotions are guilty of emotional and verbal abuse. Anger and rage communicate rejection to children. Dr. Greg Baer, author of *Real Love*, states when we yell at children what we communicate to them are these four words: "*I Don't Love You!*"[42] An individual cannot be angry and loving at the same time. When parents think their children are not listening, they yell. What is the solution? Parents talk louder and impose superior power to steamroll, intimidate, and shout the child into compliance. The assumption with yelling is that *you are not listening to me*. If I yell louder, you will hear what I am saying. Parents yelling, "*You're not listening to me*," are saying, "*You're not doing what I am telling you to do,*" which is an entirely different matter. Most children hear perfectly fine! The problem is noncompliance, not auditory concerns. The issue is power and control. The parents use power as a tool to force obedience. This tactic may work in childhood but not when children move into the teenage years.

When our children were about six and ten years old, I noticed how much more we were yelling. Once aware of the trend, Brenda and I decided to make a change. I grew up in a family with a great deal of yelling. Both of my parents struggled with alcohol at different stages of their lives. My mother suffered from severe postpartum depression after I was born. After this bout with post-partum depression, my mother was diagnosed with schizophrenia. My two older sisters screamed constantly. I grew up assuming families were *supposed* to relate to one another by yelling and screaming. Our life was one continuous drama after another. I finally realized yelling and screaming were not normal. As a parent, I did not want to replicate the reality from my childhood with my own children. If we walk into a convenience store and verbally assault the clerk, he calls 911 and we go to jail. *There is no other place or situation where society tolerates verbal abuse except in the family setting.* (With the exception of sporting events, which tolerate abuse toward players, coaches, and other fans for the price of a ticket!) Through conscious effort, our family stopped this behavior. We agreed to follow certain steps, and when matters became heated, we agreed to ease off the subject and return to discuss the issue after dinner or the next day. We committed to creating dialogue and talking openly about family concerns.

Discipline – Teaching Children to Solve Their Problems

Managing conflict and solving problems are two major areas where children become wounded in their quest for competence. Discipline is about teaching children how to solve their own problems. One erroneous assumption parents make is that punishment corrects behavior. Accountability and correction are distinctly different. What is the recidivism rate for felons who return to prison after their release? Serving the sentence fulfills accountability, but the punishment does not guarantee a change in behavior. Some of the major religious institutions, if not by design, but de facto, use this approach. Discipline needs creativity, synergy, energy and cooperation. Problem solving is one effective method to achieve discipline. If we teach our children how to problem solve, in essence the child learns to create his/her own parameters for discipline. For example, when our daughter was a senior in high school, she came to us during the first semester to report her problems with calculus. Rebekah enlisted the help of the lead student in the class who agreed to tutor her on Tuesday and Thursday evenings at a local bookstore for the next eight weeks. Rebekah indicated she would like to try this until the end of the semester. If her grade did not improve, would we help her pay for a professional tutor? Our response was, "That sounds great; just keep us posted." Her plan made sense! She identified the problem and came up with a plan to correct it on her own. That is accountability, problem solving and discipline!

We could have responded to the bad grade by rescinding the rights to the car, grounding her from the internet or taking the cell phone, but what would that approach have achieved? It probably would have made her hate me and created frustration. Specifically, punishments would not have fixed the problem. Rebekah demonstrated she understood the problem. She developed a method to create improvement and to address the concern. There was not much left for us to do than ask to be included in an accountability loop. "Keep us posted" was all we could add to the work she had done. This problem solving did not happen overnight. These were the results from strategies we started teaching Rebekah when she was seven years old! Parents need to make sure discipline *fixes* the problem instead of creating new ones. Discipline means building ways for children to see their situation and to create methods to solve their own problems. As a therapist, I see a number of aging parents with children in their thirties and forties, who still attempt to fix their children's problems. These frustrated parents never taught their children how to problem solve. As a result, the parent feels guilt, attempts to unravel the latest predicament, but most likely never will!

One dilemma parents create involves methods of inquiry and interrogation. When frustrated, parents ask children certain types of questions. These questions inadvertently place children in an emotional bind and infuse shame and humiliation. Children cannot successfully resolve this tension or find a way to win. Parents provide those in my profession with job security when they approach their children with angry voices and state, **"YOU DID X; WHY DIDN'T YOU DO Y?"**

The child inevitably feels attacked, defensive, or will feel overwhelmed with shame. The statement communicates to the child: *"You did not do what I would have done; do you realize how stupid you are?"* This approach creates frustration because neither children nor adults can change history. This question places the child in a bind that cannot be resolved and the question will "FRICK" the child. The child hears, "Because I did not do it the way *you* wanted me to do it, it must be because *I am stupid."* Unconsciously the child will either react or shut down because the question attacks the child's competence. Children frequently grow up in an environment paralyzed with fear. Often, children internalize these judgmental voices as their conscience. "How could you be so stupid? What were you thinking? Are you an idiot?" These amplified voices of condemnation will continue to play inside the mind after these children reach adulthood and may continue long after the parents are dead. Minor issues like forgetting to pick up an item at the grocery store or missing a turn on the interstate can trigger an onslaught of internalized verbal abuse. Sometimes these children grow up to be perfectionists, or hypercritical of themselves and others. They struggle to finally "get it right" and win the approval as adults they never received as children, leaving them fearful to take necessary risks. Why bother if I know I am going to fail? The bottom line of the message communicated to the child: you are stupid and incompetent for not doing what I wanted you to do and for making the wrong decision.

I believe these parents are *trying* to teach their children better problem solving skills, but the technique is ineffective. A more helpful and intentional process would include a factual, judgment free review of the facts, which provides the child with a different lens to see what transpired. This method creates vision and opens the child up to creative thoughts about problem solving.

One of my earliest childhood memories occurred around the age of five. Back in those days, milk was delivered to the front door in one-gallon glass jugs with tiny paper caps covering the mouth of the bottle that looked like a miniature nurse's hat. I was carrying two gallons of milk, one in each hand. I wanted my mother to be proud of me for being a strong young man. As I approached the kitchen she said, "Tim, I think you need to put one of those down and carry those one at a time because I think those are too heavy for you." Translated, that means, "I don't think you are as strong as you think you are and you are going to screw up." I immediately rewarded my mother's expectation and *accidentally* dropped one of the gallons of milk. Milk and broken glass spilled all over the kitchen floor. My mother, apparently having a bad day, turned and screamed at me at the top of her lungs, **"Why did you do that?"**

She was essentially asking a meaning question. She was attempting to say, "If you could explain to me why you did this, it would make sense to me!" When parents yell at their children, children feel shamed, attacked, and they do not feel safe. For example, when my mother yelled, "Why did you do that?" only a couple of responses are possible:

1) "Mom, I checked your calendar and saw today was empty so I wanted to see how you'd react to this experiment of glass and milk on the floor." (This response would have gotten me knocked into next week!)

2) Say nothing, hold my head down, and feel shame. Having not done what I was told created a skewed meaning for this event. I surmised, *"It must be because I am stupid."* My mother would have never told me I was stupid when I was five. How-

ever, this is what I *heard* as a child. These beliefs may become solidified into a wounded self if verbal abuse continues.

Choosing clarity diminishes the likelihood of a child feeling defensive or under attack. My mother missed the point. Her reaction was about meaning, not problem solving. A descriptive angle would sound something like this: "You wanted to be helpful. You were carrying both gallons of milk at the same time. I asked you to put one down and carry them one at a time. You kept going, and the one gallon slipped out of your hand." The target is to create improvement and teach the child to solve his problems. After calmly describing the situation, she might have asked, "How do you think you might improve this situation so you can do this differently next time?" This approach would encourage me to come up with my own solution. Remember, we cannot be purposeful and protective at the same time.

The Danger Zones: Parents, Siblings, School, and Peers

The four danger zones where wounds become internally organized involve experiences with parents, siblings, school, and peers. The closer the relationship with the person the greater chance the wounds will be severe.

As children, siblings and peers can shake the quest for competence. Many adults remember wishing they could *will* themselves to disappear as children, being the target of pain, ridicule and the verbal attacks of classmates. They recollect taunting and being called fat, ugly, clumsy, uncoordinated, spastic, stupid, or dumb. A child stumbling through a sentence while reading aloud to the class is sabotaged with laughter and shame. The child standing alone, the last one picked for kickball knows the intense humiliation and embarrassment of rejection. Children need assistance through these wounding experiences. The absence of "good-enough" parenting causes the child to organize his or her experiences around these injuries establishing a wounded self.

Through childhood and adolescence, peers can be absolutely brutal. From approximately seven through adolescence, the peer group exerts influence as the dominant dispenser of acceptance and rejection. When my daughter was in middle school, she came home one day deeply hurt by her peer group, a gaggle of girls, and literally grieved for several days. The group consciously decided she was the "odd one out" for the week. They treated her as an outcast and targeted their hate, rage, disgust, and shame on her. Although temporary, she became a sacrificial group scapegoat. She was slandered maliciously. School gossip "got back to her" that one of the girls said she "backwashes her sodas." For a child, sloshing your soft drink back in the can is public humiliation, shameful and disgusting. Her peer group also indicted her for being "annoying." (What seventh grader isn't?) These defects obviously reflected intense character flaws! Although, I did attempt humor in an effort to defuse her pain by telling her former serial killers Jeffrey Dahmer and Ted Bundy started out as "back-washers," it was important for her to know we understood her grief and pain and took it seriously. Sticks and stones may break our bones, but words shatter the soul.

Damage from the Danger Zones: Emerging As Young Adults

This section includes information from some of the sessions with three young adults attempting to launch. In varying degrees, each reveals wounding experiences from the danger zones. All three young adults struggled to discover, gain, or establish their competence, and made efforts to heal when they were wounded. Parents are petrified when they watch their young adults make an effort to launch. Frequently they have to allow their children to flap their wings, even fail, while they helplessly observe.

In one of the most powerful quotes I've ever read

about parenting, Martin Marty states, "Parents who make exhausting demands for the affection of their children have not learned that a family is not exclusive or permanent: a couple comes on stage; they are to reveal the family as an art form. It is not an art like architecture or painting, finished and established for eons and ages. Their art is like the ballet. This dance is danced when the curtain goes up and the spotlights illuminate the stage. Soon the floodlights will dim, the house lights will go up, and the curtain will fall. The dance is over, and the dancers move on, with memories, snapshots, and other stages ahead; parents who do not learn how to let go are doing a disservice to family relations. But if parents and children are friends, they will have been learning how to bid good-byes."

As teenagers grow into late adolescence and young adulthood, parents find it difficult to let go. Parents do not feel safe when children are not making responsible choices and decisions. Parents also feel powerless when they see their young adult children make mistakes. Their efforts to correct them become frantic.

Kimberly

Kimberly's mother, Carmen, was in her mid forties when we first met. Carmen was a divorced mother of three and worked in sales. She was extremely fragmented and depressed following the break-up of the first significant relationship since her divorce. We worked together in counseling for approximately a year. She put her life back together in an amazing fashion. For the next several years, I occasionally heard from her and met for a session or two in order to work through an issue or concern. Overall things were going well for Carmen.

I received a message one Monday from Carmen. She and her ex-husband had been with Kim, their 18-year-old daughter, in the emergency room over the weekend. After a fight with her mother, Kim had gone into the bathroom and later lay across her mother's bed with the bedroom door open. Carmen was glad her daughter had calmed down, and did not sense any danger.

Moments later Carmen's ex-husband, Stacey, called frantic from his cell phone to ask how Kim was doing. He was on his way over. Carmen was puzzled and did not understand his urgency. She was dumbfounded when Stacey revealed that Kim had called and said she took an overdose of sleeping pills. Carmen immediately went into the room and tried to wake Kimberly. Stacey arrived, and they carried Kim to his car. They laid her down on the back seat, and drove to the local emergency room. The physician determined the number of over-the-counter sleeping pills ingested was probably not lethal. Kim was given charcoal and a night to remember. She spent the remainder of the evening on or near the commode as she expelled the sedatives.

During the session when Carmen relayed this painful incident, she interrupted her own story with a dilemma occurring at the precise moment we were meeting. Kimberly was at the administrative offices of the high school withdrawing from school. Carmen's words were filled with agonizing desperation, "What am I going to do?" Stacey was an attorney known for his uncontrollable temper, was not aware his daughter was dropping out of school. Carmen knew he would be enraged. An honor student four months from graduation, Kim and her best friend Michelle had decided they were going to finish school at the vocational technical center and get a job. Kim was 18, and by definition, a legal adult. Carmen could not stop Kim from quitting school. Carmen felt helpless. She could do nothing.

Carmen recalled a number of incidents over the last several months that led to this momentous crescendo. By checking school records Carmen discovered Kim had skipped most of her classes prior to Thanksgiving. At the start of the school year Kim had wrecked her automobile beyond repair and was without transportation. As a result, she became dependent upon peers for rides. Mother and daughter battled constantly over curfews. Kim thought she should be allowed to stay out until three in the morning, the time most of the area nightclubs closed. When Kim was admitted to the emergency room, a drug screening was ordered, which was thankfully negative.

The precipitating event of this downward spiral occurred when her boyfriend flunked out of a local university and returned home to the New England area. The argument that triggered her trip to the emergency room was over Carmen's assessment of Michele, Kim's friend, and her negative influence. Carmen "laid down the law" and forbid her daughter to spend time with her and "hang out." According to one school official, Kim and Michele were joined at the hip, always seen together. Their relationship consisted of a "twin-ship", and each belonged to the other in a sorority of pain. In this twin-ship, their personalities had become hopelessly enmeshed.

Carmen was baffled and perplexed. She could not understand why her daughter laid across her bed and then *called her father* to let him know she had taken the sleeping pills while Carmen was in the next room! For Carmen this was a major violation of a justice issue. Carmen rescued her daughter from the "wicked step-mother" three years earlier and brought her to her home. Carmen stood up for Kimberly time and time again over the brutal verbal abuse she received from her father and stepmother. In the emergency room, Stacey railed on and on about how *stupid* Kim was for taking the pills. He continued on a relentless tirade, which was consistent with the way her father dealt with her throughout her life. "How could you be so stupid? Look how fat you are! You will never amount to anything! Look at you – you're throwing your life away." The prophecies were indeed becoming self-fulfilling.

In an attempt to create meaning, I hypothesized to Carmen that Kim may have called her father because it was consistent with what I had known of her over the last several years. Time and again Kim tried to connect with her father and continued to fail. Perhaps the reason she called was that she had not given up. She was still trying to connect. As previously mentioned, an individual deprived of positive empowerment, can discover destructive ways to realize their significance. In the logic of the developing self, *negative attention is better than neglect.*

Although some may agree that the daughter's behavior lacked intelligence, Stacey ranting about her stupidity in this time of extreme emotional vulnerability certainly could not prove to be helpful or beneficial in any way. Stacey's anger in that moment directly connected to his anxiety concerning his daughter's disregard for the issues involving her *safety* and *competence*. Stacey might have thought his anger would "wake her up," make her "snap out of it," or motivate her. The rage only served to create additional shame. The experience compounded Kim's wounded self: "Something must be wrong with me; I never can get what I need."

Jacob

I received a call from a mother, who along with her husband ordered their 22-year-old son Jacob home from college. Both she and her husband were concerned Jacob was depressed, and felt he may have an alcohol problem. Jacob attended school in South Carolina and was majoring in economics. He had two younger sisters, one attending a state school, the other in junior high school and living at home. Jacob's parents requested I help him with his communication skills and to be his advocate in any way I could. They also felt Jacob needed help in dealing with his anger.

Jacob entered the room and had to duck to clear the doorway. He was a towering young man, the size of a basketball power forward, and he overshadowed his father who stopped in briefly to deliver insurance information. I outlined the issues his mother and father had discussed with me over the telephone, and we began our work by addressing their concerns. Jacob gave me an overview of his previous semester. He had done extremely poor. He flunked one class because he never showed up, and barely passed the other two. He indicated he hated going to class. He even knew the material, but believed attending class was a waste of time. Jacob indicated he had missed a couple of his early classes (10:00 a.m.!) because he had been out partying. He did not believe his drinking was excessive. Now that he was back in his parent's home, "everything they said or did" made him angry. He described himself as being in a constant state of a "low boil." Jacob reported that most of his time was spent reading, watching television and doing little else. This particular morning he was angry with his mother for waking him at nine o'clock with the announcement he would follow their schedule while he was at home.

The underlying reasons for Jacob's anger became readily apparent. Jacob worked hard to please his parents and very much wanted their approval. He had been attending college for almost four years. His parents picked the school for him and the choice had never been the school he wanted to attend. He tried to make the best of the situation. When he did occasionally come home, he hated every minute under his parent's watchful eyes. His main coping strategy was to withdraw and retreat to his room. He rarely conversed with his parents and felt any comments would solicit intrusive lectures on what he should or should not do in any particular situation. This was the case over Thanksgiving and now it was January, and he was back at home again. When his parents found out about his grades, they telephoned the administrative official. The office told Jacob's parents he was on academic probation and unable to graduate. Jacob knew the information was incorrect, but no matter what he said, they refused to accept his assessment of the situation. His parents ordered him to return home, which he did. He was seething with anger. Most of his friends were in the fraternity back at school, and he felt isolated. When he did run into people he knew, they would ask why he was home, which would prompt him to tell the story, which was embarrassing and shameful to him.

At our second session, Jacob reported things had been going better with his parents, and by the end of the hour, the issues were becoming clearer. I decided to apply a strategy with Jacob that I usually use with adolescents, not young adults. I thought developmentally this was a good fit, but he proved me wrong. I explained to Jacob the three issues that terrified his parents, and they were not alone. Parents are universally frightened about their children's sexuality, particularly in this age of deadly diseases. Parents are afraid of alcohol and drugs and realize these substances are readily available anywhere. Lastly, parents want children to get the best possible education. If Jacob wanted to be in control of what was happening with his parents he needed to manage *their* anxiety about these issues. Simply put, Jacob's decisions violated the parental expectations about these big concerns. Jacob's parents did not feel safe about his decisions. They became anxious, reactive, and controlling. Jacob felt incompetent or like "a little boy" when his parents exerted control over him. When Jacob's parents became anxious about his behavior, they forced him to return home. As long as he was financially dependent on his parents, one survival strategy for Jacob was to manage *their* anxiety. Jacob began to understand what fueled his parent's behavior. He began to re-frame and reformulate the problem in his mind. He felt anger because he messed up, he was being controlled, and "was being treated like a little kid." His own sense of confidence and competence to manage the situation immediately improved as he now viewed the home territory as doable.

    Between our second and third meeting, Jacob decided he no longer wanted to manage his parent's anxiety or earn his parent's approval. He decided not to succumb to the pressure of financial dependence upon his parents. His parent's financial support was connected to a list of conditions. His parents proposed he could return to school for fall semester if he agreed to live on campus, attend all his classes, stay away from alcohol, and the list went on. Jacob decided to apply for his own financial aid and obtain his own loans in order to finish school, thereby severing his economic dependence with his parents. Jacob was asserting his independence and flexing his competency muscles.

Jacob's dad called me and expressed his concern Jacob was making these decisions for all of the "wrong reasons", i.e. he simply wanted to get out of the house as quickly as possible and get back with his friends. Although this was something I clearly heard from Jacob, I also heard his desire to go ahead, finish school and get on with his life. The father requested I intervene on behalf of his mother and himself. I truly felt for Jacob's parents, but their care and protective nature were getting in the way of letting their son succeed or fail on his own terms. "Letting go" is no easy task.

Tonya

Tonya, a young woman of 25, came to me for treatment of an eating disorder. She was five feet, eight inches tall and weighed 125 pounds, and she believed she was overweight. By no stretch of the imagination could this woman have been overweight, except within her own mind. Tonya always knew when she was putting on weight because her clothes would not fit the way she wanted them to fit. She would not let her fiancée put his hand on her stomach because it would "anchor" her feelings about being fat. She was certain if she could get to her ideal weight of 120 pounds, all would be right with the world. I asked what it meant for her to be 120 pounds, and she told me she would feel more confident. Once she identified the meaning behind being thinner, I posed two questions for Tonya. What other ways can she achieve that feeling of confidence? Is there something in particular she would like to feel more confident doing?

Tonya informed me she had "low" self-esteem and problems making decisions. When people say they have problems making decisions, they usually mean they are fearful of making "wrong" decisions or *choices that will make them feel like a failure.* The decisions we make may not be as difficult as the *consequences* of those decisions. The fear, or threat, involves making a "bad" decision. Avoiding decision-making postpones the fear of failure and any external or internal self-blame. The underlying need is to be seen as being competent; failure makes us feel stupid.

When Tonya mentioned a problem with self-esteem and decision-making, I asked her if she was *currently* struggling with making a decision. She mentioned buying a dress for the office Christmas party. She asked the sales person if she could take the dress to her workplace, to get their coworker's collective opinions on her selection. Tonya could not trust her own judgment about the dress and needed the mirroring input of coworkers. Gaining approval on the dress reflected approval of Tonya! *If they liked the dress, they would like her.* She made the sales clerk promise she could return the dress if she received any negative feedback. Tonya also recalled several occasions when she wanted to purchase items, like clothes, but indicated she would begin putting things back before she could make it to the cashier. Tonya revealed that she felt conflicted about her counseling appointments. She believed that therapy was expensive, but important. She was determined to follow through.

Tonya and I discussed these three stories in depth. I eventually proposed she did not have a problem making decisions at all. I asked a few leading questions and she began to see these incidences reframed and refocused in a different context. In terms of putting the clothes back before reaching the register, Tonya realized this was actually helpful. She would think about the clothes she already had, did not wear, and ask herself if she needed more. As for the counseling, she was determined to "work through her problems" and this was okay. The Christmas dress and the need for feedback from coworkers had more to do with the desire to "fit in", be accepted, and not "stick out." She indicated feeling wounded when one co-worker stated jokingly, "Well, if you're going to wear that, I guess *I* won't be going." The statement was meant to flatter Tonya, signifying how attractive she looked in the dress. Instead, Tonya felt wounded by the idea this may cause someone to miss the party, and she would be at fault. She would blame herself.

Tonya began to understand the enormous amount of energy she consumed through these ongoing "mental gymnastics." Feeling competent was easier by losing weight than understanding these uncomfortable circumstances and situations. In other words, losing five pounds was easier than fixing what was underneath. Tonya began to remember experiences from her family of origin. She had been primarily raised by her grandmother. Tonya never felt able to gain her grandmother's acceptance and approval. The condemning voice she heard when she made "bad" decisions was the voice of her grandmother. Her father left her mother when she was a little girl, and she had no memories of him. She was very special to her grandfather. He died when she was a teenager. Her mother had a multitude of problems and now consistently borrowed money from Tonya. In spite of all she dealt with, Tonya amazed me with her ability to function. During one of our sessions, she produced a letter she wrote to her mother. Notice the role reversals taking place. Tonya wrote this letter to her mother *when she was 12 years old.*

Mom,

The reason I blamed you for part of my room being messy is because I don't like it when you smoke or take drugs, and I especially <u>hate it</u> when you yell at me. So therefore I keep my room messy because I am mad because you don't talk to me or act like you care about me. This is what gets me so upset. You don't even pay attention to me when Bruce is down here. All you do is smoke pot and tell me to go to my room. You <u>constantly yell</u> at me and it makes me so mad I can't even control myself. And the way you do drugs and smoke makes me just want to run away. I don't see why you don't go to a treatment center where they can help you straighten your life out. You're never going to get anywhere in life if you do all those things that messes up your life. Try something before I go crazy! You wouldn't have to <u>complain</u> about not having <u>money</u> if you would<u> save it</u> and not spend it on drugs. I have nothing to say to you unless you straighten up <u>at least</u> a little bit.

Love,
Tonya

P.S. - I hope you take this seriously because I wrote it seriously!

As Tonya worked through her personal web of distortions, she began to gain insight about how these experiences skewed her perception of her present, her reality, and more importantly, herself. I attempted to impress upon her that her weight would be secondary to feeling good about her self. Once she took hold of this concept, she may find the weight issue would take care of itself. I invited Tonya to begin to notice what else was happening in her life when she began to obsess about losing weight. I asked her to "slow down" her thinking. Tonya discovered that obsessing about her weight was directly connected to her anxiety about handling situations competently.

She also obsessed in social situations when she wanted approval. Tonya's concern about her weight gradually waned as she learned new ways to enjoy herself and realize a greater sense of her own competence in life.

The Role of Depression

Let us now explore how the unconscious mind begins to link "similar" experiences of failure. These experiences, when collected, may cause us to spiral down into a tunnel of despair, depression, hopelessness, and helplessness. The unconscious mind elicits a logic that projects the past into the future, and the future becomes the present. "My life has always been bad, it will always be bad, and it is bad now." As a brief review, in Chapter 1 and 3, I described the **"FRICK"** principle and what happens when we become stuck, embedded, or enmeshed. The acronym stands for:

1) **Frustration,** which is externally focused at an object, person, situation, or a cir-

cumstance when you can't get "it" to do what you want it to do. I blame someone or something else.
2) **Reactivity,** when current situations evoke strong emotions from unresolved issues in the past. Hysterical is always historical.
3) **Internalization**, when frustration is interjected within the self. I blame myself.
4) **Conflicted thoughts, feelings, or emotions**, when I am thinking one way and feeling another way and I am struggling to resolve the internalized conflict.
5) **Knowledge**, or self-awareness that one or more of these four things is happening

Let's look at this principle as a way to understand some of the dynamics of depression. The list above represents our reactions to being stuck or enmeshed and is often necessary for new growth to occur. Many of us experience aspects of this FRICK principle every day. With depression, the main operative components are internalization and conflicted thoughts, feelings, and emotions. When more than one of these components is operative for an extended period (two weeks or longer), there is a potential to create the "perfect storm" for a diagnosis of clinical depression. Depression that persists for weeks, months, or years will assume a nearly impenetrable "logic" that establishes a depressive state of mind. In a depressive state of mind, the depressed individual will project the *past* into the *future*. Untreated, prolonged experiences of depression elongate, distort, and exaggerate the past. The past is then projected into the future and the loop is completed. The present becomes bracketed between the horrible past and an anticipated more-of-the-same dismal future. "It has always been (past) bad, it is always going to be (future) bad, and it is bad now (present)!" Getting out of bed, loading or unloading the dishwasher, buying groceries, preparing meals, or going to work, all seem like overwhelming experiences. The smallest tasks produce feelings of being overtaxed, overwhelmed, and overloaded. Managing everyday matters seems like climbing insurmountable mountains. A prayer by a depressed person would sound something like this: *"Give us this day our daily dread."*

Relationships require two things: energy and other people. The individual battling depression must make the effort to interact for a couple of reasons. First, spending time with others requires planning, organizing, inviting, traveling to or from home and cleaning house. These are logistical components of social behavior. Inviting people over involves planning a meal, going to the store, preparing a meal, and taking care of the cleanup. Ultimately, social behavior requires making the decision whether or not he or she even *wants* to be with that individual. This decision can be complicated by real or imagined wounds from the past and may trigger a fear of future wounding. "Why bother being with _____ if all he or she does is put me down?" Decisions are more difficult because the self distrusts its own judgment because of fear associated with failure. "Why decide to do anything if the only thing I do is screw up?" All this takes for granted the depressed person has the energy to get out of bed, take a shower, get dressed, and shave or put on make-up. These aspects create further "retraction" of the self, until the only get-up-and-go left is just enough to keep the vital organs in a survival mode.

Depression, for example, is similar to what happens when a human being has suffered a massive injury and has lost a major amount of life-giving blood. The circulation of blood will then be routed to the major organs in order to insure survival. In May of 2003, Aspen mountaineer Aron Ralston, 27, used a pocketknife to amputate his own arm and free himself from a boulder weighing 800-1,000 pounds. The boulder fell and trapped him for five days in a remote desert canyon in eastern Utah. Although Aron could have bled to death had he not stopped the blood flow, people can still live and function without feet, hands, arms, and legs but not without a liver or a pancreas. Under these dire and desperate circumstances, blood is circulated to critical areas of the body. *Depression involves the cumulative experiences of hopelessness, helplessness, and despair, which in turn have created a massive internal injury.* With cumulative unresolved grief, depression behaves like tumbleweed. Tumbleweeds gather momentum and grow in size, picking up more debris as it travels. Other unresolved lifelong experiences tend to be "collected" and become a part of the larger mass as these experiences accumulate and tumble through the self. Major loss or life events tend to unmask the veneer of denial when we are forced to confront these experiences. The withdrawal **from** relationships and **into** the self is a means of *rerouting the flow of energy in order to sustain survival.*

This is especially true when internalization (the **I** in **FRICK**) or interjecting frustration and blame within the self, is a dominant method of dysfunctional coping. "It's my fault. I can't ever get anything right. I am just a big screw-up. See, this just proves it . . . again!" In clinical depression, the collective experiences of individual failures become enormously inflated, linked together, and grow exponentially like an emotional tapeworm until it forms a wounded self or a victim identity. Although these persons may have valid experiences of victimization, if these initial wounds are not healed, all new experiences can further reinforce perceptions of reality that are skewed, reactive, and distorted. New experiences will be viewed through the distorted lens of victimization. This might be summarized as, "Look what *they* did to *me*. It just keeps happening over and over again and again!" Each new experience sticks like Velcro to the previous one since the unconscious mind does not separate past and present because it all *feels* the same.

All emotions have an energy associated with them. If you are living in a state of aware consciousness, you may find yourself walking into a room and you can "feel" if someone is angry or anxious. In the same manner, you walk into a room and experience positive expressions associated with joy or laughter. I am reminded of this any time I hear a baby or a small toddler laugh an authentic laugh. Their laughter immediately creates the same laughter within me. In this sense, emotions are highly "contagious." Emotions can also become "trapped" in family systems, organizations, or institutions. For example, notice the "morale" of employees when downsizing and cost-cutting measures happen in the workplace and a regular round of pink slips are passed out. Depression becomes systemic. When a business dives into protective mode, everyone feels a similar emotion. One of my reactions to sitting with people who are severely depressed is that I will often get sleepy. My unconscious mind will literally attempt to "shut down" rather than to have these feelings projected *into* me. It works this way in order to protect me from *receiving* these feelings. When this begins to happen, I do my own internal checklist and determine if I felt tired or sleepy *before* the person came into my office. I know intuitively the depressed feelings are not being "held" by the sojourner. The individual is trying to get me to hold these feelings for him. I usually will stop and ask the person if he is able to identify what he is feeling in that moment. As the person begins to own their feelings and experience his own pain, my own energy returns. Severely depressed people have withdrawn as a means of survival and often look unconsciously for other people to hold their pain and to "borrow" energy from available resources. When someone is affected with severe depression, the person affected may become like an emotional vampire, sucking the life out of his relationships. The only joy he may know is in stealing joy from others.

One must understand how to distinguish between *having* a feeling and *being* a feeling. We frequently build identities around our feelings indicating when we are feeling what we are feeling then we must be that feeling! This answers and fills in the "I am" statement with a feeling. I am sad, happy, lonely, depressed, and so on. The self then becomes identified as *being* a *feeling*. Later we will explore one of the mistakes made by creating identities with our feelings.

We have feelings, but *we are not our feelings*. Emotions change. No one emotion can be sustained indefinitely. The dilemma is a double bind. The depression creates self-rejection *of* the self *by* the self. How does this dynamic work? By projecting these feelings onto other persons, the self-fulfilling prophecy becomes complete. "Nobody wants to be around me (they reject me) when I am depressed. I'll just drag everyone else down (I reject me)." The statement may hold an element of truth. What the depressed individual is conveying is, "How could anyone possibly want to be around me when *I* don't want to be around me?" Think of this last statement as an x-ray. Let us hold this picture up, clip it in front of the light, and examine the fracture in human consciousness. "I do not like myself" is now the problem. This poses a colossal dilemma of identity.[j] If there is an "I" and a "myself" the one "me" has been split in two. Which one am I? Am I the "I" I do not like or is the "myself" someone different? Does this mean the very essence of human nature is that we are schizoid or bi-polar? Is there one or two of me? Neither "I" nor "myself" like each other, and they live in the same place! Imagine a two-headed cobra, continually biting itself and injecting venom into its own bloodstream! Depression creates self-rejection *of* the self *by* the self.

For persons struggling with a *wounded self,* the identity becomes organized around protecting the collective wounds, and depression is the ever-present companion. Depression does serve a function, role, and purpose. Depression becomes activated as a means of survival because of the perception of a threat. We withdraw *from* other people, or we draw *within* because we feel wounded and vulnerable. Depression attempts to create safety within the self. This amplifies the **C** in the **FRICK** model of conflicted thoughts, feelings, and emotions by establishing

---

[j] It also provides another example of understanding "splitting" in human consciousness, which I described, in the previous chapter with my daughter Rebekah when she was home from college.

the bind that works this way: If I withdraw as a means of trying to insure my safety or to protect myself from failure, I will fail by refusing to try. We will *succeed* to guarantee our safety, but *fail* the competency test![k]

Authentic Emotional and Spiritual Growth

Authentic emotional and spiritual growth follows the pattern in history and creation of death and resurrection. There may be days, weeks, or even years of life when we experience periods of "incubation." Something may be slowly churning within in order to create new awakenings. We move toward enmeshment when experience creates discord and dissonance within the self and the soul. When experience is troubling, creates suffering, and is difficult to accept, we may ask *meaning* questions: "Does this make any sense to you?" "Why did this have to happen?" We may ask *justice* questions: "What did I do to deserve this?" "Why am I being punished?" We may ask *competence* questions: "Why didn't I see this coming?" "How could I have been so stupid?" These are the questions created by new experience. These questions cause us to evaluate, re-evaluate, or even dismantle our theory, ideology, philosophy, and theology. These questions force us to examine our personal lens and look extensively at our history, experience, ideas, and beliefs. These questions take us to our core and reveal the self and the soul. Our own human tragedies are frequently passports to new territory and a gateway for all our tomorrows. The death of one self-understanding may be the labor and delivery room for a new birth, a new dawn, a new day, and a new beginning.

Enmeshment, when sufficiently intense, creates a type of death experience and allows us to enter a new matrix of meaning. Enmeshment is a period of incubation when the cauldron stirring in the soul becomes restless and agitated.

---

[k] Truancy and skipping school frequently involves students failing classes where they feel they can't succeed. Why would I want to go to class if I don't "get it" and I end up feeling stupid and incompetent?

This is more like cooking in a crock-pot than a microwave oven. These experiences create opportunities for receptivity and an awakened vulnerability to change, growth, and discovery. If we are willing to stay with our pain, we can progress to new places on the journey.

Barry, the college instructor I previously mentioned, came to see me after his second wife came home one day and announced she wanted a divorce. Amanda basically said to Barry, "girls just want to have fun." She had begun staying out late after work and had become the emotional confidant of a male coworker going through a divorce. Barry was either blind, oblivious, or in denial, and he never thought any of this was a cause for concern. He never saw it coming. It came out of left field and hit him like a brick. After our third meeting, Barry brought a poem he wrote:

Deep End

I can't touch bottom.
I strain downward.
Pointing my foot like a knife,
Praying for the touch of something solid.
Struggling to keep my chin above the lapping waves,
Waves from my own thrashing,
Echoing off the distant sides of the pool.
My jerky movements spin me in slow circles,
The safety of the cement lip
A hopeless constant radius.
I know if I spread my arms in surrender,
My legs will slowly rise and I will float,
Drifting to shallower water
But I can't touch the bottom
And my panic enfolds me.
My fingers rip at the water's flesh.
My eyes burn with chlorine and tears of frustration.
I don't belong here.
I learned my lessons.
Water pours down my throat.
Shivering on the surface of the warm cement,
I heave up the last of the water,
Then I am still.
I hear my breath.

I hear my heart.
I stare up into the huge blue sky.
I cannot touch the bottom.

Barry is struggling to keep from drowning in the waves of his own thrashing. As he looks at the cement border around the pool, he is caught in helplessness and despair, surrounded by "a hopeless constant radius." He struggles with conflicted thoughts, feelings, and emotions; he knows he will be able to float if he can "spread his arms in surrender." This impulse runs counter to his need for safety, expressed by his frustration and his inability to touch bottom. Floating would mean "going with the flow," but surrender is too frightening. The solid bottom of safety remains beyond the touch of his toes. Barry alternately shifts between the reactive emotions of anxiety and anger as he cries out, "My panic enfolds me" and "My fingers *rip* at the water's *flesh*." Since water has no flesh, I wondered if the water was a substitute for Amanda. Barry gets to his pain as his "eyes burn with chlorine and the tears of frustration." "I do not belong here" is his protest to injustice. I should be some place other than here. I have learned my lesson before and now I have to swallow it all over again! This pain takes him under, or so it seems, until he gets out of the pool, chokes out the water, and becomes still. Although he still cannot touch bottom, a metamorphosis is taking place. He began the lament by praying for something solid and through the course of this experience, he has now moved from chaos to calm. Barry listens to his breath and his heart. In doing so, he sees the "huge blue sky." He seems calmed although he still cannot reach the bottom. Barry feels safe as he lets his soul breathe. He moved inside a new matrix of meaning and toward the mystery.

The Logic of Depression

Depression has its own embedded logic. To penetrate this logic requires agility. Reversing the downward spiral of despair requires connecting with the sojourner with his/her current reality, building empathic bridges, and crossing the bridges to untangle the internal tumbleweed. Strategically this involves unraveling collective experiences and dealing with each individually. This strategy requires *segmenting* the experiences and the *meanings* attached to each one. Ms. Z., a young mother in her mid-thirties came to see me with a variety of physical ailments.[1] Several months after we began working together, Ms. Z. began to recall some intense experiences of sexual abuse from childhood and adolescence previously denied and repressed. After the defense mechanisms of self-preservation began to fail, nearly every day brought to consciousness another horrific recollection from her past. Ms. Z. was caught in the downward spiral of depression.

During one visit, I listened as she told a story about her nine-year-old son yelling at her. He did not have clean socks. "He never yells at me," she stated. As I prodded her to examine what this meant for her, she said it meant *she was a bad mother*. This was a premise I would not accept. The correlation fit the "logic of depression" and made perfectly good sense to her, but to me it sounded absurd. If she had said she beat her children to a bloody pulp, or locked them in the closet for days without food, I would have to agree with her. I began to drive a wedge in her equation of "no clean socks equates to bad mother" by separating the *meaning* she connected to her son's statement about the socks. In her mind, this equation was clear since she had not done the laundry because of her depression. Because she felt bad, she used her son's yelling as a way of saying *I am bad.* Notice how *identity* becomes connected with a *feeling*, and in this instance, depression. "I feel bad" morphs into "I am bad." I did not agree with her logic, and so I told her what this experience *meant* was her son did not have any clean socks, period. I also added he probably wanted clean socks since he was used to wearing socks to school. If he did not have any

---

[1] Ms. Z's story will be told in greater detail in Chapter Six, *Our Search for Healing*

clean socks, he might not be ready to get to school on time, which in a sense would make him feel incompetent. I suggested she go to Wal-Mart, buy several bags of socks and keep them around the house for such emergencies. Because this young mother had the economic means to do so, I also suggested she hire someone to do the laundry twice a week if this was the problem. The effect of this type of "segmenting" was to keep her from taking another daily experience and letting it further enlarge the emotional hairball her depression had created.

Relational Competence

The ongoing quest for competence is carried into adulthood. This quest not only involves the development of careers and jobs, but also carries into our relationships. Miraculously, most of us are able to survive the slings and arrows of childhood and adolescence. In the transition from adolescence to young adulthood, emotional scar tissue may appear from the residual effects of these experiences into our adult relationships.

Relationships frequently become the playground for unresolved pain. In the previous section on the role of depression, the **FRICK** principle is primarily centered on internalization and conflicted thoughts, feelings, and emotions. In terms of relationships, the triggers are more often frustration and reactivity. Frustration is anger expressed at an object, circumstance, situation, or individual when I cannot get it to do what I want it to do. Reactivity occurs when something in the present touches unresolved pain from the past. We react with more emotion than is necessary or required.

As a counselor, I am constantly amazed at the number of marriages and relationships stuck in an orbit of reactivity, rage, and revenge. Once stuck in these patterns, sojourners find it difficult to break into new orbits without the intervention of a third party. Psychotherapy can assist to identify these patterns and provide alternative ways to express thoughts and feelings in ways that are purposeful, helpful and beneficial, as opposed to the *known* patterns, which are reactive, hurtful and destructive.

More than half of all marriages fail. Most adult men and women in this country are in their second or third marriage, sometimes even more. Having had more than one marriage partner can create a set of alternating reactions if problems occur in the relationship. First, there may be a tendency to bail out of the marriage *sooner* when conflict erupts and is not easily resolved. "I don't need to put up with this crap. I did not put up with it before, and I sure as hell am not going to put up with it this time, either!" The tolerance for dealing with problems may *decrease* with each relationship, and the threshold for dealing with marital pain may likewise diminish. Secondly, if an individual carries unresolved issues into a second or third marriage, the chances of the same inflamed emotional issues becoming hot and volatile again are extremely likely. "You're twice as hostile as Lois, my first wife, and I cannot believe I've made the same damn mistake again." Thirdly, having problems may make the couple extremely motivated to make the marital relationship work. The motivation may not necessarily be the result of having or not having a great or mutually shared love for each other. Instead, this may be an avoidance of being viewed as relationally incompetent. The way this is usually phrased is, "*I don't want to see myself as a two-time (three, four, etc.) loser.*"[m]

---

[m] As a general rule the depression era generation grew up with a deep commitment to marriage that embraced "till death do us part." About half of the baby boomers rejected this tenant. Generation X is the first generation to be the result of the experiment with the "blended family." Although many baby boomers had no problem rejecting the notion of "staying together for the sake of the children" when they experienced marital misery, others struggled with guilt and pain at "being the first in our family to ever get a divorce." The bonds of family loyalties can be extremely difficult lines to cross and strong motivating forces in "making the marriage work".

The Destructive Patterns: Reactivity, Rage, and Revenge

As discussed in Chapter 1, anger and anxiety are protective emotions expressed when we do not feel safe. The shift of these emotions, from physical to psychological threats, involves situations that threaten our competence and/or issues of justice.

When we work to interrupt reactivity, we seek to create awareness, assess the threat, stop reactivity, hold the reaction, and heal the pain. By diffusing reactivity, we remain conscious and purposeful and avoid the chaotic states, which result from the emotional hijacking by anger and anxiety.

The following two questions are designed to create awareness and to assess the threat:

1) Is there something that has been said that makes me feel like I have been put down?
2) Is this something that feels unbalanced or unfair?

Relationships stuck in an orbit of reactivity create marital and relational stalemates. The automatic, immediate reactions to feeling threatened have their own logic. Once this logic is exposed to the light of awareness, the logic diminishes in power, and we can *choose* other forms of reason as a means of self-expression. For example, if our significant other says or does something to demean our sense of competence, we want them to understand how we feel. The automatic, or default, reaction is to create hurt for the other person. In our desire to make the other person understand our feelings, we attack them so *they will know how we feel*. In other words, if you hurt me, I will hurt you back. Then you will be able to understand how bad I feel, in a twisted sort of way. As indicated in the previous chapter, this is the logic of revenge. We want others we care for to understand how we feel, and this makes sense. However, the *method* of communication is undesirable when we attempt to target healthy and productive relationships. The instinctual response to being attacked is usually to respond in the same manner or withdraw. Constantly picking the scabs of a wound never gives it time to heal. The ability to disclose our real self in significant relationships indicates we have successfully lowered the *fences of our defensiveness* and created trusting, caring, and empathic relationships. This is a preferable alternative to wasting our life and the potential for meaningful relationships.

We carry these wounds from childhood and adolescence into our adult lives and find ourselves reacting to this pain in relationships with other adults. These interactions often trigger intense reactions relating to our need to feel competent. When we have shared life with a spouse or a child for a period of years, it does not take long to "find out where the buttons are" and be able to push them for our own drama and entertainment. The threshold between pleasure and pain is paper-thin for many people.

Jess

Jess, a 20-year-old young man came to me for counseling. He described a yelling match with his sister. She was ten years older than he was and had played the role of his "second mother" growing up. His older sister was yelling at her twin three-year-old boys for making a mess at the dinner table. Jess cringed when he heard her yelling at the twins. For a brief moment, he probably *felt* she was yelling at him. Jess intervened on behalf of the twins and asked her "to simply talk to the boys and not yell at them." She fired back and yelled, "Who are *you* to tell *me* how to raise my sons?" She heard his request as an attack on her parental competency. His natural response to feeling attacked was to attack. Choosing to attack is an attempt to *entirely eliminate the threat*. This is accomplished by destroying the source of the threat, either literally or psychologically. If this process is not defused, it carries the potential to erupt into violence. For Jess and his older sister, the situation went from bad to worse. Although this brother and sister never became violent, they had a face-to-face shouting match. Each of them made sure the other felt terribly incompetent. Verbal violence always precedes physical violence. The mother took measures to insure this would not happen. When she had all of this behavior she could take, she separated her adult children and sent them to their rooms!

Avery and Amanda

Those with whom we share emotional oxygen create the greatest amount of emotional vulnerability. Weak spots are easily found and attacked. If we have been with someone long enough, we already know where these weak spots are located. Avery and Amanda, both teachers, came to me with mutual concerns regarding problems with their 15-year-old son.

Avery was a coach, and Amanda taught kindergarten. Their son was having anger problems, a trait he learned from his father. For many years, Avery battled problems with alcohol, but had been sober for the last several years. He discovered a new and real relationship with the "God of his understanding." Avery was a "rough and tumble" man who fit the stereotypical image of a drill sergeant. Avery was now a changed man, but admitted there were still issues from his past, which were unresolved. Occasionally his bouts of fury would surface and be expressed in conflict with his wife or his son. On one occasion, in a fit of rage, their son absolutely demolished his bedroom. A wrestling match ensued between father and son, and came dangerously close to becoming a fistfight. Amanda successfully intervened. Their son scored the ultimate blow in this battle when he told his father, "You haven't changed. You are still the angry man you have always been. All of that church stuff is just talk. You're just a fake and a fraud." His son, at an age when idealizing needs are adjusting to reality, had beaten his father without landing a blow. Avery was a beaten man.

Amanda eventually had enough. After her son graduated from high school, she divorced Avery and moved back to her home state. Avery started drinking again. In his early sixties, he was diagnosed with cirrhosis and liver failure and died in a nursing home.

Angela and Brad

This young couple, Angela and Brad, were in their mid-thirties when I met them. After our second meeting, my assessment was that their marriage closely resembled a train wreck. Their communication skills were extremely weak, and they both felt controlled by the other. I literally had to stop them from talking over the other person; this is called steamrolling. One would start talking, and the other would begin speaking as if the other person was not in the room. We identified several issues that needed to be addressed and began working.

Both believed the "bottom" of all their problems involved marital frustration in the bedroom. Angela was the youngest of four children and the only daughter of a strong Italian heritage and brought up in the Catholic Church. Brad was a "man of the world," traveling all over the world in the Navy. Brad was in business for himself, and Angela recently left the family business to obtain steady employment with benefits. He was an introvert; she was an extrovert. Angela, at age 25, was a virgin when she met Brad. Brad was convinced his wife must have been sexually molested as a child; Angela insisted she had not. Brad began complaining about their sex life during the first year of their marriage. Now it was year 11, and things were worse. Brad indicated once she was satisfied, he had better hurry up and finish because it was about to be over whether he was finished or not. Brad complained Angela never initiated making love. He felt hurt, rejected, and he retaliated in anger, which reduced Angela to tears. When I asked Angela whom she learned about anger from as a child, she indicated her father.

She began to sob deep sobs and identified that Brad's anger made her feel the way she felt when her father turned anger toward her. She felt rejection and shame because she had not pleased him and earned his approval.

Angela internalized her pain, projecting the past into the future and bracketing her present moment with hopelessness, helplessness, and despair. Angela said, "I just don't see how it is ever going to be any different. It would be easier to just start over with another person who did not see me the way Brad sees me without all of the baggage." Angela experienced dire frustration and desperation. The heart of the problem finally emerged. Angela felt incompetent in the bedroom. She felt incapable of pleasing her husband. Brad constantly compared her to former sexual partners, insisting she did everything wrong. In other words, her thoughts became his thoughts. Over the course of 11 years Brad occasionally vented his frustration by bringing up a former lover and something she had done to please him. Angela stated, "You may have only said something like that once, but *I heard it over in my mind a thousand times.*" When Brad heard this, he was dumbfounded. I told Angela it made sense she would withdraw from an area in her life where she felt failure. The unconscious mind does not encourage us to try something if we believe we are going to fail. Brad started to laugh and said, "It's the same way with bowling. Angela will not bowl because she is afraid she will make a fool out of herself, and she doesn't want to be seen this way."

The common wisdom, "If you can't do it well, it's not worth doing at all" is the wisdom of the unconscious mind. Known patterns, although they may be terribly hurtful and destructive, are at least *familiar.* Learning new patterns requires patience, empathy, and care. These qualities are by-products when relationships are purposeful, targeting mutual benefit, love and respect, and are driven by the power of synergy, energy, and cooperation. When relationships are driven by reactivity, rage, and revenge, the marriage and its participants are often exhausted, tired, and afraid.

Vocational Competence

To be viewed as competent at what we do and who we are is an ongoing human need. This is our *quest for competence.* We all want to succeed vocationally. The need is the same for the C.E.O. of a major corporation or the waiter working through school.

My son worked in a restaurant for over a year bussing tables until he turned 18. At that time, the management offered him a job as a waiter. He accepted the position with some degree of anxiety. He was concerned about his ability to manage the new responsibilities and challenges of the new position. In other words, his anxiety centered on his fear of failing. He worked three or four evenings a week, earning money to pay for a truck and some extra spending money for the many "necessities" for his stage in life. He was well liked on the job, but after eight months as a waiter, he gained the reputation of a "slacker." He wore this badge with some degree of pride. He took the easiest stations and chose to service the outside deck during the hot summer months. Sean knew few people would ask to sit outside and fight the heat and the myriad of monstrous insects. One evening a raccoon jumped on top of one of the tables, subsequently closing the deck area, and Sean came home early.

Management and coworkers tolerated Sean's "laziness" until one evening he was "written up" by one of the managers. This happened when a customer complained within earshot of the owner about the way his steak had been cooked. As his waiter, Sean thought the conflict had been resolved. At the time the customer paid his bill, he became irate and irrational, complaining vehemently to the cashier. The owner interceded and gave the man a free meal, which was probably his intended target. The customer even left a sizeable tip for Sean, which was a double message. If he were so upset about his steak, why would he tip so heavily? Sean was "written up" for not notifying the management of a potential problem. Management attempted to make *him* responsible to feed their need to be competent. Sean was placed on two weeks "probation" and during this time, the manager assigned his stations.

The next two weeks created an exponential spike in Sean's tip income. Each night of his probation period, he was given more responsibility, and he succeeded. He eventually thanked his manager for receiving the disciplinary action. Sean realized he might as well make the most of his time at work, work harder and make more money. When he realized he was skilled enough to handle the larger stations, he became more confident. As he became more confident, his competence as a waiter grew as well. This was easily measured by his increase in tip income.

The quest for competence as we reach adulthood is a key component of our search. In the workplace, when workers are not challenged employee morale can be low. Positions need to offer the opportunity for employees to demonstrate vocational competence. We may experience these moments feeling as if we are "underemployed".

Underemployment can also be the result of facing handicapped conditions due to accident or injury. When I met George, a man in his late forties, he had worked as an engineer for more than 20 years. An accident on the job led to a back injury. The injury required six different surgeries, two on his brain. Because of the injury and surgeries, George was now disabled. His income was limited to a monthly social security check and his wife's income from selling real estate. He became involved in a business as the principal partner in a muffler shop. Every day George grieved in one way or another for the challenges and accomplishments he would not achieve as an engineer. Now time stood still, his job with the muffler shop was not challenging for him, the job simply filled his time. When I met George, he was extremely angry and depressed. He missed the opportunity to express his vocational competence. George did not have the same mental capabilities since the accident. He grieved what had been meaningful for him. Nothing is wrong with working in a muffler shop, but for George this endeavor did not provide the challenge he felt he needed.

The unconscious mind will offer a defense against failure by keeping us from taking risks. Failing to take risks can make us stagnant in our search, which consequently can end in failure. There is a new offshoot of professional counseling called "coaching" which has grown in popularity. This involves working with individuals who may have become stagnant in their work or those who are highly successful and striving to reach the highest levels of vocational effectiveness. Although professional credentials are not required for this field, credentials speak the language of competence and credibility in working with persons seeking to function at higher levels.

Dale, a stockbroker for a nationally recognized firm, came to see me because he recognized some problems at work. His income was tied to sales commissions, and his partner provided more stagnation than productivity. Dale was the son of a minister; his parents worked as missionaries in Japan. He went through a rebellious adolescence and young adulthood but somehow survived. Over time, he discovered he had a drinking problem, but he made it through to recovery with the help of Alcoholics Anonymous. Once back in the United States, his mother, a school principal, always expected the worst from her son. She branded him a failure. Now, Dale found he *was* failing as a stockbroker. His view of the business partnership was dismal. Ending the partnership will cost a friendship. He also recognized how he began to slack off and lose focus as soon as he reached a monthly goal. He would dawdle away his time with meaningless, non-productive tasks. Dale was pushing against internal commandments established in his childhood. In a moment of revelation, he acknowledged it would be *threatening for him to see himself as being competent and successful.* When he understood the absurdity of this, he became more focused and allowed his passion to surface. He targeted, outlined, developed, and established a plan of productivity. More important, he followed through and implemented his plan. The icon he used for his target was a new home for his family. Dale tacked a picture of the house he wanted to build on his desk to provide a daily reminder of his goal. The house was built in less than two years!

My position shifted more to "coaching" Dale after these discoveries. I only saw him occasionally, once or twice a month, in order to create accountability. He knew he was good at what he did, and he believed he could help other people. At the center of his "mission" was to *remain focused on the needs of the people he served.* As odd as this may sound, he remained on task and more productive when he saw himself as a servant, helping other people. When he worried about his own investments, he wasted too much time, effort, and energy. He would lose site of his missional purpose, and as a result, his income would drop. The pattern was now clear. His secret was his passion for people and to remain focused on being a servant. He took on two new partners, and together they established an agenda and a method for growth of the business. The business plan produced amazing results. In two years, Dale more than doubled his income. His partners became his "peer group," and together they developed brief daily meetings as a method to maintain ongoing accountability to each other.

When I am 64

As mentioned previously, retired adults must adjust to changing lifestyles, *as meaning often shifts from doing to being.* "Productivity" and purpose undergo major shifts. Older adults begin to face issues of declining health, often with a continued loss of personal independence and freedom. Each age and stage of this process provides unique challenges in managing issues of professional, emotional, and relational competence.

I first met Benny after the death of his son-in-law. His son-in-law was killed in a tragic hunting accident. His shotgun had fallen in the back of his pick-up truck and discharged into his chest. Benny, recently retired from the fire department, had trained the new firefighters for years. At the age of 16, he ran away and left home. During World War II, Benny served in the Navy and was a machine gunner on a TBF - 1 Avenger Torpedo Bomber in the South Pacific. After the war he returned home, married, and raised three children. He literally pulled himself up from the bootstraps and rose to the number two position in the fire department. He dabbled in local politics and he was elected to serve a term as a city commissioner. He hated what he saw in the game playing and deceitfulness of politics and gave up after one term.

When I first met him, he would later recall he was "sizing me up" and working to determine whether I was "real" or not. Benny had little tolerance for what he called "show" and it had been his lifelong passion to unmask who he thought were frauds. He would do it verbally, or if necessary, with his fists. He was, as we say in the south, as rough as a cob. Benny feared no man. I was no exception.

Benny was crushed by the death of his son-in-law. He described an aching and hurting in his chest like no other he had felt before. He had always felt a swaggering sense of competence throughout his life and that he could handle anything that would come his way, but this was just too big for him to manage. He could not do it on his own, and he hated like hell to ask for help. For many years, he had been a hard-drinking man, but he had joined A.A. and had been sober for over a year. He had made the transition into retirement through his work in A.A., and this was now the major source of meaning in his life. His son-in-law's death was another matter. It made absolutely no sense to him. He could not fit the square peg into a round hole. He was stunned and in shock when we met.

After this first meeting, I apparently passed the test. Benny began showing up at church and was soon a regular fixture. He was a man of authentic faith. He would accept nothing on face value without a struggle and a fight. He questioned everything and was not a passive participant in the development of his own spirituality. He became very active with an outreach program to street people and to the homeless. His abrasive style and ability to "speak the language" caught the attention of leaders, and he was asked to volunteer and be the "doorkeeper" for the Monday and Friday feeding program, where three to four hundred hot meals were served. He would help to monitor the flow of human traffic in the building and insure things ran smoothly among the homeless and the street people. When there were moments when our clientele would get out of hand, Benny commanded their respect, and he would calm things down. He recognized many of the street people from A.A. and he worked to get an A.A. group going at the church after the feeding programs to help those who wanted to move toward recovery. In many ways, Benny became a street evangelist. He sponsored some of the most down and out individuals I have ever known. Drug addicts, pimps, prostitutes, crack heads, and street drunks all knew and loved Benny. As a favor to Benny, I would attend A.A. meetings and I was impressed with the spirituality I witnessed in the program. More often than not, they were doing a better job at being the church than we were at the church. When the building which housed A.A. burned to the ground, Benny was the president and in charge of building a new building. With tears in his eyes, he was as excited as a child would be at Christmas. He witnessed the construction of the new building with both mystery and meaning. Always, it seemed, at the right time and in the right place, there were people who would step forward to take care of framing, plumbing, electrical, drywall, or flooring needs. Benny was overwhelmed with awe and excitement. He realized the new building was building itself. In his own understanding of his faith, he was simply a conduit for an energy creating all things new in his midst. He was both proud and humble.

  Having been raised to fend for himself, Benny grew up with a chip on his shoulder, and he constantly fought demons from without and within. His fierce competitiveness was a defense against his attempts to maintain his own competence. Anyone with degrees or with letters after his name would become immediately suspect for Benny, a man who never had the opportunity to add those luxuries to his resume. The more credentials a person carried, the more Benny would want to expose his competitor's incompetence. It was a twisted sort of game he played in order to maintain his own. Now living in the phase of life where *being replaced doing*, Benny began to soften and mellow. He never lost his intensity.

The following is a brief excerpt of an interview that took place a few weeks before we moved to the west coast of Florida and away from Benny's community. I conducted a series of interviews in conjunction with concluding my doctoral project. In this segment, Benny is referencing a book he received from his daughter, which included quotable quotes from famous people. It was from Sharon, whose husband, Tom, died in the hunting accident. He is commenting on an inscription she had written on the inside flap of the book. This points to a transition that occurred in his life as he began claiming values relating to "being." Benny begins to look toward his own death by examining his core values. According to Benny, honesty is how a man will ultimately be remembered:

>"Well," she wrote on the front page or the second page, whatever it was, and said, "Dad, I don't remember hearing you make any of these statements or quotes, but *what I do remember is your honesty and your love for your family.*" Now that just got to me... still does... All she's been through with those two children, Tom and death and everything, and see, I'm very proud, and this was true in everything I've ever done, even when I was drinking, I was honest. I'll tell you; I've told my children; I've tried to teach them this if nothing else. I can remember my grandmother Barnes saying this to my uncles, and they were all alcoholics, every damn one of them, and I'd hear her say, "Boys, don't forget who you are!" That meant you were a Barnes and don't forget it! "When you go out there tonight, you conduct yourself in a certain way and a certain manner. After all, when a man dies, the only thing he's got left and will be remembered for is... is his honesty and being fair to

other people..." there's not a whole hell of a lot else we have."

I had occasional contact with Benny over the next seven or eight years. That changed one day when he left a message on my answering machine. I returned his call and he told me he had been diagnosed with lung cancer. When we talked, I learned his situation was not bright. Less than eight percent with this type of cancer survived, according to his oncologist. For Benny, eight percent was at least a chance. He moved forward with chemotherapy and radiation and fought like the machine gunner he was. He lost weight, and when I first saw him, I tried not to react to his weak and emaciated frame. He now needed a cane in order to take his next steps. Success was being measured by the amount of sleep he would get, and he would express excitement over what he called a "two Popsicle night," which was a way he could maintain his fluid intake. Benny's wife now became his nurse, and their days consisted of daily visits to the radiation center or chemotherapy lab, where an intense community had formed. Everyone was in the same boat in this community of the damned.

Even in the midst of his own pain and torment, Benny believed what he was going through was for a purpose. This added meaning to his life. He joked about death and told the hospital chaplain he was sorry, but he was not going to be the 100-dollar preacher at his funeral. He remained committed to being competent and to be used in whatever way possible, which added meaning to his life and to the lives of others. He told me about a woman who came in for her first dose of chemotherapy and radiation. She was emaciated in her appearance. He looked into her hollow eyes and saw the same fear he felt the first day he came for treatment. They lay on their stretchers, side by side, through the remainder of the day. Benny took time to listen and to calm her fears. As a veteran of the process, he helped her to anticipate everything that was going to happen. He had felt the same fear, and he used it to build a bridge of empathy to cross over and create connection. When the treatment had concluded, and the day was over, they were leaving when the woman introduced Benny to her daughter. She mustered a smile, looked warmly into his face, and told her daughter she was pleased to introduce her to her guardian angel. Benny told the story with tears streaming down his own face. His meaning had been deeply touched.

After a long battle, Benny died a few months later. He never gave up and continued to look for meaning and purpose in each day. Toward the end, he lost his continence, which was a humiliating blow to his pride, dignity, and competence. He finally was able to take these changes in stride, remembering a previous time of incontinence when he was in the Navy. He had been "shit faced drunk" and had "pissed all over himself." I sat at his side. He recognized my face, which was a special gift to me because he had been in and out of consciousness for several days. He spoke and labored with every word. I could understand little of what he said, but I met his eyes with mine, gently nodded my head in agreement, and I attempted to communicate love, care, and acceptance. The words were meaningless. The connection was made. Benny could feel it, and so could I. I still can. Benny died that night.

In this chapter, we have explored the myth of self-esteem. The unconscious mind actually collects and connects experiences that are like or similar. Symptoms associated with low self-esteem are actually indicators of a wounded self. The default position for the wounded self is deflation whereas the default position for the narcissistic self is inflation. A wounded self tends to internalize blame and a narcissistic self tends to externalize blame.

Parenting that utilizes discipline as a way of teaching children how to solve their own problems as opposed to blaming and shaming will improve and strengthen an emerging sense of competence with their children. Navigating through the danger zones includes the areas children are most vulnerable: parents, siblings, school, and peers. The damage created in these stages becomes readily identifiable when young adults are attempting to launch if these problems have not surfaced or been acted out during adolescence.

Depression frequently becomes an issue for those who carry a wounded self. The role of depression involves our need to maintain "safety first." We withdraw away from others or into the self to create our own safety. This dynamic creates a bind because we will sever life-sustaining connections we need in order to survive and flourish. However, no organism can perpetually sustain growth. Authentic emotional and spiritual growth will at times require periods of angst and dormancy that may last for a season.

We are born with a need to be competent. From the moment our lungs inhale our first breath, each age and stage in life provides challenges to our competence until we exhale our last breath. We want to carry our lunch box the way big sister does or play soccer as well as our little brother. We want to be able to say our A, B, C's and learn how to read and write. We need to see in the faces of our parents that we can do it! We want to excel in sports, chess, or computer games. We want to graduate and be prepared and equipped to live our lives. We want to succeed in our relationships, in our jobs and in our vocations. We want to raise our children in an environment of love, discipline, and nurture. We want to grow old with grace, dignity, and style. We want to die a good death.

Our connections and our significant relationships are sources of rich meaning when we move away from pretense and discover the richness of the other person as "an independent center of initiative." When we are not trying to *get* something from someone else, to *use* them for our own needs or pleasure, or we are not living in *fear* of the other person, our connections can be sources of great meaning and joy. Let us continue the sojourn as we look at how our history and experience creates ideas and beliefs that shape the lens of how we see our *connections*.

Chapter 5
The Search For Connection

Our search for connection means we are creatures created to live in community. Dr. Harry Lodge and Chris Crowley, authors of *Younger Next Year*, state it this way:

> We evolved as social pack animals like wolves and dolphins. It's not a choice. Our survival depends on being a part of a group. No one has ever gone into the Amazon jungle and found an isolated person. It is always a tribe. There is no such thing as a solitary human in nature because isolation is fatal. We were designed to be emotional creatures, which is to say that we are mammals.[43]

From social pack animals, our ancestors evolved into living in groups, tribes, clans, and eventually into city-states and nations. We are made to live in connection with one another. From the moment of birth *connection* is the most essential component to survive, grow, and flourish. Without connection, we would all die.

Separation studies have been conducted between infant monkeys and their mothers. Without an appropriate surrogate or substitute, the monkeys died. In one particular study, some monkeys received surrogate mothers. The substitutes were made either of wrapped wires, or a "softer" feel of a stuffed animal. Monkeys nurtured by the "softer" mothers survived at a greater rate than the wire monkey moms did. The correlation is clear: the "softer" the mother, the stronger the bond or the connection. This characteristic closely replicates how humans are "wired" through infancy and adolescence. A correlation exists between the current epidemic of reactive attachment disorders (RAD) and children who do not receive this basic nurturing bond in the first two years of their lives. Connection is the vital life-giving oxygen of human existence. Without connection, we would all die.

Each human is born into a unique set of family circumstances and web of connections. We enter into pre-existing immediate and extended family systems and relationships. Each new arrival whether by adoption, the addition of foster children, or through the birth of a new sibling, alters and morphs those relationships in ways that may be small or significant. Our daughter, Rebekah, was born when our son, Sean, was three months shy of his fourth birthday. Prior to her birth, we did everything imaginable to try to ease Sean into accepting this new space invader. We even resorted to bribing him, offering presents "from Rebekah" and telling him how much his baby sister was looking forward to having a big brother. Once his baby sister arrived, we discovered the futility of our efforts. Sean went with me to pick up his mother and new sister and bring them home from the hospital. As we came through the back door, my son turned to me, still unsure if this was real. He tugged on my pants leg and said, *"Daddy is she going to stay here very long?"* I looked into his face and saw he was very serious, and obviously struggling with accepting this new intruder into our home. The question initially caught me off guard. I responded with a gentle smile, picked him up, held him under my left arm, inches from my face and told him, *"I promise you she will only stay with us for eighteen or twenty years and then she will leave."* Having absolutely no concept of linear time at that age he said, *"Is that all?"* I assured him I was telling the truth. He hugged me around the neck, reassured, and took off to play. When she married 23 years later Sean gave his little sister away. He would have eagerly volunteered to give her away the day she came home from the hospital, and for that matter, many of the days that followed. Now he could do so officially and with pride!

The 18 years (give or take a few) spent at home provides relational sculpting by parents, siblings, schools, and peers as part of a growing quest for competence, autonomy, and independence. We enter into this world in a state of total dependence where others meet all our needs. If you have held an infant in your arms, especially your own, you know the flood of emotions, this stirring from the depths of the soul. This stirring of emotions contains conflicting thoughts and feelings. We hold within us awe and wonder as well as the burden and responsibility for the survival of this tiny fragile life, dependent on you for its nurture, care and survival. With the uncertainty of each step a toddler takes in this growing adventure comes the evolutionary quest for autonomy and independence. The pathways of adventure provided in childhood and adolescence create opportunities for lengthening our strides in the steps toward our independence. Unless our immediate environments are adversarial or non-nurturing, our families, schools, synagogues, and churches may provide us with rich laboratories for our learning. The different venues present us with opportunities to establish our goals, launch our dreams, and experiment in living our life until we are ready to leave the family womb and embark on our own expedition. As adults, we learn the art of inter-dependence, which feeds the soul through the nourishment of intimacy.

Connection: Belonging, Acceptance, Approval, and Identity

Belonging provides a key component of our survival as a species from an evolutionary, historical and anthropological perspective. Belonging is an instinctual need. Human beings traveled in packs. The earliest forms of community required purposeful behavior. Hunting and gathering could only be successful through established cooperative efforts. While some gathered, others stood guard and offered protection from predators. The evolution of primitive societies developed into more complex groups, clans, tribes, and eventually city-states and nations. Each social system provides different roles, rules, tasks, and responsibilities that convey identity *back* to the individual. This identity includes what it means to be part of the greater whole and establishes the rules for inclusion and exclusion.

Our quest for connection ties together two aspects of

our search. It ties together the issue of identity – *who am I* and a relational connection for belonging, acceptance, and approval - *where do I belong?* "Who am I" fills in the blank of "I am _____." The blank is frequently filled with "where I am from" stories from my history and experience. The blank can be filled with a role, duty, task, occupation, or responsibility that is usually temporary. "I am a butcher, a baker, or a candlestick maker."

Groups confer identity to those who belong and define the parameters of inclusion and exclusion. My identity with one group may exclude belonging to another. Technically, I cannot be both a Democrat and a Republican or an Atheist and a Baptist. Identity fills in the "I am _____." By filling in the blank, we disclose part of our identity. I am a Democrat, Republican, Agnostic, Buddhist, Presbyterian, Bowler, Sailor, Parent, Child, Spouse, Plumber, Artist, or Maid.[n] These identities are about "doing" and not about "being". "Where do I belong" involves a larger concept of the whole being greater than the sum of the parts. *I know who I am because I know where I belong.* In the mystery of this transaction, who or what I identify with helps to *define* me. To be a member of something larger than myself conveys a sense of meaning back to the individual and confers a component of identity.

Raymond and Audrey – A Crisis of Identity

Raymond was in his mid 50s when he was forced into retirement. He worked for 25 years in Saudi Arabia for a large multi-national oil conglomerate. The oil company had been very good to their employees. Raymond and his wife Audrey enjoyed extensive benefits through the company. With no children, the couple enjoyed a very lucrative lifestyle. They traveled all over the world on extended

---

[n] On a more personal level, *identity can be limited to a particular emotion, when we identify **exclusively** with the emotion.* This is when we fill in the "I am" blank with sad, angry, happy, weary, fearful, joyous, conflicted, etc.

annual vacations. Nearly 2000 employees were housed in a company-owned compound. "Nationals" were replacing "Patriots" within the corporation, which meant U.S. citizens were being forced out of the company and native Saudis were replacing them. The times were changing fast and this show was ending for Raymond and Audrey.

They were forced to move back to the states and had to decide where to live. For the previous 25 years, the couple had lived on the corporate compound. Now, faced with deciding where to live Raymond was immobilized. Raymond's family, a mother and a sibling, lived in the Pacific Northwest, a climate too "cold and wet," especially after being acclimated to the Saudi weather. Audrey's mother lived in Northern California, which was "too expensive". Raymond and Audrey stayed a while on South Padre Island on the Texas Gulf Coast. Although this climate was much better, the Houston area was "too crowded." Unlike Goldilocks, Raymond and Audrey never could find a place "just right."

When I met them the couple was house sitting in the Daytona Beach area for friends who still worked for his former company. Raymond had begun to experience severe attacks of anxiety and depression and had gone through a regimen of doctors, psychiatrists, and therapists over the previous year. Raymond was convinced they were making the wrong decision on where they should live and had basically shut down for nearly a year. Audrey grew weary of her husband's indecision and finally pushed Raymond to sign a contract on a house in our community. Raymond's symptoms intensified.

"We should move to Nevada. That way we could be with family members if they needed us. We could hop in the car and be at either home in a three hour drive." Audrey patiently countered Raymond's despair and told him they could be wherever they needed to be on a three-hour flight. Raymond felt tormented and tortured. The day they closed on their new home there was no cause of celebration for Raymond.

The days were long and arduous for Raymond as they began unpacking and nesting in their new home. Raymond was desperately grieving the move from Saudi Arabia. "We should have just sold everything and bought new stuff when we came here." For Audrey, each opened box brought a joyful reminder of a past event. For Raymond, each unwrapped box opened raw wounds and painful reminders of his former life. When Raymond became sad he would become anxious and overcome with the intensity of the grief he was feeling.

On the company compound in Saudi Raymond enjoyed the status of being an elder tribesman, if not one of the chiefs. He held one of the top prestigious positions in this small clan of 2000 people. He also enjoyed the status of being a scratch golfer, which placed him in the highest echelon of sublimated skill levels within the tribe. (Our more primitive ancestors would have assigned a similar status to the best *hunter* in the clan.) Raymond's primary identity came from the prestige of his position and status in the tribe. When it was good, it was great; now it was gone. He had been banished and excommunicated from the tribe. Now he wandered aimlessly trying to figure out where he belonged. He suffered guilt as he imagined he had abandoned his family; yet they did not have a problem with him living in Florida. Ultimately, Raymond felt abandoned. Every decision came with a punishing sense of failure. Everything felt like loss as he grieved the connections that brought sustenance to his soul. As Raymond discovered, all identities based upon a role, duty, task, occupation, or responsibility are always temporary. In his mid-fifties Raymond was struggling with an identity crisis – who am I and where do I belong?

Our society provides us with a smorgasbord selection of cultural choices for solving the dilemma of "who am I" and "where do I belong?" Let us look at a sampling of these entrees as representatives of the entire buffet.

HOGS, Heritage, and Football

Groups organize around a wide range of topics, interests, sports, and hobbies and define their various parameters for inclusion and exclusion. Let us look deeper into the dynamics of one of these groups to which I belong. Daytona Beach is synonymous with special events. NASCAR Speed Weeks roll into town in February and July, Spring Break for college students in March and April, and twice a year the area hosts Bike Week in March and Biketoberfest in October. For motorcycle enthusiasts Bike Week is by far the more popular of the two events. Police and members of the Chamber of Commerce estimate the annual influx of bikers at half a million. They come from all over the nation and all over the world. Local motorcycle enthusiasts boast that Main Street in Daytona Beach makes Mardi Gras in New Orleans look like Sesame Street. Most visitors end up spending at least an afternoon or an evening on Main Street watching the constant parade of people and motorcycles.

I have been riding motorcycles since I was 14. I have owned a variety of motorcycles, from dirt bikes to touring bikes. My last five motorcycles have been Harley-Davidson's. For those who own motorcycles instant acceptance is accorded those who purchase a motorcycle by other cyclists, *especially among those who own the same make of motorcycle*. Regardless of the make, motorcycle owners and riders participate in a type of spiritual or religious cult. Riding a motorcycle involves an element of mystery. On the back of t-shirts and bumper stickers during bike week, we see a familiar slogan:

> If I had to Explain it,
> You Wouldn't Understand![44]

When we cannot assign language to an experience, we approach transcendence when these attempts seek to explain through the existence of mystery. From my own vantage point, this explains what happens when a biker is engaged in a transcendent moment. Motorcycle riding, unlike traveling in trains, planes, or automobiles, places us directly *into the experience.* In an automobile, you are an *observer* – on a motorcycle you are *part of the experience.* In an automobile, we can adjust the seat or the temperature to our liking. On a motorcycle, we adjust our clothing to environmental demands. Bikers can smell the smells, feel the air, and sense a connection to everything happening. In other words, motorcycle riding forces the rider to *be fully engaged in the present moment.* Athletes and those who participate in extreme sports often discuss this in a similar way when they talk about "entering into the zone." Joseph Chilton Pearce alludes to this as "un-conflicted behavior and engagement in the present moment."[45] Usually a component of danger is involved which fully forces the individual into the present moment. For the motorcycle rider a wandering mind can very easily end up with a serious case of road rash or wrapped around a tree or in some other perilous predicament.

When riding a motorcycle the *past and the future collapse into heightened present moment awareness.* To be present in the now offers a portal to transcendence. This cannot happen when we live in anticipation of the future, i.e. not enjoying the bike ride, but only anticipating the end destination and the happiness we believe is to be had when we get "there." When we get the degree, when the house is paid off, when we take the dream vacation, when the kids leave home, when the dog dies, are all ways in which we create the possibility of happiness somewhere in the future. We mortgage the present and negate the possibility of discovering happiness in the present moment in doing so. We cannot find meaning, transcendence, or happiness somewhere in the future. We can only uncover and discover it now! Lives driven by future events miss these rare moments of awareness. These transcendent moments usher in a sacred connection of creature to creation and creator.

Back to the Harley owners and their identity, they are

known to possess a certain air of elite snobbishness. They tend to view those who own foreign bikes with disgust or disdain. This leaves the Harley owner in the "inflated" position with all others in the "deflated" mode. Official HOG (Harley Owner's Groups) chapters will not allow non-Harley riders to participate in official group-sanctioned rides. Purchasing a Harley Davidson grants immediate membership to the national HOG group. The Harley Davidson Corporation must be a Madison Avenue marketing dream. Other companies and corporations must salivate when they see the level of owner loyalty that Harley owners profess. Harley owners conduct two continuous, predictable conversations with other owners. Discussions generally revolve around the continuous improvement:

1) Of the ***appearance*** of the motorcycle: this involves the ongoing purchase of chrome, saddlebags, accessories, and other assorted and sundry items that will make the bike *look better*.

2) Of the ***performance*** of the motorcycle: this involves Screaming Eagle performance packages, breather kits, taking the stock 95 cc motor and modifying it to 103 cc or 110 cc, race tuner software, cams, pistons, or pipes that makes the bike *run faster*.

Because of the *fusion* of identity between the owner and his or her machine, the entire venture can create *confusion* between the self and the object being ridden. When blurred boundaries exist, biker and bike lose a clear sense of distinction between the self and the object. "I *have* a motorcycle" becomes "I *am* my motorcycle." The image created in the mind of the consumer makes this *fusion* a marketing dream. The consumer continues to spend money to improve the ***appearance and performance of the self*** as seen through his Harley. For the Harley owner, real improvement never transpires. Cams and chrome cannot counter-balance the effects of aging, gravity, girth, or the heartbreak of psoriasis. As far as I can tell, nothing happens to *improve the individual's character or integrity*. In the suggestive world of marketing the Harley owner succumbs to the belief that shinier, faster and more is better and thus so are they!°

Heritage

Our heritage may create for us a starting point for belonging, acceptance, approval, and conferring identity. Once we trace our heritage to a specific point of origin, we answer one aspect of the mystery of our own meaning. *If I know where I came from, I can know who I am.* Alternatively, in reverse, *I know who I am if I know where I came from.* ᵖ This connection channels a *way of belonging.* Tracing our heritage may also provide us with an opportunity to struggle with some of the issues inside this matrix of meaning.

If I were diligent in my genealogical quest, I am rather certain the heritage of the McNeil family would trace back to a particular location in Ireland or Scotland. If I pursued such an endeavor, this quest would offer to me a way of connecting the genealogical dots with my particular "clan." A family crest, a symbol of identity, would signify to those inside and outside the clan my personal lineage. Our quest to determine an ancestral heritage may be an attempt to attach some exaggerated level of significance to a group, clan, or tribe to which we claim membership. Belonging to one group may inflate my sense of significance or give me a pseudo-sense of superiority. For example, if I am able to

---

° Which is the naked truth of all attempts at marketing and advertising: to convince the consumer a product or a purchase will create an advantage over others, an elevated or inflated sense of intelligence or well-being, or a desired feeling state.

ᵖ This may become a struggle for those persons who have been adopted. They may know little or nothing about their family of origin.

trace my heritage to ancestors who came over on the Mayflower it gives the allusion of importance or superiority - "We got here *first*."

When our family moved to St. Augustine, Florida, the nation's oldest city, I attended a noon service club meeting in order to get to know new people. As I introduced myself, shaking hands, I encountered a proud descendant of the Minorcans. As he proudly explained his heritage, it meant absolutely nothing to me. Later I learned the Minorcans, from the tiny Spanish Island of Minorca in the Mediterranean, arrived in St. Augustine in 1777. The gentleman asked me where I was from and when I told him, "Jacksonville," he said with a sneering sense of superiority, *"Oh, you are from up north!"* As geographical chasms are measured, Jacksonville is a whopping 35 miles straight up U.S. 1 or I-95! The message was loud and clear: for this individual, Minorcan heritage made him superior. "I am "in" and you are not!"

When our heritage or immigration stories reveal the flight to or from suffering, enduring adversity or injustice, the stories have the capacity to be containers of transcendence. These stories reveal a progressive development: suffering produces endurance, endurance produces character and character produces hope. My Irish ancestors fled their homeland during the potato famine of 1847 to enter America on the bottom rung of the immigrant ladder. They were told "Irish Need Not Apply."

Social mobility has always been a possibility for second or third generation Euro-Americans, but a hundred years after the Civil War, the sons and daughters of slaves had to continue to fight for their Constitutional rights. Malcolm Little changed his name to Malcolm X when he realized tracing his heritage was futile. He was an Afro-American with a Euro-American name. He would rather remain anonymous than to maintain the identity of a Euro-American, knowing well that his ancestors were caught, captured, and brought to this land in slave ships against their will. Beyond our own borders, there were the fortunate few who had the foresight to flee the flames of Holocaust hate when Hitler ascended to power in 1933. In 1948 holocaust survivors and Jews throughout the Diaspora immigrated to Israel after the United Nations re-drew the maps of the Middle East and carved out the nation from Palestinian lands, creating conflict with Palestinians yet to be fully resolved.

These stories of our suffering become *containers of our character.* The narratives recall more than fact or fiction. They reveal something about us that is transcendent. One characteristic of transcendence is timelessness. Each generation strives to pass the mantle to the next generation; we live and die, but these enduring qualities of suffering, endurance, character, and hope live forever. These components transcend, go beyond, and share in an eternal truth. Eternal truth is timeless and it sews a seam stitching together generation after generation.[q] Heritage provides one criterion for belonging, acceptance, approval, and the conferring of an identity

Football

We may not be able to trace our lineage to a royal family, but there certainly are substitutes that enable us to be adopted into a clan or a tribe. Football is another one of those marketing dreams advertisers just absolutely live for! Minutes cost millions during the Super Bowl. No other sport quite captures the warrior fantasies of American men and women. I love football, and I am especially drawn to the contrasting strategies coaches employ to motivate, teach discipline, and build the cooperative component of becoming a team.

Football sublimates the two most primitive drives we have as human beings and makes those drives "acceptable"

---

[q] A clarifying distinction that needs to be made is to determine an important characteristic of these stories: (1) Are the stories instruments we need to *create a truth* we feel we need? Or, (2) Do these stories *reveal Truth*?

as long as they are contained within the rules of the game. These drives have to do with sex and aggression. In football, 11 warriors face off against 11 other warriors. Aggression is allowed as long as the act is a "clean hit." When violations occur, penalties are assessed for roughing the passer, unnecessary roughness, and in severe situations, fines and suspensions may be levied against an overly aggressive player. The target of the activity is for coaches and quarterbacks to choreograph these warriors to out-maneuver the opposing warriors and enter deep into the opponent's territory, the end zone, in this symbolic form of conquest. Points are awarded for the degree of difficulty for each act of subduing the adversary, six for putting the ball and the body over the line, three for the least of the athletes to kick the football through the uprights or one for the chip shot after a touchdown. At the end of the allotted hour for this contest, if my team subdued your team and conquered your territory more times, then my team wins and your team loses. Incidentally, although only one hour of playing time is allotted for this contest, the game can never be completed in less than three hours. The additional two hours are spent showing replays and selling the viewer stuff we do not need. This is why the marketing and advertising folks love the game of football! Games no longer end in a tie because we cannot stand it if nobody wins, so the contest goes into *Sudden Death Overtime*. Something very primitive is going on here, wouldn't you say? Now, let us add another piece of this Darwinian puzzle. We surround the playing field with half-naked women who jump up and down, jiggle and are capable of igniting any male fantasy. This is the final pen stroke to connect the marketing dots and directly access the male brain. We can sell the football fan anything from beer to trucks. Sex and aggression sell!

    During the fall season millions of college alumni and school fans of all ages dedicate Saturday to football across the United States. For diehard professional football fans, the re-enactments of wars between Babylonian city-states can be seen via professional football games on Sundays, Monday nights, and Thursday evenings. Wearing the team colors marks our identity with a city or campus. Pre-game eating rituals, known as tailgating, solidify the communal experience as rites of belonging, acceptance, and approval.

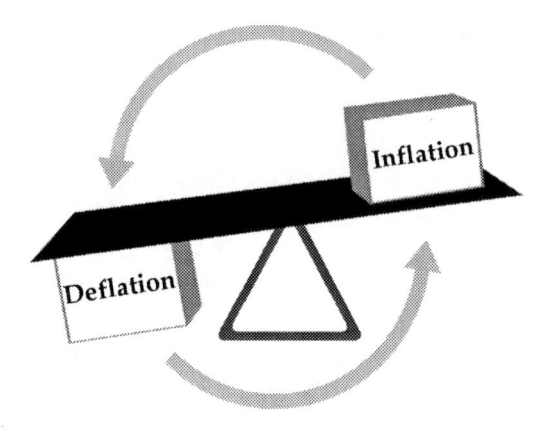

Figure 14

One of the psychological boosts fueling the inflation/deflation dynamic with sporting events is the added dimension of winning and losing. Historically, winning means victory, power, and superiority. Losing means dying. Winners are inflated, and losers are deflated. In the successful sublimation of aggression, a neighboring governor may wager to wear the team colors of her rival if her team loses. This public act of shame and humiliation seems tame when compared to the losing governor's head stuck on the end of a pole on the field!

In the football model, belonging, acceptance, and approval have clear boundaries of inclusion and exclusion and establishing who is in and who is out. In order for this model to work, one group has to be "inflated," and the other has to be "deflated."

Although these tensions in football are primarily sublimated and symbolic, this same dynamic is present when rivalries are no longer "play" but become "real." Among rivalries, the winning team is able to assert their superiority that will demoralize the defeated and deflated adversary. In subtle forms, among college or divisional rivalries, we may smile with those who portend superiority but shudder when demoralizing the adversary shifts to demonizing the enemy. This dynamic in extreme forms creates racism, terrorism, or fascism. In order to maintain White supremacy, Aryan superiority, or religious fanaticism, the deflated must be demonized, terrorized, and controlled by fear.

Group Dynamics

Our heritage, sports, and hobbies create identity transactions and opportunities to establish varying degrees of connection, which provide belonging, acceptance, and approval. The rule of thumb is the more distant the connection, the less likely a membership in the group will be life changing.

Pre-group involvement is represented by one-issue groups such as political action committees, environmental concerns, and so on may reflect how I think and feel about a particular area of my life. My only connection could be receiving a newsletter and writing checks, but I know the group is somehow "out there" representing my thoughts and advocating these positions in appropriate forums.

The level of demands required for acceptance into a group will run the spectrum of low demand (minimal involvement) to high demand (high involvement). Some groups exist with very little face-to-face interaction and loose networks of connection. For example, if I happen to be a fan of a radio talk show host, I identify with someone who is known as a local or national voice that expresses my own thoughts and feelings about a wide range of social or political views. I would also share this experience in common with the other listeners who are, in a sense, members of the same group.

By contrast, groups that lay claim to core values and ultimate concerns will create the greatest demands for loyalty, commitment, and sacrifice. The Marine Corp used a marketing campaign for new recruits that depicted square-jawed stern-faced uniform-wearing sword-carrying Marines standing at attention. The byline stated, *"We don't accept applications, we take commitments."* The higher the demand and intensity of the group the more the group will be involved in structuring and organizing an individual's life. The demands placed upon an individual who joins a bowling league and another who joins an Orthodox Jewish Synagogue are not the same. The difference involves the *levels of intensity* toward the core values, ultimate concerns, and creation of self-awareness. Bowling leagues may organize my Friday nights in direct competition to attending worship at the synagogue. Institutions and groups that demand my ultimate loyalty promise to organize or re-organize my life at the core!

The first level of group life involves a common interest, activity, hobby, or group sport offers belonging, acceptance, and approval around the interest held in common. At the most elementary level, my bowling team may help me to become a better *bowler*, but is not necessarily interested in me becoming a better *person*. Many groups that offer belonging, acceptance, and approval may not go "deep enough" for us and indeed may only attempt to meet these needs on a superficial level, unable to satisfy the deeper *longing for belonging that is transformational and life changing.*

The healthier the group, the greater the probability the group's intensity will focus on the individual member being placed, not in the role of receiving a group identity, but rather in a context for the discovery of "who I am." This distinction is critical because many groups promise core values and ultimate concerns but only deliver an institutionalized or group identity.

The second level of group life involves some type of face-to-face activity with an explicitly stated purpose to target making a difference in someone else's life. This may mean membership in service clubs, Habitat for Humanity, volunteering for disaster relief efforts, working in soup kitchens, actively involved in environmental efforts, tutoring children or adults, working with persons who have special needs, medical or dental service teams, or groups that form around in-depth studies involving life changing interest. Having interests in common with others establishes bridges of possibility for meaningful connection to take place.

Many service groups offer belonging, acceptance, and approval with the intended target to make a difference in the lives of other people. Lion's clubs target improving sight. Shriners groups provide pediatric care for children under the age of 18. The Shriner's web site states their purpose as "having fun and helping children." Certainly, nothing is wrong with having fun. I try to find a way to do this every day! Certainly, nothing is wrong with helping children! These groups target to create some form of improvement in the lives of *others* but not necessarily in the life of the *participant*. The Shriner's organization is rooted in the Freemasonry. This group dates back to when craftsmen gathered for shelter in a common lodge and became bound together by their own desire to be fraternal brothers. In this sense, belonging provides a level of safety for the members.

I once joined a service club when I was working in the inner city of Daytona Beach, Florida. The invitation to join came from someone who was both insistent and persistent. This person appealed to my sense of duty and responsibility with a certain amount of flattery. The club needed someone to help provide "spiritual direction." To underline the concern *they would even pay my dues!* It is nice to be wanted. It is nice to be needed. I joined the group and on most Thursday mornings, I woke up early to attend the breakfast meeting. I met a number of nice people during that time. If I did not wear my civic club pin to the meeting I would be fined a dollar, and the money would go to some unspecified cause. I attended an additional meeting in a neighboring community so the club could get 100% attendance for inter-club meetings. I sold football programs one evening in the pouring rain during the state high school football playoffs to raise money for the Police Athletic League. Several months after joining the organization, I received a letter from the national headquarters of the civic group. It was a fund raising letter, and it stated in the opening sentence, *"In some way our club has changed your life."* I thought about that statement for a long time. In terms of what we as members could agree upon as core values and ultimate concerns, I don't think so. I was certainly *busier* and *attended more meetings*, but I do not believe my life was changed. Not in ways I believe really matter.

I have a great deal of respect for service clubs. However, the target in service groups frequently focuses on *them* and not on *me*. The participant is not required to look inward at his/her own being, to examine his/her own character issues, or to chart a course for personal improvement. Persons may discover this level of belonging does not go "deep enough" and is unable to satisfy the deeper *longing for belonging that is transformational and life changing*. However, a commitment to make a difference in someone else's life kicks the level of involvement up a notch and fuels the possibility of the group evolving into a transformational community.

A third level of group involvement is the establishment and maintenance of transformational community. Transformational community arises when purposeful action is used to reach mutually agreed targets with energy, synergy, and cooperation. The persons reaching out are the ones who are also reached! *Lives are changed in both directions.* I become different because I make a difference.

Transformational groups target purposeful living through three core spiritual values: simple living, living non-reactively and non-violently, and living without enemies. Our western consumer culture is empty and shallow. It will never deliver what it promises. A national pancake house chain is currently advertising, "Come hungry – leave happy." I can visualize a seeker climbing a mountain to encounter a wise sage sitting on top of the mountain. The seeker asks, "What is the key to happiness?" The sage responds, "Pancakes." The message is this: consumption creates happiness. This message is so deeply embedded in our culture we often have to *step out of our culture* to see the happiness of others who consume very little. Happiness via consumption is our cultural lie.

Because of my extensive background in faith-based organizations, I have been directly and vicariously involved with short-term transformational groups. I have seen the long-term effects of lives changing in both directions. Many of these transformational groups started with an intended purpose to do medical, teaching, or construction projects throughout the Appalachian Mountains, the Caribbean Islands, Africa, Central and South America. I have witnessed hundreds of individuals experience deep and profound personal transformation as a result of these efforts. One consistent transformational theme revealed in the myriad of stories told upon their return involves seeing the fraudulent claims of our own consumer culture when viewed through the lens of a third world experience. In other words, stepping out of our culture into third world conditions creates awareness of our own cultural embedded-ness.

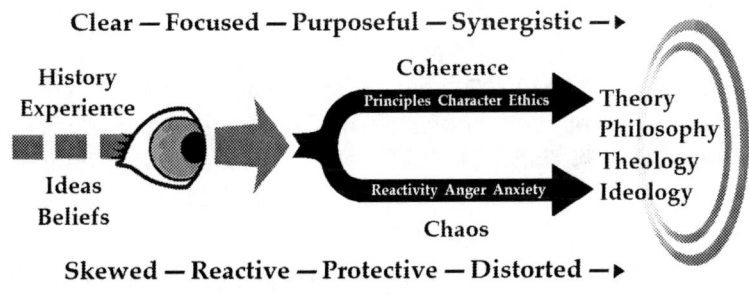

Clear — Focused — Purposeful — Synergistic —▶

History
Experience

Ideas
Beliefs

Coherence
Principles Character Ethics ▶ Theory
Philosophy
Theology
Reactivity Anger Anxiety ▶ Ideology
Chaos

Skewed — Reactive — Protective — Distorted —▶

Figure 15

As you will recall from chapters 1 and 2, our history and experience creates ideas and beliefs that establish the trajectories we will travel. Confronting our core values and beliefs may create our own personal tsunamis and the shaking of our foundations. The consistent theme in all these stories can be summarized this way: *"How can people who have absolutely nothing be so happy?"* When all the capitalist clutter is cleared away, the raw emptiness of what our culture promises to deliver and never does is exposed.

Two women, one a career church professional and the other a consultant with a national firm making a six-figure salary, reported on one of these trips they had recently made to Cuba. They were involved in bringing much needed funding to a remote area of this tiny island nation. They stayed in the home of a multi-generational household, and on the last night of the visit, an elderly matriarch of the family presented to each of these women a hand-made quilt. This matriarch was known in the community for her quilt making and this was her only means of income. She absolutely refused any payment since these quilts were a gift, and as each of these women held up the quilts, tears streamed down their faces. "They had absolutely nothing and they gave us all that they had."

Our culture has deeply embedded in our consciousness that happiness and consumption are intricately interconnected. It is a lie. I came home recently through the garage and mudroom and glanced over to the top of the washing machine. I saw a new detergent in a brightly colored box. The box read, "Gain – Joyful Expressions." I laughed and shook my head in disbelief. How anyone could connect the nonexistent dots between laundry detergent and joyful expressions is beyond me! Whether they use laundry detergents, automobiles, beer, or balderdash, marketing experts connect feelings with products. "If we buy this product we will feel this way." Fortunately, or unfortunately, this never works. We are often blind to the bombardments until we step out of this rat's maze and look at our world through the lens of a third world environment.

One of the functions of transformational community is to create awareness. We are frequently embedded in our own social and cultural enmeshment and need to step out in order to see it! After a stint in the Air Force, our son was a college student working on an associate degree in photography. He volunteered with a few others to go to a locally sponsored community known as "Family Renew." Family Renew was founded by faith-based organizations to provide short-term housing and to help families get back on their feet. In order to be admitted to Family Renew rigorous criteria must be met and maintained by the applicant families. Since these families cannot afford to pay for the usual class photos in the schools their children attend, Sean decided to take pictures of the children for no charge and to provide these photos for the parents. The afternoon he photographed the children he called to talk with his mother and me. He reflected on the experience and said, "I know I did not always have everything I wanted when I was growing up, *but I certainly had everything I needed.* I just had to call and thank you for everything you have done for me. Being where I was today made me see the world in an entirely different way." We beamed with pride when we heard his words. We knew we had passed on important and timeless values, ethics, and beliefs and he clearly got it! Several days later, he called and said he had been doing some "spring cleaning" in his small two bedroom one bath home. He indicated a growing sense of gratitude and appreciation for the things he had and a desire to do a better job of maintaining his material possessions. Lives were being changed in both directions. Stepping out of his culture into the culture of the homeless enabled Sean to see *his* world through a new lens. For Sean, the values embedded from family, the discipline he learned in the military, the skills he was acquiring from college and the opportunity to use his skills in serving the community all worked in concert and "clicked" to create a transformational community experience in creating awareness.

    Members of transformational communities are committed to core spiritual values of simple living, living non-reactively and non-violently, and living without enemies. Transforming reactive human behavior begins by intentionally creating awareness. Creating awareness involves cultivating mindfulness. Mindfulness involves knowing what we are doing when we are doing it. Self-awareness also involves living in the "ongoing awareness of awareness." Members encourage each other by living in awareness. By creating awareness, we create choice rather than living in a state of reactivity.

However, transformational group experience involves much more. This experience involves the choices we make, not the dogma, doctrine, or orthodoxy. It is about orthopraxy. Orthodoxy is about "right belief." Orthopraxy is about "right living." By living in awareness, members assist one another to assess threats, stop reactivity, hold the reaction, and heal the pain. The next chapter explores this process in detail.

Transformational groups follow the format of high demand – high intensity. The increased levels of intensity begin to approach those from our history and our primary connections: i.e. our families of origin. Primary connections are connections that have shaped us and exist within the immediate family. Relationships that re-create aspects of this intensity occur in committed relationships, therapy, group therapy, life accountability groups, or those groups that offer 12-step recovery based programs. The greater the level of intensity of the group, the greater the possibility the group may become a sanctuary for healing when members are carrying wounds from primary relationships and families of origin. Transformational groups functioning in this manner will serve as outposts for unconditional love and will help meet our needs for belonging, acceptance, and approval at a deeper level. When transformational groups are effective, they help in changing lives in *all* directions.

The highest level of group intensity beyond transformational groups involves counseling. It is also the most private and the smallest of groups. Sojourners come for counseling because their life has become **FRICKED.** They have become embedded in patterns of frustration, reactivity, internalization, conflicted thoughts, feelings, and emotions, and they have the knowledge or awareness of the enmeshment. These individuals are facing internal or external conflict. Counseling establishes an empathic environment, which holds the intensity of external and internal conflicts as they arise and creates a zone of safety. In this safe zone, an individual can be held and nudged toward new levels of personal and spiritual growth.

At times, present group conflicts serve as a screen and camouflage former wounds from our family of origin. This *prior* damage now surfaces in the form of *present* relational conflict. Strained relational conflicts frequently fuel internal conflicts. This is the nexus point where external and internal conflicts cross, converge, and intersect. External conflict involves strife, discord, estrangement, or broken relationships with a spouse, parent, child, employer, family member, or close friend. Internal conflict pushes us to resolve rear view mirror issues clouding our competence, distorting our ability to live effectively in the present, and to see hope.

Jay and Sheila

Let us look at how counseling worked as a high demand, high intensity, transforming experience for Jay and Sheila. The couple came to counseling after their divorce to explore whether or not reconciliation was possible. Having been married for a number of years, they had been trying to have a baby. They worked with a variety of fertility experts with no success. The year leading up to the divorce was a litany of agony for both of them. Failed attempts to conceive a child seemed to be at the heart of their pain, hurt, and disappointment, which is common for couples who are unsuccessful in these attempts. After being apart for a while, Jay and Sheila decided to try again to see if they could make the marriage work. This required opening old wounds.

During their work with me, an old wound opened up. Sheila brought up an issue, which demonstrated how *prior* damage had surfaced in the form of *present* relational conflict. Sheila complained about feeling ignored by Jay when they went out socially with other couples. She recalled one occasion when they went to dinner with another couple for Valentine's Day at a local restaurant. Jay became absorbed in the other couple and Sheila felt invisible. She further complained about Jay interrupting or correcting her stories. He would essentially "take them over." Sheila finally blurted, "You know, that's just like it used to be when I was growing up. My mother used to make me feel what I had to say or felt did not matter. When you treat me like that, I feel exactly like I did as a little girl. You know what they say, if you make a mistake once, shame on you. If you do it twice, shame on me. When I was a little girl I did not have any control over what they did to me, so shame on me, but I am not about to let it happen again." This was the nexus point where internal and external conflict converged.

Jay was somber, quiet, and reflective. He then launched into a story about his older brother, Mike. They were business partners and worked together six days a week. Jay spoke about growing up; the phone would ring and every call would be for his brother. This happened so many times Jay finally reached the point where he would answer the phone and when the caller asked…"Is this Mike?" Jay would respond, "Yes, this is Mike. What do you want?"

He yearned for the sense of belonging, acceptance, and approval Mike received and he did not. He felt like he was hidden in his brother's shadow. Jay was quiet and more reserved. Mike was more extroverted and outgoing. Growing up Jay would comment on or correct his brother's stories. Jay began to understand this as a compensating behavior developed as a way to expose Mike's flaws in an attempt to self-inflate by deflating Mike, thus making Jay "shine."

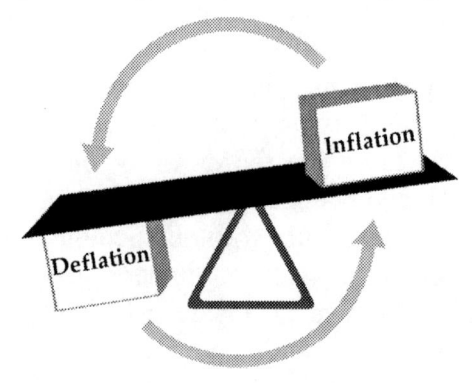

Figure 14

Being corrected made Sheila feel wounded and deflated which reminded her of the way she felt with her mother. Correcting made Jay feel inflated and powerful. Sheila had become the substitute for Mike, and Jay treated her the way he tried to treat his older brother. The internal and external conflict loops had now converged. Their work together shined new light on their relationship. They were able to interrupt a reactive pattern by creating awareness, assessing the threat, stopping the reactivity, holding the reaction, and healing their pain.

If we enter adulthood with collateral damage from our family of origin, we often find ourselves in relationships that *continue* the punishment and withhold our need for belonging, acceptance, and approval. By creating awareness of internal and external conflicts, reactive behavior can be transformed into purposeful patterns for living. Old hurts can begin to heal. In the safety of the counselor's office Sheila and Jay were able to successfully piece together how relational patterns in the present converged with their respective family issues from the past. The high intensity – high demand environment of counseling provided a transformational community for Sheila and Jay. In this community, their issues could be safely untangled and the relationship was able to heal.

Patterns of Connection in Relationships: Who We Choose and Why

As stated in Chapters 1 and 2, our history and experience creates ideas and beliefs, which in turn will establish a lens that affects how we see the world. In relationships this lens will also affect *what we see* and even more important, *what we do not see*. The family unit is the relational laboratory where we witness firsthand the experiments performed that shape our perceptions on how we deal with stress, manage conflict, solve problems, balance power, and raise children.

It is from this laboratory that we launch adolescents

and young adults into the process of dating and courtship, what I call the *"Dance of the Neanderthals."* Dating is the process through trial and error couples experiment with these issues and attempt to establish compatibility. In this experiment, couples seek to discover the answer to one question: "Can we get along with each other?" Each individual in the relationship brings an imprinted blueprint deeply embedded in the psyche from his or her family of origin. These relational impressions, imbedded, repeated, and reinforced during the formative years shapes the way we connect with others throughout our life. As we progress in our developmental patterns of physiological, psychological, and spiritual growth relationships take on different shapes and forms at distinctive ages and stages of our life. Adolescence establishes a shift in our significant connections as we move from parents to peers to seek acceptance and approval. In late adolescence and young adulthood, connections often involve unconscious *borrowing*. This *borrowing* is an attempt to find in another person what is *missing* in oneself. Marriages based upon unconscious borrowing tend to break down by mid-life. Another familiar tract is to find people who treat us in ways *familiar* with our childhood experiences. In a generic sense, we generally follow one of these four options in our own quest for compatibility:

1) Opposites attract
2) Replicate the familiar
3) Neither
4) Both

When **opposites attract**, we find people who help put us in touch with what is missing or repressed within the self. Emotions are without gender. Although males may have more testosterone, which may make them more naturally aggressive, there are no "male" or "female" emotions. When we were raising our children Brenda commented numerous times that she believed I was a better mother to the children than she was. I do not agree with her assessment, however, I believe she was referring at times to my emotional attunement to our children's needs.

We are all capable of experiencing the full range of human emotions. Crowley and Lodge state in as many words that the character played by Leonard Nimoy, Mr. Spock, from the Star Trek series on television and cinema, is not the ideal role model for men:

> "Men think they can separate reason and emotion, mind and heart, thinking and feeling. Having pulled off that amazing trick, they think they can put the emotional side on the back burner or ignore it completely. And they tend to believe they will be better men as a result. This is a mistaken notion. It is not a good idea and it is not possible. It is unhealthy and it is delusional. It goes directly against the grain as to how we were made."[46]

We do become culturally conditioned to the experience of certain emotions. Stereotypically little girls learn crying is acceptable and boys learn the opposite. Sally comes home from playing and she is sobbing. "Oh sweetheart! What is wrong? Come here and sit on my lap and let me hold you and you can tell me all about it!" Billy comes in sobbing and he hears; "What's wrong with you, you little crybaby? Did somebody take your bottle from you? Go back out there and do something about it! How are you going to learn to be a man?"

In our early developmental experiences, we quickly learn which emotions are acceptable and which emotions are not through our parents and peers. For example, Sally is out playing with a friend and comes in mad and hurt, and exclaims; "*I hate Mary. Mary took my doll! She would not give it back to me. I don't ever want to play with Mary. She is mean, and I hate her!*" Rather than just holding the child, calming and soothing her, a mother or father distressed by the intensity of their daughter's emotions might respond by saying; "You don't really *hate* Mary. You really *like* Mary.

She's your best friend. Why don't you go back over to Mary's house and play?" Therefore, Sally walks out of the house confused, and thinking, "Well, I thought I *hated* Mary but Mom and Dad say I really *like* her, and since they are bigger than me, they must be right. I guess I really do like her." Constant exposure to this type of response teaches the child not to trust his/her own feelings and emotions. Hate, rage, disgust, along with shame and humiliation are the difficult toxic emotions we all struggle to tolerate and digest. We naturally attempt to disown these emotions, projecting them on to other persons, groups, and nations or to ingest them, which may produce a somatization of illness and disease. We can literally stuff these emotions into our bodies and doing so can make us sick. If parents do not "allow" these emotions, or if they use their power to bully their children, the children quickly learn which emotions are acceptable and which ones are not. The child learns, "If I feel this way, Mommy and Daddy won't love me." The unacceptable emotions are the ones we learn to hide, disassociate, or repress. When I grew up in the Darwinian jungle, to get in a fistfight and cry would insure another beating, and include being heaped with humiliation and shame by male peers. Nothing was worse than losing a fight and showing up at school the next day! In the jungle of survival of the fittest, men learned as boys that crying is an expression of weakness. Men learn that sadness, hurt, humiliation and shame are not safe to feel or express. Culturally, these emotions are acceptable for women. In many relationships, women also "carry" or "hold" these emotions for their partner. Similarly, aggressive or assertive women are often labeled as a "bitch," a biting term used to humiliate by both genders in order to reel in traditional male traits expressed in women. In reality, emotions are not gender specific. No "male" or "female" emotions exist.

When opposites attract we find people who help us to be in touch with what is missing or repressed within the self. Extroverts find introverts. Persons who are audio or idea-oriented people, such as accountants, computer programmers, and engineers tend to find kinesthetic or feeling oriented people. Asking a computer programmer to tell us how she feels may be met with a deer in the headlights stare. In some relationships, one person does the thinking and the other does the feeling. When opposites attract we are looking for someone to be in touch with or fix what is missing in us.

When we **replicate what is familiar** we will find someone who treats us in ways that are familiar to what we have known while growing up. The hard wiring from infancy, childhood, and adolescence will often lead us to look for relationships to "plug in" to what is consistent with what we already know. If my childhood experience is punctuated by abandonment, I may choose someone who may ultimately abandon me. Abused children are at risk of abusing their own children, replicating the familiar, or partnering with someone who will continue the abuse. If parents treated us like royalty, we may look for worship and adoration.

The relationship field of dreams is frequently shattered by the dire circumstances created when the replication of the familiar re-creates and magnifies unresolved pain. We must clearly identify and successfully break these patterns of enmeshment, gain new insight, learn, and heal *before* re-engaging in new relationships. If not the result is often a serial set of relationships replicating the same unconscious and dysfunctional patterns. This pattern of replication appears to be cosmically magnetic. In deeply troubled moments of dire frustration, men and women have entered my practice in epidemic numbers with the same question about meaning for their lives: *"Why do I continue to attract the same kind of person? Is it written on my forehead? Their names change, but the circumstances and the situations are all too familiar, and it ends up déjà vu, all the same, all over again!"*

Why does it end up this way? It ends up this way because some people replicate the familiar. Men who have been controlled by their mothers find women who nag and tell them what to do. Women who have been sexually abused tend to attract men who have unhealthy sexual needs. In their current relationships, many sexually abused women report feeling as they did when they were being abused - being treated like an object, and often accompanied with scorn, shame, disgust, and ridicule. Boys who were raised to be the caregivers of their mothers or girls for their fathers end up suffering from emotional incest. Having won the shallow victory of eliminating a physically or emotionally absent parent in adulthood they become filled with a false sense of superiority, only to end up in relationships trying to be cheerleaders to depressed substitutes.

The patterns of replication can also follow our job or vocation. Chad, after many years in the role of a caring and effective chaplain, received a call to serve as a pastor in a local parish. The parish was embroiled in conflict. After several years, Chad found himself caught in the crossfire of competing factions. Chad's natural tendency was to calm and soothe the conflicted members of the congregation. Both groups wanted him on *their* side. When he tried to hold the tension and keep the groups together each group saw him as weak and ineffective. They began to attack him. Having grown up in a chaotic household with an alcoholic father, Chad began to experience the familiar feelings of frustration and failure. He tried unsuccessfully to hold the pain for his family so that "everyone would just get along," and now he felt the same frustration and failure in the parish. He could not control or fix the pain.

Neither is the compatibility option chosen as a deliberate, conscious choice about a partner. These choices align with repeatedly reactionary decision-making based on aversion, or a short list of negative traits that eliminate relationships. Since decisions made in reactivity are always driven by anger or anxiety, it does not take much to scratch the surface to uncover pain, hurt, and disappointment. "I am not going to marry someone who smokes, drinks, hangs out in bars, watches football, goes to synagogue, doesn't go to synagogue, is like my Dad, is like my Mom, etc." The neither choice is navigated through the negative. When pressed for a response an individual cannot articulate what he or she wants, but is perfectly clear about what he or she *does not* want.

Persons who find themselves back on the playing field in their 40s, 50s, and 60s tend to have a shorter list to eliminate undesirable qualities and characteristics in potential relational partners. One such dating relationship quickly ended for a couple in their early 50s. Bonnie's first husband was an attorney, an alcoholic, with a highly volatile temper. He frequently burst into bouts of rage and was verbally abusive to both her and their son. After the marriage ended, she met a highly successful car salesman. He easily charmed her; they were quickly sexually active and she soon moved in and set up household. He fit her criteria of being a "man's man" who enjoyed boating, liked to cook out on the grill, and who was also an alcoholic, abusive, and frequently burst into fits of rage. In counseling, she began to uncover the layers of her pain. Bonnie's father had been an alcoholic with a highly volatile explosive temper.

Although she had followed the "familiar" pattern based upon unconscious choices, she now set up a short list based upon her previous mistakes. Neither her previous husband the attorney, nor the car salesman had been involved in institutional religious rituals or practices. Having previously made the mistake of establishing physical intimacy before emotional intimacy, she vowed to maintain her celibacy and to shun all sexual advances, which eliminated everything but holding hands. Bonnie wanted a man who was spiritually compatible with her. She also wanted a man who wanted to have a relationship with her and not just her body. When she met Charles, a highly successful businessman, the early stages of the relationship went well with lunch meetings, phone calls, and e-mail correspondence. On the third date, Bonnie learned that Charles, although a spiritual seeker in a non-traditional sense, had serious doubts about institutional religious practices. That evening Charles tried to kiss Bonnie goodnight on the doorstep and she turned and offered her cheek. Charles soon discovered that his e-mails and phone calls were not being returned. Bonnie told Charles in a decisive moment she felt they were spiritually incompatible. She also told him she was not going to have sex until she was married. If given time they may have discovered they were more spiritually compatible than what she first thought. When Charles was trying to kiss Bonnie goodnight it raised her anxiety about sex and spiritual compatibility. Bonnie ended the relationship based upon these criteria on her short list.

Today relationships frequently begin on computer matchmaking and dating websites. The initial screening process, or dance of compatibility, is handled in a preliminary questionnaire phase. After the questionnaire is completed, the new member is presented with a computer-generated list of potential prospects based upon common interests, likes, and dislikes. Although the process intends to enhance the probability of establishing meaningful connection based upon mutually shared common interests, the process also attempts to eliminate negative components that may be aversive and reactive. This matchmaking process is only valid when questionnaires are honestly answered.

Both involve the combination of attraction and connection traits of when ***opposites attract*** and the ***replication of the familiar.*** Instead of the "either-or" of opposites attract and replication of the familiar, the answer is "both-and." These tendencies are more noticeable in relationships that are longer term. What may start out as **opposites attract** may evolve into a **replication of the familiar**. A relationship may start with the sharing of the traditional split between thinking and feeling with each partner assigned to one of these roles. When either partner in the relationship stops performing in the previously accepted role to the other partner it may trigger familiarity with a parent abandoning the family from childhood or similar type experiences.

One couple, Ben and Tammy, were married for more than 40 years when I met them. They had been compatible and had experienced very little marital difficulty over the course of raising three children. They retired from their native Pennsylvania and moved to Florida. They came to me in an attempt to come to terms with an adult "problem child." Ben brought documentation from his daughter's lifetime of difficulty and despair. Her problems first started in infancy. They had been steadily documented through her childhood, adolescence, and adulthood. Her resume included a repertoire of psychiatrists, psychologists, and psychotherapists. She had been assigned just about every diagnostic category in the manual including borderline personality disorder and bi-polar personality disorder. From the time of being a toddler, she was prone to fits of rage, fighting, and aggressive behavior. As an elementary school student, she was diagnosed as having a defiant personality disorder. As an adolescent the only way she could calm herself was through drug and alcohol abuse. She ended up in abusive relationship after abusive relationship, pregnant twice with both pregnancies ending with abortions. She had been in and out of prison and was always on the verge of homelessness. Her father always rescued her but now he was through. Her mother had handled the crises from this point forward in a limited capacity. Her adult siblings wanted little or nothing to do with their sister. They were frustrated with their parents for their co-dependant behavior and for repeatedly rescuing their sister. With tears in his eyes Ben pleaded, "What would you do if it was your own daughter? Would you let her sleep on the streets? Would you let her become homeless?" This couple had known numerous dark nights of the soul and had spent decades in despair and grief.

Their daughter had provided a continual crisis for Ben and Tammy, a by-product of which was a constant source of connection for the two of them. From a family systems perspective, I began to wonder if this child had been a symptom bearer for some dysfunctional pathology in the family and if in some way she was providing the glue to hold the family together. Although it was clear in my mind their daughter had entered the world with some form of chemical imbalance, one other thing was clear. Ben was the one who provided calming and soothing to his wife and had done so during the course of the relationship. Ben was the big picture guy and Tammy was the manager of the details. They described it as a near-perfect partnership. Ben was also the peacemaker in the family. In refusing to be the rescuer of their daughter there was a shifting in emotional roles taking place.

    After working several weeks with Ben, he asked if it would be all right if he brought Tammy with him so they could both get on the same page with issues concerning their daughter. Although initially this was the focus of our work, our attention soon turned to Ben and Tammy's relationship. 40 years of pent-up relational lava began to erupt out of this marriage. It was a paradoxical dilemma for Ben to both "calm and sooth" Tammy and confront her with his grievances, but he was now in a position to do so since he had "resigned" from his former role. Their method of dealing with conflict had been for him to avoid it and to try to do whatever it took to please Tammy. Now Ben was over it! Culminating in years of frustration, he never felt as if he had been able to please his wife. She volunteered him for fix-it jobs with neighbors and friends without his permission in order to make herself look good. She organized his time and told him what to do and when to do it. He was vehement in describing incident after incident when he consulted with her, she agreed, he thought they were in a synergistic mode, and the results were never good enough. In retirement Ben was doing some woodworking and finish carpentry and was working on chair railings in their dining room. When Tammy returned home after running errands, she did not like the results and demanded he change the position of the railings. The chair railings proved to be the straw that broke the camel's back.

    In Tammy's defense, this was the style of relating, developed over years, which seemed to work. Ben and Tammy were able to work through these issues and change their patterns of decision-making and dealing with conflict. They were able to break out of the unconscious connections involved with the **opposites attract**, and Ben was able to see that the **replication of the familiar** was not only the way he felt with Tammy, but also the way he felt as a child with his mother.

The unconscious connections involved when **Opposites attract, Replication of the familiar, Neither** or **Both** frequently become the terrain we struggle to conquer in the first half of life. Successfully passing through this developmental hoop shifts our search for connection to creating an evolved awareness in all our relationships, especially those with whom we share deeper levels of significance. These relationships hold much promise in the establishment of intimacy, closeness, and interdependence. We discover we no longer search for someone to complete, heal, or fix what is missing in us. Each of us must discover healing and wholeness within. *Quality* becomes a meaningful reality, which begins to define the importance of our connections. All souls require sustenance and replenishment from beyond and within. Once successful in the development and establishment of feeding our own soul, fully conscious relationships have the potential to add richness, emotional wealth, and meaning to our existence.

The Conscious Relationship Contract

When couples stand and vow to each other; "to have and to hold from this day forward, for better or worse, for richer or power, in sickness and in health, to love and to cherish, till death do us part," they establish the broad parameters of their commitment. However, in our naiveté, these parameters do not provide us with *effective ways, means, or methods* to live out these commitments. Most states require far more from applicants obtaining a driver's license than a marriage license.

The difference between living life with a cellmate or a soul mate becomes intentional when couples establish a conscious relationship contract. When couples learn how to keep from stomping on each other's toes, they learn how to get out of the drama and to dance their own unique dance. This contract establishes an agreement on how to deal with stress, manage conflict, solve problems, how male and female relationships balance power, and raise children. Each area is targeted with a purposeful intentionality to achieve a mutually desired result.

The Conscious Relationship Contract

| 1. Manage Stress |
| 2. Solve Problems |
| 3. Deal with Conflict |
| 4. Balance Power |
| 5. Raise Children (Blended family, ect.) |

Figure 16

Every builder uses a blueprint to build a building. A pilot would not fly a plane without a flight plan. If you became the CEO of I.B.M., G.M., or some other national or multi-national corporation you would be handed a thick document. This document would outline the specifics of when you would meet with boards of directors and stockholders. You would be expected to cast vision for the company and set direction. You would receive an outline of the rules, roles, tasks, and responsibilities of your position and what remuneration and compensation packages you would earn. This document would constitute your employment contract. But if you went to work at Papa Hull's Seafood Market and had a problem you would go talk to Papa Hull. In other words, the more *organized* a system is the greater the probability the rules, roles, tasks, and responsibilities of *how* the relationship is supposed to work will be defined. The more *unorganized* the system, the greater chance the group just makes it up as they go. On an organizational flow chart, a committed relationship or marriage falls somewhere *below* Papa Hull's Seafood Shop unless the individuals in the family system have created a conscious relationship contract.

Each component in this model requires the development of an intentional strategy for couples to establish their own methods for making their marriages work. In our present reality, relationships do not just happen. Relationships require work. The conscious relationship contract establishes a blueprint or a flight plan for couples to create a working model of *how* the relationship is going to work. This is an ongoing work in progress designed to establish an intentional environment for the continuous improvement of the relationship. The model also works in businesses and volunteer organizations. Veering off in this direction would take us off course and so a design for the conscious relationship contract will be explored in an additional work.

The conscious relationship contract provides a model for looking at the microcosm, or the particular, of managing relationships in a way that brings clarity and sanity. Against this backdrop is the macrocosm or the global context. We shall take a look at what is happening around us in the bigger picture and the effects this is having in the realm of our connections. In other words, how does the big picture affect the little picture?

Turn the Page: The Shift Of Identity Into The Post Modern Cultural Context

Some cultural historians date our present cultural shift from the end of World War II and the birth of the baby boomers. Others point to the breakdown of authority and institutional trust characterized by the radical change and social upheaval of the sixties including the sexual revolution, the civil rights movement, and the Vietnam War. Still others point toward the collapse of communism and the end of the Cold War.

From a historical perspective, major cultural shifts have always required changes in methods of transportation. Early cities usually developed on or near oceans, rivers, lakes, or streams in order to provide food and transportation. Caravan and trade routes were possible only after the domestication of camels, horses, and donkeys to carry goods to new markets. Sailing ships capable of circumnavigating the globe made it possible for western European nations to colonize the world. During the height of British colonialism, the sun never set on the British Empire. I spent an entire day in London's British museum with wide-eyed amazement; each room kept me spellbound. The British Museum contains artifacts and treasures from almost every culture in the world. The only way those British explorers would be able to please the royalty writing the expedition checks was to purchase or steal their plunder and bring it back home.

The invention of the steam engine and the locomotive eventually linked the east and west coasts in the United States by rail as well as the continents of Europe and Asia. The development of military and commercial air travel before and after WW II provided the infant stages of what is now a massive network of national and international airports along with the airline carriers who provide this service. The passage of Eisenhower's National Highway Defense Act of 1956 helped to create the infrastructure of interstates in the event we needed to move troops quickly north, south, east and west. In that defining moment, the United States decided private transportation would prevail over public transportation. Think of the staggering effect this decision made on automakers in Detroit and Tokyo not to mention foreign policy among the oil rich nations in the Middle East, which has included two Gulf Wars! If we stop to feel the earth shaking beneath our feet and consider the net results of the passage of the National Highway Defense Act, the economic and environmental impact, both positive and negative, it is staggering.

One of the net effects from all this is that we live in an era of tremendous mobility. In rural areas of North

Florida, many small towns are only ten miles from each other. The reason for the establishment of these towns within these proximities involves the *amount of time and distance to travel by a horse-drawn wagon in one day.* This type of consideration for current development of communities would be considered absurd. The transportation revolution in the last century made it possible for families to be spread out far and wide. Automobile or jet transportation make it possible for us to be anywhere in the country in a matter of hours or days. Our country's pioneers moving westward might take a year or longer to reach their destination.

From Urban to Rural

When I moved from Hollywood, Florida, a bedroom community of Ft. Lauderdale and Miami, to rural North Florida, I spent about six months trying to figure out my new environment. The rural environment was totally alien to me. Madison, Florida, is a beautiful community of 4000 in the city and about 17,000 in the county. There were more people located in a 10-mile stretch from Young Circle in Downtown Hollywood to our home than I would see in the entire county of Madison. The city's population has not wavered since the Civil War, and only recently began to grow. In beautiful antebellum homes with front porches, I would visit with people, sip iced tea, and listen to their stories. What I heard absolutely amazed me. These wonderful people would tell me stories about their parents, their grandparents, and their great-grandparents. They would discuss who was related to whom, where people used to sit in the church, and the idiosyncrasies of their ancestors.

I was baffled by these stories. I remember asking my dad when I was growing up where the McNeil's were from and he had a one-word answer, "Georgia." That was it. My father's name is George Washington McNeil and he was a junior. The best I have been able to figure out is that immigrant families would often name their children after American heroes as a way of trying to bequeath to their children acceptance in this nation of immigrants. Remember at this time shopkeepers and factories in New York City openly displayed signs that stated, "Irish Need Not Apply." In all probability, my great-grandfather was a small boy when he left Ireland, sometime during the potato famine of 1847. My mother's family, Holloway, was from England and this was all I knew about my family heritage. The heritage issue really did not matter to me.

On nearly every porch, in every rocking chair, and with every glass of iced tea, I would hear stories of ancestry dating back for generations. Why? What were they trying to tell me? I struggled to make sense and find meaning in their stories. Every person is a living human document, and I have always been fascinated and curious about what motivates, and makes us be who we are. Future mechanics are found in the garage as children taking apart clocks, radios, and power tools. Later they may grow up to do the same work with automobile engines or other repairable items. Children who enjoyed dissecting frogs in biology class may end up as veterinarians, doctors, or surgeons. My interest has always been in people. What moves us and makes us go? What gives people a sense of coherence and holds our lives together? I love people; I love listening to their stories. I never cease to be fascinated by persons who always have something to teach me.

The sense of connection is extremely strong in smaller communities where life continues to be less affected by the stress of post-modern society represented in urban cultures. Tommy, Billy, and Ashley Beggs were second-generation funeral directors in the community. Their father started the first funeral home in Madison County. They have since turned over the family business to the next generation. In the heritage of Alex Haley's *Roots*, I often teased Tommy Beggs and called him the local griot (oral historian). He could tell family stories going back several generations, and he knew the history of Madison County better than any individual could possibly imagine. He knew the formal networks of communication and the informal networks. He called me on a Thursday afternoon to tell me about the graveside service a family wanted conducted on Saturday afternoon. The service was for a woman who moved away from Madison: she had been gone for 50 years. She was returning home to be buried. Knowing both weekly papers in the community were on the stands on Thursday, I suggested the family might want to wait until Sunday afternoon. I told him I could make an announcement on Sunday to the church community. If anyone remembered the woman they could attend the service but only if they were aware of her death. Tommy said emphatically to me, "No problem." He then announced, "We'll just get an early edition of the evening news." Since I knew there was no "early edition" and there was no "evening news," I was puzzled and confused. With a grin, Tommy picked up the phone and called "Miss Clara". "Miss Clara, I need an early edition of the evening news. So-and-so has died. You remember her, don't you? She was Aunt Josie's third cousin on the Bennett side of the family, and she married that Carter fellow and moved to Panama City. That's right. She was a schoolteacher. The graveside service will be Saturday afternoon at 2:00 p.m. Do you think you can get the word out?" Tommy again smiled as he hung up the phone. On Saturday, at 1:55 p.m., I drove into the cemetery. There were 150 people milling around the gravesite waiting for the service to begin. I could not believe my eyes! This was a dire contrast to graveside services I held in Broward and Dade County when at times the only people in attendance would be the funeral director and the trustee of the estate from the bank.

The Contrasting Distinctions of Urban and Rural: Connection vs. Alienation

So what is the difference? The rural model is a *model of connection*. The urban model is a *model of alienation*. Death in a larger cultural context may go unnoticed or be anonymous. Death is important in a smaller community. Funerals become a time for connection, for telling and re-telling of stories, and for incorporating the change into the larger story of who we are as individuals and as a community. In an urban area, we may not even know our neighbors on either side or who might be in the next condo. In a smaller community, anonymity may be impossible to achieve. There were people who attended church in Madison who said the reason they came to church was *so other people wouldn't keep pestering them about why they did not attend.* The mores and folkways for social control were strong, as were the social pressures to conform. At times the price tag for connection was intrusiveness "because everybody knows and talks about your business whether you want them to or not." However, there were no truer words than: "People will talk about you all the time, but when you need them they will really be there for you." I was living in Madison during my mother's three-month hospitalization in intensive care two hours away in Jacksonville. I commuted back and forth, trying to hold together church, family, and self. The womb of care these loving people provided for me and my family will never be forgotten. As painful as that experience was, anonymity and alienation would have only made it worse. I was connected to a community of care.

One morning, in that shadowy area between sleep and wakefulness, creeping into my consciousness came the dawn of new meaning. I was beginning to understand what I was hearing and why it was important to know. They were telling me about their identity. Identity was determined by heritage. *Re-telling heritage stories maintained the connection between past and present.* Although you may get whiplash from the following sentence, what I was hearing could be succinctly stated: ***Who we are is who we were and who we were is who we are!*** In the Hebrew Bible, the patriarchal and matriarchal traditions establish the dual needs of both identity and connection. Within Judaism, the sons and daughters of Abraham and Sarah, Isaac and Rebekah, Jacob, Leah, and Rachel link the last generations in line with the first among this heritage of promise. Judaism has provided an extremely strong sense of connection, which has continued for more than 3500 years, and this faith tradition continues today. The global powers of Babylon, Persia, Greece, and Rome have long since fallen. The Byzantine era has come and gone. As previously mentioned, at one time the sun never set on British colonies throughout the world. The thousand-year reign of the 3rd Reich never made it, and the Soviet Union has crumbled. However, the religious cult and the practice of the faith of a nation that were once slaves in Egypt, continues to provide a sense of connection and coherence with twelve tribes, scattered throughout the world. The sense of connection has endured.

The insight finally began to sink in. I was beginning to understand what was making many of the people in this rural North Florida community "tick." I decided to test my hypothesis. I was invited to be the guest speaker at a noon meeting for a service club and used this opportunity to share these insights for the occasion. I spoke about how I had been perplexed at the stories I had been hearing. I spoke about my fascination with the heritage and the ancestral linkages, and cultural protocols demanded not to speak badly about anybody because everyone is related to everyone else. I told the group I had finally figured them out; *they were all Jews*.

Although by no means were either they or I anti-Semitic in any way, my listeners were visibly stunned. I used the moment of shock to let what I had said sink in and went on to speak about the importance of patriarchs and matriarchs, both living and dead. I spoke about how those stories were told over and over until they became a part of an accepted "truth," an oral tradition, finally written down lest it be forgotten. I spoke about how proud they were of where they lived and the importance of their connection with the "promised land," where generational natives often spoke about putting up fences to keep other people from entering the county. Finally, shaking their heads in agreement, they understood.

Joseph Chilton Pearce in his book, *The Crack in the Cosmic Egg: New Constructs of Mind and Reality*, writes about these phenomena in the larger context of culture, history, and myth. Pearce states,

> "Archaic cultures had a skimpy history at best, but they possessed rich myths, traditions, and symbols, giving *continuity, purpose, and meaning* (emphasis added). Ancestors, for instance, played a vital role. *Recitation of one's lineage gave a secure place in time, a sense of personal participation in a long drama* (emphasis added). Genealogy, learned from memory and a half-symbolic fantasy, often reached back to the very gods. Ancestor worship expressed an archetypal imagery indicating a cultural continuity with the whole scheme of life. One's forebears had not just "joined the god," but were, in effect, the gods themselves. Jesus' Fatherhood of God, Sonship of man, Father Abraham, and "before Abraham was, I am," indicate this shaping of a god by the whole history of man."[47]

The Post Modern Cultural Context: The Defining Differences of Identity

From this community and in this context one issue became increasingly clear to me: Identity arises from these vital connections. In the model presented by traditional modernity, *Identity flows from the sense of connection with family, both past and present.* The generational connection provides a type of linear "grounding" in time, place, and history. It also provides a way of linking the self in history to what is "beyond time" and spans the bridges of our own mortality by providing this connection. The self becomes a link in a chain connecting the past to the present and a baton to pass on to future generations.

Throughout the history of culture and civilization, connection established within family and community has provided the dominant way for individuals to meet connectional needs. It has provided a major source for *meaning* in our relationships. Within our era of rapid change, characteristic of our post-modern culture, there has been a large-scale dissolution of this component of connection. The type of connection prevalent in Madison, Florida, and in smaller communities everywhere is largely extinct and nonexistent in metropolitan urban areas. Smaller sub-communities in urban areas do not provide the same sense of belonging. These sub-communities are frequently organized around issues of *safety*. Homeowners and condominium associations band together with the intent to maintain their high standards and keep out the unwanted. Concerned citizens establish Crime Watch neighborhoods. These groups band together in an effort to protect their homes, neighborhoods and to guard against suspicious activity. Ironically, the street gang also bands together to "protect their turf." Remote rural areas in our present culture provide the last remaining remnants of the Walt Whitman World. Alienation in post-modern culture has replaced connection.

Employment opportunities were limited in this rural community. Harvesting pinesap for manufacturing turpentine had been a major revenue source in the early 1900's, but had long disappeared. A meat packing plant processed different kinds of meat for a major supermarket chain. The school system, the community college, and a prison were the current major employers. Small family businesses and a few local retail stores composed most of the local economy. Growing trees, farming, and raising livestock provided an income and livelihood for landowners.

As my tenure in this community lengthened, I began to notice trends with the young adults. Some remained at home. Many who were from families who were more economically affluent would leave town for colleges and universities. I was surprised to see many of the young adults who left for college and universities return to this rural area after obtaining an education. Employment was mostly limited to the school systems, or college graduates would find jobs in Tallahassee and commute 60 miles each way or to Valdosta an 80 mile round trip. As I listened to these returning graduates, I began to detect patterns in their stories. They often expressed conflicted thoughts, feelings, and emotions as they related to making life work in urban America.

This is what I learned and what they taught me. Life

in the corporate culture defines identity around the issue of *competence*. If we move to Houston, Charlotte, New York, San Francisco, Seattle, or Atlanta, these communities could care less who our mother, our grandfather, or our great uncle happens to be. If our primary sense of identity coheres around our sense of *competence*, our orientation in time tends to be toward the *present and the future*. If our primary sense of identity coheres around our sense of *connection*, our orientation in time tends to be *past and present*. Identity based upon competence is portable, whereas identity based upon connection is not. We can carry our competence with us, but we can't pack our relationships in a travel bag and carry them to a metropolitan area. The college graduates expressed feeling alienated, insignificant, and alone and often complained the urban jungle created too much stress and conflict.

Global Connectivity and Instant Communication: Our Means of Transportation in the Post-Modern World

The Internet may very well represent the change in transportation for the post-modern world. *No longer must I travel to expand markets or increase mobility. I can now bring the world to myself.* Satellite technology makes it possible for me to have access to any type of music or any type of movie any time I want. Cell phones are now common among middle school and older elementary children. Text messaging has created compact cryptic communication. Cell phones programmed with Global Positioning Systems make it possible for individuals to be tracked down if required by emergencies or to meet friends.

The Internet has become a major means of connection and commerce to the world. Holiday shopping requires reduced effort since a mouse is much easier to navigate than a mall. Posting resumes for jobs or relationships are common ways of networking on line. Throughout the world, our global economies increasingly become enmeshed as the

Internet continues to create a shrinking of the global village. Urban and rural areas alike now share the common bridge of the information highway as both a ways and means of connection. The Internet is one of the major sources of news and information rapidly replacing television, newspapers, and magazines. My adult children are part of a generation that never read a newspaper, and what news they get comes via the Internet. E-mail and instant messaging have become an accepted way of daily rapid communication and even these methods have become passé among young adults.

Posting or sending digital electronic pictures on line between sender and receiver creates the *visual* effects of connection. The missing pieces of the digital age are *touch, emotion, and involvement.* These traits are defining components of connection. Connection is compromised when these components are absent. As fascinating as this technology is and the worlds opened by these means, the Internet cannot replace essential human interaction and connection. Social networking programs such as Facebook, My Space, and Twitter attempt to fill the void and compensate for face-to-face connection in our post-modern world. Wall to wall on Facebook cannot replace the connection we experience face-to-face. We may be like baby monkeys in the previously mentioned experiment, but instead we are opting for the wireless surrogates.

The introduction of the Internet into our daily life has also created a myriad of new problems. Pornography, once wrapped in brown paper and sold on magazine racks, is now available in the home by a simple point and click of a mouse. Roughly 10 to 15 % of my counseling practice involves persons in trouble via the Internet. Wesley, a married male in his early 30s, reported an addiction to online chat room masturbation. (I never could figure out *how he could type and do that!*) He had a sexual problem with premature ejaculation compounded by a spouse who had difficulty reaching an orgasm. He did not feel competent in his ability to *please* his spouse sexually. Since the unconscious mind works to keep us from failure, this alternative means of pleasure and release provided him with a failsafe method of no-risk self-satisfaction. He would use his computer to go online, meet someone in a chat room, and from his keyboard to hers they typed provocative statements to each other while they masturbated. This essentially amounts to anonymous sex. We have arrived at an extremely frightful place in human history. Today, sex in the free-range open market comes loaded with the potential for sexually transmitted diseases, providing a lifetime of physical and emotional scars, or even death. What may be exceedingly more terrifying is no-risk sex without touch, emotion, or involvement. This is *alienation at its worst.*

Wesley reported feeling conflicted about this practice. He began to feel caught in the horns of a dilemma. Although this practice provided him with physical relief and reduced the stress of trying to please his wife, he would later report feeling guilty and would feel he had been unfaithful to her. His fantasy was beginning to fail. Cyber-sex is the epitome of a schizoid pseudo-connection. It is *relationship without touch*, with the exception of touch he is having with himself. The practice is also extremely narcissistic. Having this type of relationship in fantasy is essentially a relationship one has with *one's self*. In this medium, the "other person" is essentially *created in the mind of the person having the fantasy*. "Lauren," who claims to be a 24-year-old virgin with measurements of 38-24-36, could in fact, be Bill, a 270 lb. steel worker from Pittsburgh.

The Internet, our global means of transportation and communication in our post-modern cultural context, will not satisfy our basic needs for community. In fact, it presents obstacles for us with one of the defining components we face in our post-modern cultural context: alienation vs. connection.

The Post-Modern Cultural Context: Alienation vs. Connection

Our culture is experiencing a radical cultural shift in the breakdown and estrangement of primary core connections. This reality has created intense feelings of alienation, loneliness, and abandonment. In the initial meeting with a new sojourner, I usually ask a series of informal questions. I will conduct this informal inventory and ask about family members, friends, and their location. I will ask how these persons rate the *quality* of relationships they maintain with these people. I do this as a way of surveying their relational webs of connection. The quality of an individual's connection matrix is a diagnostic tool for factoring emotional distress and depression. Isolation and withdrawal are quick, down and dirty indicators of depression. The higher the level of connection in meaningful relationships directly correlates to a higher quality of emotional, mental, spiritual, and even physical health.

As I gather this information, I find the cultural context for parents, step-parents, brothers, sisters, half-brothers, and half-sisters to be commonly scattered about the country. Children rarely grow up and live in the same house, or neighborhood, with the same set of parents and friends from birth to leaving home.

In current contemporary Western cultures, we are experiencing a seismic shift in the understanding of self and identity beyond what we have known from our past. We currently live in the middle of one of the greatest cultural shifts the world has ever known. In the ongoing evolution of what Alvin Toffler called the post-industrial revolution, he was the first to tell us our culture is facing a rising tide.[48] He identified three waves of economic development. The first wave involved everything that preceded the Industrial Revolution. The second wave began with the onset of the Industrial Revolution. In Toffler's view, Western capitalism and civilization are now in the midst of another huge cultural shift, indicating a move from the industrial revolution to the post-industrial revolution. The industrial base is no longer the manufacturing of steel and the production of widgets but the brokering of information and technology.

One of the by-products of this shift is alienation. Alienation is the antithesis of connection. In essence, *alienation is disconnection.* The disconnection is from the self, others, community, and culture. Relationships become anonymous and meaningless. Individuals feel life is weighing them down, and they are drowning in a sea of social, cultural, and vocational insignificance.

Rock lyricist and performer Bob Seger expresses the cultural context of alienation in his classic hit, ***"Feel Like a Number."*** [49]

> I take my card and I stand in line,
> To make a buck I work overtime
> Dear sir letters keep coming in the mail,
> I work my back till it's racked with pain
> The boss can't even recall my name,
> I show up late and I'm docked,
> It never fails
> I feel like just another
> Spoke in a great big wheel
> Like a tiny blade of grass
> In a great big field
> To workers I'm just another drone
> To ma bell I'm just another phone
> I'm just another statistic on a sheet
> To teachers I'm just another child
> To IRS I'm just another file
> I'm just another consensus on the street
> Gonna cruise out of this city
> Head down to the sea
> Gonna shout out at the ocean,
> Hey it's me!
> And I feel like a number
> Feel like a number
> Feel like a stranger
> A stranger in this land
> I feel like a number
> I'm not a number
> I'm not a number
> Dammit I'm a man
> I said I'm a man

The song expresses the struggles of living life feeling anonymous, frustrated, impersonal and insignificant. Junk mail, the IRS, and even his employer do not know his name.

He is just another spoke in a great big wheel. The writer takes his frustration of anonymity out of the city and cries out in pain to declare his significance to the sea. Without a clear target for his grievances, he addresses the vast ocean in protest, "I am *not* a number, *dammit,* I am a *man!"*

These feelings expressed in Seger's lyrics are just under the surface of contemporary culture. You know what this is like:

- If you have contacted a business, organization, corporation, or government agency and attempted to talk to a *person* instead of an automated machine
- If you have tried to undo the quagmire of an identity theft
- If you have attempted to apply for FEMA aid
- If you have tried to contact an insurance adjustor after a natural disaster
- If you have attempted to obtain a building permit
- If you have tried to navigate through managed care to get a medical referral or see a specialist
- If you have been denied medical coverage because you have a pre-existing medical condition
- If you have had to collect child support from a deadbeat dad
- If you have been unemployed for a lengthy period of time or been downsized out of a job
- If you have had to live in your car and stand in line for a hot meal at a soup kitchen.... then you get the picture.

Alienation evokes the dull pain of despair, helplessness, and hopelessness. Underneath the layers of alienation are the need for connection, and an instinctual *longing for belonging.* The idyllic world described in the introduction of this chapter is far from the reality of those who feel torn from the fabric of the traditional forms of family and faith. The cultural duct tape of modernity, epitomized in such television classics depicting family life as *Father Knows Best* and *Leave it to Beaver,* has unraveled in our postmodern world.

Bryce

Bryce, a talented young sophomore in high school, expresses both ends of this spectrum of alienation and a longing for connection in a short story he wrote after his mother announced she was leaving home and divorcing his father. The shock, anger, and rage devastated Bryce as he searched to make meaning out of the disaster of divorce facing his family. He titled the story Linguini Salad, a sacramental meal of hope and promise he longed to share with his mother.

Linguini Salad

I had never been that attached to the idea of the family unit, at least I didn't show it. And that is now one of my biggest regrets. In the back of my mind there was always a mother, a father, one house. That is how it was and that is how it was always going to be. I know now that my assumption was wrong. Last fall I went through the most difficult time in my short-lived life. My mother made the announcement that she would be getting a divorce from my father and would be moving out. That cold night my mother told me I was in tears, in shock and enraged. I was so angry with her, but I couldn't find valid arguments to make against her decision. Only a pleading "Please!" or a "No!" would spit out of my mouth. I spent that night talking to myself, asking how or why over and over, over and over. I still don't have the answers.

She sat us down. The family watched as she wept with the knowledge of how profound an impact she was about to make on all of our lives. Those were not words that came from her mouth. They were earthquakes that shook my foundation and everything that was built upon it, until it was nothing more than merely a foundation. I stormed out of the house, out into the cold night where the only thing that was clear to me was my breath. My voice pierced the dark blue sky with words I am sure the neighbors weren't interested in. I began hurling things from the garage, an easy outlet for such difficult emotion. My mother walked out of the house to leave for the first time. After giving her explanations to my siblings she was going home, her new home. And she tried to talk to me but my ears would not accept anything she had to offer them. My father, furious for the condition his former wife had me in, was screaming, and I could understand none of it. The mini van I was so accustomed to seeing in my driveway was going on a one-way trip. The taillights blinked goodbye and she was gone. Gone for good. After screaming and throwing and punching the concrete took its toll on me I could only lay there with a terrible headache, and a broken vision of our perfect family.

After months passed, and I saw my first Christmas between two households turn into New Years, and spring turn to summer, I have gotten over the initial pain and anger (for the most part anyways). The change is starting to settle in, but I am still in the process of forgiving her or whomever it is that I am upset with. I am still uneasy with things, and my moods are much more varied nowadays; especially when I am at home or during one of the passing moments that I actually see my mom. I catch myself thinking about her, or seeing a picture of the five of us in one of those pictures you buy at a theme park when they capture you in mid-ride. I can't help but feel lost with this new life of mine.

My innocence seems far-gone now. I know that this world is not perfect. But for years, when I was just a boy without a care in the world except for what bedtime story my mom was going to read me, I thought perfection had a shot. I know now that my wishful thinking was wrong. I visited her apartment for the first time the other day. She has lived there for nearly a year. It was good to see her; it had been a while. But seeing the furniture, the barstools, the wine, the tiny kitchen, the décor that was different from what was inside the home she left only brought me back to that lonely autumn night. The tiny kitchen stood out to me. She had always hoped for a large, poolside kitchen so we could eat on the porch and enjoy the warmth of summer along with her linguini salad. You know, I would give anything for a plate of that right now.

From prose to poetry, Bryce continued to try to express his raw pain from the defining moment when his mother left on that November evening.

Sound The Alarm

This November air
Lingers to make its presence clear
Only to be ignored by clinched fists,
Primal screams
And crushed, furious eyes
On this autumn night I'm feeling the
Devastation that I
Thought we were immune to,
You and I

On this autumn night I feel the
Destruction, Europe circa 1940
But this is more than a world at war
This is me, at war with everything I know,
Barely standing on two bare feet,
Crying, screaming on cold concrete!

Bombs set to a sunny backdrop
Are still bombs
Without mercy!
Without sympathy!
Without motive!

And in the midst of this air raid
I think back to a time when
Smiles were never forced
When you and I stood
On the front lawn
Me, safe, secure, in your arms
In Sunday best

These days I don't keep the Sabbath holy
And Easter doesn't matter anymore
And I plead every night with my dreams to
Wake me, a new person, with new hope,
Resurrect me tonight!

And let me forget again that
Bombs set to a sunny backdrop
Are still bombs

    Bryce longs for a time when his world fit together, being held in his mother's arms, adorned in the wardrobe of "Sunday best." Those childhood memories are now scorched in the shock and awe of his parent's divorce. The pieces to the puzzle of faith are shattered and scattered. The Sabbath is no longer holy, and Easter does not matter any more. Yet out of his own anguish, he prays a pleading for hope and new life. "Wake me, a new person, with new hope. Resurrect me tonight."

    I began working with Bryce while he was in his senior year in high school. He became withdrawn and depressed after the break-up of his first significant female dating relationship. He presented as a quiet young man. I found it would have been impossible to read the rage that was just below the surface. He gave the impression he had quiet control of his life. I had difficulty drawing him out to verbalize his thoughts and feelings. He was the middle of three children, having an older adopted brother whom I had also worked with and a younger sister who seemed well adjusted and I had not counseled. His primary means of self-expression came through writing, but he was also a lead singer in a garage grunge band, where he screamed lyrics of frustration and rage, peculiar to this genre of music. His earlier writing was descriptive of the devastation he experienced after his mother left and the intense experiences of abandonment he felt as a result. When the girl dumped him, it brought up the previous pain of being dumped by his mother. The current target of his rage is his ex-girlfriend. The reader is warned that this is not for the faint of heart. The poem is graphically violent and the "f-bombs" are noted.

My Love Affair With Your Anatomy

I had a knife and
I dissected you, started at your chest,
Watched the blood race to your feet
And didn't let up until I was no longer amused
A familiar game, familiar players
You played the role you weren't used to
And I loved every f&*ki^g minute
I picked away at your heart
Until it resembled mine:
Black, shredded, barely beating
I watched it struggle to survive
Until I remembered that I wasn't
Ready to let you go just then
F#*k no, not that gently
Your insides aren't shit to me
So I unraveled your small intestine,
Wrapped it around your neck until
You couldn't possibly say the words I wanted you to
Then I did my best to recreate
The knots of my stomach in yours
But that blade wasn't sharp enough
And you tried as hard as you could
To fight and to live,
Almost as hard as you tried to love me
How ironic
But dear, it is difficult to scream through duct tape
And nobody heard your cries, but if they had
No one would have given a shit

You wasted your last breaths because
You, gorgeous, were as worthless as your struggles
Everyone knew it and they still do...
I easily sliced through your wrists,
And sawed through your cheekbones
One last "F#*k you!" and then your sensitive ears
Were lying on the floor, right next to my
Commitment to forever
Yours forever
And your blue (or green) eyes weren't as enticing as
I thought
So I put an end to the mystery,
Dug them out and flung them as careless
As you threw around your lips and your words

Retrieved them, held them up
To your withering body and those lonely sockets,
Let you see what you did to me
And just before you let yourself slip
I told you that there is no God
And no one that loves you
For a moment, before you slept forever,
I knew the truth, and you, dearest, were wrong
You were wrong and so was I for thinking I could
Convince you of what you made me so sure of:
Hope is useless
(I should have told you sooner)
And just before your heart stopped
I ripped it out
Ravaged through it with my teeth
And with blood dripping from my tongue
I spat it back in your face
The feeling, that feeling is what
Killed you
At least that thought is what helps me sleep at night
So I said au revoir, kissed your cold neck the way
I knew turned you on
And as your ghost resumed the twilight I remembered
The first night I lied to myself through your smile,
You dropped your fingers from my curls and
I never saw you again

I was stunned and in shock when I read what Bryce had written. I struggled with Bryce to determine if these words were a true threat. Was he planning on acting out and making this fantasy of slashing and dismemberment a reality of rage and revenge? Was this young girl in danger? Should the police be notified?

Fortunately, for all who were involved in this situation, the answer was no. How can we know? How can we tell? When do we choose to act preemptively in order to circumvent the tragedies? In my mind, it does not take much to connect the dots and draw the lines of a pathology found in what I would call *a Culture of Columbine.* This culture is capable of erupting into violence on any campus across the United States, as it did on the campus of Virginia Tech. Cho Seung Hui's videotaped and twisted tirade of hate, rage, disgust, and shame preceded the actual pulling-of-the-trigger carnage and the senseless murder of 32 innocent people. Underneath the spewing of emotional bile, underneath the trench coats, and underneath the prose and poetry, are the raw synapses and broken hearts of alienation and rejection. The fabric of faith and family, the predominant cultural glue of modernity, are sources of alienation, contempt, and despair in the post-modern world.

In review, we are born into pre-existing networks of connections that shape and mold our history and experience. Throughout our lives, we seek to find groups that will confer a sense of belonging, acceptance, approval, and identity. Group dynamics move on a continuum of low demand, low intensity to high demand, high intensity. Groups that lay claim to core values and ultimate concerns will create the greatest demands for loyalty, commitment, and sacrifice.

The healthier the group, the greater the probability the group's intensity will focus on the individual member being placed, not in the role of receiving a group identity, but rather in a context for the discovery of "who I am." At the most elementary level, a common interest, activity, hobby, or group sport offers belonging, acceptance, and approval around the interest held in common. The second level of group life involves some type of face-to-face activity with an explicitly stated purpose to target making a difference in someone else's life. A third level of group involvement is the establishment and maintenance of transformational community. The persons reaching out are the ones who are also reached! *Lives are changed in both directions*. I become different because I make a difference. The highest level of group intensity beyond transformational groups involves counseling.

The patterns we choose in relationships may follow (1) opposites attract (2) replicate the familiar (3) neither or (4) both, which includes one and two. Conscious relationship contracts establish a blueprint for relationships when systems, groups, organizations, or relationships find agreement on how to deal with stress, manage conflict, solve problems, balance power, relate to employees or raise children.

In our post-modern cultural context, we are witnessing a shift in the understanding of identity that is moving from connection to alienation. This shift is creating a re-defining of identity previously based upon historical and family connection to one established primarily by individual competence and achievement. Even though the factors may be diverse, through this shift we are witnessing increasing expressions of radical violence.

The stressors in our post-modern world heighten our sense of "readiness" as we constantly feel "on edge" and "on guard." What affect do all these toxins have on the endocrine system, immune system, and our general sense of health and well-being? How do our connections enhance healing or create disease? Do our relationships increase our quality of life or do they create ill health and sickness? What are the long-range effects of harboring negative emotions and what role does forgiveness play in healing?

Chapter 6
The Search for Healing

> Twelve ministers and theologians of all faiths and twelve psychiatrists of all faiths had convened for a two-day off the record seminar on the one word theme of healing. The chairman, a psychiatrist, opened the seminar with this question: "We are all healers, whether we are ministers or doctors. Why are we in this business? What is our motivation? There followed only ten minutes of intense discussion and they were all agreed, doctors and ministers, Catholics, Jews, and Protestants. "For our own healing," they said.[50]

In Chapter 1, our Search for Safety, I stated, "If we do not feel safe, nothing else matters." Consequently, if our *physical* health is in danger, if we are suffering from a serious illness or disease, we *do not feel safe*. I participate in a faith community which has a prayer room staffed by volunteers on a 24/7 basis. About 85% of the prayer requests received in the prayer room is for the healing of emotions, relationships, or for physical healing. The interconnection of emotions and relationships on our physical health is extremely significant along with the way we deal with stress and manage our lifestyle.

With heightened awareness, our ancestors would prepare for a hunt. They would stalk their prey. In those few crucial moments, they would enter into an extreme state of readiness when it was a matter of kill or be killed. After the hunt was completed, their state of readiness would subside until the time came for the next hunt. The prey was then hauled back to the cave.

Our bodies were never meant to withstand the onslaught and internal dumping of toxic hormones, cortisol, and adrenalin that result if our relationships or lifestyles keep us in a constant state of stress and readiness. Terrorist threats are color-coded by levels of intensity: yellow, orange, and red. The anxiety meter constantly drives the stock market.

Daily commutes turn into warfare on wheels. Drivers clench steering wheels as a substitute for the neck of the person whom tailgates or cuts them off in traffic.

In Chapter 1, I mentioned the story about what happened when I tried to teach my daughter to drive a standard transmission vehicle and the "Check Engine" light stayed illuminated. We are not meant to live in a constant state of readiness, but this is exactly what happens during a panic attack, which is the body's way of saying our "Check Engine" light is glowing brightly.

I met Julie on a mission trip to a small southern island in the Abacos chain located in the Bahamas. Julie had a real dilemma. She had phobic reactions to hurricanes, and she lived in the Bahamas. Having a phobic reaction to hurricanes in the Bahamas might be like having panic attacks at the sight of snow while living in Buffalo, New York, or Butte, Montana! Those who live in the Bahamas *will* experience hurricanes. As residents of South Carolina remember Hugo, residents of Dade County remember Andrew, and residents of New Orleans and Mississippi remember Katrina we all know that hurricanes threaten life, possessions, and create horrific devastation.

During the previous year, there had been numerous storms and Julie had traveled to Florida on two occasions to sidestep the direct pathway of approaching storms. Her panic began days in advance when the Weather Channel began forecasting an approaching storm. She feared having a heart attack and being unable to receive adequate healthcare on the remote island where she lived. The howling winds from even a minor storm would send her into the closet crying uncontrollably for hours. The challenge with Julie was to moderate her reaction to a circumstance to make her anxiety manageable.

>Hey Tim, Hope this finds you well. We are all OK. I am doing really well. I am so thankful and grateful for all your help when you were here. There's not a day that goes by that I don't think about at least

one of the many things we talked about. The difference in the way I feel is almost unbelievable. The "H" word **(Hurricane!)** does not affect me the way it once did. I can watch the Weather Channel and hear people talk about it and I don't get that sick, sinking feeling in the pit of my stomach. So far we have not been threatened by a hurricane but I feel like I have the strength and confidence to handle it. Don't even have thoughts of wanting to go away if one does come. That is quite a difference from the way I was about 2 months ago. I can never repay you or say thank you enough for everything you've done for me. I am so glad Gene brought you along for the "painting" trip. My life has truly changed because I no longer feel burdened down with that fear. It no longer controls me. It still amazes me to be able to say that, but what a great feeling.

We were not meant to live in a constant state of readiness. Human beings are the only creatures capable of holding anger and anxiety in our bodies for an indefinite time. Dumping these toxins into the body is like putting rocket fuel in a moped. Eventually the moped will wheeze, whine, freeze, seize, and blow up. The effects on our vascular and cardiovascular systems along with the increased probabilities of strokes and heart attacks are huge. In these moments of readiness, we dump toxins in our bodies that will rival damage from a lifetime of cigarette smoke!

Other animals, less evolved than we humans, do not have this problem. They seem to return more naturally to a state of being which we are intended to enjoy! When I was pre-school age, one of our favorite family outings involved going to feed the ducks. We would save stale bread and put it in the freezer. We would visit several ponds. My sisters and I would go to the pond and throw the stale bread on the water and the ducks would come and feed. Occasionally we would witness brief territorial skirmishes, and two ducks would square off, honk, and squawk at each other. As quickly as these squabbles would start, they also ended. Each of the ducks would begin flapping his wings and lift up with webbed feet just out of the water. The ducks quickly returned to the water. They would swim away as if nothing had happened. The theory is that ducks flap their wings and engage in this choreographed behavior in order to release the adrenaline and cortisol discharged into their bodies during the squabble.

Whereas other animals like the ducks, quickly release and discharge the after-effects of anxiety or aggression, humans are capable of holding it inside for five, 15, or 50 years – even if the poison makes the host sick and he knows it! People sometimes feel entitled to emotional misery. Grady, in his late 70s, refused to attend his granddaughter's college graduation because of the chance he might see his former son-in-law. His daughter and son-in-law had divorced over twenty years earlier, and his daughter had since remarried, not once but *twice*. Grady still harbored anger and resentment and was keeping score by blaming his former son-in-law for hurting his daughter. In Grady's mind, he was making a definitive statement to his former son-in-law by *not* attending the graduation. Instead, his absence only served to wound his granddaughter. She was bewildered by the pettiness of her grandfather. Resentment is the poison we drink, believing it has the power to destroy the other person. However, when we drink it, it destroys us. Individuals who carry this type of emotional pain are often slaves to addictions. They may no longer actively service their addictions, but just as they often feel entitled to their substance of choice, to dull their pain, they may also feel entitled to feelings of anger, hurt, and resentment. They have a *right* to feel this way, regardless of whom it hurts. In this instance, Grady's granddaughter suffered.

Our Bodies Remember and Hold Emotional Pain

At times, the body will hold pain and the individual may be completely unaware. Our conscious mind may forget pain, but our body will remember. When I entered the doctoral program to work on a degree in counseling one of the requirements was to set up a practice of no less than six clients per week and be involved in weekly supervision of the work. The supervision was both individual and in groups. The counseling sessions were audio taped with the client's permission. The skilled and experienced supervisors overseeing our work carefully scrutinized every word, nuance, and inflection of tone. Supervisors reviewed everything we said and everything we did not say. The process was an exciting and intense period in my life. The clinical supervisors worked with a sharp sword to cleave out and clarify the student's issues to keep our issues out of the way in order to facilitate healing for the client. Some of my own issues were beginning to stir. These issues were just out of the reach of my awareness.

Tuesdays were spent in Jacksonville and I commuted an hour and a half each way from Ormond Beach. On a Monday, I began to notice a dull ache in my left wrist. My wrist began to throb during the day on Tuesday while in class. That evening I could not sleep because of the intensity of the pain. I made a mental note to call a physician friend in the morning to see about getting an x-ray to diagnose the problem. I took an over-the-counter pain medication in an effort to secure a few hours sleep but the next morning the pain had not improved.

Wednesdays were the days I worked in my study. I took more over-the-counter pain medication but typing was difficult and painful. I finally decided to take a break on the couch and try to get in touch with what was going on with my left wrist. I began to recall a prior experience with this level of pain in my wrist. I had broken my wrist playing football in the sixth grade. I recalled the orthopedic surgeon saying the kind of break I endured might produce arthritis later in life. I wondered if this was the onset of arthritis. Again, I remembered the specifics of the experience. We were playing two on two; I was defending a receiver, and when the ball was thrown, I successfully dove through the air and knocked the pass down. When I landed on a concrete driveway the force of the impact caused the radius and ulna in my left wrist to snap. The bones protruded through the skin. There was no doubt my wrist was broken. I was in intense pain.

Since I was a latchkey child, I was the only one home. Both my parents were at work. I called my mother who was employed as a ward secretary at Baptist Hospital in Jacksonville. She in turn telephoned a neighbor. The neighbor drove me to the hospital. I sat in the emergency room for several hours and an orthopedic surgeon was called. Nurses and doctors asked me if I wanted anything for the pain and I refused to accept pain medication. In my sixth grade mind, I was afraid of becoming a drug addict, but I did not voice these irrational fears. They kept telling me *how brave I was* and what a *courageous young man I was* for enduring this pain! Interns from foreign countries kept coming to examine my arm and to run their fingers over the break. They spoke to each other in their native languages, words I did not understand. The x-ray technicians made me position my arm for the pictures in positions that were excruciatingly painful. About 10 o'clock that night, seven hours after the accident, I was taken into surgery. The bones were set, my arm was placed in a cast and I was sent home. Again, refusing pain medication I did not sleep for two nights. As the bones began to heal, the pain subsided.

I have remembered this experience my entire life. I have told and retold the story hundreds of times. What came into my awareness that Wednesday morning was the *meaning* I associated with this event. Meaning involves facts and how you interpret the facts. As I recalled this incident lying on the couch in my study 24 years later, I became aware that I was more concerned about how *my mother* was going to react than I was about *experiencing my own pain*. I was afraid my mother was going to be angry with me for breaking my arm. Although these impressions were established prior to breaking my arm, she was absolutely empathic and loving as she met me in the emergency room. She stayed by my side the entire time. When I realized I was more concerned about *her reaction* than *feeling my own pain*, I lamented uncontrollable sobs for at least 30 to 45 minutes. In reality, I lost track of time. My mother had been dead for five years when this realization struck. My body held this emotional pain for a lifetime, and now this pain was being released. When I woke up the next morning the pain in my left wrist was gone. To this day, it has never returned.

The body has a way of holding pain. Our emotions can become lodged in our bodies. As I stated in the introduction, if we do not learn healthy ways to process our emotions we may end up burying our emotions in our bodies. Think of all the ways we use metaphors to localize our emotions. "You turn my stomach." "You make me puke." "You are a pain in the ass." "I've got butterflies in my tummy." Somatized emotions, emotions we bury in our bodies, create *dis*-ease and eventually may create disease. I have had many referrals from licensed massage therapists who have sent their clients to me because of disturbing or traumatic memories evoked when the massage therapist was working on a particular area of their body.

Global Medicine, Hope, and Healing

Lifestyle habits and physical, relational, and emotional well-being are copiously intertwined. Disease, or *dis-ease*, is created from an imbalance of these factors. Alternative strategies for healing, which include hypnosis, acupuncture, massage, reflexology, herbs, supplements, diet, and exercise will continue to gain credence and credibility in the traditional fields of medicine. The alternative methodologies, what Dr. Mehmet Oz calls *global medicine*, continue to break new ground in this area. [51,52]

I attended a continuing education workshop in Orlando and one of the participants at the event was a licensed acupuncturist. About the third day into the workshop, he turned to me and said, "How long have you had sinus problems?" "Me? I've had sinus problems as long as I can remember. I've always sounded like I am talking from the bottom of a trash can." He said, "I can help you with it if you'd like to try acupuncture." I was skeptical but willing to try and the price was right – he volunteered his time and expertise at no cost. Years earlier, I was tested for allergies and I learned I was allergic to just about everything on the planet. Dust, oak, pine, mold, mildew, everything we find native to life in Florida. I took shots for a while and finally gave them up and decided to suffer with it, and to take medication during the difficult times. After we finished the afternoon session David had me lay on the floor while he inserted more needles than I wanted to know in my face, neck, and places on my legs and feet. At one point, when he inserted a needle in my foot, I could feel a strange force of energy leaving my body. I said to David, "You know, I just really felt this weird sensation coming out of my foot." "Did it feel like energy moving out of you?" he asked, and when I said yes he said, "That's Chi!" I said, "Ghesunteit." David said, "No, I did not sneeze." Then for 20 minutes, he explained to me the reality of Chi and the importance of this field in Chinese medicine. I did not understand much about the conversation. For the next three days, my sinuses were clear. This I did understand!

Krista Tippett, of American Public Media's *Speaking of Faith*, interviewed Dr. Mehmet Oz. Dr. Oz has been a regular guest on the Oprah Winfrey Show and a leader in the field of medicine, embracing the combination of alternative and Western approaches in what is becoming known as integrative medicine. He now hosts his own television program. Dr. Oz calls this developing field *global medicine*. He is the director of the Cardiovascular Institute at Columbia University and has innovated tools and techniques, including the use of robotics, which are revolutionizing the field of cardiac surgery. As a surgeon at New York Presbyterian Hospital, he has introduced mind and energy-oriented therapies like meditation, reflexology and massage into the operating theater and recovery room. He is the author of *Healing from the Heart*. The following is from that interview:

DR. OZ: Hypnosis is a therapy that is, I don't think, even that unconventional anymore. But we have studied it in numerous different settings. There are many other individuals across the country that have also done work along these lines to demonstrate that hypnosis can play a role in ailments as varied as hypertension to the chance of having pain after a procedure. So I divide the alternative therapies into two basic camps. There are the alternative therapies where you put something in your mouth — you know, herbs, vitamins and all those things — and let's leave those to the side because those really get into the science and medicine of what we're doing.

MS. TIPPETT: OK. And even homeopathy, would that be in that category?

DR. OZ: I would put homeopathy in that group as well, although, of course, homeopathy works in a very different way. And then there're the therapies where your mind plays a role. And what we're really trying to do is to figure out how to get your mind and, perhaps, elements of your mind that we don't understand working with you. So let's take a big area of energy. Whether energy exists or not at the macro level — the level of the human being — is a difficult thing to tell. But we define life at the level of the cell by whether or not you have an energy level in the cell that's different from the energy level outside the cell. That's what life is. So if you aggregate those cells together into an organ, the heart, and you put those organs together into a body, the human, why would we think that we wouldn't have energy that's measurable and could be affected to make you feel better? In fact, why would we not think that disturbances of that energy might cause some of the ailments that we cannot today put a name on? So that's why I think therapies like acupuncture and Tai Chi and acupressure and even the use of some of these medicinal treatments like homeopathy, which may affect energy levels, could actually be an important advance for us in medicine. If nothing else, it widens the vista of opportunities that we have in the healing arena. The big challenge is it's very difficult for folks to invest the resources to truly study these modalities. And because they are underfunded, it's often impossible to envision a mechanism to truly "prove," quote/unquote, that a therapy can be effective.[53]

Dr. Oz has become an advocate for this new field of Global Medicine, a phrase he uses in order to see the different models of medicine and the human body from around the world, not in competition but rather in cooperation;

> From my perspective, what's really happened is the globalization of medicine. Now think about this: We have global media. We have global banking and finance. We have global entertainment. We don't have global medicine, and that's because medicine is a remarkably provincial process. The doctors come from their local culture. They have the same biases as their mothers gave them. And so they go out, they're practicing using therapies that they think work and ignoring ones that may work but they don't think work. And so, alternative medicine has really become the globalization of medicine. It is us incorporating healing traditions from other parts of the world.[54]

We are learning that varieties of different modalities are capable of turning on gene expression to facilitate healing in the body. Our immune system is in place and constantly fights an onslaught of attacks. What takes place when these internal switches are flipped? What happens when the host is attacked from within, cells go mad, and tumors grow to destroy the body? What happens when these switches are flipped to *reverse* the destruction and facilitate healing? In traditional medicine, gene expression can only achieve results using pharmacological intervention. Global Medicine teaches something different.

The most fascinating research I have encountered in the area of triggering gene expression is in the work pioneered by Ernest Rossi.[55] Dr. Rossi demonstrates how gene expression can be ignited to facilitate healing through hypnosis. I sense that he has deliberately cast his work in the depths of scientific research in order to avoid finger pointing from the mainstream and others who would view him as a charlatan. His language describing his work is also deliberately difficult in order to avoid trivialization and turning it into the next and latest best fad. The first stage of his work with a patient he calls **preparation.** During this phase, he asks what problems or issues the patient wants to resolve. Rossi asks a series of open-ended questions to begin to move the conversation from normal everyday talk to the more pinpointed work of a therapeutic context. The goal is not to provide relief but to arouse what disturbs the individual enough to enlist these energies in the move toward the next stage, which is **incubation.** If we were to watch a charismatic healing service on television, we would see the faith healer setting the stage in a way that creates "faith, hope, and expectancy of healing which can evoke the therapeutic states of emotional arousal, creative replay, and re-synthesis that are common to both ancient and modern approaches to healing."[56] The therapist supports the individual's journey within during hypnosis and reframes negativity as it arises. The third stage is **illumination** when a breakthrough of insight or awareness takes place, followed by the fourth stage when the therapist **verifies** the work that has been accomplished and achieved.[57]

Hope and Healing: The Power of Words

Rossi's research involving both ancient and modern approaches to healing raises the issue of the role of "faith, hope, and expectancy" in creating therapeutic anticipation. What role does hope play in healing?

When I finished my master's degree and began work as an associate pastor in South Florida, I visited a man who was a member of our faith community who had been hospitalized for tests. He was in his early eighties. He had a storybook relationship with his wife. Neither of them had been previously married. They had meaningful careers, had always lived at home, and had dedicated their lives to the care of their parents. They met in their early seventies after both sets of parents had died. They doted on each other like middle school students. They had been married for about eight years. One could finish the other's sentences and vice versa. He had been taken in for exploratory surgery. They found he was eaten up with cancer from one end to the next, and the physicians quickly closed him back up. I was in the room when the doctor came to explain the results of the surgery. "Well, we opened you up and took a peek and decided the best course of action would be to begin chemotherapy and radiation. We absolutely believe this is the best course of action, and I am confident you will improve and get better." They looked at each other, their eyes lit up, and she asked, "Really, doctor?" He said, "Really!" The doctor bid them farewell and headed out to his next stop on rounds and I followed him out the door. I was angry. I stopped him and requested a moment of his time. "Let me get this straight. You opened him up and closed him back up because he is eaten up with cancer, is that right?" He nodded in agreement. "Now, you're going to subject this man in his eighties to the torture of chemotherapy." The year was 1979 and the devastating side effects of chemotherapy were far worse then than now. "What chance do you really think he has and why didn't you tell him the truth?" I do not remember the doctor's name, but I remember what he said to me that day outside the room where the two lovebirds were cooing just inside. "I am not God," he said to me. *"What right do I have to take away their hope?"* He swiftly turned and walked away.

  I was stunned by this comment. Doctors, therapists, clergy and others who are in a position of authority can deliver words of comfort and hope or words that amount to a lethal injection. Words can heal or words can kill: defining reality strikes a delicate balance. I have always believed there is a fine line between hope and denial, and in order to live a balanced life we must be present in the tension between the two. Hope is not magical thinking, as if we believe in something hard enough our belief will make it happen. Hope is not wishing on the first star we see, or blowing out the candles on a cake and thinking we are going to open our eyes and get what we want, like healing, a relationship, a catcher's mitt, or a Porsche. Hope involves openness to mystery, a belief in the possibility of miracles, and an assurance that whatever happens we will have the faith to face the future.

Empowered by Hope - Dr. Paul L. Hartsfield

A mentor and friend of mine was in a meeting of potential candidates interviewing to become ordained clergy. During an interview, he slumped over in the chair and fell to the floor. My friend, Paul Hartsfield, was rushed to the hospital. X-rays revealed a brain tumor. He was transferred to another hospital in the St. Petersburg area and evaluated by specialists. The specialists concurred the tumor must be removed. He was scheduled for surgery the following Tuesday and released from the hospital. Sunday he told his congregation what he was facing and he calmed their fears. With Easter Sunday less than seven weeks away he asked them to envision him standing behind the pulpit on Easter Sunday morning.

When I received word of his condition, I drove five hours to the hospital and spent the day before his surgery with him and the family. Paul was my pastor when I was in elementary school and a friend for many years. When I attended the University of North Florida, preparing at the time for what I thought would be a career in law, I sensed my life was changing and felt compelled to speak with Paul. At the time, Paul lived in Tampa and I lived in Jacksonville. It was a four-hour drive, but that did not matter. Just because the Organization of Petroleum Exporting Countries had created the first Arab Oil Embargo and there was hardly any gasoline to buy anywhere, did not matter. With a calm demeanor, which would have soothed a raging sea, he listened intently as I poured out my story and my tears to him. Nothing I said seemed to phase the warmth and acceptance I felt from him. This was the first time in my brief 20 years I felt unconditional love from another human being.

I have never known anyone like Paul. He has been the most rock-solid human being I have ever known. At the hospital, I was inwardly anxious and his wife and eldest son were outwardly anxious. He was not anxious at all. I arrived at the hospital early the next morning. I rode with him in the elevator and accompanied him as far as the operating room door. Never once did I detect the slightest expression of fear from him. In fact, he calmed everyone else. We anxiously waited in the surgical waiting room, and many hours later the surgeon came to report the tumor was successfully removed and the pathologist had performed a frozen section. The tumor was benign. I drove home and then returned in a few days while he was recuperating from the surgery. With his head bandaged in a turban, Paul looked like a sage from the Middle East. I commented about his lack of anxiety concerning the surgery and asked if he was in denial. He simply smiled at me and said, "I gave up being anxious a long time ago. I just knew whichever way it went everything would be okay." Easter Sunday morning, just as he asked his congregation to envision, he stood right there at the pulpit where he said he would be. That's hope!

Spontaneous Healing: Encounters With Mystery

Krista Tippet interviewed Dr. Rachel Remin, author of *Kitchen Table Wisdom*, on National Public Radio's *Speaking of Faith* series. In the interview, Dr. Remin discusses the limitations of science and medicine, and goes on to document a case involving a person who experienced healing beyond the limits of scientific knowledge. She states:

> I think we are recognizing the limitations of our science. That phrase, "living better through science," there's no question we are living better through science, but to live well is going to take something more than that. If I look at myself, without the eight major surgeries and the many medications, and I still take many medications that keep me alive, I wouldn't

be here, but with only these things, I'd be an invalid.

Objectivity is cognitive in a funny kind of way. But the thing that seems important in order to understand life we need to look at it through many different dimensions. Sometimes we understand another person the best and know how to help them the best when we are not objective. . . objectivity is a bias, just like anything else.

This happened at Sloan-Kettering many years ago when I was an intern. We had a man come into the hospital to die. People used to come into the hospital to die when there was no hospice movement then, if your care was too difficult to achieve at home, you were admitted to the hospital to die and this man came in riddled with cancer. He had an osteo-sarcoma and his bones looked like Swiss cheese; all of these lesions were cancer and there were big snowballs of cancer in his lungs and in the two weeks he was with us in the hospital all of these lesions disappeared. And they never came back, Krista. Now were we in awe? Certainly not! We were frustrated! *Obviously someone had misdiagnosed him*, so we sent the slides out to pathologists all over the country and the pathologists sent back the slides saying, "classic osteogenic sarcoma," so then we had grand rounds; the slides were shown, the x-rays were shown, the man himself was shown and the conclusion of this large group of doctors was the chemotherapy which had been stopped 11 months before had suddenly worked. Now the embarrassing part of this story is that I believed this for the next fifteen years and I never questioned this conclusion. I think too great of scientific objectivity can make you blind.

Krista Tippet then asked Dr. Remin, "What do you think now?" Dr. Remin responded, "*I think that this was one of the purest encounters with mystery I have ever had in my life.* It makes me wonder about who we are, what's possible for us, how this world really operates . . . I have no answers but I have a lot of questions and those questions have helped me to live better than any answers I might find."[58]

Dr. Oz relates a story he tells from his book about a

woman with a bleeding ulcer. Because of the religious beliefs of the family, they would not allow her to receive a blood transfusion.

There was a Jehovah's Witness who was brought into the emergency room having a bleeding ulcer and a problem that we actually do a pretty good job dealing with these days. But she was a smallish woman, and by the time she'd come to see us, she had lost almost all of her blood. So the solution is pretty obvious. You rush her to the operating room, fix the bleeding ulcer by putting a suture in it, but you have to give her blood in order to have something to carry the oxygen around the body to keep her going. And the family, when I came in to talk to her, said that they did not think she'd want the blood. And I said, "Well, that's good and all but, you know, you realize we're not kidding around here. She's going to die if she doesn't get this blood."

So I rushed her off to the operating room. And after having given the patient's family and her a pep talk about the fact that we needed to get the blood into her — and she had become unconscious by now — so while she was off there, I made this last plea to the family, and I said, "I'm going to do this surgery, and I'll be back to get your permission. You need to sign these forms so I can give the blood." So I went off and did the operation. By now her blood count, her hematocrit was about four, which, by the way, healthy animals start dying at a blood count of nine. She was at four, and *she should already have died.* And she was already having evidence of her heart and other organs failing because they did not have enough blood in them.

So I came out to get the permission from the family, and I was horrified to find that they were unanimous in their decision not to do this. They were condemning their mother and grandmother to death. I was flabbergasted. And only then did I really have the epiphany. They weren't telling me that they did not believe me. They weren't telling me that they did not love their grandmother or mother. What they were telling me is there was a deeper love, a deeper belief that transcended what I was telling them by which they were living their lives and that no matter how logical it seemed that she should get the blood, they did not want the blood. Well, of course, as the story turns out, the woman who was going to die that evening hung out for another day and then another day and then another day, and she finally went home. And she never did get that blood. And although I would never recommend, in the future, for someone not to get the blood, it was to me a very revealing experience because I began to recognize that as dogmatic as I thought I could be with my knowledge base, there were certain elements of the healing process I could not capture. And even if I was right in the science, I could be wrong in the spirit.

Ms. Tippett: So did her recovery really defy what you had been learning all those years in medical school?

Dr. Oz: *Her recovery made no sense at all.* And I don't want to get into the issue of why she recovered because there are so many hypotheses you could offer for that. But without any question, she was the first in a long series of patients, because, you know, once you realize this is happening around you, you start paying attention a little differently. You start picking up subtle clues from patients who may not be willing to share their spiritual burden with you, but now that you've expressed interest, they're willing to do that. And that, for me, became a wonderful trip, especially as I began to specialize in heart surgery, in particular, some of the sickest types of heart surgery with heart transplantation and mechanical heart devices.[59]

Jeremy, Conner, and Ms. Z

Her recovery made no sense at all. Neither did Jeremy's recovery. I met Jeremy, his brother, mother and father, when I lived in Madison, Florida. While I was living there, Jeremy left and entered a three-year photography program at Daytona State College in Daytona Beach, Florida. Years later when I left Madison his mother gave me one of his framed and numbered photographs of a sunset on Dog Island located on the Gulf of Mexico. This photo continues to be one of my favorites. Jeremy worked his way through school tending bar and doing whatever he could to get by; he finished his formal education and stayed in Daytona for a while, eventually moving to Orlando then finally to Atlanta in an attempt to establish a name and reputation for himself as a photographer. Soon after moving to Atlanta, he was having a horrible time making ends meet. A series of bad breaks followed Jeremy like a dark cloud. A thief broke into the warehouse where he stored his expensive camera equipment and stole everything. Like a carpenter without a saw, the theft left Jeremy without the tools of his trade. Jeremy started dating a woman who suffered from anorexia and bulimia, and he found himself in a "policeman's" role, monitoring her trips to the bathroom so she would not purge after eating a meal. Having moved to Atlanta to seek his dream he soon discovered his dream had turned into a nightmare. Jeremy was caught between a rock and a hard place: he could not make a living and was in a difficult emotional state.

Jeremy's illness began with a depleted immune system and a series of cold and flu-like symptoms he could not shake. He went back and forth to the doctor. For over a month, he took antibiotics but he could not get the infection cleared up. He finally tried a different physician who placed him on a seven-day treatment, which brought some temporary help. For the six weeks he suffered with the flu, he lost a great deal of weight and could not gain it back. He began drinking milkshakes in an attempt to keep up his weight but his condition only worsened. He began having blood in his stool along with intense intestinal cramping and diarrhea, and he diagnosed himself with a hemorrhoid. Without a job and medical benefits, he called his parents and his mother agreed to get him to a surgeon in Tallahassee and pay for the procedure. Too weak to drive, his parents arranged for him to fly to Jacksonville. When his father picked him up at the airport, he hardly recognized his own son in his emaciated state. He told him he "looked like Jesus." His father's first shocked reaction was that his son must have AIDS. His father was not the only one that would erroneously reach this conclusion.

The first surgeon examined Jeremy and said this was not a hemorrhoid and he would not touch it. They showed the doctor a photograph that had been taken just a few months earlier when Jeremy was working at a "Glamour Studio," and the physician immediately began questioning Jeremy if he "liked having sex with men." He bore down on him, trying to get him to admit his homosexuality.

Like a bad nightmare, Jeremy and his parents had to wait over the weekend while the diarrhea continued to worsen and weaken him. The sight of his son in this condition and the stench from his illness made it impossible for his father to be able to stay in their condo in Tallahassee. On the following Monday they found another doctor who immediately admitted Jeremy to Tallahassee Memorial Regional Medical Center. His initial diagnosis was that Jeremy was extremely malnourished. The physician's assessment was right on target, and he indicated if Jeremy had stayed in Atlanta another week he might have slipped into a coma. A colonoscopy revealed Jeremy's colon and intestines were blood red and ulcerated. The diagnosis was Chrohn's disease, a condition that had been aggravated by drinking milkshakes in his attempts to gain weight. What made Jeremy believe he had hemorrhoids was that his colon was literally pushing inside out. One of the first procedures was for intravenous fluids to be pushed into his body. Four different bags were set up which included fats, lipids, glucose, and antibiotics. The physicians determined there were too many IV's going at once and the decision was made to put in a central line into his chest and attach it to a major artery. After about a week, the site where the port entered into Jeremy's chest started leaking and turning red. He kept telling his caregivers there was something wrong. The port was first re-stitched, and a new one was later implanted to replace the first one. Overnight, Jeremy's condition worsened. He went into respiratory distress just a few hours before he was scheduled for surgery to remove six feet of his intestines. Sepsis had set in from a staphylococcus infection and Jeremy was barely able to breathe. Jeremy was gasping for breath and he was rushed to Intensive Care.

One of the nurses in ICU was a friend of Jeremy's mother. The nurse called his mother and said, "You'd better get over to the hospital right away." A devout Roman Catholic and a person of spiritual integrity, Jeremy's mother drove as fast as she could to the hospital. She was in distress because she wanted her priest to be there with her. As she pulled into the parking lot she found herself praying for her son and added, "Thy will be done." She was running across the parking lot when a car was coming right at her. For a moment she thought she was about to be run down before she could get to see her son for the last time. In the car was the young priest from her parish who had previously anointed Jeremy when they had prayed for his healing.

They went immediately to the ICU and when the pulmonary physician entered the room, he indicated they were going to put Jeremy on a respirator. The physician told Jeremy's mother they needed to "get somebody with her." The signs of Jeremy's death were imminent.

Father Tom and Jeremy's mother prayed for Jeremy and again anointed him, a procedure used in rites of healing when a small drop of oil is rubbed onto the forehead. Jeremy opened his eyes and thought they were administering "last rites." He smiled, looked at his mother and said, "Everything is going to be all right." Jeremy's mother, a licensed psychotherapist in the state of Florida, heard her son's statement through her own pain and said to him, *"Don't tell me everything is going to be all right!"* She thought her son was acting out co-dependency. While he was lying on his deathbed, she thought he was trying to reassure her and emotionally take care of her. She left the room crying, believing this was what he was trying to do.

What Jeremy's mother did not know was what had just happened to him. What Jeremy saw was a familiar face of a former parish priest. Father Ron, a family friend and professional peer of mine, had been a young priest in Madison. He had died a few years earlier of pancreatic cancer. Father Ron had appeared to Jeremy, and Jeremy felt him gently place his hands on his shoulders. No words were spoken. Nothing was said or heard.

The healing was instantaneous. Jeremy was moved to a private room and discharged after a few days. There were no surgeries and no respirators. Four years later, Jeremy was designing houses in a community south of Daytona Beach. He has a greater appreciation of life. The close brush with death has made Jeremy realize, "I have not fulfilled my spiritual obligations." He has been involved with retreat groups in his denomination, a powerful experience of covenant and community, where he has served others and has shared his story.

Like the man who had been diagnosed with classic osteogenic sarcoma, Jeremy underwent a spontaneous healing. Although Dr. Remin is now a pioneer in the field of integrative medicine, she explains from the perspective of traditional medicine, "If we can't explain it, it did not happen."

Modern pharmacology isn't the only reality that triggers gene expression. How else do we explain that in certain blind studies, placebos have nearly the same effect in turning on gene expression? Since the breaking of the genomic code in the year 2000, we are only at the beginning of being able to determine what turns on and off gene expression. I was having a conversation with a friend of mine who practices in the medical field as a podiatrist. I asked him what he thought about reflexology. Reflexology dates back to ancient Egypt and China and adheres to the belief and practice that pressure points in the feet and hands correspond to different organs and areas of the body. Massaging and manipulating these areas can promote healing and relief in areas of distress. Since he sees feet all day I was curious what he had to say on the subject. Grinning, he told me a story about attending a trade show a few years earlier. Persons marketing every imaginable product or trade related to the care of feet were present for the show. Strolling the aisles he passed by a reflexologist and she asked if he would like a demonstration. He sat in the chair, took off his shoes and she began to work on one of his feet. She quickly found a tender spot and he jumped. She looked up at him and smiled. "This is the area that correlates to your liver. So you were out drinking last night?" He felt like a schoolboy caught by his mother. He had been out with friends the previous evening and by his own admission had indulged in one or two too many libations. He became quiet for a moment and said, "You know, we're going to look back at what we are doing today in medicine fifty years from now, and we'll clearly state it was barbaric. We look back at what physicians did in George Washington's day when they applied leeches. It won't be any different when we'll look back at what we are doing now. What we basically know how to do is to cut, burn, and poison." I was stunned by his comment and observation. The intervention involved with the orthopedic surgeon who used his skill and expertise for resetting my broken arm was certainly required and necessary. What else is?

Conner

Connor Hatch, a successful dentist in the Daytona Beach area, developed an aching pain in his right arm and shoulder in December of 1979. The area was first treated with a couple of cortisone injections but with no relief. After X-rays were taken of his neck Connor was treated for a vertebrae problem with traction at home in the evenings. The pain continued and in February of 1980, his physician, Dr. Cabreza, ordered a chest x-ray. A tumor the size of a tennis ball was found in the apex of the right lung. The next day tomograms were done and sent immediately to a surgeon, Dr. Delaughter. Connor was admitted to the hospital for a lung biopsy the next day. Tests revealed a large cell undifferentiated tumor involving the brachial plexus, which was deemed inoperable.

Connor was released from the hospital and was sent to the M.D. Anderson Oncology Clinic in Houston, Texas for a second opinion. After 10 days of testing, the verdict was the same. The tumor was inoperable, and Connor was told he had a year, maybe two, to live. Connor was sent home for radiation therapy to help relieve the pain and was placed on Methadone for pain relief. Connor underwent five weeks of radiation therapy and tests showed the tumor had responded only minimally. Still suffering from a great deal of pain Connor dropped from 180 pounds to 120 pounds. The radiation treatment was stopped.

Approximately two weeks after the radiation stopped Connor developed severe abdominal pain. He was sent for a CT scan and an IV push. Once again, tests revealed a tumor, this time encapsulated in the kidney. He was hospitalized immediately. Because of the extreme weight loss and general deteriorated physical condition, doctors inserted a nasal gastric tube. For a week, this was Connor's source of nutrition to strengthen him for surgery.

In May of 1980 Dr. Delaughter, Dr. Jones and Dr. Brown performed surgery. The tumor was not encapsulated; it was everywhere. They removed his left kidney, a portion of the bowel, other pieces of the tumor and performed a colostomy. Doctors also discovered malignant lymph nodes around the aorta but did not remove the nodes due to the possibility of excessive bleeding. Connor's family was told he had two weeks to a month to live. After three weeks, Connor was sent home to die. He weighed 86 lbs.

Once home Connor sold his dental practice, his boat, paid for his funeral and prepared to die. He went through several weeks of depression. He began to push himself to try to function. He pushed himself a little at a time. He began to put on weight and was getting a little stronger, but still taking the Methadone for pain.

Nine months later, due to unrelated circumstances, a radiologist took a chest x-ray and discovered the tumor in his lung had disappeared. Connor was set up for a CT scan to check the remaining tumor and lymph nodes. Nothing showed up abnormal on the scans. Dr. Delaughter suggested Connor undergo exploratory surgery to tag any possible malignancies for radiation. Dr. Delaughter performed the surgery since he knew what he was looking for. He could find nothing to tag; instead, he re-sectioned Connor's intestines together to eliminate the colostomy. He was sent home to recuperate.

Connor remained on disability for five years. Each year following he had x-rays and nuclear studies done, and there was no recurrence of the cancer. In 1985, Connor opened his dental practice again. He did have a partial bowel blockage in 1991 that did not require surgery and the following year another blockage did require surgery, performed by Dr. Tolland. Dr. Tolland found a duodenal ulcer. In 1998, Connor had two coronary artery bypass grafts performed by Dr. Holt. The arteries had 80% blockage, and an aneurysm was discovered and repaired. Connor retired in May of 1998. In 2006, Connor traveled to the Denver area and toured the southwest with varying degrees of elevation. He reported shortness of breath and chest pains, and an emergency heart catheterization was completed indicating blockages. Several stents were placed in the arteries around his heart.

I have known Connor and his wife for more than 20 years. He is sort of like the Eveready Bunny – he just keeps going, and going, and going! Connor, like Jeremy, will describe to you the miraculous spontaneous healings they experienced as the result of prayer. In each situation, these persons were being supported by a strong connection to a faith-based community. This raises a great deal of interesting questions – for example, why some people experience healing and others do not. I wish I could answer those questions. What I do know is the effect a future with hope can have on a situation. Hope is purposeful. Hope targets a positive outcome. Hope creates anticipation. Hope directs us toward the future.

Connor, for one, was not in denial about his condition. He came home from the hospital, sold his practice, his boat, paid for his funeral and prepared to die. By the same token, Connor remained hopeful. As we face the future, we have two options. Either we will face the future with hope, or we will face the future with fear. Hope is purposeful; fear is reactive and chaotic. Connor assumed whatever happened, he would be prepared and equipped to deal with reality as it unfolded. He was empowered by hope.

The Transformation of Suffering into Healing

Ms. Z., a 35-year-old mother of three, came to see me for supportive psychotherapy after being referred by her surgeon. She had been diagnosed with trigeminal neuralgia, an extremely painful ailment that causes severe pain in the lower jaw area. The attacks can be triggered by chewing, wind blowing against the face or the attacks can begin with no apparent cause. Many people suffering from this disease are misdiagnosed with dental problems. Patients may even go through a series of root canals or extractions before the ailment is correctly diagnosed. Ms. Z. was fortunate that her neurologist diagnosed the problem before unnecessary dental work was performed. Her symptoms were being held in check with a series of medications. The use of medications troubled Ms. Z. By profession, Ms. Z. was a registered dietician and she prided herself by keeping physically fit through rigorous exercise and a vegetarian diet. One of the side effects of the medication kept her white blood cell count at low levels, a condition that had to be constantly monitored.

Since the birth of her third child, Ms. Z. had been through a series of medical problems and surgeries. Six months after the birth of her third child, she had a series of bladder spasms that were extremely painful. Not long after the bladder spasms, she was having terrible menstrual periods that would linger on for weeks. Her periods would barely stop before they would start again. She had a hysterectomy and developed an internal hemorrhage requiring an additional surgery to repair the bleeding. She lost large amounts of blood and if she had not been taken back into surgery, there was danger she would have bled to death. The lab reports from the uterus and ovaries were negative, and there was no sign of any abnormality that could be detected. After recovering from the hysterectomy she started developing problems with what she thought was her gall bladder. Her symptoms were so acute and descriptive of this type of problem she convinced her surgeon her gall bladder needed to be removed. When the gall bladder was sent to the pathology lab for an examination the pathologist's report indicated there was no detectable problem. The report was so troubling to her surgeon that he later told me he kept the report in his coat pocket for two days, trying to figure out what to do with the information. After recuperating from the gall bladder surgery, Ms. Z. then developed the trigeminal neuralgia symptoms. She was referred to a neurological surgeon at Shands Hospital, an excellent training hospital in Gainesville associated with the University of Florida. An experimental brain surgery was suggested to relieve her facial pain. Research has discovered many trigeminal patients have a cranial artery pressing against a nerve, believed by many to cause the disorder. When Ms. Z. went for the operation, the surgeon discovered her cranial artery was not pressing against the nerve but after the operation Ms. Z. reported her symptoms had abated; surgery was a success, until six months later when the facial pain returned.

It was two months after working weekly with Ms. Z. before she reported to me the "real reason" she had come for counseling. After her symptoms had returned her surgeon reported to her spouse, also a physician, that he thought Ms. Z. was suffering from depression. The neurosurgeon in Gainesville agreed. When both her surgeon and her husband talked to Ms. Z., she became extremely angry with them. She had not told me this story until now because she was "testing me" to see if I would figure it out. Since I had not mentioned this in two months she was now ready to ask me point-blank if I thought she was suffering from depression. Since I knew how strongly she had reacted to both her husband and her surgeon, I had decided I would not "side with them," but rather I told her I was not sure, and I asked her what she thought about it. From this point forward, I would only jokingly refer to depression as "the D word." The "D" word was as inflammatory to her as any string of profanities might be to a nun being spewed from the mouth of a sailor! It was as repulsive to her as vomit. At this time I had no clue what her sense of threat was concerning a diagnosis of depression, but I knew this was extremely disturbing and I was hoping to find out why. I was willing to be patient and see what would happen.

After a few months, Ms. Z.'s story started to unfold. She had been a lieutenant in the Army Reserve and was about to be called to serve during Desert Storm when she learned she was pregnant. The pregnancy forced her to resign her commission. After the birth of her first son, she gained 35 pounds. She only needed to lose five pounds to get back to her target weight, which she did in short order. She vowed she would never be fat. Ms. Z. had always envisioned she would have four children, and while her son was a toddler, she became pregnant with her second child. During her second month, she began spotting and her obstetrician ordered her to slow down with her exercise and "take it easy." She followed the doctor's orders, but had trouble accepting the advice because the regimen she had followed during her first pregnancy had proven successful. While at the beach, jumping waves with her toddler son she "felt something tug" and began spotting. The week before she had an ultra sound and her infant son was safe and growing in the protection of her womb. After the incident at the beach, she returned for another ultra sound. This test determined the heart of the fetus was no longer beating and that he was dead.

She blamed herself for his death and no amount of comforting was able to console her. The usual "it was not meant to be" did not work for her or "you already have a son, and you can still have more children," meant absolutely nothing to her. Her son was dead, and in her mind, it was her fault.

Ms. Z. grieved daily until she became pregnant with her next child, and when she began spotting, she followed all manners of caution. She gained more than 50 pounds during this pregnancy. She was ordered to bed after 31 weeks and lived in complete terror she would lose this child and end up blaming herself. A daughter was born a few weeks premature but was healthy and survived. She became pregnant again about a year after her daughter was born. She followed the same regimen. She again spotted early in the pregnancy and she was ordered to bed at thirty-one weeks. She carried this child to full term. During both of the latter pregnancies, she lived in a constant state of anxiety and panic. She feared she would have a miscarriage and end up blaming herself. After the miscarriage, being pregnant was not a condition that made Ms. Z. feel safe but instead posed a constant threat of danger.

As for her family of origin, Ms. Z. was the second of three children raised in a military family. Her father had been a high-ranking officer in the U.S. Air Force. She had been a military "brat" and had lived all over the country and never any place for long. Her father was the stereotypical military officer portrayed in Patrick Conroy's, *The Great Santini*, a book I had her read. She read the book with great difficulty and pain. She was angry with me for "making her read it." Her father ruled the family with a military hand and his word was law. Emotional problems were not allowed in the home, although physical problems were acceptable. There was very little affection demonstrated to her as a child and she held an impression from her childhood that her mother did not want to be a mother and did not really want to have children. When Ms. Z. had her hysterectomy and came close to bleeding to death her mother never showed up at the hospital to see her. Ms. Z.'s older sister became sexually promiscuous as an adolescent and her younger brother later became an alcoholic. Ms. Z.'s role in this dysfunctional family was to be the perfect child, but no matter how hard she tried, she could never quite be good enough to win the affection and approval of her parents. She excelled in academics and on the cross-country track team. She could never recall a time when either parent showed up for a track meet or when she was commended for her academic effort. She was always expected to do more. It was never enough.

After working with her for about six months, I started seeing Ms. Z. twice a week as she began to experience more of her sadness and grief as it all began to come to the surface. During a time close to the end of one of our meetings, I ventured a risk that ended up being a tremendous blow to Ms. Z. I suggested one of the reasons she may have had all of her *physical* problems was because she had been taught she was not allowed to have *emotional* problems. Emotional problems were not acceptable to her father or mother. I commented to her that being pregnant was not a condition of joy but instead it provided a constant state of terror. When the bladder spasms did not work in eliminating sexual contact with her husband, the hysterectomy certainly ended the threat of her being pregnant forever. I then asked her to think about her gall bladder metaphorically, that the gall bladder is the sac attached to the liver that contains excess gall or bile, and that she had certainly been "holding in" an emotional stench for a long time. I then suggested she might also think about the trigeminal pain in her jaw in a similar metaphorical fashion, and that the pain was now attacking her in the jaw, in a sense urging her to speak and discuss her experiences. On her present pilgrimage, she was certainly being encouraged to do so. Ms. Z. had a glazed-over expression on her face and she retreated into silence. Since our time was now up, she left. I worried for two days I had delivered too big of a blow for her to assimilate all at once, and I thought I might have lost her.

Ms. Z. did come to the next session and indicated she had thought about dropping out of therapy, which was my worst fear. Although she experienced deep wounding with me, it was a gentle enough nudge to move her on to where she needed to go. She reported feeling an intense amount of shame and an enormous amount of sadness. She felt shame at thinking her illnesses may "all be in my head." She could not understand how she had gotten this way. I told her it was all right to be sad. For nearly the entire session, she sobbed deep expressions of emotional pain. "No one has ever told me that before," she said.

When Ms. Z. reported experiencing shame, I began to think we were close to a deeper mystery to understanding her anathema about the "D" word. Shame is an emotion we experience when we learn the needs we are trying to have met are inappropriate or unacceptable. In the home, we look to our parents to "mirror" our experience of self. If I learn certain needs are unacceptable then shame is the emotion that "covers" the need seeking to be met. Shame covers the unmet need like a blanket, and when shame is experienced in therapy the expression of the unmet need is beginning to surface and the blanket is about to be removed.

As this happened with Ms. Z. she began to remember something that had happened when she was four years old. It was one of her earliest memories. Her family was living in Okinawa where her father was stationed. In great detail she began to remember "a little girl wearing a red dress" going down the street to where some boys were playing. One of the boys had a German shepherd on a leash and she asked the boy if she could walk his dog. She reported she could see the little girl walking the dog when the dog spotted another dog and took off running, dragging her across a gravel road. She remembered seeing the little girl taking a shower, her face and dress covered in blood, and going to the hospital to get her shoulder x-rayed and to learn she had a broken collarbone.

Sleeping in the same room as her older sister, she would always sleep on the left side of her face so she could see the light underneath the doorway. In this posture, she could see where her parent's room was located, and when she did, she felt safe. Because the left side was now sore and bandaged, she could only sleep on her right side, which meant she would have to face the wall. As a child, she knew monsters lived inside the wall. Being rather ingenious, she begged her mother and father to let her sleep at the foot of the bed so she could then face the "correct" way and see the light underneath the door. She was instead told she was foolish, there were no monsters in the wall, there was nothing for her to be afraid of and she was being silly and childish for thinking this way. Desperately wanting her parent's approval, she obeyed their wishes and bawled herself to sleep. During the entire time Ms. Z. relayed this story she spoke of "the little girl" in the third person. It took until midway into our next session before she could identify the little girl as "me." The disassociation she had with this experience was still present. However, she was approaching the awareness of knowing she was now safe and that she would be okay.

Ms. Z's parents did not intend to create a traumatic experience for her. What she learned was that her fears were "irrational" and she could not trust adults to be able to comfort her or to provide calming and soothing for her when she was in distress. She clearly learned "she was not supposed to feel that way" which was the same message she received from family and friends when she miscarried her child. Although the two events occurred 27 years apart, they still "feel" the same, as the unconscious mind links together experiences that are like or similar.

What followed from this discovery was beyond the scope of imagination. Shortly thereafter Ms. Z. reported a dream. She was in the military during wartime or during a military drill, she was not sure which it happened to be. Crawling under barbed wire on her back, she noticed a man crawling on top of her. She was troubled by the dream and thought the man in the dream was her father. She soon began having recalls in dream fragments as well as when she was conscious and awake. She first remembered her dad coming into her bedroom one night while he must have been drunk. He must have thought he was in the bathroom because he exposed himself and began to urinate in the corner. I tried to reassure Ms. Z this was probably just an isolated incident and he must have mistaken her bedroom for the bathroom. I was wrong. What followed was a peeling back of layers and layers of sexual abuse that began about the time of the incident with the German shepherd. What began with fondling as a young child ended up with the entire range of abuse by late childhood, early adolescence and throughout her teenage years. For nearly two years, Ms. Z. recalled horrific incident after incident.

A child learns how to survive these experiences through defenses called splitting, denial, repression, and displacement. The *splitting* involves the two distinct worlds the child has to live in. The nightmare world is the world when Daddy comes in the bedroom to terrorize the child. The other world is in the morning, when the sun is shining brightly and everyone is at the breakfast table. Daddy says, "So sweetheart, how are the Cheerios this morning?" This is the world where everybody acts "normal." The child learns how to adapt to a severed reality by splitting these realities in two. Splitting is when the "good daddy" plays games with me. The "bad daddy" is the one who comes into my bedroom at night.

Since everything that exists in the "normal" world is the world everyone else lives in, the other world must not be real. What follows with this pattern is denial and repression. *Denial* involves "this did not happen." *Repression* is "I am going to push it way down." *Displacement* is the other coping mechanism. If you cannot run away and you are not strong enough to overpower your attacker, the only other option is simply to "go away." One popular saying we hear when people are "spaced" is to say, "The lights are on, but nobody is home," or "The arm is down, and the bells are ringing, but there is no train." Ms. Z. would speak about going to a meadow, a lush lovely meadow filled with beautiful yellow daisies. This was the place she would go to in order to "feel safe" when she was being repeatedly raped by her father. During the course of our work together Ms. Z. was gradually able to trust a new reality where she began to feel safe in the context of the holding environment provided in counseling. As this began to happen, the walls holding up the facade began to crumble and she began the hard work of facing what had actually happened in her childhood and adolescence. No longer equipped with the tools of denial and repression, her experiences began to surface and she experienced intense post-traumatic stress. Any incident, thought, or feeling could trip the trigger for reliving an original traumatic event of rape and incest. Her life had become a minefield. Each step risked detonating an emotional explosion that would implode her into her own personal holocaust and hell.

This was an extremely intense time for Ms. Z. as she walked through the valley of the shadow of death and abandonment. At times, she felt like giving up and experienced deep suicidal feelings. She shared her experiences with an inner circle of friends and once wrote of her frustration in working through the healing process:

> "If one more fellow Christian tells me I have to "let go" of whatever the issue happens to be at the moment, whether it be anger, bitterness, resentment, fear, unforgiveness, grief, etc, I think I am going to scream! They expect my "letting go" to be instantaneous, as if I can just say the words, and I will have "let go" of the issue. They have implied, sometimes explicitly, that perhaps my lack of faith, or my lack of obedience, or even my lack of theological awareness might be the obstacle to me "letting go." They seem unable to grasp that "letting go" often times, if not always, is hard work, if it is to be an authentic "letting go." Letting go is hard work."

Letting go *is* hard work! Ms. Z. and her husband decided to confront her family about the abuse and to nobody's surprise, it was denied. Both she and her husband did not feel safe being around her father, especially since they had two young daughters. Relationships became strained and irretrievably broken. Her family treated her as if she was mentally ill. They related to her with an attitude of condescension. They "were praying for her and hoped she would soon get well and get over all of this," continuing to mask their denial. Her sister wrote:

Dear Little Sis,

Just wanted to let you know how much I'm thinking of you. Hope you had a good Thanksgiving. We had a great time at Grandmother's. Everyone asked if I had heard from you. Grandmother and I told each other we can only keep praying for you and your healing and that we will all be waiting for you with open arms and we will rejoice when you come home. We know that God works for the good in all things for those that love him. I thank God in advance for healing our family and bringing us back together. We are here for you.

Sister

She waited until the next day to respond to her sister:

Dear Big Sister,

Please do not send me any more e-mails. I am saddened that I have to say that. I had hoped we could maintain a relationship. But I am moving forward and it is obvious from your notes that you are choosing to stay behind in denial. I get the impression that you think my healing will result in reconciliation with the family. In actuality, my healing is carrying me further from the family. My healing is occurring because I have acknowledged that our father raped me. I have acknowledged it, and am working through the devastating results of it, and am being healed. I have chosen not to be hindered in this process by those who continue to deny the truth of what happened. I have come to realize that includes you. If you want to pray for healing, I would suggest you start by praying for the healing of yourself, Dad and Mom. None of you will ever experience the wholeness God desires for you if you choose to live in denial. But that is for you all to work on among yourselves. I am moving on. Good-bye.

Little Sis

During the intense recall phase, Mr. Z. became equally frustrated. These are trying times for any marriage, even the healthiest of relationships. Sex frequently becomes a source of relational conflict. Intense memories are often triggered in the bedroom during this phase. What might start as a romantic evening ends up with intense sobbing and grief. Mr. Z. called me, and we went to dinner one evening at his invitation. His question was blunt and to the point: *"When is this nightmare going to end?"* I told him, "It will be over when it is over and not before." Many women who relive the trauma experiences struggle with whether or not to share them with their spouses. The spouses often have their own agonizing issues with the perpetrators of the abuse. They frankly grow weary of the tediousness. Many tire of hearing the stories, or would rather not hear about it at all. Other women find it horrid to begin to think about telling their experiences with their spouse present, and the spouse will often feel left out of the process, neglected, and uninformed.

 Although alternative modalities are involved in brief therapy trauma resolutions, I was not able to use these methods effectively with Ms. Z. Another sojourner who I mentioned earlier in the chapter, Julie, was able to overcome her panic attacks involving her fear of hurricanes in two, two-hour meetings. Ernest Rossi documented the healing of a woman with rheumatoid arthritis in a demonstration session before an audience of therapists. One of the amazing aspects of this encounter is that the entire session lasted just under one hour![60] I attempted to refer Ms. Z. to someone I know who works in some of these alternative modalities and who was more qualified than I, but she refused and wanted to remain working with me. Once the level of trust had opened enabling the deepest levels of disclosure to take place, the thought of opening these wounds with another person was considered dark and foreboding for her.

 Many women prefer living a life of celibacy after their dormant terror is awakened and no longer hidden. One woman I worked with who was molested by her father, a clergyman, suspected this was her point of entry into the lesbian community. She had been a schoolteacher and had entered the gay lifestyle after college. Her abuse stayed out of her conscious awareness until uncovered during the course of her work with me.[r]

The case of convicted serial killer Aileen Wuornos is a good example of this. Wuornos's father, Leo Dale Pittman, was a child molester and a sociopath who was strangled in prison in 1969. Wuornos was pregnant at age 13.[61] She dropped out of school and shortly thereafter left home. She began living a life filled with drugs, alcohol and prostitution. She was arrested and charged with the death of Richard Mallory on January 9, 1991, and pleaded no contest to the deaths of five other men. She was convicted of the death of Mallory and was sentenced to death by the State of Florida and died by lethal injection on October 9, 2002. The killing of these men was probably substitutes for the man who committed the initial abuse – her father.

Sexual abuse and specifically incest may very well be the next closet door that will open, and the victims will come out to tell their stories and seek healing. Since the trial of O.J. Simpson, our nation has focused on the horrors involving domestic abuse. Domestic violence had previously been largely neglected or ignored until the graphic details of the trial were made public. *Experts indicate 20% to 40% of women in the United States have been sexually abused.* The discrepancy in the statistics is the result of this being a crime that goes untold. Memories recalled in therapy are not admissible as evidence in court. Therapists must be extremely careful not to "suggest" the possibilities of sexual abuse. I have never suggested it and have never brought it up until the person I am working with makes this discovery. Incest is a crime that may go undetected for decades and the perpetrator will never be brought to justice for the crimes committed. In many states, an adult having sex with a child under the age of 12 is considered punishable by life in prison. When sexual abuse begins and is habitual and

---

[r] According to research by *Lesbian London* magazine (1992) and *Project Sigma* (1990), one-third of lesbians and two-thirds of gay men have their first same-sex experience before the age of 16.

repeated, it frequently starts with fondling a child between the ages of four and six followed by forcing the child to perform oral sex and later intercourse by the age of ten to twelve.

One reason the stories remain untold are the threats the child receives. In the situation involving the woman whose father was a clergyman, she was told something terrible would happen to the family and it would be her fault. For Ms. Z. and countless others, these women are subjected to all manners of abuse, including physical violence, verbal humiliation and at times, torture. If the child does not respond in the manner expected the onslaught begins. The abuser wants to believe the child *wants* to have sex with him. Ms. Z. recalled being choked by her father in a fit of rage, telling her he would kill her if she ever told anyone what happened. This is a sufficient reason for a child to bury these memories. Do you understand the bind? In the mind of a child, this reality becomes seared into the soul with the hot iron of rage and hate: *"If you talk, you will die."* This is a common threat for a child to hear from a father when a father is sexually abusing a child. To overcome an internalized commandment this strongly embedded takes courage and strength. You can also begin to understand the connection with the trigeminal neuralgia and her stabbing jaw pain. Something needed to be expressed. Her jaw was the battleground for the pain and the internal conflict. The way her unconscious mind was at war with this issue may have been expressed as, "I need to talk, but if I do I will die."

Letting go is hard work. It cannot be reduced to trite clichés and superfluous slogans. Ms. Z. talked and she did not die. She grieved the loss of her innocence, her childhood, her family and the love of her father she never received. She grieved the loss of her second son. She grieved the lost years of not being present to her children because of her physical ailments. She shed a river of tears. She went back to school, received a master's degree and began a new career. This journey was a long, difficult and arduous process. At one time Ms. Z. was nearly an invalid when a windy day or a boat ride could trigger an attack of trigeminal neuralgia. The physical pain and the symptoms are now gone. There have been no more surgeries. Ms. Z. was healed. She had dealt successfully with the emotional turmoil, the trauma and her own personal holocaust that was lying just underneath the surface It had come to the foreground in the only way she was allowed to express it - as pain. Ms. Z. was healed.

Healing and Forgiveness

The pathway to forgiveness is through the pain, with no shortcuts. What we know in our mind takes time and hard work for the migration to move from the head to the heart. Forgiveness for Ms. Z did not happen as relational reconciliation. She could not return and play "let's pretend it never happened and I am the crazy one" with her family of origin. Families do not create entitlement to relationships. The fifth commandment states "Honor thy father and thy mother that thy days may be long in the land the Lord thy God giveth thee."[5] This is the only commandment that comes with an implied *curse*. In other words, if you *do not* honor them your days will be *short!* This commandment had a necessary function in the social order of the day: children were to take care of their aging parents. However, honor has to be *earned*. How could Ms. Z honor a father who had horribly dishonored her? Honor is not an entitlement that comes with the office of parent. When we are children, we do not have a choice: we have to have a relationship with our parents. As adults, we get to choose with whom we have relationships.

Ms. Z struggled long and hard with the issue of forgiveness. Her father violated issues of personal and social justice to the core. He robbed her of her innocence and betrayed a sacred trust. He inflicted and infected her with years of somatic distress. Why should she forgive him? After a long and painful struggle, she figured it out. She did not do it for him. She did it for herself. She experienced forgiveness

---

[5] King James Version, Exodus 20:12

when she was able to accept what had happened. It came to her as a gradual awareness when she realized she was no longer carrying around toxic emotions. Forgiveness came as a product of the process.

Most of us will never have to face the horror Ms. Z. had to face. Yet healing and forgiveness are delicately intertwined for each one of us. Learning to *practice* forgiveness, as a daily discipline, is essential to maintaining our spiritual identity and equilibrium. Forgiveness is a matter of daily forgiving reality for being the way it is. When Jesus taught his followers to pray he taught them to practice forgiveness on a daily basis.[t] The inability to forgive means the present becomes filled up with the past. It effectively distorts our ability to be *fully present in the present*. It will immediately take us out of the realm of being purposeful into reactivity, which is always chaotic and driven by anger and anxiety. Because the unconscious mind does not maneuver well by separating the past from the present any present concern of competence or justice can trigger an entire string of these issues from the past, creating an internal tipping of emotional dominoes.

Forgiveness is not only about the big things: it is about all things! After we built our present home, the tile started coming up on the floor six months after the first year warranty had expired. We placed little pieces of blue tape on the tiles that were coming up so we would not step on them. We began the process of attempting to get the builder to come back and make the repairs on the blue-taped tiles. For about four months, there were countless phone calls, letters and voice mail messages before we were able to achieve an

---

[t] Revised Standard Version, Matthew 6:9-15 "Pray then like this: Our Father who art in heaven, Hallowed be thy name. Thy kingdom come. Thy will be done, on earth as it is in heaven. Give us this day our daily bread; ***and forgive us our debts, as we also have forgiven our debtors;*** And lead us not into temptation, But deliver us from evil. For if you forgive men their trespasses, your heavenly Father also will forgive you; but if you do not forgive men their trespasses, neither will your Father forgive your trespasses.

agreement with the builder about the situation. Every morning, half-awake and half-asleep, this trek of about 20 feet was like navigating an obstacle course. I would make my way from the bedroom to the kitchen trying to step on the healthy tiles and miss the blue-taped tiles to turn on the coffee pot and begin the day. The temptation would have been to look daily at those blue-taped tiles and to go off on a tangent; "That builder, look how stupid and incompetent he is! He does not even know how to put down a tile floor and now he is taking advantage of me. It isn't fair! People like that should have their contractor's license revoked. Do you think I am going to put up with this nonsense?" It would have been very easy to play the role of the victim, blaming and accusing the contractor for violating the principles of justice and competence. Instead, I chose to forgive the tile for being the way it was since there was really nothing I could do about it other than what I was doing. The contractor was very gracious and he eventually repaired the tiles. A year and a half later, it happened again. This time we reached another agreement; the contractor agreed to pay for the tiles and we paid another person to do the installation. (If a surgeon were responsible for an act of malpractice, would you want the same surgeon to go back and fix the problem again if it was not done correctly the first time?) With the exception of the tiles, the builder built us a wonderful home. The tile flooring was just a minor part of the total construction. During the same time, in spite of the tiles, because of the boom in real estate the total value of our home doubled. Did we deserve this good fortune? No. When the real estate market fell through the floor, did we deserve this bad fortune? No, not any more than we deserved having to deal with the tiles – twice!

    Forgiveness has to do with accepting reality as it is. Non-acceptance of reality creates unnecessary negativity and resistance. We use up more energy to *resist* something than it takes to *accept* it. When we practice acceptance and forgiveness, we pull reality forward. When we resist, we push against it because it does not meet our expectations of *what we think it should be!* The key to spiritual and emotional growth is the acceptance of reality at all costs!

Dread vs. Joy

Dread, for example, is the negative response to what is. Dread meets the present moment with resistance. I have spent more time in a dental chair than most people would spend in three lifetimes. I have had a cracked tooth from a baseball bat (yes, it hurt), bridgework, crowns and periodontal disease. I had a bridge collapse (only in my mouth) and implants installed. I have my teeth cleaned every three months. I do not dread going to the dentist, periodontist or the oral surgeon. I worked through the importance of self-care early when a sign on the wall of my dental hygienist read,

"You Only Have To Floss The Ones You Want To Keep."

When the time comes to see one of these specialists I look at the calendar, note the time and day, get to the appointment and the work is done. The painful part is paying for the work! I do not look at the calendar three weeks ahead and begin worrying about whether it is going to hurt, and I do not wish I had some other place to go other than having to be in the dentist chair on that day. These mental gymnastics create negativity and resistance making the experience worse than it is. You will only create more unnecessary suffering by adding the added drama of dread and worry. In reality, you can only be where you are. You cannot be where you are not! If you are trying to be somewhere other than where you are, you are creating resistance and non-acceptance of the present moment, which happens to be the only moment you have. If you are stuck in traffic and running late for an appointment, then just be stuck in traffic. The universe is not going to suddenly swallow up all the cars in front of you and transport you immediately to your destination! Non-acceptance of where you are and what you are doing in the present moment will only create negativity within you, which you will then seek to discharge and release in ways that will magnetize someone else with all of this same negativity. Joy and dread cannot occupy the same place at the same time. If you *increase **dread***, you diminish the possibility for joy. If you *increase **joy***, you diminish the possibility of dread. I cannot say that I am necessarily *joyful* about going to the dentist, although I could be. My dentist has gone on numerous medical mission trips to Africa, the Caribbean, Central and South America. He has been a dentist for more than 30 years and has been on one of these expeditions nearly every year of his professional life as a way of giving back his gifts and talents and as a caring member of the global village. He and members of his team will set up shop in a village or in a remote area and people will walk for days to stand in line in order to receive dental care. The care these people receive is rather basic, from early in the morning until dusk the team mostly pulls teeth. These people are grateful and appreciate for being able to get the dental care they so desperately need and relief from chronic pain. I may not be joyful about having to go, but I could be and I can certainly be at peace about doing it. Dread cascades negativity and is the non-acceptance of what *is* in the present moment, which incidentally, is the only moment you have.

Dread occurs when you judge the present moment or anticipate the future with resistance. You judge it as being bad. "I don't like it." "I don't want to do this." "This really isn't my idea of having a good time." "I don't deserve this." Spiritual teachers from throughout the ages have taught three basic teachings common to all traditions:

1) Live without judgment
2) Live simply
3) Live non-violently without enemies

It may be that others see you as an enemy, but you do not have to react to anyone in that manner. When you judge a circumstance or a situation as being bad, you make it into something more than what it is. In response to a beggar who complains he is poor, even in giving thanks, Shakespeare's Hamlet responds, *"There is nothing either good or bad, but thinking makes it so."*

Forgiveness is the ability to accept and forgive reality for being what it is. Dread is the non-acceptance of the present or an anticipated future you judge with negativity, which cascades negativity within you. When you eliminate dread, you increase the probability of joy. When you discover this life, you will discover abundant life: you will discover your destiny. You will discover the one life lying underneath the life you are living. Abundance is not about what you possess, but about what possesses you!

Where Healing Begins : CASHing In For Inner Peace

Inevitably, the question arises: how do you get there? The answer is you cannot "get" there. You can only "be" there. As I indicated in the introduction, abundant life is hard work. A process has emerged in my work. Engagement in this process usually comes when we have reached a point of surrender and nothing else is working. At this point, we may be willing to try anything to get out of our pain. In my experience, the only way out of pain is to go *through* the pain. However, pain does not have to be the only motivator. You have to find the incentive that works for you.

When I was growing up, my parents would frequently determine where we would shop based on which stores offered green stamps. Grocery stores and gas stations would provide S & H green stamps with the purchase of their products. As a double bonus, gas stations frequently offered sets of dishes (with a pre-determined amount of fill-ups) along with stamps. In today's world, incentives for making purchases are frequently offered by credit card companies rather than retailers.

S & H green stamps were collected, sorted, and glued into books. As a child I would spend hours thumbing through the S & H green stamp catalogue or "wish book" as it was called. I would flip through the pages and dream of purchases I might one day be able to exchange for the stamps. Completed books could be traded in at S & H green stamp redemption centers for a variety of different catalogue items. The more expensive the gift, the more stamps were required for the exchange. My wife's grandmother used S & H green stamps to purchase an end table lamp we received for a wedding present.

Exchanging the stamps for goods provided a phenomenal incentive to buy from merchants offering green stamps. What if we could trade in our inefficient gas-guzzling super-sized SUV for a lean, green, energy-efficient hybrid? What about trading in a hovel for a home?

What incentive would it take to entice you or someone you love into **CASHing** in reactive living for inner peace? Golfing legend Bobby Jones once said, "The narrowest fairway you will ever hit is the five inches between your ears." Would being at peace with yourself and your world be enough of an incentive? If you are not motivated by incentives the question may be as basic as this: are you tired of creating suffering for yourself and for other people? What would you be willing to do in order to avoid being hijacked by intense emotions? How would you go about **CASHing** in your anger?

If you follow the theory, behavior is either purposeful or protective. It cannot be both. If you have fallen into protectiveness, your behavior will be driven by reactivity, anger, and anxiety, which are always chaotic. If you eliminate chaos you increase the probability you will be purposeful and at peace with yourself. Our world, for the most part, is insane. We must choose to be sane in an insane world.

The following acronym is an attempt to *describe* a process. This process is not stagnant but rather dynamic. To break out of old patterns requires hard work, even if these patterns create discomfort for us or for others. How long this process takes will depend upon you, your history and experience, and the degree in which you are living in the "readiness" scale. If on a scale of one to 10 your anger and anxiety runs a consistent eight or higher, you may take longer to throttle back. Or, it may be much quicker because you may be tired of being driven by these emotions and are truly ready for change. For most of us this may take a lifetime. This process usually requires and includes the help and assistance of family members, friends, and often the counsel of wise persons we can learn to trust for guidance, feedback, and support. We need trusted friends who will tell us the truth about ourselves.

>   Creating awareness
>   Assessing the threat
>   Stopping reactivity
>   Holding the reaction and healing the pain

Creating awareness involves *creating self-awareness*. It means knowing we are doing *what* we are doing *when* we are doing it! It involves the integration of thinking and feeling, thought and emotion. In Buddhist traditions this is called creating mindfulness.

If you have ever had the unfortunate experience of running over someone's pet, you know exactly how terrible this feels. It feels horrible to hear and feel the "thump" under your rear wheel only to look in the rear view mirror and see "Fluffy" flatter than a pancake. The only humane thing left to do is to stop and knock on the neighbor's door and relay the news to the grieving neighbor. If we had a choice, what we would rather do is "Get Fluffy out in front of us." If we can *see* Fluffy, we will have choices. We can slow down, turn to the left or right, honk the horn, or if we are sick, we can slam on the accelerator and run Fluffy down. Once we can "see" Fluffy and Fluffy becomes a part of our awareness we can then make decisions about how we want to *respond*. If we do not see this coming, our only choice is to feel bad about it *after*.

This **first key** component to creating awareness is

slowing down reactivity. Decreasing reactivity increases self-awareness. Self-awareness is about knowing *what* I am doing *when* I am doing it! Therefore, self-awareness creates the possibility of choice. If I am hijacked by intense emotions, "I" am no longer in control. I am bound and gagged to a seat in the back of the plane. The *emotion* has temporarily taken over the plane, commandeered the pilot's seat and is flying my plane off course. If we cannot "see" Fluffy, or what triggers our responses of anger and anxiety, we will only be able to *react*. If we choose to follow a pathway toward transcendence this type of reacting will no longer be a choice!

A **second key** component of self-awareness is this: ***Check your mirrors***. We cannot change if we cannot see what we are doing. Mirrors create awareness, and awareness creates self-awareness. Looking in the mirror is frequently painful. Chances are we may not like what we see. Mirrors tell truth and do not lie. If we are standing naked in front of a full-length mirror, we cannot hide bulges and wrinkles. However, this is not about our *outward* appearance. The mirrors you will need are other people to help you see yourself as you are seen. They will assist you in being your mirrors if you enlist their help. If you want to know and hear truth about yourself, ask your immediate family members, your coworkers or your three closest friends. Do other people see you the way you see yourself? Do they think you are toxic or tame? Do they see you as being even-tempered or do they see you as someone who tends to fly off the handle over minor things? If the wait staff in a restaurant does not serve the correct order or if the soup is cold do you tend to make a big drama out of this situation? Do you become irritated or agitated when you have to wait in lines? Do you believe your time is more important than other people's time? Do you tend to become reactive when people are driving more slowly than the speed limit? Do you find yourself offended by minor acts of injustice? Can you hear yourself saying, "How can they let *those people* get away with *this*? It is not fair! Somebody ought to *do something* about it!" Do you tend to see yourself as superior and other people as inferior? Are you prejudiced against other people? Do you intensely dislike or hate ethnic groups other than your own?

    If you are going to enlist the help of family or friends, you must pledge to be non-reactive to the telling of truth. Our family or friends may be fearful if they believe the telling of truth will create reactivity in us. If this is the case, they will simply reassure you and tell you what they think you want to hear. People must feel safe. We lie when we want to protect and as you will recall, we cannot be purposeful and protective at the same time. They will lie if lies will protect them.

    Let us hold up the mirror for Trenton and his family. Trenton, a young man of 19, came and sat on the couch across from me. He told his story. He came looking for direction, not in terms of, "Do you know the way to San Jose?" but rather, "What happens after the party is over? What am I supposed to do with my life?" "Why am I carrying around so much pain?" He told me he was going to stop playing video games. "All I've been doing is killing things on the computer for hours: this can't be right." Darwinian emotions were being stirred up within him: kill or be killed. He went on to say he does not watch the news anymore because of all the bad news. The first time Trenton came to see me was the day after the Virginia Tech massacre. He turned off the television so that his grandmother would not sit mindlessly watching the carnage and absorb it. This was an attempt to protect her and him from the pain.

    Pain was the theme of his story. Pain has a way of awakening us to deeper truths about our family, our world and ourselves if we can learn to stay with our pain. This young man had gotten into some trouble and was awakening to issues of faith. His story was cosmically coincidental because it was so similar to my own. I could see myself in him when I was at his age and stage of life. The empathy bridge had already been built.

Our stories were similar, yet different. His parents had divorced after a lengthy marriage, primarily, I had gathered, because of their difficulty with ongoing unresolved conflict and the ***inability to process toxic emotions:*** hate, rage, disgust, and shame/humiliation.

Since the beginning of time, we have tried to figure out what to do with these emotions. These four emotions were the driving forces that put Jesus on the cross. We have sacrificed people, sacrificed animals, symbolically spit on goats and run them over cliffs. We project these emotions onto other people, other nations and other races, and conveniently deny our own shadows. When these emotions are trapped in a family system, a child often becomes the identified carrier of the toxins and he/she looks for ways to escape the pain. Someone ends up as a family kidney, attempting to purify the poison.

"My folks, they love me, they are good people, but sometimes my Dad just goes off on me. He always comes back later and apologizes, I don't really think he means it, but he keeps doing it over again." Earlier in the week, his father awakened him at 6:30 a.m. and raged about a minor item, clearly over-reacting to a trivial incident. The son had left a few things in his own car: a gym bag, empty soda bottle, etc. "He really has a thing about keeping cars clean. I just stood there and took it. That's what I have to do." After he had been the lightning rod for his father's rage and rectified the situation with the car, he went back to the bathroom and noticed his father had left a mess in the sink with shaving materials, combs, brushes, etc. The pandemic problem of our collective human dysfunction is that we will overlook our own flaws in order to focus on the flaws of those we can see rather than our own. Our own flaws remain hidden and invisible to our self-awareness. We will focus on removing the spec in our neighbor's eye and miss the cross beam blinding our own vision.

The **third key** to self-awareness involves checking for **blind spots in our mirror**. When we become indignant, reactive, incensed or enraged concerning another person's behavior, it may be because of something we do not like about ourselves that is hidden from our own view. Trenton's father became enraged about the gym bag and soda cans Trenton left in his car, yet he was oblivious to the mess he left in his sink.

Incidents that help create awareness can be major, or even minor, sources of irritation. Irritation is symptomatic of emerging awareness. This new awareness can become a dilemma, or a challenge for change. One morning after my workout at the gym, I was in the locker room cleaning up for work. A young man came in, opened his locker and removed his toothpaste and toothbrush from his duffle bag. He set them on the sink, turned on the water and proceeded to fiddle with his gym bag while wasted water ran down the drain. He checked his teeth in the mirror, rearranged his personal belongings and the water continued to run for several minutes. I felt uncomfortable and mildly annoyed; I tried to think of something to say to improve the situation. I drew a blank. I had only seen this young man a couple of times before and never had a conversation. What could I say to him to encourage the conservation of a valuable resource? Although I could not come up with the right words to intervene, what I did come up with was this: *I do the same thing when it comes time to get in the shower.* I turn on the water and wait for it to get hot before I get in. I was annoyed by *his* behavior but it was also something about *me*.

We cannot *change* what we cannot *see*. Mirrors create awareness, and awareness creates self-awareness. Trenton's father knew he was repeating his toxic behaviors evidenced by his constant apologies. He was stuck in a cycle of reactivity. He had not learned how to *stop* his reactivity or *hold* his reaction. He continued to *project* his pain and use his son as a lightning rod. If we project our pain, as this father did to his son, we project hate, rage, disgust and shame/humiliation *on to* and *into* others. Without owning our own pain, we simply create more of it. When we scream at each other, we temporarily release those intense feelings. However, if we do not deal with the intense feelings another crescendo will build again in a week or two. It will happen again. When we use a verbal club, the screaming communicates these four words: **"I don't love you!"** You cannot *love me* and *yell at me* at the same time! To hear the emotional content of screaming and the message underneath the words is extremely painful. To hear "I don't love you" creates emotional paralysis and relational handicaps. "What's wrong with me that my father doesn't love me?" Trenton's father will need to look long and hard in the mirror and see the messages he is giving to his son if he really wants to break the cycle. At some point Trenton will not take it anymore. He will choose to leave or stand his ground and fight back. Here lies the risk: *verbal violence always precedes physical violence.* Fortunately, this incident did not escalate to the next level but the future holds no guarantees. Violence within the family frequently erupts during these repetitive cycles.

The three keys of self-awareness are slowing down reactivity, checking our mirrors and checking for "blind spots" in our mirrors. What we do not like in someone else may involve something we do not like about ourselves. The next three phases of this process are closely related and intertwined. Assessing the threat, stopping reactivity and holding the pain are stages of self-intervention. When we are **assessing the threat** we ask, "What is the threat?" By asking this question, we are working to *slow down* the automatic response. We are deliberately interrupting the automatic reaction so we can determine the *extent* of the threat.

The very nature of threat involves the *immediacy* of it. When the alarm rings at the fire station, the fire fighters go through a pre-arranged drill, which has been established by practice, practice and more practice. The purpose of the practice is to improve efficiency and create ritualistic responses. If my house is on fire the last thing I want is for fire fighters to be running around in circles because someone could not find his/her boots. The bell rings and the fire fighters react with ritualistic behaviors designed to improve response time and get to the fire quickly and safely. In much the same way when a situation or experience internally "rings the bell," we react automatically. Our internal mechanisms are equally efficient in order to secure our safety. If the situation were not a threat, it would be perceived differently.

Let us look at another example again using a fire. If you and I were sitting together in my office and the building was on fire I could not imagine saying to you, "Well, the fire is in the southeast corner of the building, and we are sitting in the northwest corner of the building. The building construction is concrete block. It will take a temperature of 1200 degrees Fahrenheit in order for the fire to burn through the walls and there are three concrete block walls before the fire will reach us in this part of the building. The wind is blowing at ten to twelve miles per hour from the northeast. Now, with my calculator I can tell you with the present wind speed I can guesstimate the fire will reach this part of the building in the next twelve to fifteen minutes. Since we have this much time before the fire will set this part of the building ablaze, why don't we just sit here and finish our conversation?"

No amount of logic would calm or soothe you if you smelled smoke. Because fire is a threat to our immediate safety, we would never think this way. We do not have internal mechanisms, working like parliamentary procedures, when it comes to evaluating a threat. These internal mechanisms would not call a committee meeting, study the situation for two years and take a vote. We would yell FIRE and get out of the office!

This internal mechanism within the unconscious mind fires autonomically and automatically. It does this not only to what is instinctual. It also fires in this manner in accordance to our cumulative *learned* experiences. Our history and experience also shapes how we perceive threat. In "slowing down" this process, we are making a deliberate intervention to *interrupt* the reaction and determine the *extent* of the threat. An individual will have a different response to different types or levels of "threat" such as:

1) Someone is "flipping you off" in traffic three lanes over because they do not like the college team you happen to support with bumper stickers.
2) Someone is holding a serrated hunting knife at your throat and threatening to slit your esophagus wide open if you resist or make a sound.
3) Your spouse asks you a question about whether or not you want to go out to eat, and you respond, "I'm sick and tired of always having to do what *you* want to do!"

What is the extent of the treat? Is it a threat founded in reality? Is it a threat to my immediate survival? Is it a threat to how I feel about myself? As we begin to slow down our autonomic and automatic responses, we can begin to interrupt the reaction and *move* the triggering response from the *unconscious mind* to the *conscious mind*. If we do not "see" what is coming, we do not have choices in terms of our response. We can only *react* to the situation *unconsciously*; that is, out of the realm of our immediate awareness.

When the issue of safety is not connected with what is tangible (a fire), anger or anxiety may be triggered because of a perceived attack on our *psychological safety*. As indicated in Chapters 3 and 4, assessing the threat will involve one of two questions:

1) What is happening that feels imbalanced or unfair?
2) What is happening that makes me feel stupid or incompetent?

As discussed in earlier chapters, if you discover reactivity in another person and you are working to respond and not react, ask the question, "Is there something I've said or done that feels unbalanced or unfair or have I said something that makes you feel like I've put you down?"

Let us explore how **assessing the threat** helped to create awareness for Anita and her own personal growth. I first met Anita when she came to counseling because she thought she was "embarrassing her husband." Anita was aware her reactivity to certain situations did not seem to merit the level of intensity she was discharging. She realized this and came ready to work. Her presenting issues involved two incidents expressing a parallel theme. The theme involved her response of anger and rage when she felt "people were taking advantage of me." These situations involved scenarios when she had a skewed, reactive, and distorted sense of justice. The first incident she reported happened while she was waiting in the car for her husband to return from shipping a Christmas package. After waiting in the car for 15 or 20 minutes, she stepped out of the car and went inside to see what was taking so long. She found one clerk servicing a line of customers backed up to the front entrance. Her husband was next in line. She went up to the clerk and let her have it! The second incident involved a pimply-faced teenage girl at a fast food restaurant who did not correctly assemble Anita's order for grease and fries. In Anita's situation, her meaning making of these benign situations created chaos and distorted interpretations. Anita reacted to the teenager at the fast food restaurant and the woman working as a shipping clerk because she thought they *were out to take advantage of her*. She was treating Siamese kittens as if they were saber-toothed tigers. She reacted unconsciously from an autonomic level, and therefore, she reacted *automatically*. Anita knew something was wrong, and she came to counseling to figure it out and get things straight.

Anita was an extremely bright woman, an educator, who taught simultaneously as a visiting professor at a college and a university. The oldest of three children she had been an educator all of her adult life. She had earned her master's degree and her Ph.D. by the time she was in her early thirties. She was now 49 years of age and had moved from a large northwestern town to escape the cold winters and enjoy partial retirement with her husband of eight years. This was her first marriage and his second.

Back in the northwest, Anita had risen in the ranks of public education. She had accepted a position as an assistant school superintendent in a town where she had previously lived. Anita earned the reputation of being a ruthless administrator. She was someone no one wanted to cross. Through the course of our work together, Anita realized *nice* administrators would order her to be his/her attack dog and to "take people out." She began to express shame and she felt like she had been duped.

Anita realized through the course of therapy that accepting the new position as assistant school superintendent was a way for her to end a 12-year relationship with a man who was the same age as her father. Alan, although married and with a family, served as her mentor and lover for this period, and Anita tutored him toward a graduate degree. In the relational bartering, the trade-off in the relationship was that Alan provided Anita building strength for her ego and an encouraging "atta girl" attitude. Alan was, according to Anita, the antithesis of her father. Alan was gentle, kind and supportive. Anita began to understand that her relationship with Alan was an attempt to repair the damage her father had done to her. Anita described her father as moody, bombastic and attacking. One of Anita's earliest memories of her father was when he took her to a department store to return dress shoes that hurt her feet. When the store refused to take the shoes back, her father ended up in a complete and total rage. The event culminated with her dad taking the shoes off her feet and throwing them at the salesman! Anita remembered all the stunned faces of the adults and walking home barefoot from the store. Alan served as a type of "transitional object" for Anita. This relationship provided her with an opportunity to grow and evolve until she no longer needed what he was able to offer her. Anita was stunned when Alan started appearing in her dreams. Over several months, he was "killed off" in her dreams, appearing as an aged man driving a jalopy travel trailer, which was falling apart and dropping parts as it ambled down the road.

As Anita began to understand her anger, she realized she would often experience and direct it in ways similar to how *her father* would discharge *his rage*. In this respect, she had become very much like him. She unconsciously adopted his paranoid view of the world. He frequently told her, "People are *always out to take advantage of you*, and so you have to look out for yourself." In recent months, she had received several critical reviews from students in one of her undergraduate classrooms. At one point in time, she would have bore down and gone for the jugular. Now, without the 'benefit" of her rage, she floundered and became anxious. She no longer had the important support of supervisory personnel in her present teaching positions to guard her flank. Gradually this type of performance anxiety began to ease, and she became increasingly comfortable in her work as a professor. Conflict no longer became something requiring her to *win at all costs,* no matter how many bodies were left lying around. She no longer took things personally when students came late to her class, did not show up or whined and displayed narcissistic attitudes about how "special" they were as they pleaded for preferential treatment.

The work required Anita to look intently at how her history and experience had created ideas and beliefs that had her traveling on trajectories that were skewed, reactive, and distorted. This required painstakingly examining the role her father and mother had played in how she had been "shaped." In Anita's family, each member learned how to tiptoe carefully around her father's rage. Preventative measures were used so no family member would disturb the rage-aholic. The slightest minor incident would easily provoke and set him ablaze. Her mother coped with her father by becoming detached and indifferent. Anita recalled a relationship that ended with a young man while she was in college. She called broken and grieving in despair in search for empathy and care from her mother. Rather than empathy, what she received from her mother was indifference: "Oh well, this is nothing to fret about. Just get over it." Later her mother came to see her for a visit and she took her out to buy new furniture.

Her dad always had to "be in control," although frequently more often than not he was out of control. Being in control even included his death. During the holiday season several years earlier, he had been diagnosed with a terminal illness and he lived until the beginning of Spring the next year. He wrote a letter to his wife, crawled into the bathtub, put a handgun to his head and pulled the trigger. Blood and brain tissue is much easier to wipe up from tile and porcelain than from carpet or bedding. Rather than losing control of what was happening to him, he chose instead to take his own life.

Anita worked through a lifetime of grief and pain with her usual persistence and determination. At times her determination bordered on compulsiveness. She did the work in therapy in one year, which ordinarily would take most people two or three. For Anita, her learning contract was not going to be a matter of acquiring a few new skills. Anita was not content unless she was going to complete a total overhaul.[u]

Stopping reactivity involves making a conscious effort to stop the behavior. When I was in elementary school, we received training each year during the annual fire safety week. Fire fighters would come to school, and we would watch films and take field trips to the local fire station. At the end of the week, we children would receive a "Jr. Fire Marshall" safety badge to pin on our shirts. We were told not to play with matches and how to report a fire if we saw one. We were told how to "break the glass in case of fire" and the

---

[u] Managed Care insurance companies are biased toward "anger management" models of treatment rather than models that encourage transformation. Frequently this involves getting the symptoms bridled and the bit back in the mouth in ten sessions or less. *Re-formation* requires a total overhaul, not just a change in spark plugs.

consequences of what would happen if we broke the glass and there was none. If we were with someone whose clothing was on fire, we were to instruct them to "stop, drop, and roll" in order to extinguish the flames.

When people are caught up in reactivity, they are literally on fire. They feel entitled to their rage and hold family members, loved ones and total strangers as unwilling hostages. They spew incendiary material and belch fire and brimstone. They live for the next reactive moment, then the next and the next. They love drama and create it whenever they can. These people only truly feel alive in these moments. Like Anita, their reactivity meters are off the graph and the slightest blow to their physical or psychological safety will set them off.

Stop, drop, and roll may establish a helpful mantra to stop reactivity. In order to cross the empathy bridge persons must *stop* their reactivity. They must seek to understand, "How is this person being affected or infected by my tirades?" Pamela and Tom were in their mid thirties when I first worked with them. Pamela came first because of an issue involving a previous therapist and something the therapist had said. Pamela was the mother of two small children and her husband Tom was a man who sometimes would enter into bouts of rage, usually in response to the chaos small children bring to a household. Pamela had asked the therapist, "Do you think Tom will ever change?" The question expressed her anxiety and concern about her husband's ability to transform his anger. The therapist responded, "Maybe by the time he is in his third marriage."

Here again is another example of the power of words mentioned earlier in this chapter. A counselor must *choose* his or her words with *wisdom and precision*. The expression of his opinion created an impression for Pamela that her husband's anger was untreatable and impossible to change. Pamela lived with the same kind of hope as a condemned felon. The words of the therapist kept her in solitary confinement. She felt her situation was hopeless and her husband would never change, at least until two wives later.

He could have just as easily said "inoperable brain tumor." He had poisoned her with hopelessness for her marriage and the safety of her children. When Pamela came to see me, she essentially came seeking a second opinion. When she asked me, "Do you think Tom will ever change?" the same question she had asked the previous counselor, I told her "I don't see why this should be a problem." The sense of hope and release was enormous for Pamela. She looked at me dumbstruck and told me what the previous therapist had said.

Pamela had left Tom and had taken their two small children with her. The precipitating event, the straw that was breaking the back of this marriage, involved Tom and one of his bouts of rage. A former lifeguard and a physically fit man, Tom took his five-year-old son's "See and Say" toy and smashed it into a thousand pieces when the boy would not share the toy with his sister. The violent action terrified the small boy. Later when Tom had calmed down Pamela was calming and soothing their son. With tears streaming down his face, he looked up to his mother and said, *"What if Daddy does that to me?"*

The child was bright enough to understand the toy was a substitute for him. When he saw the demolished toy, he wondered aloud to his mother, "Am I going to be next?" When Tom realized and understood he had terrorized his son, he broke. He recalled stories of shame and humiliation he had experienced with his own father. As a young adolescent his father would make him put on boxing gloves. His father would put on his gloves. The garage was the ring. His father would then proceed to beat him mercilessly to a bloody pulp. Bullies become bullies usually because someone bullied them. Tom realized he was beginning to do the same things to his son that had been done to him and it had to stop. He would have to learn how to stop, drop, and roll to hold the reaction and seek healing for the pain he had been carrying all those years.

Holding the reaction - Stopping reactivity does not mean we are simply sealing off these emotions and denying their existence. Stopping reactivity is not about repressing emotions. Stopping reactivity is about *holding* these emotions and not projecting them on to other people or internalizing them. When we *project* these emotions onto and into others, *they* become the ones who end up holding the pain, as Trenton's father was doing with him when he was raging about the gym bag he left in the car. When we *interject* these emotions within the self, we may end up suffering from a number of somatic illnesses or diseases that are created by internalizing this type of toxic emotional distress just as it was with Ms. Z.

When we are *holding* these emotions, we will be willing to explore what is pulling the triggers and heal the hurt that is causing the reactivity. When we are *holding* these emotions, the question to ask is this: *"What is it about the present situation that is triggering unresolved pain from the past?"*

Jack's story may help us understand these critically important distinctions. Jack, an attorney, came to see me with his wife after news of his extra-marital relationship became public, and Lori, his spouse, found out. The "third party" was an attorney who Jack had hired in his firm. In reality, Jack had been seduced. Jack did report after the encounter he felt "dirty," and came home and showered in an obsessive manner. The description of his behavior was not much different from women who have reported incidences of rape. However, this was where Jack was attempting to hold conflicted thoughts, feelings, and emotions (The "C" in FRICK). He was also infatuated with his younger associate. Jeannie was much younger than Jack was. She was just a few years older than his eldest son was and young enough to have been his daughter. He was mesmerized by her skills and abilities as an attorney, and in many ways Jeannie mirrored how Jack saw himself when he was her age. Jack felt as if he had some real help for the first time in his many years in his law practice. He fell "head over heels" in love with Jeannie, or so he thought. After a few months Jack was able to say, "I don't think the problem is Jeannie; I think the problem is me."

As we went below the surface Jack revealed he had been raised in an abusive home. His father had been an alcoholic who had been both verbally and physically abusive to him. Jack carried many bad memories and ill feelings toward his father. Jack had experienced problems with anger all throughout his adult life. His wife and two sons at times feared him because of his occasional expressions of rage. After one such experience, nearly eight years previously, Lori *warned* her husband about these outbursts. She threatened him by telling him she would take their two sons and leave him if it ever happened again. Jack "changed" instantly and became a very even-tempered man. When Jack remembered what had happened in response to his wife's threat, he realized the extra-marital relationship had awakened *all* his feelings. He had learned from his wife's threat to repress his anger. As is the case, a person cannot repress *one feeling* without *other feelings being involved in the connection.* Although often given to working long hours, Jack further adopted a stance of being a workaholic, and he buried himself in briefs and billable hours. Now in the depths of a mid-life crisis Jack knew he was in trouble.

Jack recalled from his history and experience what it was like when his dad had targeted his anger at him. Jack recalled feeling victimized from being the recipient of his dad's verbal tirades and abuse. As an adult, the victim became the perpetrator in his role as a husband, father and attorney where he could use his power and assume the role of bully. When his wife threatened him with abandonment, he learned how to repress his anger. The affair blew the manhole cover off the sewer of his rage. Any repressed emotion is like a beach ball. If we sit on a beach ball in a pool or in the ocean, we know we can sit on it for a while. Eventually, however, Newtonian physics will prove to be true, but in the reverse. "What gets pushed *down* must come *up.*" The beach ball will ultimately win.

Jack's anger was often amplified out of proportion to the circumstance and situation and he would become reactive. Whenever a response to a situation elicits a reaction "greater than" what might ordinarily be understood as "normal," this over-reaction indicates a high probability that unresolved issues have been activated from the past. This is a key point in understanding reactivity: *something in the present triggers old pain from the past.* (Reactivity or the R in FRICK) The unconscious mind has a difficult time understanding that traumatic experiences are in fact "over." These "issues" will often surface in relationships or with people where the response may be "similar" to prior experiences. Couples generally learn how to locate the "buttons" of their mates and how to push them. If an adult, who was raised in a critical environment and was constantly scolded has a spouse who is critical of a meal or who only gives minimal notice to a commission bonus, in that moment the spouse can trigger 20 years of unresolved pain by a word, the tone of voice or body language. The present situation "automatically" triggers the old pain, and the hijacking takes place. If the heat is "hotter" than it should be, we have probably found one of our own "hot spots". These sensitive issues, because the unconscious mind does not understand the previous experiences are "over," will continue to surface in a variety of ways: usually in relationships, dreams and reoccurring or obsessive thoughts.

Healing the pain - When we are *holding* these emotions, we will want to explore what is pulling the triggers and healing the hurt that is causing the reactivity. When we are *holding* these emotions, the question we will ask is this: "What is it about the present situation that is triggering unresolved pain from the past?" What is the threat? The first aspect of threat involves the triggering of the instinctual autonomic responses of anger or anxiety. The second aspect of threat involves the triggering of these same reactions by what is our *learned* reaction to threat. In order to understand and defuse anger and anxiety and move toward a cure at the core, we must move toward an evolved sense of our own consciousness and the healing of the pain that lies underneath these emotions.

Anger and anxiety are the sentinels guarding the

gateway to our pain. The cure at the core occurs when these sentinels lay down their weapons and the underlying hurt is healed. When our hurt is healed, our pain gives birth to meaning. Let us look at two different situations involving the healing of pain, the first involving anxiety and the second involving anger.

Laura was a woman in her mid-thirties, happily adjusted in her second marriage, and by her appearance, she seemed to be someone who would have nothing but happiness in store for her. By profession, she was an attorney although not practicing law at the time. She was highly intelligent, articulate, stunningly poised and attractive. Laura's physical beauty was intimidating and brought her a great deal of unwanted attention. She had become something of a recluse given her daily struggles with panic attacks, which she kept a secret. Driving in an uncertain area or jogging beyond the sight of her home might trigger one of these terrible ordeals when her adrenalin would take over, her breathing would become hyperventilated and her heart would race out of control.

Within two weeks, we had Laura's panic attacks under control, and Laura began to make plans to drive across the state to visit her brother and nephews she had not seen in some time. She continued in counseling to explore issues of her own personal growth and we worked together for about six months. During this time, Laura explored issues involving her history and experience as we explored life in her family.

Her father was a salesman who was gone a great deal of the time. This meant she would be left at home with her younger brother and her mother. As a child, Laura was often extremely confused by her mother's behavior, which frequently went beyond the bizarre. As an adult many years later, Laura could only begin to understand the depth of her mother's diagnosis as a schizophrenic. Home was hardly a place where Laura and her brother felt safe. One of Laura's earliest memories was around the age of five when she was in the kitchen, standing on a stool making peanut butter and jelly sandwiches for her brother and herself. Laura's mother came into the kitchen and in an unprovoked rage began chasing Laura around the house with a butcher knife. In the safety of my office, Laura experienced her terror and fear as fresh as if it was happening again for the first time.

One of the immediate targets I wanted to aim for was for Laura to understand *the trauma was over*. Her safety was no longer a threat. She had survived, and she was okay. I assisted her in an exercise to help her make this distinction concrete and real. I asked Laura to close her eyes and envision the scene with her mother chasing her around the room. This time, I told her instead of a knife her mother would be chasing her around the room and attempting to stab her with *a banana*. As she envisioned this scene, Laura began to smile and laugh. Her terror was immediately relieved. No one has ever been stabbed to death with a banana. She was able to see the humor in this event and to know her mother was no longer a threat to her safety.

Laura was perplexed and baffled that at such a young age she had to look after herself and her brother even to the point of having to prepare a meal. This seemed quite normal and natural to her at the time, but in retrospect, she could see the distortion. Although no other single incident stood out in her mind, Laura indicated this episode was a representative experience of her childhood years. It demonstrated her ongoing struggle to find safety in a chaotic household. Her main means of survival was to get out of the house and to take her brother with her. Often when they would return hours later, they might find their mother acting as if nothing had happened. She might instead be loving and caring. This bizarre shift further added to her confusion because she could never be sure if her mother would be crazy or calm. When Laura was older, she would report these experiences to her father. He would discount them and would do nothing to "get that crazy woman away from us." In school, Laura learned she could be a good student and worked hard as a way of channeling her energy in hopes of receiving positive recognition. One of her greatest disappointments came when she graduated from college and her father chose not to attend.

Laura responded well to psychotherapy and soon felt she had taken care of her concerns, which had haunted her for many years. Her panic attacks remained under control for over a year, until one day, she called me on her cell phone, driving on Interstate 95 right in the middle of a panic attack! I felt like an air traffic controller trying to land an airplane while the pilot is slumped over in the cockpit and some well-meaning passenger is fumbling with the controls. In essence, this is what happens when a panic attack takes over. The emotion hijacks the person and takes over control. This attempt to bring relief for Laura over the telephone was limited. What worked was doing what she needed to be doing in order to feel safe. This meant getting her back on the road and moving in the direction of home. It was then the symptoms subsided and Laura felt better. We did meet for a few more times. As a post-script to this story, I recently saw Laura and she reported she had been free of panic attacks for 10 years.

Leland was a 40-year-old man who came for psychotherapy because of his need to clarify his life's purpose, to wrestle with his sense of vocation and to tackle some of the existential "blues" he associated with his career. Leland saw himself as being stuck in his present predicament. He considered a wide array of options. He struggled with whether to remain in his present occupation, teach philosophy, do computer programming or become a psychotherapist. Leland married for the first time in his mid-thirties. He reported a loss of wanderlust because as a married man he no longer was able to enjoy the freedom he once had.

Over an extended time, Leland worked hard on his issues and came to therapy each week raring to go. He explored his issues with his family of origin. Leland was the oldest of four children. His father remained temporarily behind when he, his mother and siblings moved to Indiana from New York State. With dad back in New York, in mid adolescence Leland became the "man of the house." His mother became more absorbed in alcohol and Leland took care of things, including his mother. Leland agreed the "critical voice" which often intervened in his thinking was closely paralleled to the voice of his father with whom he could never do anything right. Leland reported a longing for his father's approval and remembered with anger and regret what happened when a neighbor's son graduated from high school. Leland's father spent hours talking with this neighbor's son about his dreams, his goals, and aspirations - a conversation which never happened between Leland and his father.

Leland came to counseling one day and reported an experience he recalled many years ago when he was a young boy. His father was outside, climbing a ladder when he looked through the window and saw Leland trying to put sugar on his breakfast cereal. Leland spilled sugar on the table and in his bowl. To his horror his father came down the ladder and into the house in a full blown rage and told his young son, "If you can't eat your breakfast without spilling sugar all over the place, then by God you'll *just never get to eat again!"*

Leland sobbed as he re-experienced this moment when his father had tattooed him with toxic emotions. I was struck with the absurdity to think a child would be forbidden to eat due to a slight error in coordination! From the best evidence I can tell, eating is a physiological need driven by either survival or pleasure. Not eating is usually not an option.

Leland struggled with anger as well as depression. He reported an incident in which his spouse had not followed his advice concerning the purchase of new tires for her car. He had researched the tires, done his homework and she decided to do something else other than what he recommended. When his wife reported this to him, he pulled off to the side of the road and began pounding the steering wheel with his fists. He told me he felt like a "little kid having a temper tantrum." Leland reported his depression would begin on

Sunday evenings when he knew he would have to get up the next day and go to a job he hated. Usually there would be some form of conflict with his wife on Sunday evenings, a ritual they both learned they could use to set their watches. Leland never felt adequately appreciated, by his wife, his employer, his peers and occasionally by me. As all married persons occasionally do, he was not sure he had married the "right" person. He did not know if his vocation was meaningful enough for him or if he should change course and direction. When the time for making decisions came Leland would gather volumes of data and information and get stuck as to which way to go. He lived in fear of making a "wrong" decision. He would end up in a sea of regret and sorrow. His attempts at avoiding *making* decisions were an attempt at avoiding making a *wrong* decision. He lived in fear of failure.

Leland decided to go back to school at night and work to become a therapist. He had to take several undergraduate courses before he could be accepted into graduate school. One undergraduate professor shook Leland to the core when she questioned his commitment to become a therapist. She told him if he wanted to become a therapist, he should quit his job and move out of state to attend another school, which had a reputation for graduating some of the best therapists in the nation. This feedback bothered Leland because now he thought he might have made a wrong decision.

Now well into her forties Leland's wife became pregnant and they became parents to a son. Leland was going to school three nights a week, working as a student counselor one night a week and studying most of the weekend. He constantly complained about never having enough time to do anything. He called and made an appointment and laid out his life as it was going. He asked if I thought it was okay if he decided to give up his dream of becoming a therapist. There is an old story that goes; "How many therapists does it take to change a light bulb?" The answer is, "I don't know, what do you think?" Leland indicated he was happier with his work and seemed to be enjoying it more. He felt like he was missing his son's childhood. Missing his son's childhood might provide him with regret he did not want to carry. He decided to quit school.

For Leland, the internalized threat was far more complicated. As the oldest of four children, he had assumed more responsibility than necessary when he was growing up. As a teenager, he became the "man of the house" taking care of his younger siblings and his alcoholic mother. It was a role in which he was never adequately appreciated and one which left him hungering for mirroring and recognition. His over-critical internalized voice of conscience was the condemning voice of his father. His paralysis in decision-making involved his efforts to keep from hearing his father's condemning voice, a weapon he used on himself and occasionally on other people. Feeling safe was something Leland knew little about because for many years he was haunted by the internalized voices of self-condemnation. The healing of his pain did not happen with a flash of insight, but by doing the painstakingly slow and methodical work required by therapy.

To my surprise, ten years after our work together I received a graduation announcement. Leland had received his master's degree in counseling and was working on his internship to become a marriage and family therapist.

The Key To Transformational Healing: What We Do With Our Pain

The key to transformational healing involves what we do with our pain. We have three options when dealing with pain. We will either numb it, transmit it, or it will transform us if we learn how to hold our pain. We will *numb* our pain with alcohol, drugs, pornography, television, food, sex, the internet, or other obsessions, compulsions, or addictions.

I worked with Jill, a spiritual sojourner, who was also a compulsive workaholic. She had wrestled with her weight most of her adult life. She was like a hummingbird and was always in constant motion. Hummingbirds must continually be eating to maintain the energy they exude. This is where the comparison stopped. She was constantly in motion but rarely ate anything but a piece of fruit, nuts, or a protein bar during the day. She always kept 15 plates spinning in the air at once. She lived in fear and anxiety that the plates would all come crashing down at once. However, at night, when things began to slow down, she began to notice a pattern creeping into her awareness. One day she reported to me, "I go and go and go all day but then around 9:00 p.m. at night I go into the kitchen and I start *grazing*. All day long, I keep disciplined eating patterns but at night, I cannot. Why do I do this?" I paused for what must have seemed like an eternity for this woman who wanted a quick answer so she could get on to the next thing to check off of her list. I said, "I do not know Jill. That is a great question! Why do you do this? I paused for a while to let the question she asked to sink in and saturate. I then asked Jill, "What would happen if the next time you had a compulsive thought to go and graze if you asked yourself what you were feeling? Is there something emerging within you that you do not want to feel? Are you feeling boredom or anxiety? Are you trying to calm and sooth?" Whatever the compulsion or addiction, these are important questions to ask ourselves if we are trying to avoid, deny, or repress emotions. The compulsion or addiction will temporarily mask what we do not want to see or feel.

    If we are *transmitting* our pain, we are looking for a target to blame. We will constantly be on a search to find new targets and scapegoats to *project* our pain. Todd, a successful architect, was approaching fifty when he came to work with me. He had been married for eighteen years and was the father of three children. He came initially to counseling because of a marital demand. He needed, he said, "to work on himself." However, most of his complaints were about his spouse. He complained about his wife's relationship with their older daughter. He complained about what was not happening in the bedroom. He talked about his mother who lived in a neighboring community. "Everyone knows she is crazy." His mother's hate and rage would always manage to find a moving target that would become the focus for her to discharge her projectile toxicity. She was always at war with one of her offspring, their spouses, or her grandchildren. When she would tire of one tirade, she would start another one.

Todd presented in counseling as very professional. He was also very guarded, calculating, and cautious. He carefully chose every word he spoke. I knew of Todd from having previously worked with his spouse and his two older children. After working with him for several months, Todd's behavior became worse. He had been a binge drinker and would go months without drinking but then he would go off the wagon. After slowly building bridges of empathy after four months, he finally opened up to admit an addiction to pornography that started when he was a teenager. The addiction had continued throughout his marriage. He also liked to go to strip clubs. The latter behaviors had stopped abruptly four years earlier when he confessed to his wife but the drinking was getting worse. He blamed his wife for the compulsive behaviors because she did not meet his needs. Todd's wife called me frantically one day and reported an incident that had occurred the previous Friday evening after too much to drink. "He is like Jekyll and Hyde! You would not believe the obscenities and the profanities that came out of his mouth. He has blamed me for everything that is wrong in his life including our daughter. I am afraid he is about to totally loose it. I told him this morning I want him to move out." Todd was stuck in a pattern of numbing and blaming. The numbing was no longer working and the blaming was becoming more frantic and intense in a last ditch effort to divert his pain. His defense mechanisms were breaking down and we were beginning to stand on a perilous precipice fifty stories high and woozily looking down at people as ants on the streets below. Would he crash and burn or pull out of the dive and begin to soar? It is an endless, futile search to find the relational vomit bags to hold our toxic emotions. In order to experience transformation, we must learn how to hold our own pain rather than to numb it or project it on to others.

If we are allowing it to transform us, we have to be willing to experience our pain. As a pastor and as a pastoral counselor, I see psychotherapy as a spiritual pilgrimage. It involves a gradual de-layering of impressions that have come from our experiences. Like peeling back the layers of an onion..... you will shed some tears, but the fruit of the onion enhances the quality and flavor of your recipe. Our experiences have shaped and molded our lives. Many times these impressions and events are distorted and painful. We would rather not remember them, but the frequent results are that these impressions are getting in the way of the present, usually in the form of relationships that may be "like" or "similar" to our original experiences. We are condemned to continue in the same patterns in our relationships until we are aware of these patterns. Not dealing with them often results in replicating the same relationships or events. These events or experiences may be pushed out of consciousness. These experiences will function as a magnet to "like" or "similar" circumstances, until the original pain is resolved. Increasing awareness creates new possibilities to make purposeful choices and beneficial change. However, we cannot change what we do not see. One way of seeing *sin* in this model is to see it as unconscious behavior. We do not know why we are doing it but we just keep repeating the same mistakes and we become stuck and enmeshed in what does not work. (Romans 7:15)

If we allow our pain to transform us, we will learn how to hold and allow our pain to bring healing. Glimpses of the soul are seen from time to time throughout this process. When the distortions of the false self are worked through, the soul is further exposed. A new energy will begin to radiate from within. A trained observer will see it in the eyes of the one who is in the tractor beam of transformation, for the eyes are the windows of the soul.

At times, this process feels like death. It actually is the death of the false self. There may be extended periods of mourning and grieving.[v] Friends, family members, and others who are a part of the network of relationships may not understand. They may seem indifferent or even hostile. Change does not occur in a vacuum. Change creates anxiety. Change will disturb the equilibrium in a family system. Other persons in the network of relationships will be affected by your growth and change. They will sometimes fight to return the family system to the previous familiar dysfunctional patterns. For other family members who did not necessarily "sign up for these changes" the dysfunctional patterns are at least *known* and *familiar*. At times, you will feel like a salmon swimming upstream. If you are on a spiritual expedition, you will learn how to resist these forces of entropy that will be working to reverse the current and to return the tide toward the familiar. If we are able to uncover our spiritual reservoir (John 4:14) and release this new energy, what is "beyond" will touch what is "within" and the soul will drink from wells that will provide the wisdom and energy to press forward and to create new meanings.

In summary, if our health is in jeopardy, we do not feel safe. In the field of Global Medicine, we need to establish openness and dialogue with alternative methodologies that facilitate healing and activate gene expression. Our bodies hold emotional pain and can turn disease into disease. There is strong evidence to correlate a connection between healing and forgiveness. Practicing forgiveness is not only about the big issues but presents a daily challenge! CASHING in reactive living is a process that involves creating awareness, assessing the threat, stopping reactivity, holding the reaction, and healing the pain. Transformational healing involves what we are doing with our pain. We will numb it, transmit it, or it will transform us if we learn how to hold our pain and lead us to healing.

---

[v] Christianity is essentially about going ahead, dying now, and getting it over with so we can learn to live in the one true life. (Mark 8: 34-35, John 12:24, Romans 6:5)

Chapter 7
Transcendence

> "This is your last chance. After this, there is no turning back. You take the blue pill - the story ends, you wake up in your bed and believe whatever you want to believe. You take the red pill - you stay in Wonderland and I show you how deep the rabbit-hole goes." *Morpheus to Neo in the motion picture movie, "The Matrix"*

> "The world we see and experience in a state of fear, rage, dire emergency, competition, or struggle is quite different from that which we experience in a state of harmony and love."[62]

When the Dalai Lama came to New York City in 2003, he gave a four-day teaching to sellout crowds in the Beacon Theatre. The glittering marquee over the entrance proclaimed, "On Stage: The Dalai Lama... Coming soon, Twisted Sister and Hot Tuna." The day after the teachings, the Dalai Lama gave a talk at Central Park. Under a brilliant sky, the East Meadow was blanketed with loyal fans, spiritual seekers, and the simply curious. An enormous stage bracketed by huge videotrons was erected for the occasion. Those who could not find space in the grassy fields peeked through dense foliage from beyond the tree line. All told, 100,000 people came for the event of the season. This was a mini-Woodstock choreographed by actor Richard Gere. Only Billy Graham and Pope John Paul II have drawn more people in Central Park.[63]

Why? Why has there been such a tremendous response to these three spiritual leaders? Why have persons been drawn to these three like magnets, like moths to porch lights? What is it about these spiritual leaders that draw loyal fans, spiritual seekers and the simply curious? Do we admire them from a distance or believe they have something we all desire? Do we revere them and believe they have unraveled the great mysteries? Do we believe they have lived their lives with a force of spiritual integrity? How do we make sense of the millions of mourners who stood in front of televisions and lined the streets of Rome when John Paul II died?

I will return to these questions at the end of the chapter, but for now, let it suffice to say that this chapter is about the red pill. This chapter is about transcendence. Once the dawning of awareness begins, there is no turning back. Here there is a far richer meaning than the ordinary maintenance of the mundane. Spiritual pilgrims approach their sojourn with a sense of sacred awe, wonder, and an appreciation of the mystical. *For the spiritual pilgrim meaning comes from living in the mystery.*

Easily Amused and Comfortably Numb

We are so easily bored and so easily amused. A consultant friend of mine told me about a job he had in Philadelphia. A certain high-rise office complex opened and there were immediate complaints that the elevators were too slow. He was hired to find the problem and offer solutions. He and his team rode the elevators, timed their trips from the bottom floor to the top floor and back again. They timed the express elevator and they timed stopping on each floor. Armed with this information they rode other elevators throughout the city and compared the data. They discovered no appreciable difference between the elevators in the new building and the elevators in comparable buildings throughout the city. They concluded that the people were bored. The recommendation he made to the building owners was to put mirrors at each stop. The owners agreed. Once the mirrors were installed at each landing, the complaints about slow elevators stopped immediately. The problem was solved.

Transcendence is not about going up the elevator and looking *at* your self; transcendence is about being anywhere and looking *within* yourself. To look within allows us to see what goes beyond and reaches to the stars! This new vision opens the windows of our soul and illuminates us from within. This is cosmic consciousness and a dance between immanence and transcendence. Transcendence is about the "beyond" and immanence is about the "within." This chapter discusses connecting the two, and sorts out the pseudo, the substitutes and the imposters from the real thing. Preoccupation with how things *look* will never take us into the looking glass. This fixation keeps us stuck on form and missing the essence! All forms are highly unstable and are in various stages of growth, decline and decay. The pages you are reading will wither and rot. The MP3 or compact disc technology you use to listen to these words will be outdated in a matter of time. The automobile you are now driving and maintaining will be stripped of its reusable parts, crushed and compacted, and rusting in a junkyard in 10 or 20 years. In five years, 15 years, 50 years, or perhaps longer, we will be rotting corpses. So much about the maintenance of the cultural mundane is about appearance, about how things *seem*.

The Difference Between Glamour and Beauty

In sorting out the pseudo, we must ask one question in our search for transcendence: Does the *form* allow the *essence* to shine *through the form?* Our culture deliberately confuses glamour and beauty. Can you see the *eternal* in the *temporal?* Let us examine the distinctions between the two and clarify the confusion. Beauty is an essence shining through the form. Glamour is a weak substitute with little or no essence. Beauty nourishes and feeds the soul. Glamour is anorexic and bulimic and offers empty calories. Beauty is immanent and radiates from within; it emanates through a flower, the face of a child, and even through the wrinkled countenance of the aged. Glamour surgically removes the wrinkles or covers them with make-up. Glamour is fearful of death and fights to hide it. Beauty never dies. Beauty is timeless; glamour is temporary.

Let us look at this from the perspective of one person and see how this confusion is culturally embedded in our consciousness. Julia, a 66-year-old widow, called me on a Thursday morning at the request of the hospice chaplain who had been with her through her husband's death. When I suggested a time the following week she said her issue could not wait until then, so I offered her a noon appointment. She needed an answer *right away* and could not wait through the weekend. Julia was tiny and petite, barely five feet tall and under 100 pounds. She wore no make-up and had shoulder length gray hair. She had a simple beauty that shined through her but she was not in touch with it. She lacked awareness of the beauty I saw. Julia's husband of 45 years had died three years earlier. She described a satisfying marriage. His death from Melanoma had been quick. The cancer had metastasized from his leg to his lungs and brain. They were high school sweethearts and they had married right out of school. He had been a pilot for one of the major airlines. He left her financially comfortable. The problem she was now facing involved a man she met who was five years her junior. He was previously married and divorced twice. His second wife was also five years older than he was. Julia explained her dilemma. She had been seeing the man for just over two months. She was convinced he would lose interest in her. "I know that my body is changing. Over the last several years, gravity has taken over in some places. I exercise and walk every day. I know I will never be fat. He is so good looking! Why would he be interested in me? I just know he will leave me for somebody else in a few years when he gets tired of me and I am no longer attractive to him. I have broken it off several times but we keep getting back together. I am miserable without him and fearful when I am with him. I just know he will leave me. He needs to find somebody younger."

I told Julia she wanted a microwave answer to a crock-pot solution. This one needed to bake and stew but she wanted it right away. After ascertaining her new boyfriend's financial stability, and how they had discussed "what if" scenarios involving pre-nuptial agreements and segregated assets, I told Julia she might have linked together two separate issues. S*he had issues of abandonment connected to what she perceived as her diminished marketability as an object of desire.* Her fear was she would become *disposable* once she was no longer seen as *attractive.*

Julia is not alone. Men and women alike are embedded with similar fears. As we seek to sort out the pseudo, the meaningless and the mundane from the real, we begin with the realization that we are embedded in our own culture. Residents of the nations of Somalia and Sumatra are also culturally embedded, but their embedded-ness is *different* from ours. Our culture constantly bombards us with trivial pursuit, and creates what Paul Tillich calls "false absolutes." The culture confuses the basics necessary to grasp and be grasped by transcendence. Western culture markets glamour for beauty and confuses the two by offering glamour as a commodity and a pathetic substitute. We are seduced by the substitutes, and marketing agencies bank on this fact. Marketing agencies lull the culture into unconsciousness, which is pervasive and epidemic.

How do these ideas become entrenched in our consciousness? Let's take a slice from our cultural pie. Rock star Bon Jovi appeared as the featured guest for the pre-race show at the Daytona 500, which is the premier event of NASCAR and also known as "The Super Bowl of Racing." I was a guest of the France family and I would be watching the race from their suite at the start-finish line. We watched the pre-race festivities along with 200,000 other people in attendance and 37 million watching via satellite around the world. The pre-race activities and the race were televised live on NBC. During a commercial break the 300 or so folks who were chosen to crowd around the stage while Bon Jovi performed were turned loose and allowed to take their positions in and around the stage. While the television commentators scrutinized the race strategies of the different drivers and teams, the NBC television stage crews were working hard to deploy their Bon Jovi strategy. Who is going to be standing directly *behind* Bon Jovi and receiving most of the camera shots and her 15 seconds of fame? We studied this activity with binoculars to insure we were actually seeing what we *thought* we were seeing. First, the stage crew removed the *men* from behind the stage. Secondly, although it was a cool and drizzly February day in Daytona, the men were replaced with young attractive women wearing mostly tank tops and halter-tops. Third, they had these women rehearse jumping up and down, presumably in an attempt to avoid a "wardrobe malfunction" such as the one that occurred with Janet Jackson and Justin Timberlake at the Super Bowl in 2004. Two women, quite overly endowed, presented a problem of DD proportions. The lines of decency had clearly been drawn; they wanted *jiggle* but not *exposure*. The stage crew worked fast and furious, and found two jackets for these ladies to wear over the top of their halter-tops. The two women were strategically placed off to one side, just in case of a button bust so to speak. Bon Jovi came out and performed his three songs and the ladies behind the stage performed as well. They jiggled and jumped up and down, just as they had been choreographed to do, right on cue. There were no double exposures or wardrobe malfunctions. The stage crew had successfully done their job, and the media had once again embedded our psyche with another unreal, "real" slice of a real event.

The media constantly bombards our boredom with cheap tricks to keep us entertained in order to sell us the next thing we do not need. If we look *into* the mirror, what do we see? What do we see *beyond* appearance? What do we see when we look *within?* Can you readily observe and make distinctions between beauty and glamour? Do you recognize the beauty in others and in yourself?

Snorkelers and Divers

We can categorize people into two fundamentally distinct types: snorkelers and scuba divers. Some people are happy to snorkel on the surface and view the bottom from a distance. The snorkeler occasionally dives down, but due to the limitation of air supply, they cannot stay submerged very long. When the water is too rough, the snorkeler will stay in the boat. A snorkeler sticks to conversations revolving around news, sports and weather. If you are a snorkeler, you may want to go ahead and take the blue pill and head back. Chances are if you have gotten this far into this expedition, you want to keep on going. Perhaps you have always wanted to become a scuba diver but did not know how. Scuba divers are not content to stay on the surface. Scuba divers want to plunge into the depths of the ocean and explore life up close and personal. Scuba divers thrive on meaning and connection. They are motivated to dive deeper to discover their destiny. They want *more* out of life. This *more* is not about consumption. It is not *more* in the sense of *more of this* or *more of that*, which is the way our western culture tries to "feed the need." This *more* is about what lies underneath, down below, deep within. How do we discover an identity (our *real* self) that transcends appearance, possessions, the roles we play, activities we engage in, feelings we possess, or the body we occupy?

As previously stated, transcendence is about the *beyond* and immanence is about the *within*. How can something as innocent as our identity become a substitute and deter us from establishing an authentic integrated spirituality? "I am a millionaire" or "I am homeless," means our identity has to do with what *we have* or what *we do not have*. Since I have never seen a U-Haul attached to the back of a hearse, we can surmise we cannot take it with us. If we settle for an identity based on material possessions, hobbies or activities, the roles we play, the relationships we have or do not have, our feelings or emotions, or our physical appearance, we will miss transcendence. These forms of identity are *temporary* and highly unstable. They have to do with, "I have this, I do this, or I feel this." Let us explore some common areas where we misidentify our identity.

We are *Not our Possessions*

Author and speaker John Ortberg tells of an experience with his grandmother when he was growing up. His grandmother was one of the most saintly, loving and caring individuals he had ever known. However, she was absolutely ruthless, like an offspring of Leona Helmsley and Donald Trump, when it came to playing Monopoly.[64] She would methodically pick him apart and acquire every piece of property in the game that requires the acquisition of all properties in order to control the board. Each time she beat her grandson she would tell him, "Someday you'll learn how to play the game."

That someday came one summer at 10 years of age when he linked up with a friend and played daily until he mastered the game. With the same ruthlessness John learned from his grandmother, he now turned on this nurturing soul with sheer delight. Vividly recalling that day John remembered her final demise took place at Marvin Gardens. It was there he took her last dollar, crushing her in defeat. However, she had one more lesson to teach her grandson. As she stood up from the table, she said, "*Now remember, it all goes back in the box.*" He wanted to have the board bronzed in order to memorialize this moment in time that brought him the greatest joy he had ever known. However, the joy would not last. "All of the money, the deeds, the player tokens, the houses and hotels, even Boardwalk and Park Place, must go back in the box. The next time the game is played they will be bought, sold, and bartered all over again. It all goes back in the box."

Ownership is actually an illusion. We never truly *own* anything. It all goes back in the box. Deeds, cars, bank accounts and all of our stuff are literally reassigned to someone else once we are dead. The next time you ride by an automobile junkyard, remember that every one of those smashed rusted vehicles piled on top of one another was someone's dream. The oil was changed, the exterior was polished and the car was detailed with care but not anymore.

It all goes back in the box.

We never truly *own* anything. If anything, what we have truly *owns us*. By this, I mean the time, effort and energy required for maintaining what we possess begins to possess us. I assembled a swing set for my children when they were small. At the bottom of the instructions, a risk management attorney had successfully inserted a disclaimer: "All nuts and bolts should be tightened *on a weekly basis* in order to insure the safety of your children." On top of every other detail I needed to manage in my life this task needed to be placed on the calendar and managed religiously. If I did not and my children were injured on the swing set, the injury would be my fault.

We were living in North Florida when we bought our first piece of real estate, a river lot on the Withlacoochie River. The Withlacoochie empties into the Suwannee River (the same river Stephen Foster memorialized with, "Way down upon the Suwannee River...") four miles down river, which in turn empties into the Gulf of Mexico at Yankeetown. The lots had been in the same family since 1902. The man who sold the lot swore to me no flood had ever occurred during the entire time his family owned the property. In the next three years, we had *two* floods, perhaps making up for lost time.

I loved going out and working on this land. My father-in-law and I tore down an old slave shack (which gave me tremendous joy), and we reused the ten and 12-inch wide hand-hewn yellow pine boards for a deck we built together. We eventually moved a repossessed mobile home my brother-in-law found in Jacksonville on to the property. I dug the water hook-up after we moved the trailer in, and we were set up. I sat in the trailer one afternoon, reading, when I heard little squeaking noises. Much to my horror, I saw a small family of a half-dozen mice who apparently moved into the trailer without my knowledge or permission. I chased the mice back to the furnace area, lit the furnace in an attempt to smoke them out and I nearly burned the trailer to the ground. The lot and trailer were quiet, picturesque and accessible *only by boat after a flood*. Like Scarlet O'Hara in *Gone With The Wind*, I would grab a handful of the river sand and feel it slip through my fingers, knowing this place would always be my *Tara* - as long as I *made the payments and paid the taxes*. However, I felt as if I had sold the proverbial boat when that river land sold, the happiest days of my life being the day I bought the property and the day I sold the property. So much for the Tara myth: owning real estate does not provide safety and lasting fulfillment.

We have possessions, but *we are not our possessions*. The economic depression of the 1930s and the material deprivation of WW II were the most obvious events to shape my parents' generation. During this time, there were people watching stock market numbers drop, and as their wealth vanished, they felt as though they no longer existed. Because of their financial devastation, they literally jumped out of windows. If my identity were based on the numbers on a ticker tape or a bank account, I would theoretically cease to exist once the numbers dropped to zero. If you confuse your net worth with your personal worth, there is no reason to live if the numbers reset to zero. To these people suicide was a logical conclusion.

The deprivation of this entire generation was devastating. For many this deficiency created a lifelong struggle for safety. For many acquiring wealth equated to safety. The more an individual had, the safer he or she felt. Hoarding is a protective measure to insure a sense of safety. Hoarding creates false illusions. Safety cannot be obtained through hoarding because one can never acquire enough.

The last words my mother spoke to me before she went into surgery were, "If I don't make it out of this, *do not throw anything out."* She lived for another two and a half months in the intensive care unit, on a respirator, unable to communicate. After her death, we helped my father clean out the house. Her words finally made sense. We found over $13,000 in cash stashed in drawers and old pocketbooks. In one suitcase, she had placed $1,000 in an envelope. She also wrapped the envelope in tin foil. Supposedly, in a fire the money would not burn up. We felt like we were participating in a scavenger hunt. Mother always said she was saving up for her divorce. My mother did not trust banks, and if the bottom fell out again, she was prepared. I was stumped looking through a closet in a back bedroom when I found a *case* of toilet paper. I thought about conducting a séance to communicate with my dead mother. I was trying to "make meaning" and to figure out what she was thinking when she purchased a *case* of toilet paper. We needed to conduct a psychological autopsy to figure out this mystery. Then I remembered, after the second Arab oil embargo in 1979 gas prices shot through the roof. There were long lines at the gas pumps. Johnny Carson, of The Tonight Show fame, predicted in his monologue that our next shortage would be *toilet paper*. Sure enough, a panic ensued and a shortage followed. In the back of my mother's closet, we found one of the reasons for the shortage. She was not going to do without. She tucked away her own reserve. The world could go to hell, but the McNeil family was going to wipe!

    My mother was a simple woman. As an adult, she worked as a waitress in a restaurant and donut shop. When she was hired as a ward clerk in a hospital the position was the closest she would come to her career aspiration. She always wanted to be a nurse, but never made it. She never finished high school. Because of this, she always felt I would be ashamed of her. As a little girl, she grew up in a series of Methodist parsonages. When we moved into our home when I was four years old she said, "I ain't moving again until they move me out feet first." Her words came true.

    In 1934, her father was not paid the entire year, although church members would bring vegetables from their gardens and an occasional chicken. When Papa retired in 1945 that same church he served in 1934 sent representatives to his retirement celebration and paid him that full year's salary, which they could not afford to pay during the depths of the depression. Another telling incident that helped to shape my mother's lens for how she saw the world happened when her oldest brother, who later became a very wealthy man and self-made millionaire, came home from Wofford College. He was working his way through college selling magazine subscriptions. He found his parents sitting at the kitchen table drinking hot water. When he asked them what they were doing, Papa said, "We're *pretending* we're drinking coffee." My uncle left in disgust, vowing he would never live in poverty; he did not.

My father's story was not much different. His father was a carpenter and farmer. Their house burned down when he was five and the only items saved were the mattresses. Like my mother, he was one of seven children. One of his younger sisters caught pneumonia in the chill of that winter night when their house burned down and she later died. My father always said, "We moved every time the rent came due." He tells gut-wrenching stories every Christmas about walking five miles with his brother to the Florida Theater in downtown Jacksonville where the poor children would stand in line to sit on Santa's lap. He, along with the other children, was given a bag with an orange, some nuts and a toy. Every year my parents went all out at Christmas, partially I am sure to repair their own hurt about Christmas disappointments.

The economic depression and WW II radically shaped what Tom Brokaw has called "The Greatest Generation." The safety needs of that generation were first threatened economically and then politically as young men were sent to fight a war to save the world from tyranny. Initially the depression created a foreign policy stance of global isolationism that forced us into withdrawal in order to take care of ourselves. The bombing of Pearl Harbor changed that isolationism overnight. The values forged out of these experiences were varied, including sacrifice, a deep appreciation of all material possessions, and perhaps a skewed sense that safety and happiness could be achieved through acquiring possessions. No matter how many or how few possessions we have in life, we *are not* our possessions. They all go back in the box.

We are *Not our Feelings*

Although this may come as a shock to many people, especially therapists or counseling junkies, we *are not our feelings*. Our emotions can teach us a great deal. Our feelings are certainly an important component of what partially enables us to be human. To *see* a sunset is very different than to *feel* a sunset. I would not trade anything for the feelings I felt when I married, the joy I felt when my children were born, the grief I experienced when my mother died or other feelings I have felt in a million other day-to-day experiences. I have met individuals who are cut off from their emotions and have done so because of an inherent risk. They are afraid of their emotions, and *feeling their emotions becomes a threat*.

Feeling is a way of knowing, but not the only way of knowing. Bandler and Grinder were the first pioneers in the learning theory they labeled as *Audio-Linguistic Programming*. Through their captivating study of the work of Milton Erickson, they concluded each human being has one dominant way of perceiving the way he or she sees the world. We each have methods of learning and perceiving in place, but one method tends to be more dominant.

Bandler and Grinder indicated that the dominant ways of this knowing are primarily audio, visual, or kinesthetically oriented. The language or actions of the person or persons we are with will disclose their dominant ways of perception. Audio dominant persons are idea or concept driven. By profession, these individuals tend to be accountants, computer technicians, engineers or in professions which have a high concentration of technical skills as opposed to "people skills."[65] They present themselves in a formal way. When Tim Savage of LEAD Consultants worked as a local church pastor, he concluded audio dominant people would traditionally sit in the back of the church. When they would leave he might hear them say, "Thank you very much; you've given me something new to think about." They would then bow at the waist and leave.

Visually dominant people usually sat in the middle of the church. Their orientation was more toward how things *look or appear*. As they exited the church they would say, "You've given me a new way of *seeing* an old issue, and I really have a different *vision* for myself. By the way, doesn't the choir look nice in their new robes?" The kinesthetically oriented people predominately sat down front in the sanctuary. When they left they would say, "Did you really *feel* the spirit move today? It just felt really awesome." Their departure usually included a request for a hug, or the hug was just taken anyway. Kinesthetically oriented people and audio dominant individuals drive each other crazy. Savage found when working with this mix on committees, audio dominant folks champion themselves as realists and kinesthetically oriented people feel they are more spiritual. Audio dominant people make decisions by projecting outcomes based on income and expenses. Kinesthetically oriented people make decisions based on "faith" and "how the Spirit is leading us."[66]

One of the problems with identifying with our feelings is that our *feelings are subject to change.* For this reason to identify our self with our feelings is, at best, risky business. Why would we want to confuse the identification of the self with the feelings we feel? The risk of doing this is if we experience a particular feeling, we become *that feeling*, at least in the moment. Have you ever caught yourself saying, "I am tired," or "I am depressed," or "I am lonely," or "I am angry," and you believe this is who you are?

I worked with an older unmarried couple that came to see me. She was 80 years old and he was 75. He wanted to get married and she did not. Both had outlived their previous spouse with whom they had been married for many years. They each enjoyed the companionship of the other, and they spent a great deal of time together. The man finally grew tired of going home every night; he eventually ended up sleeping over and finally moved in with this woman. A tragic reality for older couples is that if a couple gets married, pensions can be forfeited if those pensions were connected to the incomes of a deceased spouse. Being married for this woman meant she might lose her financial security if her new husband were to die. He felt the guilt, which came from "living in sin" and not being married to this woman. They were **FRICKed**, with a special overload of conflicted thoughts, feelings and emotions, caught in the bind of a moral dilemma.

    One of the first statements this woman said to me when they came and sat on my couch was, "He is depressed." I quickly shot back to her, "No, *he is not.*" She looked shocked and said, "*He is too* depressed." Equally unimpressed I stated again, "No, *he is not*!" At this moment, I saw the frustration build up in her face, and I thought she was going to get up and club me with her purse. She blurted out, "He's been in the hospital for three weeks, he's had medications and shock treatments and he is too depressed!" I looked back at her and said, "He may have been in the hospital for three weeks, had medications and shock treatments, but he is *not* depressed!" It was then I explained to her he may have been *feeling* depression, but *he was not depressed.*

    I take depression seriously. I have worked with hundreds of people through all types of depression, including the dark night of the soul variety, which comes from working through abandonment depression. I have been on suicide watches with sojourners who teetered on the edge of this world and the next, hanging on by a mere thread. I believe in throwing every weapon in the arsenal against this slippery slope, which slides the self into the black pit of despair. I have seen transformational results from individuals taking serotonin uptake enhancing medications. These medications provide enough relief to allow the process of counseling to be more effective. Over recent years, the humanization of electro-shock therapy has also proven beneficial for the most severely depressed. I definitely believe in taking depression seriously.

    What I was not going to take seriously with this couple was their misidentification of feelings as an identifier for the self. Feelings change, but the self and the soul stay fairly constant, unless we are subject to constant states of fragmentation. We *have* feelings, but we *are not* our feelings. Identifying the self with our feelings is not the method to define who we are at the core. Feelings change but our core remains constant.

Christine was a 29-year-old woman and a graphic design artist by trade. She came to counseling with a need to work through issues. For most of her adolescence and adulthood, she had learned to numb her pain by self-medicating with alcohol and cocaine. She stated she had been *clean* for six months. Christine moved to our area from Maine where she previously lived with her mother. She had seen a therapist twice a week while she was living there. We scheduled our second meeting for the following week, and a half hour before the appointment she called to cancel. I returned her call. She was frantic. She told me she had done something horrible. She was too embarrassed to come. I told her this was all the more reason to come. I told her she was wasting time and to come right away, even though she would be late. When Christine arrived, she explained two days after our initial visit she had gone out for some beers. She was feeling as if she could handle drinking. Two days later, she did it again. When she awoke the next morning, she went out, bought crack cocaine and smoked it all.

I saw Christine at her absolute worst. She was coming down fast and crashing from her high. It was a dreadful scene. She yelled and screamed, repeatedly using the "F" bomb and she directed much of her hostility toward me. Christine missed her previous therapist and claimed she was in love with him. She was embedded with reactive issues involving justice and meaning. Life was not fair; she did not understand the point of it all. It did not make any sense to get up, work, pay bills and live with someone she did not love. "What's the point of it all?" she screamed at me. She demanded me to tell her the secret of life and blamed me for withholding the answer from her. Finally, in utter disgust, she scowled, claiming she was in the grips of a demon. Her self-diagnosis may have been accurate. What came next was absolutely terrifying. She screamed, "I HATE MYSELF!" Christine was expressing the extreme split in human consciousness. Is there two Christines? Which one is she? Is she the "I" or the "Myself" she hates? The two-headed cobra was again continually biting itself and injecting venom into its own bloodstream! Christine was FRICKed! She was injecting herself with a lethal dosage of toxic emotions.

Our feelings are always subject to change. To identify the self with our feelings would have been tragic in Christine's situation, or for that matter in any situation. We have feelings, but *we are not our feelings*. Limiting our identity by misidentification of the self with our feelings is a lamentable mistake.

We are *Not our Relationships*

When my son was 19 years old, in his mind, to stay home on a Friday night was a punishment worse than death. If given a choice, staying home on a Friday night would have been worse than death row at the state penitentiary. As for his sister, 15 years old at the time, my wife and I wondered if we needed to have the telephone surgically removed from the side of her face. Many, if not all 15 year olds today have their own cell phones. For her fifteenth birthday, she wanted caller ID. After one family evening night out, we returned home and she had received no less than 20 phone calls!

You may recall this time in your own adolescence. The identification with a peer group is extremely strong. The importance of peer acceptance cannot be overstated. The group provides an identity for its members at a time when structures of the self are not yet fully in place. Each group has unspoken conditions and terms of acceptance. The more formal the group, the more likely those conditions are conscious, spoken and known. To the extent these groups provide an identity for the individual members, the probability is greater an individual will fragment at the possibility of being excluded or denied acceptance by the group. The need for peer acceptance, of course, is not limited to adolescence.

Hannah initially came to counseling to work on two issues. One issue involved her unresolved grief over the death of her husband, a longer-term issue. An immediate issue involved her struggle with several people in the gated golf community where she lived. Hannah had been a cheerleader in high school and college, and by her own admission, she was a "people pleaser." The gated community where she lived was a contained system, much like in a small town. The informal hierarchies of power were extremely dysfunctional. After spending a year in a self-imposed exile, staying at home and grieving the death of her husband behind closed drapes, Hannah began to venture slowly back out into her neighborhood community. She was an avid golfer, having played on the golf team in college, and she again picked up her clubs and started playing. She began to spend time with a male friend who later became her companion. Hannah took care of the man's aging mother on many occasions, but after a year in the relationship, she realized the relationship was not working. She chose to end the relationship. Hannah was cast as a social pariah and the censure she received in this community was beyond her wildest imagination. The way the members of her group framed this threw her for a loop. Word got back to her she was being labeled as someone who "did not care about old people," evidenced by the fact she had *abandoned* this man's mother in her hour of greatest need! She was the victimizer, and he was the victim or worse yet, this man's poor helpless mother was the victim. Other individuals circulated rumors. Two vicious comments, which got back to her through the relationship grapevine and bothered her the most, were that she was promiscuous and that she was a "bitch." To be called a "bitch" is one of the most biting criticisms many women feel to the core. Hannah was terribly distraught over being rejected, slandered, and scorned. She was considering moving from her gated community to another location. I suggested to her it would be much easier for her to adjust to the situation than it was for her to move, and if things did not improve in six months she should then consider the possibility of moving. Hannah could not understand why anyone would not like her and how "anyone could believe those lies about me." Hannah worked hard in counseling. She could not control how other people saw her but she could regulate how she saw herself. She chose not to move and she remained a resident of her community..

The fact of the matter is this. We have relationships, but *we are not our relationships.* Relationships are connections, which confer identity. The self involves "I." Relationships involve "we" or "us." When relationships end or terminate, the mistake often made confuses the "we" with the "I." If I have limited myself by defining who I am to a relationship then I have narrowly focused my identity and lost sight of other extremely important components of both self and identity. We have other roles and identities rather than the one in question, but if this is the way we have *limited* our identification by identity, then these other components will remain unseen and hidden.

In a relational transaction, something more is transpiring in the merging of self with another. This something more is the *borrowing* of another person to fill in the gaps of what is missing in me. This is the dynamic described in Chapter 5 of "opposites attract" or "replicating the familiar." These relationships are predominately unconscious when a person does not see the other person as "other," or as *"an independent center of initiative."* When these unconscious contracts break down, it comes as a result of someone I desperately need to fix what is missing in me no longer is working.

Ms. B., a woman in her early forties with two adult children, came to see me because of problems she was having in her relationship with her second husband, which is something of an understatement. Several years earlier she had been driving down Interstate 95 in her van and looked in the rear view mirror. She witnessed her husband having sex with her daughter on the rear bench seat. "That isn't happening," she told herself, and quickly shut it out of her mind. Three years later, she was now acknowledging it *did* happen and she began to experience intense anger toward him, as you might expect. Before this revelation Ms. B. was so psychologically "merged" with her husband she could never be angry with him. If Ms. B. wanted to be *angry* with him, it meant she would have to be *separate* from him. When they married, her husband told her, "You don't even have to do the thinking anymore. I'll do the thinking *for* you." Counseling was tedious and much like separating co-joined twins merged at the hip. She had been stuck in this psychological merger with her husband for many years, and now she was disentangling from the mess. It was a fascinating process to observe. She described one occasion when her husband was upset with her. Ordinarily she would have hurriedly gone to apologize, even when the disagreement was not her fault. This was something she would do in order to smooth things over and quickly move back to the safety of the previous merger. Her husband went upstairs. He was playing his electric guitar, using the instrument as an outlet for his frustration. She remained downstairs. She was sitting in a chair, literally clutching the arms of the chair so she would not give in and go upstairs. The harder and the faster he played, the harder she had to hold on to the arms of the chair to keep from going upstairs. She was learning to **CASH** in reactivity by creating awareness and holding the reaction. Finally, the music stopped, and when it did, Ms. B. was able to relax. Shortly thereafter, he came down and apologized to her. She was ecstatic! It was a breakthrough experience for Ms. B. She was free of her identity based upon, "I am my relationship."

    In the process of working through grief during either divorce or death, the grieving is not only for the loss and missing of the *individual*, but also for the way this other individual *functioned* for the one grieving. The surviving loved one must now be able to provide for him or her what was previously borrowed from the now missing person. One woman I know became extremely angry and frustrated with her dead spouse when she was repeatedly having car trouble. Her grieving triggered justice issues. "Damn it, he was the one who always took care of these things! Why do I have to be stuck doing this crap?" If the person who is now dead or gone was the one to provide the calming and soothing, the one grieving must now discover how to do this on his or her own. Grieving can also be a process of *transmuting internalization*, when the individual begins to internalize some of the functions which were previously "borrowed" in the marital or relational "merger."

Again, we have relationships but *we are not our relationships.* Melanie, a registered nurse, came home to take care of her parents when her father was diagnosed with colon cancer. After going through both surgery and chemotherapy, he died a very slow and difficult death. He took nearly a year to die. In just a few months after her father's death, her mother was also diagnosed with colon cancer. Melanie went through the same process with her dying mother. The mother died less than a year after her father.

Melanie was emotionally spent after providing constant care for her parents for over two years. She had been their only source of care giving. She soon went back to work. After about four months of working at a local hospital, she decided to have a complete physical to make sure she was in good health. A mammogram produced a slight concern, which troubled the radiologist. The radiologist asked Melanie to come back in four months to re-check the spot. Melanie was not concerned since there was no family history of breast cancer. In four months, the spot had not grown, but neither had it gone away. She indicated her willingness to have a biopsy and approached her surgeon about doing the procedure. After studying the x-rays, the surgeon did not believe there was cause for alarm and indicated this to Melanie. When her surgeon told the radiologist he did not think there was any cause for concern, the radiologist told her surgeon if he did not do the biopsy he would not be able to sleep at night. The surgeon called Melanie the next day to say he thought it best to schedule the procedure.

The surgeon did the biopsy of a small nodule located in one of Melanie's breasts. The nodule was buried in some fibro-cystic tissue. This was the reason the surgeon thought there was no cause for alarm. The biopsy was positive and confirmed she had a rapidly destructive cancer, which had to be removed. When the surgeon shared this news in the recovery room Melanie immediately covered her hands over her face in shame and wept uncontrollably. Someone from a cancer support group came to offer her care. When the volunteer arrived for her visit, Melanie reported feeling uncontrollable rage at the woman. The volunteer had simply come to express her concern and to outline the possible scenario for her treatment, which would include surgery and chemotherapy.

The surgery was conducted and 10 lymph nodes were taken from her armpit to determine if the cancer had spread into her lymph system and metastasized throughout her body. Having been a nurse all her adult life and having taken care of her dying parents, Melanie was fragmented and mad at God "For letting this happen to me after all I have been through." Her reactivity was caused from the unfolding of the events tripping the triggers of the justice issue. From her point of view life was now unfair because of "all she had been through." She could not begin to think about the possibility of undergoing chemotherapy treatments after the surgery. Her oncologist was very patient and understanding. After several months, she went back and scheduled the treatments for her chemotherapy. Again, she expressed the same anger and rage she had felt toward the volunteer after her initial biopsy, but this time she was directing these feelings toward the oncologist. The oncologist suggested to Melanie she get some counseling in order to be able to explore why she was so hostile toward the process.

Melanie did not take long to figure out what had been troubling her about her rage. In her mind, she had equated chemotherapy with death. Both of her parents had received chemotherapy and both had died. She began to see she was the daughter of her mother and father, but *she was not her mother and father*. She was different. She was unique. Both of her parents had died of *colon* cancer. This was *breast* cancer, and it was *not the same*. When she could clearly *see* the distinctions between herself and her parents, it all made sense to her, clicked into place and the emotional threat to her safety was eliminated. Melanie made it through chemotherapy. She is now a cancer survivor having bested the five-year window.

As Melanie learned she was "not her parent's" we also learn "we are not our children." Brenda, my wife, and I were standing in line at the grocery store buying a few items. The day happened to be the day of our 25th wedding anniversary. My cell phone rang and our son said, "I did it. I just enlisted in the Air Force." He answered my few questions with "Yes sir, no sir," language that sounded foreign. He could have been speaking Zulu for all I knew. "How long did you sign up for?" "Six years. I get an extra $200 a month for signing up for the additional two years." "You WHAT?" I came as close to fainting as I ever have in my life, yet we knew this was coming. We did not know the recruiter would talk him in to an extra two years. When he got out of high school, he tried college, went through a series of dead end jobs and was struggling with what to do with his life. I had gone with him to the recruiter. He needed to lose weight in order to get in and he did. He was to leave to go through boot camp in six weeks at Lackland Air Force Base in San Antonio, TX. We thought we had a few more days with him in early October when the recruiter called and said he had to be in Jacksonville **that night** before midnight. We hustled to get him ready. Friends dropped in and out all afternoon and early evening to say good-bye. When we arrived at the hotel where he was going to be staying that night, other new recruits were showing up and saying their good-byes. When it was time for us to leave, Brenda and I were overcome with deep grief and sadness. The next day I cleaned out and re-organized the garage in my attempt to organize my pain while Brenda furiously cleaned house. He finished boot camp and we went for graduation. The Air

Force sent him to school, and after training, he was stationed at a base just six hours from where we lived. When he would come home for a visit, we experienced the sadness again whenever he would leave. After September 11th and the invasion of Afghanistan he was stationed in Incerlik, Turkey, which at the time was the Air Force Base to enforce the no fly zone over northern Iraq. Sean was in the Red Horse division and he was trained as a plumber. Red Horse is a mobile construction team that would be deployed to set up temporary bases in the field. We feared what every parent fears when they have surrendered a son or a daughter to the military. This e-mail arrived as I was writing this section. It expresses those same fears by another anxious parent:

> My son has been shot in Falujah. I wanted to get everyone to pray for my son Chad. Today, Sunday, I got a call from the Army that my son had been shot in the head. I am asking for all your prayers. He was in a Humvee going through Falujah fighting and a gang of militia fighters fired on the Humvee and hit Chad in the head. The driver got him out of the city and took him to Baghdad. He was in fatal condition, but now has been upgraded to stable critical. His dad and I are on standby to fly to Washington then on to Germany as soon as the military calls us to go. The Army is trying to stabilize him enough to fly to Germany and at that time we will leave. Please pray that my son will not have brain damage and that he will be restored and healed by the grace of God. I ask for you to pass this prayer request on so there will be many prayer warriors praying for him. Thank you so much and I will try to keep you updated on his condition.

Two years after Sean joined the Air Force his sister went off to college. We moved Rebekah into her dorm in Lakeland, Florida, two hours away. I would hang up clothes in her new closet and sob. I would work on shelves and sob. I put her computer together and sobbed. Brenda and Rebekah went off to a local store to pick up a few items, and I stayed behind and sobbed. Finally, after about five hours of this, we decided to leave. I could not take any more and we did not think Rebekah needed to have to deal with all of my pain. Heading back to the east coast, it was not until we were at least an hour away that I could finally stop sobbing.

No one ever told Brenda and me letting go of our children was going to be so difficult. They were never ours in the first place. We were chosen and privileged to bring them into the world, raise them and release them. We had to let them go in order for them to discover their own destiny. They were never solely our possession. We did not *own* them. They never were "our" children. They were on loan. They belong to the universe in order to discover their place in it. Our grief and sadness had more to do with signaling our role as parents was ending. Our biological purpose had been fulfilled. We were letting them go and surrendering an identity that comes from being "Mom" and "Dad." We could not protect our son from bullets or our daughter from boys.

We are *not* our relationships. We *have* relationships, and all relationships will change, evolve and eventually end. No other human being can fulfill what is missing within; no relationship can do this, even the most devoted between a husband and wife or a parent and a child. If you think you have discovered otherwise be assured it will only be temporary, until you realize the illusion and experience the disillusion.

We are *Not our Activities*

We push and strive in childhood, adolescence and young adulthood to become "independent centers of initiative." In later years of young adulthood and middle age, we learn, hopefully, to become "interdependent" through the process of discovering our soul and self. We ascend, raise children, create, accomplish and achieve; and as quickly as we have ascended, we begin to descend. Children grow up, launch and leave. We become downsized or outsourced. Someone 20 years younger is hired at half the salary. We experience changes in our health. Family members and friends become seriously ill or die. Retirement is forced. The descent continues. In our later years, we may have to surrender our pride and further become dependent on others to watch after us and to take care of our needs. We are often delivered a crushing blow when the day comes and we can no longer drive. The day I took the car away from my father was one of the most difficult jobs I have ever undertaken. Our roles switched that day. I remembered times he had taken *my* driving privileges away and now I was taking *his*. In our years of declining health we may need the assistance of retirement living, assisted living, adult congregate care or long-term nursing home care. I once visited a combination assisted living and nursing home and recall getting in the elevator. I looked on the floor and noticed the rug. The rug stretched the length of the elevator floor. It simply said "Tuesday." With dementia and Alzheimer's potentially facing each of us, orienting us to the day of the week is certainly a stark statement of the direction our potential dependence is heading. The road to our own personal demise is often difficult. I had the privilege of being with one wonderful saintly 83-year-old woman who was dying of congestive heart failure. Velma was a retired nurse. She knew what was happening to her and had been on the other side of the hospital bed thousands of times in her crisp white uniform and starched cap. On the day before she died, she was gasping for every breath and drowning in her own fluids. Velma pulled down her oxygen mask, looked me in the eye, and said, *"Dying isn't for sissies."*

Through the span of our time on earth, a variety of activities, hobbies or things we enjoy doing provide meaning for our lives. As a teenager, I remember telling my mother, "If it was not for surfing, I don't think I would want to live." It was a crushing blow to her. She thought I was suicidal. What I was trying to convey to her was exactly the opposite. Surfing was an activity that gave *meaning* to my life. Every fiber of my being felt fully alive when I caught a wave, dropped in, bottom turned, and did roller coasters or found my way into the tube. She did not understand. She did not want me to *organize my life around an activity*. Her wish was for me to "go deeper." Although I still enjoy this activity, I hardly organize my life around surfing. The dozen or so times I will go surfing are now during the summer when the water temperature is 75 degrees or warmer. Now I enjoy watching others do what I would do, paddling out during hurricane conditions or in the winter with a wet suit and the water temperature under 60 degrees.

We have activities, but *we are not our activities.* Actor Christopher Reeves of *Superman* fame enjoyed horseback riding as a hobby until he had a terrible accident that left him paralyzed from the neck down and living in a wheelchair. The fact he was no longer able to jump horses *did not mean he existed any less.* His life radically changed after the accident. He became an international spokesperson for advocating stem cell research. He was no less of a person after the accident than he was before. What it did mean is that he could not jump horses anymore.

To create an identity based upon an activity will extremely limit who you are as a person. Professional football players are rarely able to play beyond the age of 40 because of the inevitable injuries and repeated surgeries they must endure in order to play the sport. Eventually the body says, "No more." Every athlete will face the moment when his or her skill levels no longer will enable him or her to play sports competitively. At the age of 30, I started running as a way to manage my weight and deal with stress. Seven years later, playing a pick-up game of basketball with friends, I tore cartilage on both sides of my right knee along with the anterior cruciate ligament. The orthopedic surgeon told me this injury would end the career of a professional athlete. I do not run 10K or 20K races anymore but I do occasionally manage to hobble two or three miles; instead, I opt to use the cardiac equipment at the gym every morning.

We are not our activities. I am always amazed by the vast number of people who live only for the moment of their activity. They look forward to doing what they enjoy doing and everything else amounts to wasted time until the activity can be repeated. I pulled up to a stoplight next to a man in a big truck, complete with knobby off-road tires and a gun rack in the rear window. I motioned for him to roll down his window and when he did, I said to him, "Be fishing!" He looked at me as if I were crazy and said; "Huh?" and I repeated what I had said. He said, "What do you mean?" I told him his bumper sticker on his truck said he would rather "Be Fishing," so *"Be Fishing."* He spat out a wad of something, rolled up his window, shook his head and drove off when the light turned green. For this gentleman at the traffic light fishing is his *way of being*. Sailing, fishing, golfing, bowling or any form of recreation bumper stickers convey a sense of *identification of the individual with the activity* and suggest *no other components of life really matters*. The activity is more important than any other life function to these owners of the bumper stickers. We have activities, *but we are not our activities*!

We are *Not our Bodies*

Don't get me wrong. Our bodies are important. If we take good care of them, they might last a long time. At the beginning of the twentieth century, life expectancy in the United States was 47 years of age. As we have moved into the 21st century, our life expectancy is now beyond 77, and will continue to increase. Our bodies help us get around. Our bodies provide us with many pleasures and increasingly with age, many frustrations. I had always enjoyed perfect vision until I wrote my doctoral dissertation. I began to notice the change in my vision after looking at a computer screen for hours. I would turn off the machine, walk away and it would take several minutes before my eyes adjusted to the change. My entire visual world would be blurred and out of focus. First, it was reading glasses. Next, it was progressive lenses. Eventually, if I live long enough, it may be a German shepherd and a stick with a red tip on the end. Death occurs at different rates of speed to different parts of the bodies.

No matter how well we treat ourselves, what diets we

undertake or how much we exercise, our bodies will eventually wear out. Further advances in nutrition, exercise and medical technology may stretch our life expectancy to 100 years or even 125 years. According to Genesis 5:27, "The days of Methuselah were nine hundred and sixty-nine *and he died."* I am not sure how time was measured in those days but the point is this, Methuselah is still dead. From the moment we are born, we begin the process of our movement toward death. The length of the expedition may vary. The results are inevitable. Ultimately our bodies are not who we are.

Comedian Jerry Seinfeld indicates he believes the one thing constant about human experience is we are always *moving.* Since we are always moving, the other constant is we are always looking for boxes. You go to stores and ask, "Do you have any boxes?" Seinfeld attended the funeral of a friend. As he was sitting at the funeral, he caught himself thinking, "Now, that's a nice box. I bet my stereo would fit perfectly in there. I wonder if I could use it when he gets through." Our death is our final, last move when we get six of our best friends to help carry our last big box. This box, however, is only the container for the container, the part that is eventually disposable.

Let me explain. My grandmother, Nanny, as her grandchildren affectionately knew her, was one of the saintliest persons I have ever known. She was married to Papa, who was a Methodist minister in the South Georgia Conference. I never knew Papa but I do have a collection of his sermons, his books and a picture, which is absolutely priceless to me. In the photo, he is baptizing me on their 50th wedding anniversary. He died of a stroke a few months before I turned two years of age. From his writings and family stories, he must have been a stern man. Stern is a polite way of saying he must have been as stubborn as a mule and hardheaded to boot. There were several churches in his ministerial career that asked Papa to move, but they always wanted Nanny to stay.

Each year at Christmas, an uncle from Tampa would

send Nanny a box of oranges. On one particular Christmas gathering, I asked Nanny if I could help her fix breakfast for the extended family that gathered for the holiday celebration. In the flurry of activity that accompanied cooking breakfast Nanny cut the oranges and laid them on the counter for me to squeeze, between tending to the toast cooking in the oven and stirring a great iron skillet of scrambled eggs. I stood on a stool and squeezed the oranges, at least two or three, before I grew tired. I showed her the container, which must have held at least 10 ounces of juice, and asked Nanny if she thought this would be enough for everyone. She assured me it was. I was dispatched to round up the rest of the family for this morning feast. We all gathered at the huge breakfast table. Nanny had placed trivets on the table where she set plates of country ham and sausage, a steaming pot of grits and an iron skillet filled with scrambled cheese eggs. Her last item to bring to the table was *a full gallon pitcher of freshly squeezed Florida orange juice.* My mouth was wide open. A miracle had occurred greater than the story of the little boy with the loaves and fishes and the "feeding of the 5000." My Nanny had "blessed the juice," and it had somehow multiplied. I was absolutely dumbfounded. "How could this be?" I thought to myself. Then came a moment I had not anticipated. It would be *my* moment. Nanny, in front of the entire extended family turned to me and said, "Tim squeezed the juice." The family broke into spontaneous appreciative applause, and Nanny winked a knowing wink at me. More than liquid sunshine and vitamin C went down my throat that morning. This saintly woman fed a four-year-old boy the warmth and love of narcissistic nourishment. She made me feel 10 feet tall!

    Three years later, the day after Christmas, the extended family gathered again. This time we were in a hospital surgical waiting room. Nanny had phlebitis and blood clots had formed in her leg. I wore my brand new Cub Scout uniform that had arrived just in time for Christmas and tried to be brave for my younger cousins. They gave Nanny a "spinal" we were told; we did not know what that meant except she would be awake during the surgery. She heard the surgeons say they had to "saw up higher in order to get it all." Today she would have been given Coumadin, a blood thinner and sent back home. Nanny never went back home. She moved into a nursing home.

Visits to see Nanny were never the same. They were usually day trips which involved taking her out to lunch on a Sunday and staying late into the afternoon. She was never fitted for a prosthetic device so a wheelchair was her only mode of transportation. Getting into and out of the car required extensive effort. We always feared Nanny would hit her head either coming or going, and we would warn her to be careful.

She never changed. She watched her "stories" on television, kept up with the goings on of the other residents and could beat anyone at dominoes. Occasionally she would have what she called "blue days," but they were infrequent. The phone rang late one night and it was the fateful call we all hate to get. As an adult looking back, I see the way my family reacted as strange. The reaction bordered on hysteria. There was literally weeping, wailing and gnashing of teeth. At 13, I saw my father cry for the first time, sobbing deep expressions of grief. My own hurt was worse than anything I had ever felt before. After the committal at the graveside, we started the slow walk to the cars. The cemetery workers began shoveling dirt on top of the casket and the youngest grandchild said to my uncle, "Who is going to help Nanny with her wheelchair when she gets to heaven?" In his own fashion, he responded to his daughter and expressed our collective hope: "Sweetheart, she won't need any help. *She'll have wings!*"

Although her mobility changed after having her leg amputated, I did not notice much change in my grandmother. The reason for this was *my Nanny was not her leg.* She had a leg, and for many years, she had two, but *she was not her leg.* If anyone would have gone up to her after the surgery and said, "Where's Nanny?" she would have answered, "Here I am!" "But your leg is missing!" "That's right. My leg is missing, *but I am not my leg.*"

We have limbs, but we are not our limbs. Every day in this nation, hundreds of individuals have major organs removed or transplanted. We have organs, some we can live without and some are duplicates. Having duplicates makes it possible to live with only one lung or one kidney. However, we are not our organs. When John Wayne Bobbitt was "dismembered" by his enraged spouse, and it was surgically reattached, every male in America cringed with castration anxiety. The reason for this cringing is greatly suspected by most women, because many men *believe they are their penis!* I am here to set the record straight. Men *have* a penis, but we are *not* our penises!

We have bodies, but we are not our bodies. Although varying degrees of difference exist and debates continue about our "essence" being expressed through our "form," every major world religion points toward this reality. The Apostle Paul wrote in his second letter to the Church at Corinth, "We hold this treasure in earthen vessels." Our bodies are our "vessels," our containers for the self, the soul and the spirit.

The Life Within Our Life

Death today largely remains hidden in our culture.[w] While I was working at a hospital my last year of high school and first year of college the morgue was located across from the Emergency Room. The sign on the door read, "Conference Room F." Hospitals certainly did not want anyone to think that people truly *died* there. Since the turn into the twentieth century, technological advances in science and medicine have greatly changed the way our culture deals with death. In the year 1900, 80% of all people died at home and 20% died in institutions. Today those numbers have been reversed. In the early 1900's, when a death occurred, a

---

[w] This of course is with the exception of the tabloid-like Nielson rating wars that demand the most gruesome tales of death be told in the first eight to ten minutes of any local news broadcast in any major city in the United States.

local carpenter would make a casket, and the body would be viewed at home. Families would gather to wash the body of the deceased and prepare it for burial. This would not happen today. Today, the law in most states requires these duties to be delegated to the funeral home industry.

With the development of pre-natal care, along with the eradication of diseases and development of vaccines used during infancy and childhood, these measures have all but eliminated death in the early stages of life. The discovery of penicillin provided the medical community with the first weapon for fighting infections, and today more than 300 antibiotics are on the market. Immune suppressing drugs make organ transplants possible. Without these drugs, the body would reject donor organs. Cardiovascular by-pass operations are as common today as tonsillectomies were when I was a child. Balloon angioplasties and the insertion of stents have radically limited many invasive heart surgeries. These medical advances have greatly enhanced our potential for a longer and healthier life. However, these advances have had certain adverse effects on our culture. Death was fairly common in all age groups for our turn-of-the-previous-century-ancestors, and therefore *death was far more familiar than it is today.*

I have been fortunate enough to be present with more than a hundred people when they were taking their last breath. Unless we die suddenly by accident, murder, stroke, or by a heart attack, a miracle of metamorphosis takes place in the last 72 hours of life. Just as labor pains are involved in bringing us into the world, the body experiences labor pains as it shuts down and finally releases our life. When a person releases his or her last breath and life leaves the body the transition is clearly visible. The body immediately becomes ashen and gray. Within a matter of moments, rigor mortis begins to set in. In these sacred and solemn moments, in a tangible yet spiritual way, *life is released*, and the cocoon is left behind.

In a section of the interview Krista Tippett held with Dr. Mehmet Oz, described and cited in the previous chapter on Healing, Krista probes with Dr. Oz this very same phenomena.

> Ms. TIPPETT: People who are close to death often experience a sense of a reality — of another level of reality. And I wonder, as a surgeon who is sometimes with people in those moments when they're hovering between life and death, do you experience something palpably?
>
> DR. OZ: I don't normally experience the near-death element in part because I'm pretty busy trying to prevent the death. But there is no question that you sense a deep-seated loss when a patient dies. And it doesn't go away. You can hide it and bandage it better as you get more experience dealing with death. But when someone leaves and you did not want them to leave or you don't think they wanted to leave, the sense of loss is deep. It's a coldness that's inside of you, and it takes another person to get rid of it, either the family member of the patient or your own family, in my case, frequently where I go for recharging. But that is a very draining experience, and it's something that I suspect one day we'll be able to put numbers on and measure and quantify. But for today, I would just call it sadness, a cold sadness.
>
> Ms. TIPPETT: You mean the body is still there, physically everything is in the room that was there before, but something non-tangible...
>
> DR. OZ: It's something non-tangible, un-measurable. If I were using a "Harry Potter" analogy, I'd say there was one of those goblins that had come in and stolen my very *chi*, my very essence.[67]

For many physicians, the actual experience of the death of a patient frequently feels like a personal failure. Goblins do not steal our essence. Our essence, our very being, is released and returned to the Creator. We are this life. Our destiny is to discover this life *now*, not just in the moment of release from the body.

A Critique of Cultural Christianity

Authentic spirituality is about discovering our life in the one true life. In this life, we have life. This life is the life seeking to be expressed through us *now*, through all of the days of our sojourn on this earth.

Cultural Christianity substitutes oppositional energy as a weak pretender for authentic spirituality. Oppositional energy requires the formation of enemies and operates within the tension of right-wrong, good-bad, winner-loser, and love-hate. It requires the formation of enemies and the demonizing of others to create a false sense of unity.

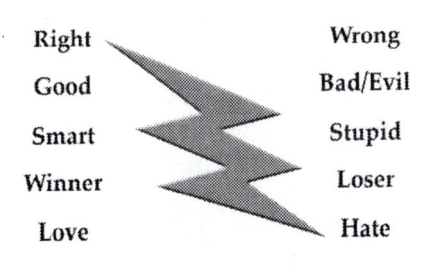

```
Right            Wrong
Good             Bad/Evil
Smart            Stupid
Winner           Loser
Love             Hate
```

Figure 11

Oppositional energy poses as an imposter for true spiritual empowerment, interrupting the rhythm of the dance between immanence and transcendence, the "beyond" and "within."

In primitive and regressed Cultural Christianity, much like in early childhood, reward and punishment are the primary motivators. Accept the principle, the person, recite the correct words, be spared the wrath to come and get your ticket punched to heaven. Avoid the *punishment* and receive the *reward*. The emphasis is pushed into the *future* and my life is never changed *now*. In this way, Cultural Christianity invalidates the value of discovering our destiny and identity as spiritual beings *now* because it is preoccupied with avoiding punishment in the *future*.

I attended a crusade held by a nationally recognized evangelist in Tallahassee, Florida. One evening, before the main speaker took the podium, the "warm-up" talked about the importance of each decision you make because *you never know which day may be your last*. He illustrated his point with a story about a man who attended the crusade the previous evening. His body had been found lying next to a train track in Lake City, Florida, some 90 miles east of Tallahassee. A train had hit the man and he had died. The speaker went on to say a commitment card had been found in his back pocket, indicating he had been present at the crusade the previous night and he had made a "decision for Christ." With this announcement, the crowd broke into thunderous applause with shouts of praise. The man by the train tracks *had been saved*. I sat in my chair in stunned disbelief. I could not believe what I was hearing. Meaning is about facts and interpreting these facts. As mentioned in Chapter 2, meaning is about three grocery carts at the bus stop. What do the carts *mean*? Why are they there? I interpreted the facts in a way entirely different from the speaker's interpretation. This was not a cause for celebration but a cause for sorrow. The story was not about a grand slam walk off victory but rather a huge swing-and-a-miss strikeout. A man had come to a community-wide religious event, hurting and looking for help. He went through the motions of doing what he was told to do, and when his pain was not relieved, he stood in front of a train. Perhaps he now felt assured so he was free to commit suicide and go to heaven. For members of the crusade, the story represented a soul snatched from hell and saved at the last possible minute. I found the story extremely tragic and sad. The prescribed formula for getting the man "saved" blocked the community of faith from *hearing this man's cries of pain.*

    The applause spawned from the reward-punishment model of a success story. The man's ticket had been punched, and he was now on the Amtrak to heaven. He was looking for relief from his pain, which he eventually received. He may have been looking for something else. What would happen if we took the reward-punishment angle out of the motivation and the win-lose position out of the equation? Would this push us into the present moment?

Richard Rohr tells the story of a nun walking on the streets of New York City. While out one day, she walked into the path of an angel on the sidewalk. The angel is carrying a pail of water in one hand and a torch in the other. The nun asks the angel what she is doing and the angel replies, "With the torch I am going to burn down the mansions of heaven and with the pail of water I am going to douse the fires of hell, *and then* we are going to see *who loves God.*" You may recall we cannot be purposeful and protective at the same time. Squirrels will be gathering nuts or running away from predators. They cannot do both at the same time. Neither can we. Falling in love with God is purposeful. Fearing God is protective. How do you fall in love with someone with whom you are afraid? Does divine judgment at the end of time point toward a hope we have as humans for a grand finale resolution in our *Search for Justice*? You may get away with what you are doing *now* but in the end, you will get what's coming to you? Without justice in *this* life, do we push justice out to the future so that everything seems fair in the end?

Removing the reward/punishment angle takes away one more oppositional force in the win/lose dynamic. Once an individual is stuck in win/lose as the only way of seeing the world, *winning means nothing if somebody doesn't lose!* Winning means triumph over something or someone else, presumably our enemies. Jesus taught his followers to live life *without* enemies. This means living in a surrendered state of consciousness where we choose not to accrue anger, hurt and resentment over real or perceived injustices. For most of us, this sounds like an impossible possibility or a nirvana naïveté. Those who choose to take the highway of transformation see this as the only option in the maintenance of spiritual integrity.

Another imposter to authentic integrated spirituality is a fear-based reactive cult of Christianity attempting to move into the mainstream. This movement has created a strange combination of spiritual narcissism and rapture theology. A host of end-time cults sprouted up in the twentieth century and moved into the mainstream, such as Seventh Day Adventists and the Advent Christian Church, but the recent era of this movement began with Hal Lindsey's *The Late Great Planet Earth* (1970) and more recently the *Left Behind* series. These movements interspersed a formula of fear and fiction in a broad interpretation of apocalyptic literature, found in the Book of Daniel in the First Testament and the Book of Revelation in the Second Testament. Referred to as the "Beam Me Up, Scotty" movement, the broadly held belief is that the end of the world is a foregone conclusion. If the world is going to hell in a hand basket, what could possibly create a best-case scenario? The answer to this apocalyptic dilemma is that there is only one way to get off this sinking ship. The "Beam Me Up" movement strives to convince the true believers they will be able to play their, "Get Out Of Suffering Free" card and fly up, up, and away. Christians will be beamed directly up to heaven while the rest of the rotten scoundrels on earth will get what is coming to them. Christians at the end of time will be spared all the gory mess. They will be winners and everyone else will be losers. This theology appeals to those with a need to feel inflated and superior, and quietly masks a form of spiritual grandiosity. The movement also encourages withdrawal from the problems of the world because it is all going to go to hell anyway. What matters is that *we* get to be special, we get what we want and to hell with everyone else.[68]

Again, when we look to the future, we see either fear or hope.[69] The two aforementioned approaches are driven by fear. In the reward–punishment model, life is about fleeing the wrath to come and getting the cookie. In the rapture model, the world is basically going to hell anyway, and here is a way to avoid future suffering. We can be beamed up just as the Klingon Empire begins their attack. Both approaches avoid the issue at the core of authentic spirituality: transformation.

Transformation

Transformation is about my life being changed *now*, not pushed off into the future. Transformation comes as a result of holding the tension between our two natures.

Figure 17

Annie, a personal trainer, works out and trains her clients in the gym where I exercise. In this image, Annie is working on her biceps. This visual *external* image represents the tension we experience *internally* when we are working to "hold" both our human and divine natures.

In a televised two part P.B.S. series two characters, portraying the work of Sigmund Freud and C.S. Lewis were in an imaginary dialogue involving their life's work. Although their life spans did overlap, they never met. Scholars in attendance participated in round table discussions debating the different views of these two historical giants. The actors delivered speeches from the written works of the characters they portrayed. Freud was a proponent of atheism and C.S. Lewis promoted a perspective of the Christian faith. When I watched the series, what became apparent to me was these two individuals saw human beings from totally different viewpoints. Freud was an interpreter of human experience from the basis of *who we are as animals* reducing our drives to sex and aggression. C.S. Lewis looked at human beings as made in the image of God, Imago Dei. They were both right. Ever since Adam and Eve woke up in the Garden and discovered their nakedness, we have been trying to reconcile the differences of our two natures. When each of us awakens, we will do the same. Our confessional paradox is that we are both human and divine.

The work can be hard and painful. The Second Testament writer Paul, largely responsible for the first century spread of Christianity around the Mediterranean Basin, described this process in a way that parallels Jesus' experience in death and resurrection. Paul describes a mystical connection between the suffering of Christ and our own suffering. The connection embodies a process demonstrating an acute awareness to living in this tension.

> "For I do not do the good I want, but the evil I do not want is what I do. Now if I do what I do not want, it is no longer I that do it, but sin which dwells within me. So I find it to be a law that when I want to do right, evil lies close at hand. For I delight in the law of God, in my inmost self, but I see in my members another law at war with the law of my mind and making me captive to the law of sin which dwells in my members. Wretched man that I am! Who will deliver me from this body of death?"[x]

If we apply the **FRICK** principle to Paul, he is clearly frustrated and struggling with conflicted thoughts, feelings, and emotions. Paul undoubtedly suffers from internal conflict. He is attempting to live in this tension and to hold onto both natures. He wrestles back and forth. It takes him into a state of wretchedness. Wretchedness is extremely difficult to market in Cultural Christianity. Holding this tension transforms Paul from the inside out.

These ongoing experiences of transformation are what push us deeper into our divine identity. These ongoing experiences take us into the knowing that comes from being. The deeper knowing of who we are lies in the discovery that we are a small tributary seeking to flow into the underground river of a new reality. This river runs far

---

[x] Revised Standard Version, Romans 7: 19-24

deeper than the roles we play, the positions we have, or what or whom we identify. Discovering the deeper knowing that comes from being has to do with "I am," and becoming comfortable with this before we fill in the blank! We will get to this in a moment, but let's take a look at what dams this up.

The most predominant game in town is fighting the constant battles of the ego and being stuck in the dynamics of inflation and deflation. In mathematics, this dynamic is communicated in the "less than" and "more than" symbol of the triangle on its side:

Nine is greater than two, 9 > 2
Eight is greater than six, 8 > 6.

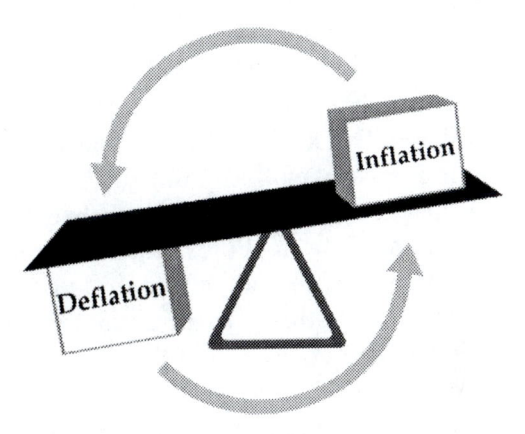

Figure 18

Inflation is whatever I use that will give me a temporary sense of feeling superior to others. Men tend to do this through competition; in business, sports, leisure activities, or hobbies. "My team can beat your team." "My motorcycle is faster and has more chrome than yours." Women tend to do this through comparison and contrast. "Can you *believe* what she is wearing? Doesn't she see how fat that makes her butt look?" We can temporarily feel superior if someone else's butt is bigger than our own. If the butt is smaller, we might hear a comment, "She's probably anorexic." Persons struggling with addictions rapidly cycle through the inflation/deflation paradigm and the addicting element provides the inflation mode. Persons addicted to drugs, alcohol, or prescription painkillers get to the inflated mode with their drug of choice. They become deflated when the party is over. The party always ends. Gambling provides the (potential) thrill of victory and the inevitable agony of defeat. Winning inflates and losing deflates. The house always wins. The inflation/deflation dynamic may also involve the size of my bank account, the prestige of the schools I attended, the degrees or titles I have, the house I live in, the clothes I wear, the car I drive, the importance of my job or vocation, the power I have, the circle of influential friends, self-conceit about physical appearance or beauty or anything else that temporarily inflates me to make me feel superior. If my intelligence temporarily inflates me then I may make life miserable for others by pointing out to them how *stupid* they are. Think of the humor that is built around this issue whether it is jokes that point fun at ethnic groups or blondes. "I sure am glad I am smarter than those dumb blondes!" The blondes, Irish, Poles, Italians, you name it, become deflated which of course, in turn, inflates me.

The inflation/deflation dynamic can be over something as silly as washing your car and then noticing everyone who has a dirty car and feeling superior because *your* car is clean and *theirs* is dirty! Or, because you have attended Mosque, Synagogue or Church *you feel superior* because *you* went and *you* are, by rite of attendance, now closer to God and *your neighbor is not!* I may even begin to feel special if I get eight green lights in a row and believe I must be aligned with the forces of the universe and the gods are smiling at me.

Religious groups are not exempt and frequently communicate the inflation/deflation dynamic with such language as, "Are you saved?" The "saved" communicate in their experience an inflated superiority, and the "unsaved" are therefore deflated and inferior. In the language of transactional analysis, it would be expressed this way: "I am okay, you're not okay, and if you become like me you'll be okay." Life becomes a constant juggling act to manage these circularities in order to stay in the "up" or inflated position. It takes a phenomenal amount of effort to play this game. The game is so deeply embedded in the collective cultural consciousness most people are not even aware of the cycle or what purpose the dynamic serves.

In the deflated end of the seesaw, persons who live on this end constantly battle depression, helplessness, hopelessness and despair, especially if they have experienced this state for prolonged periods of time. They project the past into the future and make it their present moment. "It has always been bad; it is always going to be bad and it is bad now!" The slightest annoyances can send someone spiraling downward. These persons will then take new experiences to validate feelings of worthlessness and incompetence. "See, I told you I was no good! This just proves it again!"

Chelsea, a 39-year-old professional worked in city government. She had a long history of being abandoned in relationships. Neither Chelsea nor her older sister knew who their biological father was. When she was 17, Chelsea asked her mother the "who" question. Her mother slapped her and repeatedly hit her about the head as Chelsea covered her head with her arms. Her mother is currently being treated for cancer and undergoing chemotherapy. The existential clock is ticking and projections are not optimistic that the cancer will go into remission. Chelsea recently asked her mother again, "My sister and I would *really* like to know who our father is." Undoubtedly the issue still generates a great deal of pain for her mother because the answer was, "He did not want you; he never wanted to know you. Why would you want to know who he is?"

Chelsea has been through two marriages, both ending in divorce, and has a child from each marriage. She is presently in a relationship with an attorney from a neighboring central Florida town. She sees him about twice a month. They have dated for seven months, but her male friend has not introduced Chelsea to his two children. "I want to ask him again about this, but I am afraid my *request* will sound more like a *demand*. I feel like I have a right to it! And there is this other voice I hear inside my head and I want to say to him, 'What's the matter, am I not *good enough* to meet your children?'"

Chelsea was aware that her trigger had been tripped on the justice issue. Her attorney friend had been to *her* place and had met *her* children, but she had not met his. She felt entitled to meet his children. In an attempt to make meaning out of this experience, she shifted into reactivity, which made her feel deflated. Underneath the layers of the self are deeply embedded images of *not being good enough*. The turtle was poking its head out of the shell!

The False Self

Wounded Self ⟵⟶ Narcissistic Self

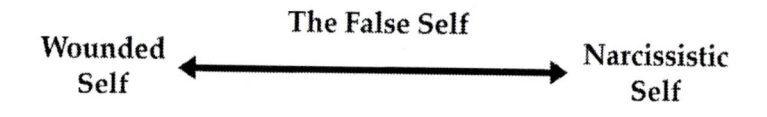

Figure 19

The paradigm for the false self has previously been introduced. Under multiple layers, the false self covers our deeper hidden identity as spiritual beings. The false self will operate on the continuum and we will carry aspects of both but one tends to be more dominant in our way of interacting with the world. Remember, one key feature in understanding the way the false self works involves the way we process blame. Do you internalize blame (turtle or wounded self) or externalize blame (narcissistic self or skunk)?

How does this self develop? The formation of these individual types comes about in a variety of ways. From development in infancy, some children seem to possess a natural ability to draw other people to them. We have all seen infants with a beaming countenance who have come into this world pre-packaged with an attractive physical appearance. These children nonverbally communicate to the world "notice me," and we do! In addition to "notice," the nurturing environment around them also tends to be overly responsive to their needs. A healthy family environment will facilitate a child's growth out of their entitlement fantasies, as must happen to all children in order to become healthy adults. Children who do not cycle out of the entitlement fantasy often develop into "The Little Prince," "The Little Princess" or simply "The Golden Child." Their accomplishments and achievements may begin to outdistance others and they may be repeatedly told they are "smarter than, prettier than, more athletic than, or more special than all other children." These experiences may create expectations that over-dramatize the child's own healthy narcissistic development. In dysfunctional families, this may further be exacerbated by parental mistakes such as a mother telling her son, "You're much smarter than your father. He never did amount to anything but *you* won't be like him. You'll be great." A father can inflict the same damage to his daughter with similar results. The child begins to believe she or he has "won" the struggle by defeating the opposite sex parent, as described in Freudian drive theory, and the grandiosity of the child gets notched up to the next level. Only danger and trouble lie ahead.

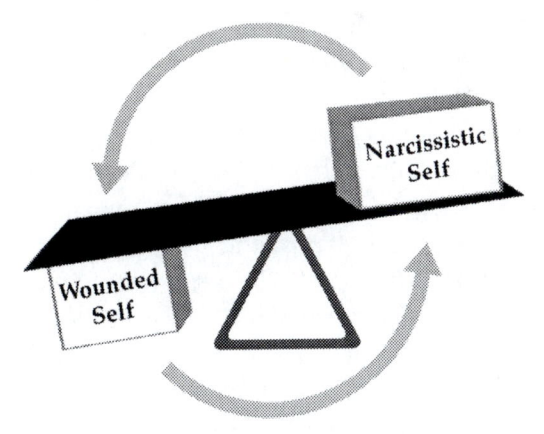

Figure 20

For a wounded self the opposite scenario is in place. The child cannot elicit a favorable response to his or her needs from the immediate environment. The infant is hungry, cold, hot, wet or dirty and cries out as a way of expressing and expecting his needs to be met. When the nurturing environment does not elicit a "good enough" response the theory and image the infant begins internalizing is, "If I can't get what I need there must be something wrong with me." With a non-nurturing parent, the split occurs within the infant as the infant sees the nurturing parent as good and his own self as bad. As the child grows and develops through childhood and adolescence this internalized image becomes reinforced by impressions created from other experiences, which validate and enlarge these perceptions. A child's pre-school song best expresses this posturing, "Nobody likes me, everybody hates me, and I guess I'll go eat worms!" When a child is growing up in this type of environment *shame* becomes the dominant emotional experience. The child learns when they express their needs that their needs are "wrong." These children learn certain feelings or emotions *are not acceptable*. These needs will then become repressed. The children feel shame, which *covers* the expression of the need. They will grow up feeling something is wrong with them for having these needs or feelings. Whenever I am working with an adult and the adult begins to experience shame, I know we are close to uncovering unmet needs.

    The default position for the wounded self is deflation and for the narcissistic self is inflation. Persons who have a narcissistic self expect to be treated as "special," and when they do not receive this treatment, they often resort to rage. "Don't you know who I am?" Persons who have a wounded self often have a victim mentality even if they have never been victims. "Look what she did to me! Can you believe this? Everybody treats me this way!" Persons with a narcissistic self are constantly in need of being the center of attention. Those who surround them often feel they are trying to inflate a hot air balloon with hundreds of holes. No matter how much they pump, it will never be enough. For those who live with persons who carry a wounded self, they constantly feel like they are pouring water in a colander. It will always be empty. Nothing will ever fill it up.

Beyond The False Self: The Question of Identity

When it comes to your own identity before you fill in the blank of I am_____ (Mother, Father, Butcher, Baker, or a Candlestick Maker) you must first wrestle with the issue of "I am." "I am" is the present tense of the verb "to be." God is saying, "I am the present tense of being." Each human *being* is an extension of divine *being*; therefore, you are that in your essence before you are Mother, Father, etc.

In a story from the First Testament Book of Exodus, God calls Moses from a burning bush to go to the Pharaoh of Egypt and tell him, "Let my people go." Moses had been raised in the house of Pharaoh, murdered an Egyptian for his mistreatment of a Hebrew slave and left Egypt with an outstanding warrant for his arrest - he was **not** eager to go back and face certain death if he was arrested, fingerprinted, and his true identity discovered. Moses had entered the witness protection program, married, changed jobs and was content with day-to-day life the way it was. Since Moses was not sure about the statute of limitations for a murder case and did not carry any diplomatic credentials as an ambassador from any of the neighboring nations, and he also had a speech impediment that caused him to stutter, he sought to convince God this going back to Egypt deal was a bad idea. God needed to summon someone else for this suicide mission. To say Moses was resistant to God is putting it mildly. However, this was not a request; God chose Moses and was not taking no for an answer. Moses eventually grew weary and conceded saying, "Okay, if I do this, whom shall I say sent me?" God responds to Moses, "Tell him 'I AM,' sent you." God is saying, "I am being," and by extension so are you!

Created in the Image of God

What we notice, appreciate, and encourage will grow,

no matter how dismal the environment may be and against all odds. This is the nature of how the universe is marvelously made and how human beings are created in the *Imago Dei*, or the Image of God.

I was home, hungry, and so I went to the kitchen and opened the refrigerator door, looking for half of a sweet Vidalia onion I had sliced a week earlier to adorn a hamburger I had retrieved from a previous grilling. I opened the vegetable bin in the very bottom and the very darkest part of the refrigerator, and I was surprised when I slid the door open. In a plastic storage bag, the onion had three green shoots about an inch in length. I looked at it stunned. Against all odds and in the darkest possible location this onion was attempting to grow. I put the onion on the counter, stared at it for a few moments, and I began talking to the onion. In fact, I started shouting encouragement to the onion. "You can do it! Way to go! That's fantastic!" My children came out of hiding from their bedrooms, saw what I was doing, shook their heads, and returned. "What's your Dad doing?" Brenda asked the children. Rolling their eyes, together in unison, they said, "Oh, nothing, he's just *talking to an onion*."

I simply did not have the heart to cut off the growth and disregard the effort that went into making this growth happen. My hamburger went onion-less. The onion was rescued, placed in a pot out on the back porch, and it grew like gangbusters when it was placed in an optimal environment for growth to occur.

If this imprinting for growth is in an *onion*, how much more can this be within each of us who are created in the Image of God? What happens when those who are taken out of the dark and dank places and allowed to flourish in the light of a new consciousness, a new reality, to create a new heaven and a new earth?

In this model of anthropology, human beings are created in the image of God who is pure being. By our very nature, we are born with an innate kinship connection and desire for the discovery of our destiny. As we grow and begin to accept this realization of our own destiny, we accept our connection as sons and daughters of the great "I AM." This is the life lying beneath the life hidden by the false self. This is the tributary seeking to merge with the underground river of a new reality. This is the being in humans seeking to connect to the Being of the Creator and creation. The destiny we seek to discover as the source of life emerges, concurrently coinciding with the death of the false self.

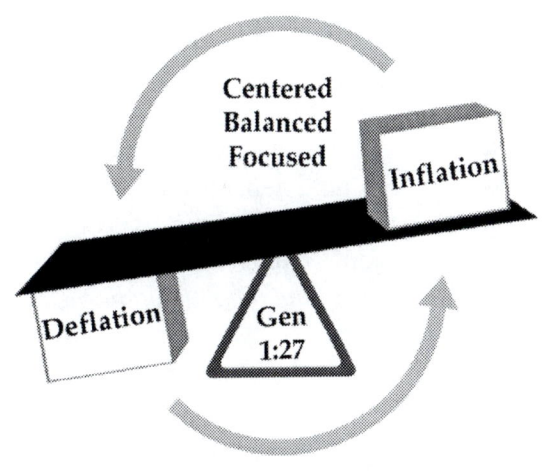

Figure 21

In the center of the seesaw, up and down have little variation. From this position, we can discover our identity beyond what we identify with *externally,* and see who we are *internally.* When we attempt to manage the false self and live on the outer ends of the seesaw we will constantly be in motion, up or down depending on win-lose, success-failure, gain-loss, right-wrong, good-bad, and love-hate. All the drama of life is out there on the end seats. When we judge circumstances external to the self as favorable, we may be granted a few moments of happiness; and, when we judge circumstances external to the self as non-favorable, these circumstances will define our misery. *Good* is what you perceive as favorable and therefore inflates. *Bad* is what you perceive as unfavorable and deflates. Your happiness now depends on whether the good outweighs the bad. In order to keep the good inflated you will need to be in control of the universe and direct the course of destiny which is not your responsibility!

Does this mean bad things will never happen? Of course not! As long as we live east of Eden bad things will happen. There will be swine flu, bird flu, epidemics, debilitating disease, earthquakes, tsunamis, floods, hurricanes, tornados, hunger, holocausts, wars, violence, murder, rape and all manner of human brokenness. Yet, if events such as these push us to release our attachment to our false self and force us into a deeper knowing of who we really are, is it really bad if these circumstances drive us individually and collectively into a higher consciousness and transformation of our identity? What if all human suffering is pushing us to evolve? As Dr. Leo Buscaglia once said, *"Suffering ceases to be suffering when we accept it as part of the human condition."*

Suffering: Why Should I Be Exempt?

Why do we believe we should be exempt? In the Christian tradition, Jesus stands in the center of human history and dies a tortured death. In language that may be confusing to those outside this faith Christians believe Jesus was the Son of God. It is not that Mr. and Mrs. God got together one day and decided to have a boy. The terminology is meant to describe a relationship. If the son of God was not given an exemption or a "get off the cross free" card, why do we believe we should be granted an exemption from suffering? It is not that God willed Jesus to die on a cross, any more than God would will the same for your life or mine. If God threw Jesus under the bus, so to speak, this would be divine child abuse. God is not a murderer. To follow this line of reasoning, God would be responsible for flying the planes into the World Trade Center, the Oklahoma City bombings, the Challenger Shuttle disaster and the heartbreak of psoriasis. The cross confirms the reality of suffering in human history and affirms that the very nature of God *is to raise up who or what gets crucified*. We do not get off the hook. What this does mean is Jesus came to show us *this is how it is done!*[y]

Externally we have very little control over what happens to us. Internally when our tributary flows into the deep underground river of this new reality, *our life* is connected to *the source of life*. The split is repaired in human consciousness because there is no longer a "me" and "life". Life is liberated and lived out *through* me. Once consciousness and awareness begin to shine a light on the false self, the inflation/deflation dilemma begins to collapse and the false self withers and dies. The real self, grounded in being, illuminated with intelligence greater than our own begins to replace all of the former ego functions and fills the voids of human existence. The immanence of this life and light radiates from the inside out.

Think about it this way. If you were on board one of the ships with Captain Menendez in July of 1565 crossing the Atlantic during an early season hurricane, being tossed at sea from pillar to post, chances are you too would become frantic and fear for your life just as those original sailors did. If you were in the same ocean today under similar circumstances but instead you were in a submarine, would it matter what was happening on the surface? The winds could be howling and waves could be churning up 20 feet with driving squalls and pelting rain. Down below, deep down beneath the surface, outside the realm of up and down, inflation and deflation, there is calm.

---

[y] Revised Standard Version, Romans 6:3-5 "Do you not know that all of us who have been baptized into Christ Jesus were baptized into his death? *We were buried therefore with him by baptism into death, so that as Christ was raised from the dead by the glory of the Father, we too might walk in newness of life.* For if we have been united with him in a death like his, we shall certainly be united with him in a resurrection like his."

The Sharing of Divine Attributes

In the creation stories told in the First Testament God places the divine signature on human beings at the beginning of creation. There are two distinct visual pictures of "image" and "breath" offered in these poetic expressions, which seek to unmask the mystery of our connectivity to God. In Genesis 1:27 the text states, "Then God said, 'Let us make man in our image, after our likeness.'" Is this a literal understanding that humans have been made to look like gods? Does the reference to "us" point to an early glimpse of polytheism? Is this a reference to an undertaking of such great importance God would consult the "heavenly host" in the creation of a human being? Theologians have debated the concept of being made in the image of God for centuries. Let it suffice to say, for this context, the statement is meant to convey a *sharing of nature and attributes* between the divine and the human. This includes communication, thought, the potential for good and a shared partnership in creation. It also includes the potential for human beings to share in divine attributes such as unconditional love, forgiveness, empathy and our ongoing quest to absorb these qualities in our own process of transformation.

In Genesis 2:7 the text reads, "And the Lord God formed man of the dust of the ground, and breathed into his nostrils the breath of life; and man became a living soul." The Hebrew word translated as "soul" is *nephesh*, from the verb *naphash*, which means *to breathe*. For the ancient mind, this was a very literal connection. It was easy for them to make the direct correlation between breath and life. Before the advent of modern medical technology, when the body stopped breathing, life ceased to exist. Breath, therefore, is the property of God. This is a direct way of understanding human beings as being *"breathed"* by God, which is crucial and critical for the maintenance of life. Breathing is a primary function of human existence. Breath vividly demonstrates the essential *connection* we have with our Creator. We have been created to be in such an intimate relationship with the Creator so much so that we breathe the Creator's breath! This means living in a relational posture that allows God to "breathe" us. We were created to live our lives on Divine life support!

You have been invited to join this journey of transformation. What you choose to do is up to you. .Nobody can do this *for* you. You must do it for yourself. Shortly after boarding a plane prior to takeoff, we have all heard a flight attendant make the safety announcement. You know the speech. The attendant points to the emergency exits, reminds you about the seat cushion as a flotation device, and instructions for a loss of cabin pressure. If the oxygen masks drop due to a sudden change in pressure, first put the mask on your own face….then assist your child or the person sitting next to you. Do not be concerned about the breath of others, until you have initiated your own life-saving measures. You need not be concerned if someone else is getting it or if you will be making the journey contingent on the commitment of someone else. "I'll put my mask on, if you put yours on" does not work when it comes to the Creator. You cannot do this for your wife, husband, mother, father, daughter, son or neighbor. Neither can you *wait* for them. Get your mask on first!

At the beginning of the chapter I posed a series of questions as to why there has been a throng of humanity that have flocked to hear and to be in the presence of Billy Graham, Pope John Paul II, and the Dalai Lama. Why have masses of humanity been drawn to these persons like moths to porch lights?

Is it possible that these spiritual leaders awaken something within us? This may sound tricky, but have you ever had somebody tell you something that brought new awareness to *something you already knew?* Some refer to this as an "Aha" moment, *"I already knew that . . . I just did not know* that I knew it!" Somewhere deep within, you *already knew it,* but *awareness* brought the *knowing* to a *conscious level,* which then *deepened the knowing!* These spiritual leaders work like a tine on a tuning fork.

When this tine is struck-
It strikes a frequency and resonates –
With what we already know –
And it attunes itself with
Truth we hold within.

We recognize truth with the truth. *It is the awareness of truth recognizing itself,* a claiming at the innermost awareness of who you are. We all *belong* to this truth. When you discover this truth, this knowing, you discover your destiny. This knowledge is not about data, or about doctrine, nor is it about regurgitating meaningless information to qualify you to be the King or Queen of Jeopardy or Trivial Pursuit. In fact, this knowledge is not about *information* at all: it is about *transformation*. We are not human knowings – we are human *beings*. *Knowing* comes from *being*. *Living in the mystery is about being in the Being.*

History and Experience – Yours and Mine

My history and experience created ideas and beliefs that shaped the lens of how I see the world. My maternal grandfather was a Methodist minister in the South Georgia Conference. I have a sermon he preached in 1922 when he publicly denounced a lynching. I am proud to be a part of a tradition of protest and justice. My paternal grandfather worked as a farmer, a carpenter and he practiced the faith of the Seventh Day Adventist Church. My father was raised in this tradition that observes the Jewish Sabbath and kosher dietary laws. My maternal grandfather performed the wedding for my parents. I was raised in the Methodist Church. Today I am a Christian by call and by choice. My faith is the foundation for my character, ethics, principles and ideals. My faith creates purpose, meaning and synergy in my life. When I fall into the chaos track, hijacked by reactivity, anger and anxiety, the agility test works the same for me. Abundant life is hard work!

Your history and experience created your ideas and beliefs that have shaped the lens by which you see the world. I wrote *Discover Your Destiny* as an invitation and a challenge to live purposefully by moving out of chaos and into coherence. The theory, philosophy and theology are not concerned about the nuances of orthodoxy but rather the particulars of orthopraxy. In other words, *Discover Your Destiny* focuses on "walking the walk" and not "talking the talk." You only have this one Life. If your *heart* is right, you will live in *harmony* with life.

God does not come pre-packaged in a single flavor. How can we experience the rich diversity God has placed on this planet if the only flavor is vanilla? No tradition can lay claim to a sole monopoly on absolute faith or absolute truth.[z] Throughout history, world religions have built schools, hospitals, and prophetic voices have critiqued the cultural conscience. In the darkest moments, they have sanctioned war, slaughters, massacres, and left in their wake a trail of blood and tears. The righteous intolerance of "true believers" vilifies others to justify "holy violence." We can no longer tolerate this intolerance. We must learn to celebrate religious diversity, peacefully co-exist, and renounce the insanity of warrior god ideology and theology.

Let us get to the heart of the matter: Authentic faith is not about the finger but rather it is about the finger *pointing to the moon*. There is not *one* holy and apostolic finger! The truth contained in all expressions of faith is only realized when these traditions become transparent and point us toward and reveal the one Creator of the Universe. *"Truth belongs to one who shows the readiness to ask for it - who opens the doors of his heart and calls for it."*[aa]

Authentic faith, in whatever form, is about a heart

---

[z] To claim otherwise is to establish one tradition in the superior or inflated position and others in the inferior or deflated position. This dynamic does not represent authentic spirituality but rather the work of the ego by creating the polarization of consciousness driven by oppositional energy..

[aa] http://www.oshorisk.dk/books_music/EnglBooks/12-Upanishads.htm

transplant. Authentic faith forces us to face our shadows and deal with our pain, not to project our pain on to others. Authentic faith is about *being in the Being*. Life in the global village means the entire cosmos is sacred space. We and we alone make sacred space profane. If you would not dream of spewing the toxic emotions of hate, rage, disgust and shame/humiliation in your church, synagogue, mosque or other holy place why would you do so at home, school, work or on the road? Every space is sacred and even more so once you discover the sacred space without and within.

You will see the future with either hope or fear. Hope is purposeful. Fear is protective. This Hope I speak of is not about what you desire. It is not about your dreams or your aspirations. It is not about wanting to put goals on your "to do" list, your "wish" list or your "bucket" list and checking them off as they are accomplished. This Hope is about a new earth, a new day, a new dawn, and a new beginning. This Hope is about a vision for a new reality that is *breaking into the present from the future*. When we are captured by this Hope, it works like a tractor beam pulling us forward into all of our tomorrows. This Hope never fails. It never tires or grows weary. It does not slumber, and it does not sleep. It is timeless and eternal. It calls us out of numbness or unconsciousness to say yes to this Hope. Right now, it is tapping on the window of your soul.

Whether you live in India or Indonesia, Africa or the Americas, Europe or the Middle East, one thing is certain: Governments can no longer guarantee safety for their citizens. If you truly desire to feel safe in an unsafe world, then safety must first be discovered within.

Transformation is an internal process that creates alignment with this new reality. The evolution within creates transformation from the inside out. From the internal, we will build new external forms and formulas for structures, systems, and governments to resonate with this new reality. We will be purposeful in hitting these new targets with energy, synergy and cooperation. We will transcend reactivity, and inspire life with new meaning. We will seek to maintain this vital balance in every aspect of life and in all our relationships. We will experience the emergence of an inner competence born in humility and hope, not based on arrogance or bravado. We will seek significance in our connections with others. We will relate to people as individuals with whom we share humanity and a vision for this new reality. We will want to grasp this elusive "other" and be grasped by it! We will want to recognize the one whose signature is on every sunset has also embedded the divine DNA in our very soul.

Every person on the planet is a pilgrim. Some are actively seeking. Some have settled for chasing cultural carrots while others have become comfortably numb. If you choose to accept the resonating of truth and its claims on your life, you will get to seek and see how deep the rabbit hole goes. You will continue searching, becoming, and evolving. Seekers will become finders. Together we will herald a new day, casting out fear and empowered by Love. Together we will call for the revolution of a new reality, a new destiny. This is a new call, not a call to war, but a call for a *revolution of transformation*. Revolutions begin from the bottom up, not the top down. Peacemakers will become ambassadors of this new reality and issue the clarion call to global leaders to cure us from the warring madness. The revolution begins *now,* in this moment, when you make your own leap of faith.

Epilogue
The Dumbo Dilemma:
Taking the Leap toward Transformation

In the early 1990s, I attended an annual denominational meeting of clergy and laity. Reports are received, votes are taken, and budgets are adopted. Little did I know, or was I prepared, for what was about to happen. The Mystery was about to surprise me in the midst of the mundane. Author Kurt Vonnegut might have said it this way: *"and so it goes."*

I sat down with the father of a close friend who at the time was the Senior Pastor of a large membership church in Palm Beach Gardens, Florida. We spoke informally. By the end of the conversation, contingent upon completing an interview process, he offered me the position as the Director of the Community Counseling Center, an outreach of his church. I was stunned. I had not planned on this happening.

The following week I went to attend graduation ceremonies in Louisville, Kentucky, where I received a doctorate in counseling. My family traveled with me to mark this rite of passage. While driving north on Interstate 75 through Florida, Georgia, Tennessee, and finally Kentucky, I was very quiet. The closest image I can use to describe how I felt was like a *radar dish*. I was trying to pick up any sign being sent from the universe. I listened for any word, phrase or faint signal which might provide my family and me a sense of direction about *what to do* or which direction to take. I felt like every nerve, every cell and every fiber of my being had been placed on red alert. I listened to my soul. I listened to myself. I kept wondering if the *timing* was right. I remembered a story about a Greek statue. The statue was of a man who stood crouched and ready to run. He had a lock of hair in the front and his head was shaved in the back. The name of the statue was *Opportunity,* symbolically indicating if we do not grasp opportunity when it faces us, there is nothing we can do once it has passed. Was this an opportunity to grasp or to pass? I felt the "C" in "FRICK" with conflicted thoughts, feelings and emotions. Although I felt uneasy, it made sense to pursue this vocational shift after working diligently for three years to obtain an advanced degree.

After the graduation ceremony, we drove home. The following week I went to Palm Beach Gardens and I interviewed for the position. Palm Beach is one of the most upscale, affluent communities in the state of Florida. I received a royal welcome. I interviewed one evening and I was scheduled to meet the next day with a real estate agent to look at houses. This would be a major step for my family and me. Housing would no longer be provided. There would be no safety net for this high wire act. I would have to give up the security of having a guaranteed roof over my head. Everyone who is "self-employed" knows the feeling.

There were a couple of hours open between appointments the next morning. I decided to spend some time meandering in the mall at Palm Beach Gardens; something I had been told I should not miss. The landscaping was meticulous in every detail. The interior of the mall projected a spacious *feng shui*. There was a generous expression of overhead glass and windows, which bathed the marble flooring with available sunlight.

I was walking in the mall when I strayed into a store specializing in Disney animated portraiture. While browsing the pictures I was captivated by a particular lithograph depicting a scene, from all things, the movie *Dumbo*. I stood hypnotically in front of the lithograph and was mesmerized into a trance. Dumbo stood on the edge of a cliff with terror on his face and fear in his eyes. Four black crows were off to the side, laughing in an uproar at the possibility of this elephant's attempt to fly. One lone black crow feather stood in plain view inside the extended tip of Dumbo's curled trunk. In Dumbo's cap, as if on top of the crow's nest of a sailing ship, Timothy, the mouse, stood at attention. With an undaunted look of fierce determination, Timothy pointed for Dumbo to ignore the laughter of the crows and to *make the leap over the edge.*

I stood in front of this picture lost in the moment and oblivious to my surroundings. Tears were streaming down my face. I *knew* what Dumbo felt. I could *feel* Dumbo's fear. It was my own. I had to jump. Which way would I jump and in what direction?

A young saleswoman came up and politely started speaking to the back of my head. I heard her say, "You must be interested in the Dumbo lithograph." She started to tell me a list of details about the picture: when Disney made the movie, the writers, the producers, and the celebrity voices of the characters along with a myriad of other information. My Dumbo trance had pushed the playback button on her pre-recorded sales speech. It was like being on the summit of the Empire State Building and the tour guide was telling me the amount of concrete, steel and construction hours it took to build the building when I was contemplating jumping off the ledge. I kindly turned to her and said, "No, let me tell you what this picture *means*!" When I turned to face her, the youthful saleswoman saw my tear-streaked face. She stepped back, startled, and quickly apologized. She must have thought I was a total nut case. Admirers of art are often moved to tears in the Louvre Museum in Paris or the Vatican Museum in Rome but probably not very often in a Disney store! I had made her anxious. She did not know what to say or how to respond. She excused herself and quickly found someone else to assist.

In this moment, you may very well be standing on the edge of your own cliff struggling with discovering your destiny. Understandably, you may feel protective. You may have a list of "what if" questions. You may struggle with change – changes in your vision for tomorrow, changes in your surroundings, your relationships, changes around you and changes within you. Your past may be holding you in chains. Your future may be filled with dread, worry, uncertainty or fear. You are not sure what will happen because you may not be in control. What would happen if you surrendered your life to the one true Life?

Now is your moment. The tines of the tuning fork

have been struck. They are vibrating at a perfect pitch. The source of all Being is resonating with the being within you. You are being breathed by the Creator in this very moment. The divine design for your life is holding your history and all of history. It is the Alpha and the Omega, the beginning and the end, the past and the future. It holds each moment of your past and yet it is breaking in from the *future* into your present moment.

You have been created in the Imago Dei, the Divine Image, and God intends this purpose for you. The intentional purpose of the divine design is to absorb and conquer chaos. This design is accomplished because this *internal* energy vibrates at a higher frequency attuned to the energy emitted from the *Eternal*. Love replaces reactivity, anger and anxiety as the energy within and surrounding your existence.[bb] You enter into this divine design when you chose to surrender your addiction to chaos and the ensuing drama it creates. You will then be empowered by love until your own chaos has been absorbed and conquered.

When this divine purpose meets your receptivity, a reunion takes place. You return to the source of Life, the one Life, from where you came. Before this reunion takes place, there must be surrender. Surrender is not a sign of defeat. It is a signal of strength. Surrender invites you to relax and relinquish control of your life. When you loosen your grip, stronger arms will surround you, steering your ship's wheel, as you sail toward the sunrise of all of your tomorrows.

Whatever your resistance, whatever your reason, make the leap anyway! Go ahead and jump! Your destiny is not about a location, it is about a place: it is about a place within! Say *yes* to this one Life! It is your destiny!

[bb] I Corinthians 13: 13 "So faith, hope, love abide, these three; but the greatest of these is love." Revised Standard Version

Appendix
Narcissistic Personality Disorder

The Diagnostic Statistical Manual IV Edition describes a Narcissistic Personality Disorder as containing the following characteristics:

1) Has a grandiose sense of self-importance (e.g., exaggerates achievements and talents, expects to be recognized as superior without commensurate achievements)
2) Is preoccupied with fantasies of unlimited success, power, brilliance, beauty, or ideal love
3) Believes that he or she is "special" and unique and can only be understood by, or should associate with, other special or high status people (or institutions)
4) Requires excessive admiration
5) Has a sense of entitlement, i.e., unreasonable expectations of especially favorable treatment or automatic compliance with his or her expectations
6) Is interpersonally exploitative, i.e., takes advantage of others to achieve his or her own ends
7) Lacks empathy: is unwilling to recognize or identify with the feelings and needs of others
8) Is often envious of others or believes that others are envious of him or her
9) Shows arrogant, haughty behaviors or attitudes [70]

Lasch describes the narcissist as follows; "The narcissist divides society into two groups: the rich, great, and famous on the one hand and the common herd on the other. Narcissistic patients, according to Kernberg, are afraid of not belonging to the company of the great, rich, and powerful, and of belonging instead to the 'mediocre' by which they mean worthless and despicable rather than 'average' in the ordinary sense of the term. They worship heroes only to turn against them when their heroes disappoint them. Unconsciously fixated on an idealized self-object for which they continue to yearn,... such persons are forever searching for external omnipotent powers from whose support and approval they attempt to derive strength."

Lasch further states, "(The narcissist) sees the admired individual as 'merely an extension of themselves'... The narcissist admires and identifies himself with 'winners' out of his fear of being labeled a 'loser'. The narcissist cannot identify with someone else without seeing the other as an extension of himself, without obliterating the other's identity."[71]

Notes

[1] On Saturday, the 8th, the general landed with many banners spread, to the sound of trumpets and salutes of artillery. As I had gone ashore the evening before, I took a cross and went to meet him, singing the hymn *Te Deum Laudamus*. The general marched up to the cross, followed by all who accompanied him, and there they kneeled and embraced the cross. A large number of Indians watched these proceedings and imitated all they saw done. The same day the general took formal possession of the country in the name of his Majesty, and all the captains took the oath of allegiance to him, as their general and governor of the country. When this ceremony was ended, he offered to do everything in his power for them, especially for Captain Patino, who during the whole voyage had ardently served the cause of God and of the King,

[2] http://www.fordham.edu/halsall/mod/1565staugustine.html

[3] Eckhart Tolle, *The Power of Now* (Novato: New World Library, 1991), 103.

[4] Gil Bailie, *Violence Unveiled, Humanity at the Crossroads* (New York: Crossroad, 1995).

[5] http://www.cacradicalgrace.org/conferences/tension/post/powerpoints/TwoWaysofKnowing.pdf

[6] Cormac McCarthy, *The Road*, 2006, (New York: Alfred A. Knopf, 2006).

[7] Karen Armstrong, *The Great Transformation: The Beginning of Our Religious Traditions* (New York: Alfred A. Knopf, 2006).

[8] Karen Armstrong, *The Great Transformation: The Beginning of Our Religious Traditions* (New York: Alfred A. Knopf, 2006).

[9] Mihalis Kakogiannis and Nikos Kazantzakis, *Zorba the Greek*. Directed by Mihalis Kakogiannis (Los Angeles: 20th Century 1964).

[10] Queen, *Bohemian Rhapsody*.

[11] Quoted from a Bumper Sticker!

[12] Robert Kegan, *The Evolving Self: Problem and Process in Human Development* (Cambridge: Harvard University Press, 1982), 174.

[13] Malcolm Gladwell, *Blink: The Power of Thinking Without Thinking,* New York, Back Bay Books, Little, Brown, and Co.

[14] Babylon, LTD. "Latin Dictionary," http://www.babylon.com/define/112/Latin-Dictionary.html (accessed May 29, 2009).

[15] Gordon MacKenzie, *Orbiting the Giant Hairball: A Corporate Fool's Guide to Surviving With Grace* (New York: Viking, 1996).

[16] Michael Veeck, *Fun Is Good: How to Create Joy & Passion in your Workplace and Career* (New York: Rodale, 2005).

[17] Malcolm Gladwell. *Outliers: The Story of Success* (New York: Hachette, 2008), 149-150.

[18] *The Graduate*, Embassy Pictures, released December 21, 1967

[19] Greg Baer, *Real Love* (New York: Gotham, 2004).

[20] Brooks Atkinson, *At The Theatre*, New York, *New York Times*, February 11, 1949.

[21] Arthur Miller, Death of a Salesman, First performed February 10, 1949, Morosco Theater, New York City, N.Y.

[22] Joseph Chilton Pearce, *The Crack In The Cosmic Egg: New Constructs of Mind and Reality* (Rochester: Park Street Press, 2002), 19.

[23] Paul H. Ornstein, The Search for the Self, Selective Writings of Heinz Kohut: 1950-1978, International Universities Press, Madison, Connecticut, p. 757-761

[24] Joseph Chilton Pearce, *The Biology of Transcendence: A Blueprint of the Human Spirit* (Rochester: Park Street Press, 2002), 73.

[25] Gil Bailie, *Violence Unveiled: Humanity at the Crossroads* (New York: Crossroad, 1995), 93.

[26] John Savage, *The Apathetic and Bored Church Member: Psychological and Theological Implications* (Pittsford: LEAD Consultants, 1976).

[27] *Speaking of Faith "Truth"* NPR, October 27, 2005.

[28] *Speaking of Faith "Truth"* NPR, October 27, 2005.

[29] Gil Bailie, *Violence Unveiled: Humanity at the Crossroads* (New York: Crossroad, 1995), 4.

[30] *60 Minutes II "Abuse Of Iraqi POWs By GIs Probed"* CBS News, April 28, 2004.

[31] Gil Bailie, *Violence Unveiled: Humanity at the Crossroads* (New York: Crossroad, 1995).

[32] Gil Bailie, *Violence Unveiled: Humanity at the Crossroads* (New York: Crossroad, 1995), 90.

[33] Daniel Goleman, *Emotional Intelligence* (New York: Bantam Dell, 2005), 124-126.

[34] *Speaking of Faith "Science and Hope"* NPR, July 7, 2005.

[35] *Speaking of Faith "Science and Hope"* NPR, July 7, 2005.

[36] *Speaking of Faith "Science and Hope"* NPR, July 7, 2005.

[37] Michael Basch, *Understanding Psychotherapy: The Series Behind the Art* (New York: Basic Books, 1988), 25.

[38] Eckhart Tolle, *A New Earth: Awakening to Your Life's Purpose* (New York: Penguin Books, 2005).

[39] Robert Schuller, *Self-Esteem: The Next Reformation,* Word Books, Waco, Texas, 1982

[40] *The Lion King,* Walt Disney Pictures, Released June 15, 1994

[41] Michael Basch, *Understanding Psychotherapy: The Series Behind the Art* (New York: Basic Books, 1988), 77-78.

[42] Greg Baer, *Real Love* (New York: Gotham, 2004)

[43] Chris Crowley and Henry S. Lodge, *Younger Next Year: A Guide to Living Like 50 Until You're 80 and Beyond* (New York: Workman, 2004).

[44] Robert Pirsig, *Zen and the Art of Motorcycle Maintenance* (New York: Bantam Books, 1981).

[45] Joseph Chilton Pearce, *The Biology of Transcendence: A Blueprint of the Human Spirit* (Rochester: Park Street Press, 2002), 10-20.

[46] Chris Crowley and Henry S. Lodge, *Younger Next Year: A Guide to Living Like 50 Until You're 80 and* Beyond (New York: Workman, 2004).

[47] Joseph Chilton Pearce, *The Crack In The Cosmic Egg: New Constructs of Mind and Reality* (Rochester: Park Street Press, 2002), 134.

[48] Alvin Toffler, *The Third Wave* (New York: William Morrow, 1980).

[49] Bob Seger and the Silver Bullet Band, from the album Stranger In Town, Capital Records, May 1978

[50] Robert Greenleaf, *Servant Leadership* (New York: Paulist Press, 1991), 36.

[51] Andrew Weil, *Spontaneous Healing: How to Discover and Enhance Your Body's Natural Ability to Maintain and Heal Itself* (New York: Ballantine Books, 1996).

[52] Bill Moyers, *Healing and the Mind* (New York: Bantam Doubleday Dell, 1993).

[53] *Speaking of Faith "Heart and Soul: The Integretative Medicine of Dr. Mohmet Oz"* NPR, June 22, 2006.

[54] *Speaking of Faith "Heart and Soul: The Integretative Medicine of Dr. Mohmet Oz"* NPR, June 22, 2006.

[55] Ernest Rossi, *The Psychobiology of Gene Expression* (New York: W. W. Norton, 2002).

[56] Ernest Rossi, *The Psychobiology of Gene Expression* (New York: W. W. Norton, 2002), 401.

[57] Ernest Rossi, *The Psychobiology of Gene Expression* (New York: W. W. Norton, 2002), 398-424.

[58] *Speaking of Faith "Listening Generously: The Healing Stories of Rachel Naomi Remen"* NPR, August 11, 2005.

[59] *Speaking of Faith "Heart and Soul: The Integretative Medicine of Dr. Mohmet Oz"* NPR, June 22, 2006.

[60] Ernest Rossi, *The Psychobiology of Gene Expression* (New York: W. W. Norton, 2002), 337-390.

[61] Office of the Clark County Prosecuting Attorney, *www.clarkcountyprosecutor.org/html/death/US/wuornos 805.html*, Jefferson, IN. (accessed June 2007).

[62] Joseph Chilton Pearce, *The Biology of Transcendence: A Blueprint of the Human* Spirit (Rochester: Park Street Press, 2002), 10-20.

[63] His Holiness the Dalai Lama and Victor Chan, *The Wisdom of Forgiveness: Intimate Conversations and Journeys* (New York: Riverhead Books, 2004).

[64] John Ortberg, When The Game Is Over, It All Goes Back In The Box, Grand Rapids, Michigan, Zondervan, August 26, 2007

[65] Richard Bandler and John Grinder, *The Structure of Magic: A Book About Language and Therapy* (Palo Alto: Science and Behavior Books, 1975).

[66] John Savage, *The Apathetic and Bored Church Member: Psychological and Theological Implications.* (Pittsford: LEAD Consultants, 1976).

[67] *Speaking of Faith "Heart and Soul: The Integretative Medicine of Dr. Mohmet Oz"* NPR, June 22, 2006.

[68] Robert Jewett, *Jesus Against the Rapture* (Philadelphia: Westminster Press, 1979)

[69] II Timothy 1:7 "For God hath not given us the spirit of fear; but of power, and of love, and of a sound mind." Revised Standard Version,

[70] *DSM V, The Diagnostic and Statistical Manual of Mental Disorders*, (Arlington: American Psychiatric Association, 1994), 661.

[71] Christopher Lasch, *The Culture of Narcissism: American Life in An Age of Diminishing Expectations* (New York: W.W. Norton and Company, Inc., Warner Books Edition, 1979), 85.